Constitutional Law

The daring publisher, Universal Law Publishing Company, among the foremost in the law publishing field and progressive in venturing to bring out rare legal literature of avant garde *character has rightly enriched the* corpus juris *of India*

Justice V R Krishna Iyer
Random Reflections, page 14

Constitutional Law

Dr. Justice AR. Lakshmanan
Former Chairman, Law Commission of India
Former Judge, Supreme Court of India

Foreword by

Justice Tirath Singh Thakur
Judge, Supreme Court of India

Justice K.S. Radhakrishnan
Judge, Supreme Court of India

Universal
Law Publishing Co. Pvt. Ltd.
NEW DELHI - INDIA

2012 Edition

ISBN: 978-93-5035-168-0

Published by
UNIVERSAL LAW PUBLISHING CO. PVT. LTD.
C-FF-1A, Dilkhush Industrial Estate,
(Near Azadpur Metro Station) G.T. Karnal Road,
Delhi-110 033
Tel.: 011-47082254, 27438103, 27215334
Fax : 011-27458529
E-mail *(For sales inquiries)* : unilaw@vsnl.com
E-mail *(For editorial inquiries)* : edit@unilawbooks.com
Website : www.unilawbooks.com

Recommended citation: Dr. Justice AR. Lakshmanan, *Constitutional Law* (New Delhi: Universal Law Publishing Co. Pvt. Ltd., 2012).

Computer Typeset at Aesthetic and *Printed* at Deepak Printers, New Delhi.

Justice T.S. Thakur
Judge
Supreme Court of India

10, Krishna Menon Marg
New Delhi-110011
Ph.: 23018989
23018082

FOREWORD

In a Sovereign Democratic Republic like ours, with a written Constitution, the Superior Judiciary plays an extremely important role, not only as an independent arbiter of all disputes, brought before it but also as the fountain source of what is often called the Judge-made law. Parliamentary legislations, whether in the realm of municipal laws or amendments to the Constitution, are by a process of judicial Interpretation made effective for achievement of the objects underlying the legislation or struck down if found to be falling foul of the constitutional scheme. Disputes about the true meaning of the provisions are settled and doubts are dispelled by judicial pronouncements, declaring the law on the touchstone of time-tested principles of interpretation. It is not therefore uncommon to see the legislature intervening to bring an amendment in situations where the judicial pronouncement is not seen to be promoting the object which the former had in mind. Equally well recognised is the principle that the legislature can by law remove the basis of a decision rendered by the Superior Courts, in order to overcome or neutralise its effect. This interplay between legislative exercise on the one hand and judicial review on the other provides the life-breath to a dynamic and vibrant constitutional scheme of governance where rule of law is the ultimate guarantee for the security of the citizen and his rights. Notably judicial pronouncements of the Apex Court are, by the mandate of Article 141 of the Constitution, binding on the courts in the country as the law of the land.

Justice Lakshmanan is known as a quick, sensitive and knowledgeable judge in the legal fraternity. He has been prolific in his pronouncements, covering almost all disciplines of law. His tenure as a High Court judge, as Chief Justice of the Rajasthan and Andhra Pradesh High Courts and later as a judge of the Apex Court has been an extremely productive period. Law reports bear ample testimony to the kind of work that Justice Lakshmanan has done, leaving hardly any branch of law untouched. His tenure as Chairman of the Law Commission has seen the submission of as many as thirty-three reports on a variety of subjects and enactments. The Judge has now decided to publish his pronouncements as a Judge of the Supreme Court including one where he wrote a dissenting opinion. These pronouncements speak for themselves and bear testimony to Justice Lakshmanan being at home in the field of constitutional law as much as he is in other branches.

I compliment the author for this endeavour and hope that the decisions will provide assistance to the members of the Bar and students of law alike in understanding and applying the principles that are settled thereby in appropriate cases that may come their way.

New Delhi, 2012

T.S. Thakur

Justice K.S. Radhakrishnan
Judge
Supreme Court of India

7, Ashok Road,
New Delhi-110001
Tel.: 23074324

FOREWORD

The past decade has been a period of transformative constitutionalism in which the Supreme Court of India has played a significant role. The Constitutional mandate envelopes all spheres of the nation's life—political, social and economic, however the realization of this mandate has not been absolute. The Supreme Court of India and the High Courts of the country have persistently tried to remedy the disconnect between the Constitutional rights and their realization. Justice AR. Lakshmanan's compilation of his judgments on Constitutional Law undeniably reflects the Court's involvement in every sphere of human life and also depicts the process of initiation of a constitutional morality in the country.

"Justice AR. Lakshmanan on Constitutional Law" is a valuable compilation of 15 judgments authored by him, among others, during his tenure as a judge of Supreme Court of India. The judgments deal with various aspects of Constitutional Law and examine highly intricate and sensitive issues. The compilation elucidates the judicial treatment of issues such as Secularism, Limits of Affirmative Action, Fundamental Freedoms and Reasonable Restrictions, amongst others. These issues have been the center stage of various ongoing debates and Justice Lakshmanan's lucid reasoning while balancing opposing interests can resolve many misconceptions of the society regarding the interpretation of the Constitution. Justice Lakshmanan's treatment of the issues reflects the much needed appreciation of the intricate social, economic and political setting in India and aids in the development of a constitutional morality. The present scenario of the country requires a display of sensitivity towards the diverse background. Justice

Lakshmanan's views in his judgments can be extremely important in inculcating this much needed attitude.

With his rich experience at the Bar, as the judge of various High Courts and then the Chief Justice of Rajasthan and Andhra Pradesh High Courts, as a judge of Apex Court and the Chairman of the Law Commission of India, Justice Lakshmanan, possesses a keen understanding of the intricacies of the Constitution, which is well reflected in his interpretation of Constitutional Law through his judgments. Justice Lakshmanan is one of the few people who have combined his responsibilities on the Bench with academic work of high quality. Justice Lakshmanan's previous publication including the "Neethiyin Kural" ("Voice of Justice"), "The Judge's Speak" and "My Own Judgments-Volume I" have been extremely well received.

This compilation is a very useful companion for judges, advocates, law students and academicians. The compilation of judgments of a varied nature, reflecting a myriad of issues in Constitutional Law is a novel and laudable attempt. The compilation is a thought provoking and instructive publication for anyone interested in understanding and appreciating the scope of India's Constitutional Law.

New Delhi, 2012 **K.S. Radhakrishnan**

Dr. Justice AR. Lakshmanan

Former Judge, Supreme Court of India, Former Chairman, Law Commission of India
Chief of Panel - Indian Courts of Arbitration for Sports (ICAS)

Office: Dev Regency, 1st Floor, No. 11, First Main Road,
Gandhi Nagar, Adyar, Chennai-600 020.
Phone: 044-24423188 Fax: 044-42121858
e-mail: justicearl@yahoo.com / jusarlakshmanan@gmail.com

PREFACE

By the grace of the Almighty, I had the opportunity of serving in four High Courts of our country from the year 1990 to 2002 before I was elevated to the position of a Judge in the Supreme Court of India. During these years, while I was in Tamilnaldu, Kerala, Rajasthan and Andhra Pradesh, both as a Judge and as the Chief Justice of the States, I was invited by many forums to preside over and deliver lectures on varied subjects. I fully utilized these occasions into useful opportunities.

In-depth studies in various subjects as the occasions warranted were necessary. I made thorough studies of the subjects and delivered these speeches. They are on various fields like Law, Spiritualism, Art, Education, Sociology, Feminism, Environment Protection, Patriotism etc. They were in Tamil and English as well.

Not only did I take pre-operative care, but also took much post-operative care in preserving these speeches all these years. With modesty, let me claim that the number of speeches delivered by me may be more than 470.

Some of my friends insisted the need of preserving these speeches in a Book form, so that it may be permanent and also useful for the Society and as a result, this book is now in your hands.

I have been a Member of the Bar for 22 years and a Member of the Bench for 18 ½ years in four different High Courts and in the Supreme Court. All these years, I felt happy while arguing cases as a lawyer and hearing and disposing of cases as a Judge of various High Courts and the Supreme Court and also delivering lectures on various topics of importance.

I cannot claim any heredity in the legal profession. I had a humble beginning in the profession. I am a first generation lawyer. I had to struggle hard, particularly in the beginning, to survive in the profession. I was appointed as a Government Pleader by the State of Tamilnadu in the High Court of Madras in the year 1989. I was nominated as Senior Advocate by the Govt. of Tamilnadu to impart training

Residence : 2/448, third Street, Karpagambal Nagar, Kottivakkam,
Chennai - 600 041, Phone : 24518888
Cell : 91769 20022, 93111 12222, 99418 11111, 87544 76797

Meenakshi Illam, No. 6, Alambattar Street, Devakottai - 630 302.
Sivaganga Dist. Tamilnadu. Phone : 04561 262248

to a select Law Graduates belonging to Backward Classes under a Scheme formulated by the Govt. of Tamilnadu. In June 1980, I was appointed as a permanent Judge of the Madras High Court.

I have been extremely fortunate in having had the affection and goodwill in abundance of every member of the Bar and of my esteemed colleagues on the Bench. All these years, I can humbly say, I believed in humility, honesty and hard work.

A compilation of some selected lectures/speeches delivered was made and released as a Book in Tamil titled "**Neethiyin Kura**l" (Voice of Justice) by His Excellency Shri Surjit Singh Barnala, the then Governor of Tamilnadu. His Excellency, Shri A.P.J. Abdul Kalam, the former President of India gave the message of greetings, which speak volumes of the high nature of content of the speeches. The English version of the book is titled "**Voice of Justice**" which contains 116 speeches. The Hon'ble Prime Minister of India, Shri Manmohan Singh was kind enough to give the Foreword to the Volume I of Voice of Justice on 25th July 2006. The former Chief Justice of India, Shri Y.K.Sabharwal has given the Foreword to the Volume I of Voice of India.

For my "**Voice of Justice"** (Volume II), Shri K.G. Balakrishnan, the former Chief Justice of India and the Hon'ble Home Minister, Shri P.Chidambaram (former Finance Minister) gave the Foreword.

I was appointed as a Judge of the Supreme Court in the year 2002 and after my retirement, appointed as Chairman of the 18th Law Commission of India. During this period, I participated in many Seminars and Conferences in India and also abroad and delivered many lectures and speeches on various topics. The book titled "**The Judge Speak**s" has been published by the famous Publishing House of Delhi namely, Universal Law Publishing Company Pvt. Ltd.

The said book "The Judge Speaks" was launched at the Rashtrapathi Bhawan by Her Excellency, Smt. Pratibha Devisingh Patil, the President of India. The Hon'ble President has also given a message on 3rd March 2009. The former Chief Justice of India, Shri K.G.Balakrishnan and the present Chief Justice of India, Hon'ble Mr Justice Altamas Kabir, also gave their Forewords.

As a Judge of the Supreme Court, I disposed of 6,862 matters, out of which, the number of matters I presided over was 1,026. This is apart from the disposal of 1,432 regular matters, of which I presided over 472 matters. Out of the plethora of Judgments, the Judgments mainly relating to **Arbitration, Business and Commercial Laws** have also been compiled and the book was launched by the Hon'ble Speaker of Lok Sabha, Smt. Meera Kamar at the Indian Institute of Public Administration, New Delhi. The Hon'ble Mr Justice V.S.Sirpurkar, the Judge, Supreme Court of India and the Hon'ble Mr Justice P. Sathasivam, the Judge, Supreme Court of India gave their Forewords in the Book.

As the Chairman of 18th Law Commission of India, I have submitted 33 reports (202nd to 234th Report) which were also published in the form of a book by the Universal Law Publishing Company Pvt. Ltd.

The Book on "**Labour and Service Laws**" is the compilation of 54 selected Judgments authored by me and concurred by other Hon'ble Judges. This was printed and published by Universal Law Publishing Company Pvt. Ltd – one of the reputed and leading Publisher of Law Books.

After a deep thought and appreciation, I have organized to get the collection of Judgments on Constitutional Law also printed into a presentable and publishable book.

Judiciary has played a crucial role in development and evolution of society in general and in ensuring good governance by those holding reins of power in particular, perhaps, there can be no two views about the significance of the role expected of judiciary, vis-à-vis the goal and good governance in a free society.

The transformation of India in the last decade as an economic power-house and its integration into the globalized trade and commerce has brought some stability and hope for those in governance. Development and progress of our nation hinges upon technology, commerce and most importantly, faith in legal processes to enhance equity and resolve disputes in a peaceful manner. Thus, our fast paced growth in technology and commerce cannot be sustained if our people lose faith in legal processes and the rule of law. We must necessarily introspect on how, in an ancient civilization such as ours, respect for the rule of law , has been withering despite the relative improvement in our economic position since Independence and technological advances that we have achieved. Consciously or unconsciously, society has elevated the Judge to a carefully protected eminence. Common citizens acknowledge and regard Courts as sacrosanct, right from the Magistrate's Court to the Supreme Court. Indeed, a Judge is an epitome of manners in men as the highest personage of law. As the Chairman of Law Commission of India, it was incumbent upon to reflect on the state of administration of justice in our country, on the performance of the third branch of Government, on its relentless efforts to improvise on the implementation of the tasks assigned to it under the Constitution of India and the need for necessary changes in the Indian legal system as and when the need arises.

The present attempt is the compilation of the Judgments mainly relating to the "**Constitutional Law**", which I am sure, will serve as a ready reckoner for Professionals, Law Teachers and Law Students. It is the compilation of 15 selected Judgments on Constitutional Law authored by me and concurred by other Hon'ble Judges. This compilation deals with various current topics. This is being printed and published by Universal Law Publishing Company Pvt. Ltd – one of the reputed and leading Publisher of Law Books. Mr Manish Arora, the Director of Universal Law Publishing Company Pvt. Ltd. also printed my Volume 1 and 2 of Voice of Justice and "The Judge Speaks" and the Arbitration, Business and Commercial Laws.

I wish to place on record my sincere thanks to Hon'ble Mr Justice T.S. Thakur and Hon'ble Mr Justice K.S. Radhakrishnan, the Judges of Supreme Court of India, for conveying their blessings by giving the Forewords to the book in spite of busy schedule in their assignments.

March 2012 **Dr Justice AR Lakshmanan**

CONTENTS

TABLE OF CASES

J

K

L

M

N

T

U

V

W

Commissioner of Police
v.
Acharya Jagadishwarananda Avadhuta

AIR 2004 SC 2984: 2004 (2) CTC 690:
JT 2004 (3) SC 224: (2004) 3 MLJ 28 (SC):
(2004) 3 SCALE 146: (2004) 12 SCC 770
Civil Appeal No. 6230 of 1990
Decided on 11-03-2004

Coram: Hon'ble Mr. Justice S. Rajendra Babu
Hon'ble Mr. Justice G.P. Mathur
Hon'ble Dr. Justice AR. Lakshmanan

Judgment by: Hon'ble Mr. Justice S. Rajendra Babu

FACTS: In *Acharya Jagdishwarananda Avadhuta* v. *The Commissioner of Police, Calcutta,* (1983) 4 SCC 522, the Supreme Court held that *Tandava* dance in public is not an essential rite of *Ananda Margi* faith. Subsequently Ananda Murti Ji - founder of that order prescribed to perform *Tandava* dance in public as an essential religious practice in *Carya Carya,* a book containing the relevant doctrines. Based on this, *Ananda Margis* sought permission of the Commissioner of Police to perform *Tandava* dance in public. The Commissioner accorded permission to take out *Tandava* dance without knife, live snake, trident or skull. This was challenged by the respondents before the Supreme Court.

ISSUE: Whether performance of *Tandava* dance in public is an essential and integral part of *Ananda Margi* faith?

HELD: The practice of *Tandava* dance in public is not an essential part of *Ananda Margi* faith. Essential part of a religion means the core beliefs upon which a religion is founded. Essential practice means those practices that are fundamental to follow a religious belief. The test to determine whether a practice is essential to the religion is to find out whether the nature of the religion will be changed without that practice.

JUDGMENT

S. Rajendra Babu, J.

1. This is second round of litigation. In the first round of litigation question raised before this Court was whether performance of Tandava dance in public is an essential practice of *Ananda Margi* order or not. This court in *Acharya Jagdishwarananda Avadhuta* v. *The Commissioner of Police, Calcutta,* MANU/SC/0050/1983, (*First* Ananda Margi case), held that *Tandava* dance in public is not an essential rite of *Ananda Margi* faith. Subsequent to the first case, it appears that Ananda Murti Ji - founder of that order prescribed to perform Tandava dance in public as an essential religious practice in *Carya Carya,* a book containing the relevant doctrines. Based on this, *Ananda Margis* sought permission of the Commissioner of Police to perform Tandava dance in public. The Commissioner accorded permission to take out Tandava dance without knife, live snake, trident or skull. This was challenged by the Respondents herein before this Court by filing Writ Petition (Civil) Nos. 1317-18 of 1987. This Court with the following observation disposed it of:

> "We are of the view that these cases should appropriately be examined by the High Court keeping in view that has been said by this Court in the Judgment in *Acharya Jagdishwarananda Avadhuta* v. *The Commissioner of Police, Calcutta* reported in MANU/SC/0050/1983. Petitioners are at liberty to go before High Court."

2. Firstly a Single Judge and subsequently a Division Bench of the Calcutta High Court arrived at the conclusion that taking out *Tandava* dance in public carrying skull, trident etc., is an essential part of *Ananda Margi* faith and Commissioner of Police could not impose conditions to it. This decision is now under challenge.

3. When this matter came up for consideration before this Court, a Bench of two learned Judges made an order on 13.11.1992 as follows:—

> "After hearing the parties for sometime and having considered the decision of the three learned Judges of this Court in *Acharya Jagdishwarananda Avadhuta* v. *Commissioner of Police, Calcutta* MANU/SC/0050/1983, we are of the view that this is a matter which requires consideration by a Constitution Bench of this Court. Hence, we request the learned Chief Justice to constitute the Bench as early as possible for hearing of the matter".

4. On 4.12.2001 a Constitution Bench of this Court considered this matter and noticed that (i) that the Bench does not express any difficulty in following the earlier judgment, (ii) that they do not set out any substantial question of law which requires the decision of a Constitution Bench since that order merely stated that the matter should be heard and decided by a Constitution Bench. The Constitution Bench felt that in those circumstances there was no justification for hearing the appeal by the Constitution Bench and therefore placed the matter back before the two learned Judges for final disposal who in their turn made a reference to a Bench of three Judges.

5. The relevant question herein for consideration is whether the High Court is correct in it's finding that *Tandava* dance is an essential and integral part of *Ananda Margi* faith based on the revised edition of *Carya Carya*. A bench consisting of three judges of this Court in first *Ananda Margi* case arrived at a unanimous conclusion on facts that *Tandava* dance in public is not an essential and integral part of *Ananda Margi* faith. In order to arrive at this conclusion this Court *inter alia* took the following four aspects into account.

1. Shri Prabhat Ranjan Sarkar otherwise known as Shri Ananda Murti, founded a *socio*-spiritual organization claimed to have been dedicated to the service of humanity in different spheres of life such as physical, mental and spiritual, irrespective of caste, creed or colour, in the year 1955.
2. Ananda Marga contains no dogmatic beliefs and teaches the yogic and spiritual science to every aspirant.
3. Tandava dance was not accepted as an essential religious rite of *Ananda Margis* in 1955 when that order was first established. It was introduced for the first time as a religious rite in or around 1966.
4. Ananda Marga is a religious denomination of the *Shaivite* order, which is a well-known segment of Hindu religion.

6. After taking into account of all the relevant facts, including the above, this Court held:

> "...Ananda Marga as a religious order is of recent origin and *Tandava* dance as a part of religious rites of that order is still more recent. It is doubtful as to whether in such circumstances *Tandava* dance can be taken as an essential religious rite of the *Ananda Margis*. Even conceding that is so, it is difficult to accept Mr. Tarkunde's argument that taking out religious processions with *Tandava* dance is an essential religious rite of *Ananda Margis*. On the basis of the literature of the Ananda Marga denomination it has been contended that there is prescription of performance of *Tandava* dance by every follower of *Ananda Marga*. Even conceding that *Tandava* dance has been prescribed as a religious rite for every follower of the Ananda Marga it does not follow as a necessary corollary that Tandava dance to be performed in the public is a matter of religious rite..."

7. By the above finding this Court was categorical in it's judgment that Tandava dance in public is not an essential part of religious rites of *Ananda Margi* faith. The conclusion arrived at by this Court regarding the non-essential nature of *Tandava* dance to *Ananda Margi* faith was principally based on the fact that the order itself is of recent origin and the practice of dance is still more recent. Court even went to the extent of assuming that Tandava dance was prescribed as a rite and then arrived at the conclusion that taking out Tandava dance in public is not essential to *Ananda Margi* faith. After arriving at the above ratio, the Court further added that—

> "...In fact, there is no justification in any of the writings of Shri Ananda Murti that *Tandava* dance must be performed in public. At least none could be shown to us by Mr. Tarkunde despite an enquiry by us in that behalf."

8. This observation cannot be considered as a clue to reopen the whole finding. By making that observation the Court was only buttressing the finding that was already arrived at. The learned judges of the High Court wrongly proceeded on the assumption that the finding of this Court regarding the non-essential nature of *Tandava* dance to the *Ananda Margi* faith is due to the non-availability of any literature or prescriptions by the founder. The High Court is under the wrong impression that an essential part of religion could be altered at any subsequent point of time.

9. The protection guaranteed under Articles 25 and 26 of the Constitution is not confined to matters of doctrine or belief but extends to acts done in pursuance of religion and, therefore, contains a guarantee for rituals, observances, ceremonies and modes of worship which are essential or integral part of religion. What constitutes an integral or essential part of religion has to be determined with reference to its doctrines, practices, tenets, historical background etc., of the given religion. (See generally the Constitution Bench decisions in *The Commissioner* v. *LT Swamiar of Srirur Mutt,* 1954 SCR 1005; *SSTS Saheb* v. *State of Bombay,* 1962 (Supp) 2 SCR 496, and *Seshammal* v. *State of Tamil Nadu,* MANU/SC/0631/1972, regarding those aspects that are to be looked into so as to determine whether a part or practice is essential or not). What is meant by 'an essential part or practices of a religion' is now the matter for elucidation. Essential part of a religion means the core beliefs upon which a religion is founded. Essential practice means those practices that are fundamental to follow a religious belief. It is upon the cornerstone of essential parts or practices the superstructure of religion is built. Without which, a religion will be no religion. Test to determine whether a part or practice is essential to the religion is - to find out whether the nature of religion will be changed without that part or practice. If the taking away of that part or practice could result in a fundamental change in the character of that religion or in its belief, then such part could be treated as an essential or integral part. There cannot be additions or subtractions to such part because it is the very essence of that religion and alterations will change its fundamental character. It is such permanent essential parts what is protected by the Constitution. No body can say that essential part or practice of one's religion has changed from a particular date or by an event. Such alterable parts or practices are definitely not the 'core' of religion where the belief is based and religion is founded upon. It could only be treated as mere embellishments to the non-essential part or practices.

10. Here in this case *Ananda Margi* order was founded in 1955. Admittedly, *Tandava* dance was introduced as a practice in 1966. Even without the practice of *Tandava* dance (between 1955 to 1966) *Ananda Margi* order was in existence. Therefore, Tandava dance is not the 'core' upon which *Ananda Margi* order is founded. Had Tandava dance been the core of *Ananda Margi* faith, then without which *Ananda Margi* faith could not have existed.

11. There is yet another difficulty in accepting the reasoning of the High Court that a subsequent addition in Carya Carya could constitute Tandava dance as essential part of *Ananda Margi* faith. In a given case it is for the Court to decide whether a part or practice is an essential part or practice of a given religion. As a matter of fact if in the earlier litigations the Court arrives at a conclusion of fact regarding the essential part or practice of a religion – it will create problematic situations if the religion is allowed to circumvent the decision of Court by making alteration in its doctrine. For example, in *N. Adithayan* v. *Travancore Devaswom Board,* MANU/SC/0862/2002, this Court found that a non-Brahmin could be appointed as a *poojari* (priest) in a particular temple and it is not essential to that temple practice to appoint only a brahmin as poojari. Is it open for that temple authorities to subsequently decide only brahmins could be appointed as poojaris by way of some alterations in the relevant doctrines? We are clear that no party could ever revisit such a finding of fact. Such an attempt will result in anomalous situations and could only be treated as a circuitous way to overcome the finding of a Court. If subsequent alterations in doctrine could be allowed to create new essentials, the judicial process will then be reduced into a useless formality and futile exercise. Once there is a finding of fact by the competent Court, then all other bodies are estopped from revisiting that conclusion. On this count also the decision of High Court is liable to be set aside.

12. In the result, we respectfully adopt the finding of this Court in the first *Ananda Margi* case and allow the instant appeal. Since we find that practice of Tandava dance in public is not an essential part of *Ananda Margi* faith, there is no need to look into any other arguments advanced before us. The order in the Writ Petition as affirmed by the Division Bench is set aside and the Writ Petition is dismissed.

13. Before parting with this matter, it is necessary for us to refer to the observations made by this Court in *Bijoe Emmanuel* v. *State of Kerala,* MANU/SC/0061/1986, because reference to three Judges' Bench has arisen on account of these observations. In *Bijoe Emmanuel's* case (supra) this Court adverted to the decision of this Court in the earlier round of litigation in *First Ananda Margi* case (supra) and observed as follows:—

> "The question in that case was whether the *Ananda Margis* had a fundamental right within the meaning of Article 25 and Article 26 to perform Tandava dance in public streets and public places. The court found that Ananda Marga was a Hindu religious denomination and not a separate religion. The court examined the question whether the Tandava dance was a religious rite or practice essential to the tenets of the Ananda Marga and found that it was not. On that finding the court concluded that the Ananda Marga had no fundamental right to perform Tandava dance in public streets and public places. In the course of the discussion, at one place, there is found the following sentence:
>
> > 'Mr. Tarkunde for the petitioner had claimed protection of Article 25 of the Constitution but in view of our finding that Ananda

Marga was not a separate religion, application of Article 25 is not attracted.'

The sentence appears to have crept into the judgment by some slip. It is not a squinter to the reasoning of the court on any of the issues. In fact, in the subsequent paragraphs, the Court has expressly proceeded to consider the claim of the Ananda Marga to perform Tandava dance in public streets pursuant to the right claimed by them under Article 25(1)."

14. We respectfully agree with what has been stated above in *Bijoe Emmanuel's* case (supra) insofar as the First *Ananda Margi* case is concerned. As noticed therein, these observations are not the basis of the reasoning of the court on any of the issues. Therefore, it would not affect the final outcome of the case.

The appeal is allowed accordingly.

A.C. Lakshmanan, J.

15. This appeal stems from the judgment and order dated 08.11.1990 passed by the Division Bench of the Calcutta High Court in F. MAT. No. 1451 of 1990 dismissing the appeal filed by the Commissioner of Police with a directive to the effect that "The Police Authorities should permit the *Ananda Margis* to perform the *Tandava* dance in public processions on the occasion of their principal religious functions listed in prayer (b) of the writ petition on their undertaking to maintain peace and discipline on such occasions." The Division Bench affirmed the judgment and order dated 07.05.1990 passed by the learned Single Judge of the said Court allowing the writ petition of the respondents herein with a declaration that "Tandava dance as prescribed for the followers of *Ananda Margis* is an essential and integral part of the religion of the said religious denomination and that they have a right to perform such a dance in public on the occasions prescribed in this behalf subject to the restrictions under Articles 25 and 26 of the Constitution of India and the Police Authorities have no jurisdiction to impose ban on such a dance."

16. This case has a long and chequered carrier. The facts are stated as under.—

17. Ananda Murtiji introduced *Tandava* dance requiring it to be performed daily by an *Ananda Margi* as one of his religious rites.

What is Tandava Dance:

18. According to the Ananda Margis, Lord Shiva was the originator of Tandava dance and introduced it about six thousand five hundred years back for physical, mental and spiritual upliftment of every human being. *Tandava* dance is to be performed with a skull, knife and Trishul. It is also customary to hold a lathi and a damroo and sword. Dancer may also use live snake in place of skull in day time and fire mashal's or damroo during night time. *Tandava* dance lasts for a few minutes where two or three persons dance by lifting one leg to the level of chest and then bringing it down and lifting the other. Ananda Murtiji by incorporating *Tandava* dance in the system of beliefs of Ananda Marga wanted to bring it to its original glory. *Tandava* dance symbolises 'life' and 'death'. The skull represents death and the knife represents life. The *Ananda*

Margis are followers of *Shaivite* order within Hindu religion and Ananda Murtiji directed performance of Tandava dance as one of the prescriptions of religious rite to be followed by an *Ananda Margi* in private life and public places.

19. The respondents took out a procession with human skulls, daggers, trident etc., on 10.08.1979. According to the police, the procession was to take out violating prohibitory ban in regard to carrying of those articles in processions in public streets. In that circumstances, the Police Authorities declared the assembly unlawful and the police force was compelled to intervene. The Commissioner of Police, Calcutta made repetitive orders under section 144 of the Code of Criminal Procedure, 1973 since August, 1979, directing that no member of a procession or assembly of five or more persons should carry any fire arms, explosive, swords, spears, knives, trident, lathis or any article which may be used as weapon of offence or any article likely to cause annoyance to the public. This order of the Police Commissioner was challenged by the General Secretary of the Ananda Marga in a Writ Petition No. 903 of 1980 before the High Court of Calcutta. The Calcutta High Court, by order dated 23.09.1980, rejected the said writ petition for the reasons recorded therein. Again the Commissioner of Police, Calcutta made a fresh order under section 144 of the Code of Criminal Procedure, 1973 on 29.03.1982 wherein the same restraints as mentioned in the earlier order were imposed and an application for permission to take out a procession on the prohibited streets accompanied with Tandava dance was rejected by him. The said order refusing permission by the Police Commissioner was challenged by filing a writ petition under Article 32 of the Constitution of India in this Court being registered as Writ Petition Nos. 6890 and 7204 of 1982.

20. This Court passed an order in the said writ petition rejecting the same on the finding that performance of *Tandava* dance in procession in the public streets or in gatherings in public places was not an essential religious rite of the followers of the Ananda Marga. This Court also held as under:

> "The claim of Ananda Marga as a separate religion was not acceptable in view of the clear assertion that it was not an institutionalised religion but a religious denomination. *Ananda Margis* belong to the *Shaivite* order and as such they belong to the Hindu religion. Accordingly, they were not entitled to get the protection of Article 25 of the Constitution of India.
>
> The Courts have the power to determine whether a particular rite or observance is regarded as essential by the tenets of a particular religion.
>
> *Ananda Margi* as a religious order is of recent origin and Tandava dance as a part of religious rite of that order is still more recent. It is doubtful as to whether in such circumstances Tandava dance can be taken as an essential religious rite of *Ananda Margis*. Even conceding it is so it is difficult to accept Mr. Tarkunde's argument that taking out religious processions with Tandava dance is an essential religious rite of *Ananda Margis*.
>
> Even conceding that Tandava dance has been prescribed as a religious rite for every follower of *Ananda Margis* it does not follow as a necessary

corollary that Tandava dance to be performed in the public is a matter of religious rite. In fact, there is no justification in any of the writings of Shri Ananda Murti that Tandava dance must be performed in public..... .....We are, therefore, not in a position to accept the contention of Mr. Tarkunde that performance of Tandava dance in a procession or at public place is an essential religious rite to be performed by every Ananda Margi."

The petitioners have no fundamental right within the meaning of Article 25 and 26 to perform Tandava dance in public streets and public places."

21. According to the appellants, no permission was granted to the respondents' organisation for taking out a similar procession. The respondents performed Tandava dance with human skulls, knives etc., violating the conditions of permission. On 07.05.1987, the respondents made an application to the Commissioner of Police, Calcutta seeking permission for taking out procession. By order dated 25.05.1987, the permission was refused by the Commissioner of Police, Calcutta. Under Article 32 of the Constitution of India, Writ Petition (Civil) Nos. 1317-18 of 1987 was filed by the respondents in this Court challenging the said order of the Police Authorities refusing permission which was disposed of by this Court with the following observation:

> "We are of the view that these cases should appropriately be examined by the High Court keeping in view that has been said by this Court in the judgment in *Acharya Jagdishwaranand Avadhuta etc.* v. *Commissioner of Police, Calcutta* reported in MANU/SC/0050/1983. Petitioners are at liberty to go before the High Court."

22. Pursuant to the aforesaid liberty granted by this Court, a writ application was moved by the respondents praying for quashing the orders dated 20.05.1987 and 27.05.1987 of appellant No. 1 - Commissioner of Police and also for a directive upon the appellants commanding them to allow the respondents to perform Tandava dance in public procession of Ananda Marga on the occasion of its principal religious function and festival such as

(i) Ananda Purnima;

(ii) Shravani Purnima;

(iii) Bijaya Dashami;

(iv) Dipavali;

(v) New Year Day;

(vi) Falguni Purnima (Vasanttotsava); and

(vii) Dharma Maha Chakra and Dharma Maha Sammelans.

23. The respondents based their right to perform Tandava dance in procession and in public gathering on the basis of the prescription of their Guru Shri Ananda Murtiji in the recent Fourth Edition of Carya Carya Part I published in the year 1986. The writ application was heard by a learned Single Judge who passed an order allowing the writ application upon holding, *inter alia,* that Tandava dance as prescribed for followers of Ananda Marga was an essential and integral part of the religion of the said religious denomination and that they have right to perform such a dance on the occasion prescribed in this behalf subject to the restrictions imposed under Articles 25 and 26 of the Constitution of India and the Court was powerless to examine as to whether such prescription of their Guru formed essential and integral part of the religious rite to be observed by the *Ananda Margis*. Against the said judgment and order, the appellants filed an appeal before the Division Bench and obtained stay of operation of the said order of the learned Single Judge. The stay application and the appeal were heard by the Division Bench of the High Court of Calcutta on several dates. The impugned judgment and order of the Division Bench of the High Court of Calcutta was passed on 08.11.1990 dismissing the stay application and the appeal and affirming the order of the learned Single Judge of the High Court of Calcutta. Aggrieved by the impugned judgment, the appellants have approached this Court by way of Special Leave Petition No. 16233 of 1990. On 21.12.1990, this Court granted leave in this matter and directed to continue the *status quo* until further orders. A direction was also issued to expedite the appeal and to post the appeal as early as possible. On 13.11.1992, this Court, after hearing the parties for sometime and having considered the decision of the three learned Judges of this Court in *Acharya Jagdishwaranand Avadhuta etc.'s* case (supra), was of the view that this is a matter which requires consideration by a Constitution Bench of this Court. The matter was placed before the Constitution Bench. The Constitution Bench, by an order dated 04.12.2001, observed that there is no justification for the hearing of this civil appeal by a Constitution Bench and it must be placed before a Bench of two learned Judges for final disposal. When the matter came up before the Division Bench of this Court on 17.01.2002, the Bench expressed their opinion as follows:

> "After hearing the counsel for the parties at length, we are of the opinion that seemingly there is a contradiction in the order passed by the Division Bench of the Calcutta High Court (impugned judgment); the three-Judge Bench judgment in *Acharya Jagdishwaranand Avadhuta* (supra) and the order passed by a two-Judge Bench in *Bijoe Emmannuel* (supra). In the latter case, the two-Judge Bench has explained in judgment of this Court in *Acharya Jagdishwaranand Avadhuta* (supra) and held that *Ananda Margi* could claim the benefit of Article 25(1) having open the question regarding applicability of Article 25 to the *Ananda Margis*. The High Court based its decision on the latter judgment and gave the impugned judgment holding that the order passed by the appellants was violative of Articles 25 and 26 of the Constitution of India.
>
> We feel that the observation made by the two-Judge Bench in *Bijoe Emmannuel* (supra) that Article 25 did not apply to *Ananda Margis* had crept in the latter judgment by some slip does not appear to be correct. In our view, this Court in its judgment in *Acharya Jagdishwaranand Avadhuta etc.* (supra) had reached a definite conclusion that the claim of the respondents that the action of the appellant was violative of fundamental rights of the respondents within the meaning of Articles 25 and 26 of the Constitution of India had to be rejected. It is apparent from the observation made by the Court in para 15 of its order reproduced in the earlier part of this order.

Another aspect which is required to be considered is whether the High Court was right in holding that prescribing of Tandava Dance, with damroo, skull and trishul as a necessary religious rite by the *Ananda Margis* by their Guru after the rendering of the judgment by this Court would translate into a practice and the religious rites of the *Ananda Margis* or not. As the earlier judgment had been rendered by a three-Judge Bench, it would be appropriate that this aspect is also examined by a three-Judge Bench.

In order to avoid contradiction and inconsistency in the orders passed by this Court, we are of the view that this matter requires to be considered by a Bench of three learned Judges. Accordingly, we request the learned Chief Justice to place this matter before a Bench of three learned Judges."

24. As noticed earlier, the dispute started in the year 1979 between the Police Authorities - the appellants herein and the respondents' organisation and the matter was pending before one forum or the other for all these years and has now been placed before this Bench for final hearing and for resolution of the long standing dispute between the parties.

25. We heard the arguments of Mr. Tapas Ray, learned senior counsel for the appellants and Mr. T.R. Andhyarujina, learned senior counsel for the respondents.

26. Learned senior counsel appearing for the respective parties drew our attention to the pleadings, documents, exhibits marked, the judgments rendered by the High Court and of this Court on earlier occasions. Both sides have also cited number of judgments in support of their respective contentions.

27. Mr. Tapas Ray, learned senior counsel appearing for the appellants, submitted that—

(a) Tandava dance is not a religious rite or practice essential to the tenets of religious faith of *Ananda Margis* and that taking out religious processions with Tandava dance is not an essential religious rite;

(b) *Ananda Margis* have no fundamental right within the meaning of Articles 25 and 26 of the Constitution of India to perform Tandava dance in public streets or public places on their mere assertions that their Guru recently prescribed Tandava dance as part of their religious rite;

(c) The findings of the Calcutta High Court to the effect that Tandava dance is a part of religious order of that particular community and that the Police Authorities should allow the *Ananda Margis* to perform the Tandava dance in public procession on the occasion of their principal religious functions mentioned in the writ petitions are hit by the principle of *res judicata* in view of the negative decision of this Court on identical issues in *Acharya Jagdishwaranand Avadhuta etc.'s* case (supra);

(d) The subsequent order dated 01.12.1987 of this Court in Writ Petition (Civil) No. 1317-18 of 1987 to the effect that the case made out in the writ petition filed in this Court should be appropriately examined by the High Court keeping in view what had been said by this Court in *Acharya*

Jagdishwaranand Avadhuta etc.'s case (supra) has not enabled the High Court to reopen the issues already conclusively decided by this Court in the above case;

(e) In view of the fact that *Ananda Margis* is not an institutionalised religion by itself and that they are a religious denomination within the Hindu religion which is the religion they hold, the *Ananda Margis* have no fundamental right within the meaning of Article 25 and Article 26 to perform Tandava dance in pubic streets and public places as per the mandate of their preceptor Ananda Murtiji in absence of any prescription to that effect in the "Shaivite" order within the Hindu religion;

(f) Whether the 'Guru' of *Ananda Margis*, Ananda Murtiji enjoys complete autonomy under Article 26(b) of the Constitution of India in the matter of deciding as to what rites and ceremonies are essential for his followers and whether Court is powerless to determine if such particular rite or observance is an essential tenet of the religion the followers of *Ananda Margi* hold.

(g) The respondents also cannot be permitted to carry trident, daggers or knife and/or live snakes in public procession or otherwise in view of the fact that the same is bound to disturb public peace and tranquility and also such permission cannot be given as because there would be possibility of breach of public order and it might affect public health and morality. Further carrying of human skulls and indulging in dance by lifting the leg to the chest level with weapons like tridents, daggers and/or knives and/or live snakes in crowded public roads of Calcutta and its suburbs or anywhere are repulsive to public taste and morality and the unusual dancing pose would also cause fear in the mind of people specially children thereby provoking public annoyance.

28. Mr. T.R. Andhyarujina, learned senior counsel, made elaborate submissions in support of the respondents' case and cited many decisions.

29. He submitted that the issue raised in the present appeal had been raised by way of an application under Article 32 of the Constitution of India before this Court and this Court having directed the High Court to dispose of the matter keeping in view the earlier judgments of this Court, the matter is at large.

30. The action of the appellants in refusing the *Ananda Margis* the right to perform the Tandava dance was violative of Articles 15, 19, 25 and 26 of the Constitution of India.

31. In the present case, what constitutes an essential part of a religion is primarily to be ascertained with reference to the doctrine of that religion itself and the Court cannot say that a belief or practice is not part of religion. In support of this contention, he relied on the following judgments:—

1. *The Commissioner, Hindu Religious Endowments, Madras* v. *Sri Lakshmindra Thirtha Swamiar of Sri Shirur Mutt*, [1954] SCR 1005 (1028)
2. *Sardar Syedna Taher Saifuddin Saheb* v. *The State of Bombay*, [1962] (Supp 2) SCR 496 (531-532)

3. *Seshammal etc.* v. *State of Tamil Nadu,* MANU/SC/0631/1972.
4. *Ratital Pannachand Gandhi* v. *The State of Bombay,* [1954] SCR 1055
5. *N. Adithayan* v. *Travancore Devaswom Board,* MANU/SC/0862/2002.
6. *The Durga Committee, Ajmer* v. *Syed Hussain Ali,* MANU/SC/0063/1961.

32. In the present case, Anand Murtiji had prescribed a procession on six days with Tandava dance in the *Carya Carya* in the Fourth Edition 1986. This precept is binding on the *Ananda Margis* which has not been disputed by the Commissioner of Police that these precepts are mandatory for the *Ananda Margis.* [As could be seen from Volume-II page 84 para 8 of the paper book].

33. It is significant that this Court in its order of 01.12.1987 did not dismiss the fresh writ petition filed after its decision in *Acharya Jagdishwaranand Avadhuta etc.'s* case (supra). When the precepts were recorded in the *Carya Carya* and made part of the new petition, this Court ordered that this should be investigated by a fresh writ petition in the High Court which was done by the Division Bench of the High Court now and held that the precept was established as part of *Ananda Margis* religious belief.

34. It is pertinent to mention that carrying a small knife not exceeding 3" or 4" in size and a skull as symbolic items for the purpose of performing religious rites is not prohibited by any law. Besides, it must be emphasised that a knife with a blade shorter than 10.16 cm in length is not an "arm" under section 2(c) of the Arms Act. Learned senior counsel cited MANU/WB/0042/1990 and *Acharya Jagdishwaranand Avadhuta etc.'s* case (supra) which also notes that these are only 'symbolic' items.

35. There can be no question of any 'public order' being violated by the procession of *Ananda Margis* involving in the Tandava dance. The concept of 'public order' which is a permissible restriction under Article 25(1) needs to be distinguished from the connotation 'law and order'. As stated by this Court in *Dr. Ram Manohar Lohia* v. *State of Bihar,* MANU/SC/0054/1965 that every breach of peace does not lead to public disorder.

36. Learned senior counsel for the respondents relied on the decision of the Constitution Bench in *Himat Lal K. Shah* v. *Commissioner of Police, Ahmedabad,* MANU/SC/0583/1972 for the proposition of the right to carry out religious processions in public streets.

37. It has been stated by the Commissioner of Police that if *Ananda Margis* do not carry a knife, trident or skull but only perform the Tandava dance in public, there would be no objection. This is to ignore the fact that feature of the Tandava dance is the carrying of a knife, trident and skull since time immemorial. This has also been noted by the Division Bench of the Calcutta High Court in *Commissioner of Police* v. *Acharya Jagdishwaranand,* MANU/WB/0052/1991.

38. Concluding his argument, learned senior counsel submitted that the respondents are wiling to abide by any reasonable regulation in the interest of public order imposed by the Commissioner of Police in the conduct of their procession provided that the essential practice of *Tandava* dance as aforesaid is permitted.

39. The first question which needs to be decided goes to the very root of the High Court's jurisdiction in deciding the issue after the permission was given to the respondents to approach the High Court. It is clear from the language used by this Court in disposing of the petition under Article 32 of the Constitution of India that this Court itself was persuaded with the earlier judgment did not finally conclude the matter. That is why, this Court directed the respondents herein to go before the High Court and directed the High Court to reconsider the matter. As rightly pointed out by learned senior counsel for the respondents, it is significant to note that this Court in its order dated 01.12.1987 did not dismiss the fresh writ petition filed after its decision in *Acharya Jagdishwaranand Avadhuta etc.'s* case (*supra*) when the precepts were recorded in the Carya Carya and made part of the new petition under Article 32 of the Constitution of India, this Court ordered that this should be investigated by the High Court in a fresh writ petition filed by the respondents, which was done by the High Court and which on reconsideration of the entire gamut of litigation and the records and of the arguments of the counsel appearing on either side held that the precept was established as part of *Ananda Margis* religious belief. Therefore, the submission made by learned senior counsel for the appellants that the earlier judgment of this Court is final and there was no scope for the same issue to be reagitated or redetermined by the High Court has no force. Since the matter is at large, we are of the opinion that the High Court is right in considering the entire matter afresh and determining the same. The High Court was competent to consider the question whether the *Ananda Margis* can claim the benefit of Article 25(1) of the Constitution of India. Since, in our view, the said question is still open for reconsideration. This apart, this Court in arriving at its finding that the Tandava dance was not an essential part of *Ananda Margis* religion had taken into consideration the fact that there was no document to show that the Tandava dance was to be performed in public. As rightly pointed out by the High Court, there has been a factual change in the situation since the earlier judgment. The High Court, therefore, is right in holding that it has the jurisdiction to entertain the present writ proceedings.

40. This Court in its earlier judgment, took note of the fact that the practice was a recent one. No finding, however, was arrived at by this Court that by reason of the recentness of the practice, the same could not form part of religion or be a matter of religion. This Court, finally rested its finding on the fact that the *Ananda Margis* had not been able to show from any of their religious literature that the Tandava dance was to be performed in public. In fact, this Court has also recorded that the counsel for the *Ananda Margis* had been asked by the Court to produce any literature in this regard but this could not be done.

41. As far as the recentness of the practice is concerned, it has been submitted by Mr. Andhyarujina that the *Tandava* dance has been closely associated with Hinduism from time immemorial and in support of this argument he relied upon several authorities and that the Hindus in general have always believed in dance as a form of worship *vide* "Nataraja in Art, Thought and Literature" by C. Sivaramamurti. He would further submit that Ananda Murtiji was considered by the *Ananda Margis* as their religious preceptor or guru and any direction given by him was a mandate which could not be disobeyed. Therefore, the rites and rituals which would be prescribed by Ananda Murtiji would form an integral part of their religion as Ananda Murtiji was alive till recently, necessarily such directives could continue to be given until his death.

42. I am of the opinion that there is merit and substance in the contention of learned senior counsel. Although the specific introduction of Tandava dance in public procession may have been recent, this does not detract from the fact that the Tandava dance is part of the religion of the *Ananda Margis*. In any religion, practices may be introduced according to the decisions of the spiritual Head. If these practices are accepted by the followers of such spiritual Head as a method of achieving their spiritual upliftment, the fact that such practice was recently introduced cannot make it anytheless a matter of religion.

43. Countering the argument, learned senior counsel for the appellants, submitted that the concept of Tandava dance was not a part of religion but a secular activity and relied upon the decision of this Court in the case of *Durga Committee, Ajmer* v. *Syed Hussain Ali* reported in (supra). The particular passage relied on by learned counsel for the appellant is as follows:

> "In order that the practices in question should be treated as a part of religion they must be regarded by the said religion as its essential and integral part; otherwise even surely secular practices which are not an essential or an integral part of religion are apt to be clothed with a religious form and may make a claim for being treated as religious practices within the meaning of Article 26. Similarly even practices though religious may have sprung from merely superstitious beliefs and may in that sense be extraneous and unessential accretions to religion itself. Unless such practices are found to constitute an essential and integral part of a religion their claim for the protection under Article 26 may have to be carefully scrutinised, in other words, the protection must be confined to such religious practices as are an essential and integral part of it and no other."

44. This observation of this Court, in our view, runs counter to the observation of Mukherjee, J. in *The Commissioner, Hindu Religious Endowment, Madras* v. *Sri Lakshmindra Thirtha Swamiar of Sri Shirur Mutt* (*supra*). In this context, it is useful to reproduce a passage from the above judgment which explains the definition of religion in paragraphs 14 and 19 of the judgment which are—

> "We now come to Article 25 which, as its language indicates, secures to every person, subject to public order, health and morality, a freedom not only to entertain such religious belief, as may be approved of by his judgment and conscience, but also to exhibit his belief in such outward acts as he thinks proper and to propagate or disseminate his ideas for the edification of others....
>
> ....If the tenets of any religious sect of the Hindus prescribe that offerings of food should be given to the idol at particular hours of the day, that periodical ceremonies should be performed in a certain way at certain

periods of the year or that there should be daily recital of sacred texts or oblations to the sacred fire all these would be regarded as parts of religion..."

45. In a subsequent decision, namely, *His Holiness Srimad Perarulala Ethiraja Ramanuja Jeeyar Swami etc.* v. *The State of Tamil Nadu,* MANU/SC/0631/1972, this Court has held that—

> "Worshippers lay great store by the rituals and whatever other people, not of the faith may think about these rituals and ceremonies, they are a part of the Hindu Religious faith and cannot be dismissed as either irrational or superstitious."

46. Mr. Tapas Ray again submitted that the directives regarding the performance of Tandava dance was contained in Carya Carya under the heading "Social functions and festivals" and, therefore, the performance of Tandava dance was a secular activity. We are unable to accept this contention. We have already referred to the festivals at large. The Tandava dance has to be performed which are religious in nature. It is stated in Chapter 15 of the Carya Carya that our social-cum-spiritual functions will be considered part of our spiritual life. Admittedly, the original Tandava dance of Siva forms part of the Hindu religion which is said to represent the threefold processes of creation, preservation and destruction. The rhythm, postures, ornaments and the weapons used in the dance are said to be symbols of religious significance vide chapter entitled "The significance of Siva's dance from "Nataraja in Art, Thought and literature" by S. Sivaramamurthi. It is to be noticed that since 1986 Ananda Murtiji has specifically directed the performance of the Tandava dance in public procession on special occasions. This directive is contained in the revised version of the *Carya Carya.* It was placed before us at the time of hearing. In fact, this writing was not produced before this Court during the hearing of the earlier writ proceedings and that this Court had no occasion to consider the same. In our view, the performance of Tandava dance in public procession forms part of the *Ananda Margis* religion and is also a matter of religion within the meaning of those articles and that the *Ananda Margis* cannot be deprived of their right to practice their religion in the manner prescribed by their religious preceptor, except on the grounds of public order, morality and health. It is not the case of the appellants that the permission for the performance of Tandava dance in public procession has been forbidden on the ground of health. The permission has been refused on the ground of public order and morality. However, in the orders by which the permission had been refused, the Police Authorities have refused permission in terms of the order of this Court. This Court had never directed the said authorities not to accede to the performance of the *Tandava* dance in public procession. It was, therefore, wrong for the State Authorities to refuse permission purportedly in terms of this Court's orders. A close scrutiny of the order refusing permission do not contain any reference to public order or morality. However, the appellants, at the time of hearing of this appeal, tried to improve their case by affidavits which cannot at all be permitted. The reason justifying refusal of permission should have appeared in the order refusing permission itself. The only reason given was this Court's order. These reasons cannot now be modified or supplemented by way of an affidavit in the proceedings as held by this Court in *Mohinder Singh Gill* v. *The Chief Section Commissioner,* MANU/SC/0209/1977.

47. Ananda Marga had already been declared as a religious denomination by this Court *vide* judgment dated 20.10.1983 as reported in *Acharya Jagdishwaranand Avadhuta etc.'s* case (supra) at para 9 wherein it has been observed as under:

> "....Ananda Marga appears to satisfy all the three conditions, *viz.,* it is a collection of individuals who have a system of beliefs which they regard as conducive to their spiritual well being; they have a common organisation and the collection of these individuals has a distinctive name, Ananda Marga, therefore, can be appropriately treated as a religious denomination within the Hindu religion..."

48. This declaration was made by this Court after perusal of all rival contentions by both the parties, in that case also, the present appellants had made various averments about the alleged misbehavior of *Ananda Margis* and this Court placed no reliance on the said allegations. The contention that the word 'religion' under Article 25(1) of the Constitution of India does not include sect of religion of Ananda Marga being declared as religious denomination does not qualify for the same protection as religion in our view is not tenable. The learned Judges of the Calcutta High Court in their judgment impugned in this appeal has categorically dealt with the question following the decision exactly on the same point in the case of *Shirur Mutt* (supra) and the National Anthem case reported in MANU/SC/0061/1986 and *Sri Venkataramana Devaru* v. *State of Mysore,* AIR 1958 SC 255 held that a religious denomination or organisation enjoys complete autonomy in the matter of deciding as to what rights and ceremonies are essential according to the tenets of the religion they hold and outside authority has no jurisdiction to interfere with their decision in such matters.

49. It was argued on behalf of the respondents that the Ananda Marga which has been declared as a religion by this Court has been discriminated and singled out by the West Bengal Government for its ideological differences as its philosophy is based on spirituality. Several instances were pointed out by the respondents. Particulars were also furnished by the respondents in their writ petition in this regard. According to the respondents, processions of various hues are taken out regularly in Calcutta and the celebration of Muslim festival of Muharram is taken out with various deadly weapons as well as Sikh celebrations with sword fighting display in public, the procession of workers of Bharat Sevasram Sangha (a Social and not even a religious organisation) are allowed to move on horseback and carrying swords through the streets. Besides these, the example of Bolana and Gajana festivals in Burdwan, Birbhum, Murshidabad, Nadia in West Bengal, wherein a public dance with severed heads from corpses is displayed and the procession of monks in Allahabad are examples of religious tolerance in our country which has a wide variety of traditions and beliefs. The display of Tandava dance which takes only a few minutes by a very limited number of persons to display the same compared to other religious festivals. The plea of congested streets is an eye-wash in that the appellants allows other groups of other hue to move in procession in Calcutta and deny the *Ananda Margis* due to prejudice towards Ananda Marga and its philosophy. This contention was denied by learned counsel for the appellants stating that if the respondents are allowed to perform the dance on public roads while in procession which is offensive order morality are bound to create external situation endangering public life and safety which goes or bound to go out of control of the administration. Such a procession with burning torches, human skulls etc., if allowed will only be at the cost of widespread public panic, disruption of traffic, both vehicular and pedestrian and smooth movement of passers by and will give rise to the chances of rioting and other criminal offences. In our view, this contention of the appellants has no merits. If one religious denomination is allowed to carry its religious practice but another religious denomination is restrained from carrying on religious practice and almost similar religious practices, the same makes out a clear case of discrimination in violation of the principles of Article 14 of the Constitution. It was submitted by learned senior counsel for the respondents that in the procession of the followers of *Ananda Margis*, each one of them will not carry the skull and trident or knives of the aforesaid size, but only 5 to 6 members in a procession of at least 1,000 members would carry the skull and the trident and/or knives to perform the *Tandava* Dance which will be of a very limited duration, may be of 1 or 2 minutes. Such performance is likely to be repeated at the interval of say one mile and the said performance is not a continuous one. Such performance cannot by any stretch of imagination cause public annoyance or disturbance of the public law and order situation and therefore, there is no reason for the respondents to deny permission to the members of *Ananda Margis* to perform such Tandava Dance in public inasmuch as the said dance is one of the most fundamental aspects of the religious practice which the *Ananda Margis* are bound to perform as per the directions of their Living Guru.

50. According to Mr. Andhyarujina, a wrong impression is created about the religious procession by the *Ananda Margis* as if it consisted of a huge number of violent persons brandishing knives or tridents and displaying human skull or tridents terrifying the public and disturbing periodically public order in streets and that the facts are to the contrary. In regard to this submission, he invited our attention to the conditions under which the procession with Tandava dance is held by *Ananda Margis* as under:—

"1. 6 times a year on days of festivals and social functions;

2. approximately 1000 members in procession;

3. 5 or 6 members carry skulls and trident and/or knives to perform Tandava dance, which is of 1 or 2 minutes duration. This will be repeated at intervals of one mile and is not of continuous duration;

4. Knife/trident is only of 3" to 4";

5. The skull is held in the left hand and knife/trident (sometimes a torch) is held in the right;

6. Each of the items, *tandava* dance, trident/knife and skull has a deep spiritual significance;
7. The organizers of the procession have given undertaking to the Commissioner of Police to maintain peace and discipline when conducting procession and the procession will be taken only on a specified route or roads".

51. According to him, *Tandava* Dance in procession is the mandate of *Ananda Margis.* He invited our attention to para 14 of the judgment of this Court in *Acharya Jagdishwaranand Avadhuta etc.'s* case (*supra*) in which this Court held that there is no justification in any writings of Shri *Ananda Margis* that *Tandava* dance must be performed in public. On this finding, this Court held that *Tandava* dance was not proved to be an essential religious rite to be performed by every *Ananda Margi* in procession.

52. The tenets of the *Ananda Margi* are both oral and written as in the case of many religions. The fact that there were no writings shown to the Court that Tandava dance is to be performed in public, did not negative the existence of such precepts by the Anand Murthiji. As in the case of many religions any of the *Anand Murthiji's* precepts are a matter of oral prescriptions. However, in the 1986 edition of *Carya Carya* specific mention was made by Anand Murthiji of the requirement of *Tandava* dance in procession on special functions and festivals.

53. These written mandatory directions of Anand Murtiji were specifically pleaded by the Petitioner at page 9-10 para 9 and 10 of the Writ Petition. Their existence or genuineness were not denied in the reply. On the contrary, it was admitted that "the directive may be mandatory and binding on the followers of *Ananda Margis* but it does not bind the respondents.

54. The Court rightly observed that the fact that the practice is recently prescribed by Ananda Murtiji is not a reason for saying does not part of the religious practices and beliefs of the denomination.

55. I shall now consider whether *Ananda Margis* have the fundamental right under Articles 25 and 26 of the Constitution of India.

56. The Anand Margi are a religious denomination and as such are entitled to the protection under Articles 25 and 26(b) of the Constitution for their beliefs and practices including their practice of *Tandava* dance in a procession or public place. This is because, as held by this Court in several cases.

57. "Religious practices or performance of acts in pursuance of religious beliefs are as much a part of religious as faith or belief in religious doctrine. No outside authority has any right to say that they are not essential part of religion and it is not open to the secular authority of the State to restrict or prohibit them in any manner they like....." *Ratilal Pannachand Gandhi* v. *State of Bombay (supra)* citing with approval Daver, J. in *Jamshedji Soonabai,* AIR 33 Bom 122; *Commnr. HRE, Madras* v. *Lakshmandra,* 1954 SCR 1008 (1021-1022, 1025); *Sardar Syedna* v. *State of Bombay,* 1962 Supp (2) SCR 496 (531-532). In *Venkatarama Devaru's* case *(supra),* this Court has held that the right under Article 26(b) of a denomination to manage its own affairs in matters of religion includes even practices which are regarded as part of religion.

58. The exercise of the freedom to act and practice in pursuance of religious beliefs is as much important as the freedom of believing in a religion. In fact to persons believing in religious faith, there are some forms of practicing the religion by outward actions which are as much part of religion as the faith itself. The freedom to act and practice can be subject to regulations. In our Constitution subject to public order health and morality and to other provisions in Part III of the Constitution. However, in every case the power of regulation must be so exercised with the consciousness that the subject of regulation is a fundamental right of religion, and as not to unduly infringe the protection given by the Constitution. Further in the exercise of the power to regulate, the authorities cannot sit in judgment over the professed views of the adherents of the religion and to determine whether the practice is warranted by the religion or not. That is not their function [See *Jesse Cantwell* v. *State of Connecticut,* (1939) 84 L.Ed. 1213-1218; *United States* v. *Ballard,* (1943) 88 L.Ed. 1148 (1153, 1154)].

59. I shall now consider the right of the *Ananda Margis* to religious procession. In *Parthasaradi Ayyangar* v. *Chinakrishna Ayyangar,* ILR 5 Madras 304 Turner C.J. said,

60. "In India, person of whatever sect are entitled to conduct religious procession through public streets so long as they do not interfere with the ordinary use of such streets by the public and subject to such directions as the Magistrates may lawfully give to prevent obstruction of thorough fare or breaches of public peace."

61. "The power to suspend is extraordinary and the Magistrate should resort to it only when he is satisfied that other powers are insufficient. This authority of the Magistrate should be exercised in defence of rights rather than in their suspension."

62. These observations were quoted with approval by this Court in *Ghulam Abbas* v. *State of UP,* MANU/SC/0059/1981. It was observed that the authorities should not in face of such religion rights prohibit religious procession on the "facile ground of public peace and tranquility" but adopt a positive approach to protect fundamental rights under Articles 25 and 26 of the Constitution.

63. Moreover "public order" has a larger connotation than "law and order". Contravention of law to effect public order must affect the community or the public at large. A mere disturbance of law and order leading to disorder is not one which affects "public order". [See *R.M. Lohia* v. *State of Bihar* (supra)].

64. Similar processions by other communities even with use of swords *e.g.,* Sikhs, Muslims and Bharat Sevashram Sanghs have been permitted by the Commissioner of Police.

65. The Police Commissioner answers the charge of discrimination by stating that "activities of Anand Margis cannot come within the scope of religious functions or practices as compared to well-established practices festival of Muslims and Sikhs". It is not for the Police Commissioner to give his disapproval to practice of a particular sect which are in his opinion not well established. To allow any authority to judge the truth or falsity of a religious belief or practice is to destroy the guarantee of religious freedom in the Constitution (see *US* v. *Ballard*, 88 L.Ed. 1148).

66. At the time of hearing, a promise was made that the *Ananda Margis* are willing to abide with any regulatory condition imposed by the Police Authorities in their procession so long as their religious beliefs and practices of Tandava Dance in a procession are not abrogated.

67. Whilst our Constitution is neutral in religion, it at the same time, is benign and sympathetic of all religious creeds however unacceptable they may be in the eyes of the non-believers. Articles 25 and 26 embody a tolerance to all religions. This Court has rightly said

> "Our tradition teaches tolerance; Our philosophy preaches tolerance; Our Constitution practices tolerance; Let us not dilute it:
>
> It is in that spirit of tolerance that creeds like the Petitioner with their practices must be accepted in our society".

68. This Court has explained in a number of decisions that what constitutes an essential part of a religion is primarily to be ascertained with reference to the doctrine of that religion itself and the Court cannot say that a belief or practice is not part of religion. This proposition was authoritatively laid down by the Constitution Bench of this Court (Seven Judges) in *Shirur Mutt's* case (supra) as extracted in paras (supra). This is the most essential part of the fundamental right of freedom of religion. This Court in subsequent cases have followed the proposition in *Shirur Mutt's* case *(supra), Sardar Syedna Taher Saifuddin Saheb* v. *State of Bombay (Five Judges),* 1962 (Supp) SCR 496 (531-532) & in *Seshanmmal* v. *State of Tamil Nadu,* MANU/SC/0631/1972 (five Judges) at page 21.

69. In the case of *Ratilal Pannachand Gandhi* v. *State of Bombay (supra),* this Court emphasized that "No outside authority has any right to say that these are not essential parts of religion and it is not open to a secular authority of the State to restrict and prohibit them in any manner they like under the guise of administering the trust estate." This Court quoted with approval *Jamshedji* v. *Soonabai (supra)* where the Bombay High Court held, "if this is the belief of the community......a secular judge is bound to accept that belief - it is not for him to sit in judgment on that belief, he has no right to interfere with the conscience of a donor who makes a gift in favour of what he believes to be the advancement of his religion and the welfare of his community or mankind."

70. As late as 2002, this Court has reiterated this in *N. Adithayan* v. *Tranvancore Devaswom Board,* MANU/SC/0862/2002. This Court observed that "as to what really constitutes an essential part of religion or religious practice has to be decided by the Courts with reference to the doctrine of a particular religion or practices regarded as parts of religion."

71. The obiter of Gajendragadkar, J. in Durga-Committee, *Ajmer* v. *Syed Hussain Ali (supra)* to the effect that the Court may have carefully scrutinized the practices to find out whether they constitute an essential or integral part of religion is not in line with the above decisions including that of seven Judges Bench in the case of *Shirur Mutt* (supra).

72. *Seervai in Constitutional Law of India* (4th Edn.), Vol. II at page 1268 has criticized this as obiter as inconsistent with earlier decisions of this Court cited above.

73. Subject to consideration of public order, health and morality, it is not open for anybody to question the tenets and practices of religion, however, irrational they may appear to an outsider.

74. It is brought to our notice that the following observation in *Acharya Jagdishwaranand Avadhuta etc.'s* case (supra) is not correct in law:—

> "Mr. Tarkunde has claimed protection of Article 25 of the Constitution but in view of our finding that Anandamarga is not a separate religion, application of Article 25 is not attracted".

As rightly stated by this Court in *Bijoe Emmanuel's* case, (1986) 6 SCC 615 (631). This sentence appears to have crept into the judgment by some slip.

Article 25(1) states that all persons are entitled to freedom of religion. Hence every member of a religious denomination is entitled to the fundamental right of freedom of religion under Article 25. It necessarily follows that every sect or denomination is entitled to freedom of religion under Article 25. It is undisputed that under Article 26(b) a denomination is entitled to manage its own affairs in matters of religion.

The above observation in *Jagdishwaranand's case* is also contrary to the interpretation of Article 25(1) given by this Court in the Constitution Bench of 7 Judges in *Shirur Mutt* case where the Court observes that "institutions as such cannot practice or propagate religion; it can be done only by individual persons and whether these persons propagate their personal views or the tenets for which the institution stands is really immaterial for the purpose of Article 25".

75. In this context, I can also usefully refer to the decision of this Court in *Ratilal Panachand Gandhi* v. *State of Bombay (supra).*

76. I am, therefore, of the opinion that the observation of the learned Judges in the referring order dated 17.01.2002 are not correct

77. I have given my thoughtful consideration to the important questions of law posed for our consideration.

78. Article 25(1) guarantees to every person freedom of conscience and the right freely to profess, practice and propagate any religion. It may be noted that this right is not confined to citizens alone, but covers all persons residing in India. But the right to freedom of religion guaranteed by this Article is subject to restrictions which may be imposed by the State on the grounds of:

1. Public order, morality and health;
2. Other provisions of Part III of the Constitution;
3. Regulating non-religious activity associated with religious practice;
4. Social welfare and reform; &
5. Throwing open Hindu religious institutions of public character to all classes of Hindus.

79. The full concept and scope of religious freedom is that there are no restraints upon the free exercise of religion according to the dictates of one's conscience or upon the right freely to profess, practice and propagate religion save those imposed under the police power of the State and the other provisions of Part II of the Constitution. This means the right to worship God according to the dictates of one's conscience, Man's relation to his God is made no concern for the State. Freedom of conscience and religious belief cannot, however, be, set up to avoid those duties which every citizen owes to the nation; *e.g.* to receive military training, to take an oath expressing willingness to perform military service and so on.

80. Though the freedom of conscience and religious belief are absolute, the right to act in exercise of a man's freedom of conscience and freedom of religion cannot override public interest and morals of the society and in that view it is competent for the State to suppress such religious activity which are prejudicial to public interest. That apart, any activity in furtherance of religious belief must be subordinate to the criminal laws of the country. It must be remembered crime will not become less odious because sanctioned by what a particular sect may designate as religious. Thus polygamy or bigamy may be prohibited or made a ground of disqualification for the exercise of political rights, notwithstanding the fact that is in accordance with the creed of a religious body.

81. The liberty of the individual to do as he pleases, even in innocent matters, must yield to the common good. In other words, the police power of the State is founded on the theory that when there is conflict between the rights of individual and the interest of the society, the interest of the society must prevail. In an organized society there cannot be any individual right which is injurious to the community as a whole. At the same time, the police power is not absolute and must not be arbitrary or oppressive. In other words, the police power must be exercised for preservation of the community from injury. What our Constitution attempts to do is to strike a balance between individual liberty and social control. There are two limbs to religions freedom contained in Article 25. While one limb guarantees the right the other limb incorporates restrictions on the exercise of the right so that they may not conflict with public welfare or morality.

Jahova Witnesses and *Ananda Margis*

82. The principle of secularism enshrined in the Constitution touched its high watermark in the Jehovah's witnesses case, wherein this Court held that children of the Jehovah's witnesses faith need not stand-up to sing the National Anthem at school assemblies. According to the Court there is no provision of law which obliges anyone to sing the National Anthem, nor is it disrespectful to the National Anthem if a person who stands up respectfully when the National anthem is sung does not join the singing. It is true that the Constitution enjoins a duty on every citizen to respect the National Flag and National Anthem. However, according to the Court, proper respect is shown to the National Anthem by standing-up when the National Anthem is sung and it will not be right to say that disrespect is shown by not joining in the singing. Therefore, the expulsion of the children from the school for the reason they did not join the singing of National Anthem, though they do stand-up respectfully, when the Anthem is sung would be violative of Article 19(1) and Article 25(1), especially when it was sought to be done in pursuance of two circulars issued by the Director of Public Instruction having no statutory force. In the case of *P.M.A. Metropolitan* v. *Moran Mar Marthoma,* MANU/SC/0407/1995 (ex-communication case), a sharply divided Court upheld the right of the leaders of faith to ex-communicate 'fallen' believers for religious reasons – no doubt leaving it to the Courts to determine whether an ex-communicatory reason was religious or not. The principle of ex-communication is that the collective right will prevail over individual right. However, in 1995, this Court recognized the power of ex-communication as a measure of discipline. In the case of *Mohd. Hanif Quareshi* v. *The State of Bihar,* 1959 SCR 629, *Cow Slaughter* case] this Court had struck a balance between the fundamental rights of butchers to occupation and slaughtering of cows, an activity claimed to be part of the Islamic faith. While prohibiting indiscriminate slaughter of cows the Court did two things.

1. Muslim sentiments were respected and butchers retained a large part of their trade.

2. By rejecting their claim that cow slaughter was an "essential practice of Islam" relying on its own interpretation of *Koran,* the Hindus were partially appeased.

83. Here, the Court has assumed the role of the theologian after making a roving enquiry. White the decision is criticized on the ground that, once this door is opened, there is no limit to which the Court cannot go, the answer is theft the power of judicial review as a basic structure is vested with the Court and if some one has to be trusted, let it be the Courts even in matters of faith. This Court, as stated earlier, considered this question whether performance of Tandava dance is a religious rite or practice essential to the tenets of the religious faith of the *Ananda Margis.* The Court while upholding Ananda Marga satisfies all the three conditions envisaged by Article 26 of the Constitution of India and as such a religious denomination negatived their claims to perform Tandava Dance in public (1) It is a collection of individuals who have a system of beliefs which they regards as conducive to their spiritual well-being; (2) they have a common organization, and (3) the collection of these individuals has distinctive name). The specific case of the petitioners is that Shri Ananda Murti introduced Tandava as a part of religious rites of Anand Margis in 1936. What is Tandava Dance? It lasts for a few minutes, where two or three persons dance by lifting one leg to the level of the chest, bringing it down and lifting the other. When the *Ananda Margis* greet their spiritual preceptor, they perform a brief welcome dance of Tandava using skull and knife for 2/3 mts. According to them, Tandava is a custom among it sect members and it is a customary performance and its origin is over thousands of years old. Repelling the contention the Court held even conceding that Tandava dance has been prescribed as a religious rite for the followers of Ananda Marga, it does not follow as a necessary corollary that Tandava Dance to be performed in the public is a matter of religious rite. The Court went on to observe that there is nothing that Tandava dance must be performed in public. In the result, this Court rejected the claw of *Ananda Margis* to perform Tandava Dance in public streets.

84. It would be pertinent to mention that the Sikh Community carry "Kirpans" as a symbol of their religious practice and the Gurkhas the "Kukris" or "Dagger". So also, the Hindus are permitted to carry the idol of "Ganesa" in procession before immersion in the sea during Vinayaka Chaturthi Celebrations. Persons professing Islamic Faith are allowed to take out procession during "Moharrum" Festival and persons participating in such processions beat their chest with hands and chains and inflict injuries on them and the same has been permitted as a religious practice of that community.

85. Each deity presides over a certain function, has a certain consort, uses a particular vehicle, giving them a concrete aspect that appeals to less spiritually sophisticated lay people. All these insignia have a deep philosophical symbolism. What might interest us presently is that all these vehicles are mostly drawn from the world of animals, birds, and even reptiles. For example, Brahma has a swan, Vishnu has a garuda, a type of eagle, Siva rides a bull, Ganesa a mouse, Subrahmanya a peacock, and so on. The idea is only to emphasize the kinship with animals. Trees have the divinity Vanadevata. War is presided over by the Goddess Chamundi riding a lion. Sound has a divinity, the Nadabrahmam. The Goddess Saraswathi presides over music and arts. Lakshmi sitting on a lotus deals with wealth. Parvathi, the consort of Siva, rules the entire Nature. All these divinities serve to consecrate every aspect of daily life. The whole pantheon serves to emphasize the one ultimate Reality.

86. Reading and reciting old scriptures, for instance, Ramayana or Quran or Bible or Guru Granth Sahib is as much a part of religion as offering food to deity by a Hindu or bathing the idol or dressing him and going to a temple, mosque, church or gurudwara.

87. The authorities concerned can step in and take preventive measures in the interest of maintenance of Law and Order if such religious processions disturb Law and Order. It has to be held that the right to carry Trishul, Conch or Skull is an integral and essential part of religious practice and the same is protected under Article 25 of the Constitution of India. However, the same is subject to the right of the State to interfere with the said practice of carrying Trishul, Conch or Skull if such procession creates Law and Order problems requiring intervention of concerned authorities who are entrusted with the duty of maintaining Law and Order.

What is Religion

88. Religion is a social system in the name of God laying down the Code of Conduct for the people in Society. Religion is a way of life in India and it is an unending discovery into unknown world. People living in Society have to follow some sort of religion. It is a social Institution and Society accepts religion in a form which it can easily practice, George Barnard Shaw stated, "There is nothing that people do not believe if only it be presented to them as Science and nothing they will not disbelieve if it is presented to them as Religion."

Essentially, Religion is based on "Faith". Some critics say that Religion interfered with Science and Faith. They say that religion led to the growth of blind faith, magic, sorcery, human sacrifices etc. No doubt, history of religion shows some indications in this direction but both Science and Religion believe in faith. Faith in Religion influences the temperament and attitude of the thinker. Ancient civilization *viz.*, the Indus Valley Civilization shows faith of people in Siva and Sakthi. The period of Indus Valley Civilization was fundamental religion and was as old as at least Ehyptian and Mesapetomiah Culture. People worship Siva and the Trishul (Trident), the emblem of Siva which was engraved on several seals. People also worshipped stones, trees, animals and Fire. Besides, worship of stones, frees, animals etc., by the primitive religious tribes shows that animism *viz.*, worship of trees, stones, animals was practiced on the strong belief that they were abodes of spirits, good or evil. Modern Hinduism is to some extent includes Indus Valley Civilization Culture and religious faith. Lord Siva is worshipped in the form of Linga. Many symbols have been used in Hindu Literature. Different kinds of symbols and images have different sanctity. Breading of chest, arms and other parts of body represent to the weapons of symbols of Siva. Modern Hinduism has adopted and assimilated various religious beliefs of primitive tribes and people. The process of worship has undergone various changes from time to time.

89. The expression of 'RELIGION' has not been defined in the Constitution and it is incapable of specific and precise definition. Article 25 of the Constitution of India guarantees to every person, freedom of conscience and right freely to profess, practice and propagate religion. No doubt, this right is subject to public order related to health and morality and" other provisions relating to Fundamental Right Religion includes worship, faith and extends to even rituals. Belief in religion is belief of practice a particular faith, to preach and to profess it. Mode of worship is integral part of religion. Forms and observances of religion may extend to matters of Food and Dress. An act done in furtherance to religion is protected. A person believing in a particular religion has to express his belief in such acts which he thinks proper and to propagate his religion. It is settled law that protection under Articles 25 and 26 of the Constitution of India extend guarantee for rituals and rituals and observances, ceremonies and modes of worship which form part and parcel of religion. Practice becomes part of religion only if such practice is found to be essential and integral part, it is only those practices which are integral part of religion that are protected. What would constitute an essential part of religion or religious practice is to be determined with reference to the Doctrine of a particular religion which includes practices which are regarded by the Community as part and parcel of that religion. Test has to be applied by Courts whether a particular religious practice is regarded by the community practicing that particular practice is integral part of the religion or not. It is also necessary to decide whether the particular practice is religious in character or not and whether the same can be regarded as an integral or essential part of religion which has to be decided based on evidence.

90. It is not uncommon to find that those delve deep into scriptures to ascertain the character and status of a particular practice. It has been authoritatively laid down that Cow Sacrifice is not an obligatory over-act for a Muslim to exhibit his religious belief. No Fundamental Right can be claimed to insist on slaughter of a healthy cow on a Bakrid Day. Performance of "Sharadha" and offering of "Pinda" to ancestors are held to be an integral part of Hindu Religion and religious practice. Carrying "Trishul" or "Trident" and "skull" by a few in a procession to be taken out by a particular community following a particular religion is by itself an integral part of religion. When persons following a particular religion carry Trishul, Conch or Skull in a procession, they merely practice which is part of their religion which they wanted to propagate by carrying symbols of their religions such as Trishul, Conch etc., if the conscience of a particular community has treated a particular practice as an integral or essential part of religion, the same is protected by Articles 25 and 26 of the Constitution of India.

91. Therefore, Anand Margis have right to take a procession in public places after obtaining necessary permission from the concerned authorities and they are also entitled to carry Trishul or Trident, Conch or Skull so long as such procession is peaceful and does not offend the religious sentiments of other people who equally enjoy fundamental right to exercise their religious freedom. An Anand Margi is entitled to transmit or spread religion by taking out procession in public places and also carry Trishul, Conch or Skull. However, any religious right is subject to public order. The State has got ample powers to regulate the secular activities associated with religious practices. Religious activities are protected under Article 25 of the Constitution of India. No doubt, such religious freedom is subject to health and subject to laws made for social welfare. Every person has got right to follow, practice and propagate his religion.

92. The Commissioner has got power to regulate assemblies, meetings and processions in public places, etc. It specifically provides that he is entitled to prescribe the routes by which and the times at which such processions may pass, in order to keep the public places and prevent obstructions on the occasion of such assemblies, meetings and processions and in the neighbourhood of places of worship during the time of public worship.

93. Hence, to preserve public peace and to avoid damages to public properties and keeping this in mind the Anand Margis are permitted to go on procession and perform Tandva dance with symbolic skull, Trishul, knife, damroo, sword subject to the following terms and conditions:—

1. The Commissioner of police may prescribe the route;
2. REGULATION:
   - (i) The participants to the procession shall not carry wooden bars, weapons, metal rods, weapons capable of inducing violence.
   - (ii) Loud speakers shall not be used.
   - (iii) Traffic regulations should be observed.
   - (iv) Traffic should not be obstructed.
   - (v) Normal activities of common man should not be disturbed.

(vi) Objectionable slogans and illegal slogans or provocative slogans affecting others' sentiments shall not be expressed or voiced.

(vii) Processionists shall proceed in five persons row and shall keep one side of the road by keeping other side for transport.

(viii) Crackers are prohibited.

(ix) They should not spray colour powders.

94. The instructions of police officers and other regulations as above should be followed."

95. For the foregoing reasons, I am of the opinion that the appeal filed by the appellate has no merits and is, therefore, dismissed.

96. In my opinion, it is a fit case for awarding of exemplary costs to the respondents. Since the respondents were prevented from practising their religion and perform the religious Tandava dance, they were compelled to come before this Court. In this appeal, since the appellant is a Government, by taking a lenient view, I order no costs.

Sun Beverages (P.) Ltd. v. *State of Uttar Pradesh*

AIR 2004 SC 777: (2004) 9 SCC 116
Appeal (civil) 4617 of 1996
Decided on 28-11-2003

Coram: **Hon'ble Mr. Justice P. Venkatarama Reddi**
Hon'ble Dr. Justice AR. Lakshmanan

Judgment by: **Hon'ble Dr. Justice AR. Lakshmanan**

FACTS: The Government of Uttar Pradesh formulated a scheme known as 'Capital Grant Scheme' for the grant of subsidies to industrial units for giving an impetus to the industrialisation of the backward areas. In the Scheme, 'Pioneer Unit' was defined as 'Such industrial units to be set up during the period from 1-10-1982 to 31-3-1985 firstly in any part of the Tehsil or at Tehsil level where no heavy industry is established prior to 1-10-1982 and that whose capital investment is more than Rs. 1 crore shall be treated as a 'Pioneer Unit'. Registration with DGTD as medium scale industry was also the requirement. The

petitioner, had set up his industrial unit with total investment of Rs. 1,07,78,368,34 on building, land and machinery etc. He was granted cash subsidy. His unit was registered with DGTD as Medium Scale Industry. Subsequently the Government of India issued fresh guidelines and the DGTD cancelled registration of the appellant as a Medium Scale Industry and directed the appellant to approach Director of Industries, U.P. for registration as a Small Scale Industry. As a consequence of de-registration as a Medium Scale Industry by the DGTD, the Government of U.P. issued notice for recovery and called upon the appellant to refund Rs. 15 lacs as the DGTD had cancelled the registration.

ISSUE: Validity of the demand for refund of subsidy and that of the recovery certificate.

HELD: The appellant had been compelled to get the registration under the Small Scale Industries Unit on account of the change in the definition of the Small Scale Industries Unit by the Central Government and not on account of any inaction of the appellant. Hence, if on account of the change in the definition of the Small Scale Industries Unit, the appellant was de-recognised as DGTD Unit then the appellant could not be denied the benefit of cash subsidy.

JUDGMENT

Dr. AR. Lakshmanan, J.

The present appeal was filed against the judgment dated 19.05.1995 pronounced by the Division Bench of the High Court of Judicature at Allahabad by which the writ petition of the appellant bearing No. 1607 of 1988 was dismissed. The writ petition was filed by the appellant to issue a writ prohibiting the respondents from recovering Rs. 18,72,821.92 constituting cash subsidy plus interest thereon from the appellant-Company as arrears of land revenue after quashing notice dated 15.09.1987 (Annexure 8 to the petition) and recovery certificate dated 31.10.1987 (Annexure 11 to the petition).

The sequence of facts and events leading to the filing of this civil appeal are as follows:

By an order dated 30.09.1982, the Government of Uttar Pradesh formulated a scheme known as 'Capital Grant Scheme' (hereinafter referred to as 'Scheme') for the grant of subsidies to various industrial units for giving an impetus to the industrialisation of the backward areas *i.e.,* zero industrial areas of the State.

In the said Scheme, 'Pioneer Unit' has been defined as:

> "Such industrial units to be set up during the period from 01.10.1982 to 31.03.1985 firstly in any part of the Tehsil or at Tehsil level where no

heavy industry is established prior to 01.10.1982 and that those capital investment is more than Rs. one crore shall be treated as a Pioneer Unit."

In view of the aforesaid incentive Scheme, Shri Rajan Sethi (since deceased) and his wife decided to incorporate a Company for bottling of aerated waters in the backward area of the District Agra. The Company was incorporated under the Companies Act on 01.10.1983 and it had entered into a franchise agreement with M/s. Campa Beverages Private Limited on 06.05.1983 for bottling various brands of aerated waters. For the purpose of becoming entitled to the cash subsidy under the aforesaid Scheme, the appellant purchased land and building and made an investment of Rs. 17,11,845.95. The Company made further investment on installing plant and machinery in the unit. The total investment made by the appellant in establishing this unit amounted to Rs. 1,07,78,368.34 with the location of the industrial unit in a zero industrial area. According to the appellant, because of the total investments made, the appellant became entitled to cash subsidy under the aforesaid Scheme as a pioneer unit.

The aforesaid Scheme prescribed the following two conditions for grant of cash subsidy to industrial units—

(i) That it will be a 'Pioneer Unit' within the terms of the Scheme.

(ii) That it is registered with the Director-General of Technical Development.

Under the Notification issued by the Government of India, in the year 1983, a Small Scale Industry has been defined under the Industries Development Regulation Act, 1948 as one which had made an investment of up to Rs. 20 lacs in plant and machinery alone apart from other assets. As a Small Scale Industry, the appellant was liable to be registered with the Government and as a Medium Scale Industry, the appellant was entitled to be registered with the Director-General of Technical Development (in short 'the DGTD'), Government of India. The investment of the appellant in the plant and machinery exceeded Rs. 20 lacs. The DGTD was obliged to register the appellant industry as a Medium Scale Industry since the investment in the plant and machinery exceeded Rs. 20 lacs. The appellant accordingly applied to the Director-General of Industries for registration and the appellant was registered on 28.11.1984 with the DGTD as a Medium Scale Industry for the manufacture of 43.2 million bottles of soft drinks per annum. The appellant applied for cash subsidy to the Government of U.P. as it fulfilled both the above stated conditions under the Scheme. The Government of U.P., on 31.03.1986, sanctioned a subsidy of Rs. 15 lacs to the appellant and this subsidy was paid to the appellant in two instalments. An agreement was entered into between the appellant and the respondents under which the mode and method of the payment of subsidy of Rs. 15 lacs was prescribed. It was covenanted:

"1 (b). That the grantee will comply with and faithfully observe all the provisions of the said Scheme as also any other conditions imposed by the order sanctioning the said subsidy.

(c) That for a period of five years from the date of receiving the subsidy or any part thereof or from the date production starts, whichever of these dates are earlier, the grantee will allow the officers subordinate to the Director or any other person or persons authorised by the Director or by the State Level Committee constituted under the said Scheme to inspect the work for which the Special State Capital Subsidy has been given and also the machine plant, appliances, tools equipment for the procuring of which the grant has been made.

(f) That within a period of five years from the date of going into production or of the date of receipt of the Subsidy or any part thereof whichever of these dates are later. The Grantee will not change the place or location of the said Industrial Unit entirely or partly, nor enter into partnership with anyone nor change its constitution nor will the grantee effect substantial contractive disposal of substantial part of its total fixed capital investment without the written prior permission of the Director.

2. It is hereby agreed and declared by and between the parties hereto that in any of the following cases the Director shall have the right to stop further payment of the State Capital Subsidy and to require the Grantee to refund the amount of subsidy already paid and the Grantee shall refund the same forthwith together with interest at the Bank lending rate then prevailing and in the case of Grantee's failure to do so, the Director may recover the same as arrears of land revenue.

(a) Where Grantee has obtained the said Subsidy by misrepresentation as to an essential fact or by furnishing of false information/or where his industrial unit does not go into production;

(b) Where the Grantee's said industrial unit goes out of production within five years from the date of commencement of production except in cases where the unit remains out of production for short periods extending to six months due to reason beyond its control such as shortage of raw material, power, etc.; or

(c) Where the Grantee fails to furnish the prescribed statement and/or information which it is called upon to furnish; or

(d) If the Grantee commits a breach of any one of the covenants herein contained or of the Provisions of the said Scheme."

Subsequent to the registration of the appellant as Medium Scale Industry, the Government of India, by Notification dated 18.03.1985 altered the definitions of 'Small Scale Industry' and 'Medium Scale Industry'. By this notification, it was provided that if the investment of an industrial unit in plant and machinery alone (excluding other investments) was up to Rs. 35 lacs, it was entitled to be registered as a Small Scale Industry, but if it exceeded Rs. 35 lacs, it was entitled to be registered as Medium Scale Industry. In other words, the limit of investment in plant and machinery for Small Scale Industry was increased from Rs. 20 lacs to Rs. 35 lacs. The existing registered medium scale industries were given option to get themselves registered as small scale industries if they so chose within six months. The appellant was advised to apply to the DGTD for de-registration on the ground that its investment in plant and machinery was less than Rs. 35 lacs in view of the revised definition of the Small Scale Industry and the Medium

Scale Industry made by the Government of India by its Notification issued on 18.03.1985. The appellant was advised to apply to the DGTD for de-registration more than a year after the cash subsidy had been sanctioned and granted, to the appellant under the Scheme and much after the expiry of the option period. By letter dated 04.08.1987, the DGTD cancelled the registration of the appellant as a Medium Scale Industry and directed the appellant to approach the Director of Industries, U.P. for registration as a Small Scale Industry. According to the appellant, the registration could not be cancelled as the option period of six months had already expired. The appellant thereupon applied for registration with the General Manager, District Industries, Agra, for being registered as a Small Scale Industry.

On 24.09.1987, the appellant received a communication dated 15.09.1987 from respondent No. 2 calling upon the appellant to refund the cash subsidy together with interest amounting to more than Rs. 18,40,767.12 on the only ground that the unit of the appellant was required to continue to remain a Medium Scale Industry for five years from the date of the agreement and on account of the cancellation of its registration by the DGTD, the appellant had caused a violation of the scheme. It is also stated that the power to seek refund of the subsidy is also circumscribed by clause 2 of the Agreement dated 31.03.1986 executed between the parties. Clause 2 of the said Agreement has already been extracted above.

While so, the respondent without waiting for a reply from the appellant or affording any opportunity of hearing straight away issued a recovery certificate on 31.10.1987 to the third respondent calling upon him to recover the sum of Rs. 18 lacs and odd as arrears of Land revenue from the appellant. The appellant thereupon made a representation to the Government of U.P. that the said demand and subsequent recovery order were illegal and contrary to the factual position. As no response was received to the aforesaid representation and as the respondents were taking recourse to coercive processes, the appellant filed a writ petition before the High Court.

It was contended before the High Court on behalf of the respondents that the appellant has not faithfully observed all the provisions of the Scheme as also other conditions imposed by the order sanctioning the scheme and that a perusal of the terms of the scheme under which the subsidy was allowed only show that a Pioneer Unit holding DGTD registration was eligible for subsidy under the Scheme and a combined reading of the Scheme and the agreement shows that the loanee that is the petitioner (appellant) had to retain its character as a Pioneer unit holding DGTD registration for a period of five years to be computed from the year in which the disbursement of the subsidy was made. It was further submitted that after raising of the limit from Rs. 20 lacs to Rs. 35 lacs in the meanwhile, the appellant lost its DGTD registration which was cancelled on its own application *vide* order dated 04.08.1987 as a result of which the appellant was relegated to the character of a Small Scale Unit. It was further argued by the respondents that the inevitable consequence of the loss of the DGTD registration by the appellant as aforesaid was that the appellant ceased to be eligible for special subsidy paid to it under the Scheme and this indeed constituted violation of condition No. 1(b) of the Agreement. Under such circumstances, the subsidy of Rs. 15 lacs paid to the appellant under the Scheme as a Pioneer Unit holding DGTD registration became recoverable by the respondents as provided in clause 2 and clause 2(d) of the Agreement along with interest at current bank lending rate calculated from the date of payment of subsidy till the date of recovery of the amount.

The Division Bench of the High Court held that the writ petition filed by the appellant was bereft of merits and that the respondents are entitled to recover the subsidy with interest as demanded. The High Court proceeded on the basis that there was breach of the terms granting subsidy by reason of the appellant being de-recognised by DGTD.

Aggrieved by the judgment of the High Court, the above appeal has been filed.

We have perused the pleadings, the judgment under appeal, the annexures and other relevant documents and, in particular, the Scheme, notice for recovery of subsidy, certificate for recovery issued by the Commissioner and Director of Industries, U.P., correspondence between the appellant and the respondents, Sanction letter dated 31.3.1986, Agreement dated 31.3.1986, cancellation order of DGTD registration dated 04.08.1987 and the proceedings issued by the Government of India in regard to the procedure for registration of units on transfer from DGTD etc., consequent upon revision in the definition of Small Scale Industries dated 17.01.1981 and the Notification dated 18.03.1985.

We heard the arguments of Mr. Kailash Vasdev, learned senior counsel for the appellant and Mr. R.K. Singh, learned counsel for the respondents. The counsel for the respective parties reiterated their submissions advanced before the High Court. On the aforesaid facts and circumstances of the case, the following questions may arise for consideration:

(1) If an industrial unit of a Company is granted subsidy in terms of the Scheme framed by the State Government when it fulfils all the terms and conditions of the Scheme, it is open to the State Government to call for refund of the subsidy at a later stage when the 'pioneer unit' chooses to get itself registered as a Small Scale Industry with the State Government instead of remaining registered as a Medium Scale Industry with the Director-General of Technical Development, Government of India in accordance with the change effected in the definition of a Small Scale Industry and a Medium Scale Industry by the Government of India, although it continues to remain 'pioneer unit' and there is absolutely no change in the control of the State Government over the unit in the obligations, investments and assets of the pioneer unit?

(2) Whether there is any provision in the Scheme or Agreement that a 'Pioneer Unit' which had been granted subsidy must continue to remain registered with the Director-General of Technical Development for a period of five years and if it does not remain registered, are respondents I & 2 entitled to seek refund of the subsidy?

In the instant case, the following facts are not in dispute:

(1) That both the parties to this action have entered into an Agreement;

(2) That the Government of U.P. formulated a scheme known as 'Capital Grant Scheme' for the grant of subsidies to various industrial units for giving an impetus to the industrialisation of the backward areas of the State;

(3) That the Scheme provides for payment of subsidies to the industries sector in the zero industrial area;

(4) That the petitioner, in fact, had set up his industrial unit in the zero industrial area;

(5) That the industrial unit had been set up during the period from 01.10.1982 to 31.03.1985 in a backward area where no heavy industry is established prior to 01.10.1982;

(6) That the appellant's unit was treated as a Pioneer Unit within the terms of the scheme and that it was registered with DGTD;

(7) That the appellant had made a total investment of Rs. 1,07,78,368 on building, land and machinery etc., and became entitled to cash subsidy under the Scheme;

(8) That the appellant's unit was registered with DGTD as a Medium Scale Industry and that the appellant had fulfilled the conditions of the scheme;

(9) That the sanction of subsidy of Rs. 15 lacs to the appellant and payment of the same in two installments;

(10) That the Government of India has issued fresh guidelines on 18.03.1985 which provided that an industry, investment of which did not exceed Rs. 35 lacs in plant and machinery alone shall be entitled to be treated as a Small Scale Industry;

(11) That the DGTD cancelled the registration of the appellant as a Medium Scale Industry on 04.08.1987 and directed the appellant to approach Director of Industries, U.P. for registration as a Small Scale Industry and as a consequence of de-registration as Medium Scale Industry by the DGTD, the Government of U.P. issued notice for recovery of Rs. 15 lacs and again called upon the appellant to refund Rs. 15 lacs as DGTD had cancelled the registration contending that the appellant had violated condition l(b) of the Agreement.

A resume of the aforesaid undisputed facts clearly show that there has been absolutely no violation of any provision of the Scheme on the part of the appellant and that the demand for the refund was wholly illegal and arbitrary.

In this background, we have also to see as to whether the grantee/appellant complied with and observed all the provisions of the Scheme and of the covenants of the Agreement or violated any terms of the Agreement.

We have already noticed as a result of change in the definition of Small Scale Industry by the Development Commissioner, Government of India the Industrial units which had invested upto 35 lacs in plant and machinery was liable to be treated as small scale industries and that it was on this ground alone, the appellant's industrial unit been de-registered as a Small Scale Industry but it continued to be a pioneer unit in terms of the scheme to which the subsidy had been granted to the appellant. In the circumstances, the appellant stated that the question of seeking refund of the amount from them did not arise as the appellant had not violated any terms of the Scheme or of the Agreement. In our view, the High Court has overlooked the aforesaid facts and documents in this regard.

It is also pertinent to notice that subsequent to the registration of the appellant as Medium Scale Industry, the Government of India, by Notification dated 18.03.1985 altered the definitions of Small Scale Industry and Medium Scale Industry. By this Notification, it was provided that if the investment of an industrial unit in plant and machinery alone was up to Rs. 35 lacs, it was entitled to be registered as a Small Scale industry, but if it exceeded Rs. 35 lacs, it was entitled to be registered as a Medium Scale Industry. In fact, the respondents could not point out that there was any change in the investment, assets, production, land, building, plant and machinery of the appellant and that there had been any change in the control exercised by the respondent Nos. 1 and 2 over the appellant and its units. There has been no change in the obligations of the appellant.

The appellant had applied for re-registration with DGTD as a Small Scale Industry more than a year after grant of subsidy on the advise that in view of the revised Notification issued by the Government of India, the appellant was liable to be registered as a Small Scale Industry. In our opinion, the registration of a unit as a Small Scale and Medium Scale Industry is done in pursuance of notifications issued under the Industries Development and Regulation Act, 1951 by the Government of India and that the subsequent cancellation of registration by DGTD on account of change of criteria has no bearing on the status of an industrial unit as a Pioneer Unit under the scheme framed by the State of U.P.

The appellant was registered as a DGTD Unit on 21.10.1983 and the said registration continued. Thereafter, in the year 1985, there have been some changes in the definition of the Small Scale Industries by the Development Commissioner, Government of India by which the definition of a Small Scale Industries Unit has been amended and the limit of investment in the plant and machineries has been extended from Rs. 20 lacs to Rs. 35 lacs. It has also been made clear that while computing the value of the machineries, only the value of those machineries will be considered which are directly involved in the production, while the other accessories and other machineries which are used in the manufacturing process but are not directly involved in the process of manufacture were not to be included for considering the unit as Small Scale Industry unit. In this view of the matter, even though the investment of the appellant in the machineries was more than Rs. 35 lacs, but the machineries while are utilised for manufacturing was less than Rs. 35 lacs *i.e.*, Rs. 32,15,861, hence the appellant was compelled to get it registered as Small Scale Industry unit, instead of a DGTD Unit. Thereafter, the appellant applied for registration as Small Scale Industry Unit and the requisite registration certificate was granted to the appellant by the General Manager, District Industries Centre, Agra, registering the appellant as a Small Scale Industry Unit.

It is also pertinent to notice that the respondents without issuing any show cause notice to the appellant as to why the said recovery be not made against the appellant and without affording any opportunity to show cause, a call notice dated 15.09.1987 has been issued to the appellant for recovering that amount and again followed by a recovery certificate from the office of the Commissioner and Director of Industries for recovering the sum of Rs. 18,72,821.92 as the arrears of land revenue. In our opinion the entire recovery proceedings initiated against the appellant by the respondents as arrears of land revenue is absolutely illegal and in gross violation of the principles of natural justice.

In this context, we may reproduce clause 13 of the Scheme which reads as follows:

> "13. Recovery of Special State Capital Grant: The Director of Industry, Uttar Pradesh shall have power to get the Special State Grant recovered as the recovery of land revenue is done consequent to following circumstances;
>
> (a) If the Industrial Unit has obtained the State Capital Grant by giving false facts or by submitting necessary facts in fraudulent manner.
>
> (b) If the Unit has stopped the production work within five years of the commencement of the production. However, this condition of restriction shall not be applicable to such units where the production work has remained suspended for a short period of 6 months due to reasons beyond its control such as sick and shortage of power etc.
>
> (c) If industrial Unit fails to provide prescribed details and information sought for. If Director of Industries of Uttar Pradesh could not get the Special State Capital Grant recovered from the Unit under the normal procedure, then he can get the amount of loan recovered as the arrear of land revenue recovery done under the Government of Uttar Pradesh rules.
>
> (d) If the Director of any Unit who has partly or fully received the grant has to change the place of his unit or dispose of any part of immoveable property/assets within five years from the date of start of production: Clause 2 of the Agreement has been extracted in paragraphs supra.

The above two clauses mentioned the circumstances under which the cash subsidy may be recovered as arrears of land revenue. None of the said clauses is applicable or attracted in the instant case. Therefore, we are of the opinion that the entire recovery proceedings are absolutely illegal and without jurisdiction. It is not the case of the respondents that the appellant has practised any fraud or guilty of making of any misrepresentations in obtaining the sanction/eligibility. The only provision which refers for recovery of cash subsidy as arrears of land revenue is mentioned in the above two clauses and inasmuch as none of the conditions enumerated therein is attracted, the entire recovery of the cash subsidy as arrears of land revenue is illegal. Even otherwise, the allegations made in the call notice for recovery of the cash subsidy as arrears of land revenue is uncalled for.

We have carefully perused the entire Scheme which goes to show that the cash subsidy would be granted to the unit which is a Pioneer Unit *i.e.* having an investment of more than Rs. 1 crore and which has been established after 01.10.1982 and at the time of grant of cash subsidy, the said Unit should be registered as DGTD Unit. Nowhere it provides that the said industry should remain as a DGTD Unit for a period of five years mentioned in clause 4 of the call notice. A perusal of the scheme further goes to show that it has been provided in the scheme that the production should not be stopped for a period of five years but it nowhere provides that the unit should remain as a DGTD Unit for a period of five years. In fact, the appellant had been compeiled to get the registration under the Small Scale Industries Unit on account of the change in the definition of the Small Scale Industries Unit by the Central Government and not on account of any inaction of the appellant. Hence, if on account of the change in the definition of the Small Scale Industries Unit, the appellant was de-recognised as DGTD Unit then the appellant could not be denied the benefit of cash subsidy.

We have already seen that clause 13 of the Scheme and clause "2 of the Agreement has been invoked by the respondents for the recovery of the subsidy. A close scrutiny of the above two clauses goes to show that in the event of violation of any conditions, the recovery will be made as arrears of land revenue and so prior to initiating action for breach of the terms of clause 13 of the Scheme and clause 2 of the Agreement, the opportunity ought to have been provided by the respondent No. 2 to the appellant to demonstrate whether the provisions of the Scheme and the Agreement are violated or not and that having not done so the entire recovery proceedings initiated against the appellant is bad for violation of principles of natural justice.

As already observed, a perusal of the pleadings would reveal that there is no allegation regarding playing of fraud or misrepresentation in obtaining the sanction/eligibility. The argument of the learned counsel for the respondents that the appellant on his own freewill applied for de-registration *vide* letter dated 12.06.1987 and that the appellants were no more entitled to be registered under DGTD and since the constitution of the Company had undergone charge and under the changed conditions the respondents were entitled to recover the subsidy given to the appellant cannot at all be countenanced.

Having taken note of the aforesaid factual situation, we have no hesitation to hold that the respondents have acted arbitrarily and contrary to the terms of the Scheme and the Agreement and on the basis of unwarranted assumptions in seeking to recover the amounts given as subsidy to the appellant.

In the facts and circumstances of the aforesaid, we set aside the judgment of the High Court impugned in this appeal and allow this appeal. However, there will be no order as to costs.

Saurabh Chaudri
v.
Union of India

AIR 2004 SC 361: (2003) 11 SCC 146
Writ Petition (Civil) Nos. 29, 54, 57, 68, 69, 84, 85, 89, 91, 95, 98, 99 and 100 of 2003 and Civil Appeal No. 8581 of 2003
[Arising out of S.L.P. (Civil) No. 1347 of 2002]
Decided on 04-11-2003

Coram: Hon'ble Mr. Chief Justice V.N. Khare
Hon'ble Mr. Justice R.C. Lahoti
Hon'ble Mr. Justice B.N. Agarwal
Hon'ble Mr. Justice S.B. Sinha
Hon'ble Dr. Justice AR. Lakshmanan

Judgment by: Hon'ble Mr. Chief Justice V.N. Khare

FACTS: On 31-12-2002 the Delhi University issued the following Notification:

> "........It is hereby notified that for admission of P.G. Courses during the Academic Session 2003, only Delhi University Medical Graduates would be eligible against the 75% reserved seats of the students from Delhi who have taken admission in the University/States under the 15% All India quota will not be eligible to seek admission in the P.G. Degree/Diploma Courses of Delhi University against the 75% reserve seats. All concern may please be note.
>
> Accordingly the students who have done MBBS under 15% All-India quota from the University/States other than Delhi University and have applied for admission to the P.G. Degree/Diploma Courses are not eligible to appear in P.G. Medical Entrance Test 2003 to be held on 9-2-2003. They are advised to apply for the return of the Bank Draft/Cheque."

The appellants filed the writ petition in the Supreme Court questioning the aforementioned notification dated 31-12-2002 as also reservation made by way of institutional preference for admission to Post-Graduate Medical Courses.

ISSUE: Constitutional validity of reservation by way of institutional preference. Domicile as a basis of reservation.

HELD: Reservation by way of institutional preference should be confined to 50% of the seats since it is in public interest. Reservation on the basis of domicile is not impermissible in view of article 15(1).

JUDGMENT

V.N. Khare, C.J.

1. Leave granted in the Special Leave Petition.

2. The core question involved in these writ petitions and appeal centres round the constitutional validity of reservation whether based on domicile or institution in the matter of admission into Post-*Graduate* Courses in government run medical colleges.

3. For determination of the said question factual matrix of the matter, is being noticed from Writ Petition (Civil) No. 29 of 2003.

4. The petitioners who are 52 in number are original residents of Delhi. They joined various medical colleges out of Delhi for undertaking their MBBS Courses of studies against the 15% all-India quota on being qualified therefore in the All India Medical Entrance Examination.

5. The appellants intended to join the medical colleges of Delhi for their Post-Graduate Medical Courses. They applied for and were granted admission forms having regard to the decision of this Court in *Dr. Parag Gupta* v. *University of Delhi*, MANU/SC/0300/2000. In the Bulletin of Information issued by the University of Delhi, it was stated, that Candidates like the appellants would be entitled for admission in Post-Graduate Courses subject to the decision of a matter pending in this Court, i.e. *Magan Mehrotra* v. *Union of India* since reported in (2003) 3 SCALE 101.

6. A three-Judge Bench of this Court in *Magan Mehrotra* (supra) *inter alia*, therein held that apart from institutional preference, no other preference including reservation on the basis of residence is envisaged in the Constitution, in view of the decision of this Court in *Dr. Pradeep Jain* v. *Union of India*, MANU/SC/0047/1984.

7. The Delhi University on or about 31.12.2002 relying on or on the basis of the decision of this Court in *Magan Mehrotra* (supra) issued the following notification:

> "In view of the judgment of the Hon'ble Supreme Court of India dated 17.12.2002 in Writ Petition (C) No. 417 of 2002. It is hereby notified that for admission of P.G. Courses during the Academic Session 2003, only Delhi University Medical Graduates would be eligible against the 75% reserved seats of the students from Delhi who have taken admission in the University/States under the 15% All-India quota will not be eligible

to seek admission in the P.O. Degree/Diploma Courses of Delhi University against the 75% Reserve Seats. All concern may please be note.

Accordingly the students who have done MBBS under 15% All-India quota from the University/States other than Delhi University and have applied for admission to the P.G. Degree/Diploma Courses are not eligible to appear in P.G. Medical Entrance Test 2003 to be held on 9.2.2003. They are advised to apply for the return of the Bank Draft/Cheque."

8. The appellants claiming themselves to be "the residents of Delhi" and "sons of the soil" filed the writ petition in the court questioning the aforementioned notification dated 31.12.2002 as also reservation made by way of institutional preference for admission to Post Graduate Medical Courses.

9. A Division Bench of this Court having regard to the decision in *Magan Mehrotra's* case (supra) which was rendered by a three-Judge Bench of this Court, referred the matter to a Bench of three Judges by order dated 3.2.2003. However, when the matter was placed before a three-Judge Bench, it by an order dated 7.2.2003 directed the matter to be placed before a Bench of five Judges considering the importance of the matter; but no reason was assigned therefore.

10. The question which was initially raised in the writ petition was as to whether reservation made by way of institutional preference is *ultra vires* Articles 14 and 15 of the Constitution of India; but during hearing a larger issue *viz.*, as to whether any reservation, be on residence or institutional preference is constitutionally permissible; was raised at the Bar.

11. In view of the importance of the question involved, this Bench in terms of order dated 1.4.2003 directed issuance of notice to all the States and Union territories. Pursuant whereto, except State of A.P. and State of Jammu & Kashmir all the States filed their returns and were heard.

12. Shri Harish Salve, learned senior counsel appearing on behalf of the appellants raised two contentions in support of the writ petition. He submitted that in view of the equality clause contained in Articles 14 and 15(1) of the Constitution of India, reservation whether based on domicile or institutional preference would be unconstitutional. The learned counsel took us through the decisions of this Court operating in the field and urged that in view of the passage of time no reservation should be permitted either on the basis of residence or on institutional preference. Reservation on residential criteria, the learned counsel contended, is squarely hit by clause (1) of Article 15 of the Constitution of India. Placing reliance on the debates on the subject at the time of framing of the Constitution. Shri Salve urged that the 'place of birth' being synonymous with 'domicile' the observations made contrary thereto in *D.P. Joshi* v. *The State of Madhya Bharat,* MANU/SC/0012/1955 are not correct.

13. Shri Salve further contended that in terms of the constitutional scheme, reservation is permissible only when there exist compelling Government objectives therefore and that too on nominal basis if it can be demonstrated that 'rule of merit' should not be allowed to be sustained and when the class in whose favour a departure is sought to be made constitutes a homogeneous group and such departure satisfies the tests of social justice for securing equality upon comparison of such disability suffered by such class or group of persons. The learned counsel submitted that in the matter of reservation the State must scrupulously follow the requirements of Clause (4) of Article 15 of the Constitution of India, namely, that the same is needed for the weaker section of society or a homogeneous class and identified by a presidential order issued in that behalf.

14. In a case involving higher education even, Shri Salve argued, such a provision must be handled with care and keeping in view a large number of decisions of this Court including *M.R. Balaji* v. *State of Mysore,* MANU/SC/0080/1962 not more than 50% of the total seats can be reserved. The learned counsel would contend that if such reservation is *prima facie* impermissible having regard to the constitutional scheme the same would fall within the purview of 'suspected classification' and, thus, must pass the 'strict scrutiny test' or 'intermediate scrutiny test'. Any executive order providing for such reservation, the learned counsel urged, must be construed having regard to the preamble, the fundamental rights of the citizens and in particular Article 19(1)(d), as also the Directive Principles of the State Policy as contained in Part IV of the Constitution of India and in particular Articles 41 and 47 of the Constitution of India. It was argued that meritorious students suffer from lack of mobility as contra distinguished from the mobility of the employees, and are required to be protected so as to suffer any discrimination only on a specious plea of the State "our money, our people". Domicile of all the citizens of India, Shri Salve urged, should be one; as the concept of State domicile has no role to play in our constitutional scheme. He emphasized that keeping the same in view, a profile check is required to be made so far as meritorious students are concerned, as those who are born and brought up in small towns also would like to have higher education in the metropolitan towns where having regard to the better infrastructures and higher resources, the institution therein would provide a better academic pursuit for them. In terms of Article 14 of the Constitution of India, Shri Salve argued, students cannot form different class nor any such classification made amongst them would be in public interest. Relying heavily upon the observations made in paragraph 10 of the judgment of this Court in *Dr. Pradeep Jain's* case (*supra*), the learned counsel submitted that as all students are entitled to equal opportunities all sorts of reservations must be given a go by.

15. The learned counsel next contended that in any event, the students like the appellants should not be held to have lost their residential status only because they had gone out of their State of origin for pursuing their MBBS Course for a period of five years.

16. According to *Shri Salve, Magan Mehrotra* (supra), does not lay down the correct law and it is required to be overruled.

17. Assailing reservation by way of institutional preference, Shri Salve, further submitted that the very premise upon which it, is based is fallacious inasmuch as the majority of students, in view of the decision of this Court in *Dr. Pradeep Jain's* case (*supra*) having taken admission on the criteria of domicile alone, would again be considered for pursuing their Post-Graduate Studies only on that basis and, thus, reservation by way of institutional preference would amount to indirect way of doing things as the same would for all intent and purport would be based on domicile and, thus, is liable to (sic)

18. Shri Salve further contended that Delhi University or the States were required to place before this Court sufficient materials to prove that such classification on institutional preference is based on an intelligible differentia. Drawing our attention to the statements made in the counter-affidavit, the learned counsel urged that no such material has been placed except that the said practice is in vogue for a long time.

19. Shri R.F. Nariman, learned senior counsel appearing on behalf of some of the students of All India Institute of Medical Sciences (AIIMS) submitted that in view of the decision of this Court in *All India Institute of Medical sciences Students Union* v. *All India Institute of Medical Sciences*, MANU/SC/0480/2001, out of 40 students only 6 were offered admission in non-clinical subjects which the most of the students would not like to pursue, Shri Nariman urged that plight of the students of AIIMS should be considered having regard to the stand taken by or the practice prevalent in other Universities, namely, institutional preference and in that view of the matter the students of the institution are also entitled to equal opportunity to compete with the students of other Universities.

20. Shri Shanti Bhushan, learned senior counsel appearing on behalf of the students of Delhi University, on the other hand, submitted that *Magan Mehrotra's* case (*supra*) has correctly been decided. The learned counsel contended that keeping in view the decisions of this Court *e.g., D.P. Joshi* (supra), *Dr. Jagadish Saran* v. *Union of India,* MANU/SC/0067/1980 and *Pradeep Jain* (supra), it must be held that reservation by way institutional preference has held the field for a long-time. The impugned notification, Shri Shanti Bhushan urged, having been issued pursuant to the directions of this Court, it is futile to urge that the action on the part of Delhi University in following the same has resulted in arbitrariness. According to the learned counsel reservation by way of institutional preference is not only a matter of convenience but also forms part of the educational policy. If such a policy is not allowed to have a little play, a student while undergoing different courses of studies may have to take admissions in different parts of the country where for he would face problems involving different languages, different cultures and different environments. It may not be feasible even for the parents of middle class family to send their children out of the State. Furthermore, the learned counsel contended that the chances that the local students would serve the local people cannot be completely ruled out and, thus, such a criteria cannot be said to be illogical or bad in law.

21. As regard application of strict scrutiny test, Shri Shanti Bhushan relying on or on the basis of the decision in *Shri Ram Krishna Dalmia* v. *Justice S.R. Tendolkar*, 1959 SCR 279 submitted that this Court has laid down the law that the constitutionality of a statute must be presumed and onus to prove that the statute is unconstitutional is upon the person who asserts the same. Only two tests, namely, as to whether the classification is reasonable and based on an intelligible differentia stood the test of time and there is no reason to deviate therefrom. Shri Shanti Bhushan argued that reservation by way of institutional preference had been holding the field since this Court decided *Dr. Pradeep Jain's* case (supra) and nothing has been pointed out by the petitioners to show that the said principle should be departed from.

22. Shri A. Mariarputham, learned counsel appearing on behalf of Delhi University, supplementing the arguments of Shri Shanti Bhushan, submitted that reservation by way of institutional preference is a definite and identifiable criteria and in that view of the matter it satisfies the test of valid classification as contained in Article 14 of the Constitution of India. The reasons assigned in support of the institutional preference in various decisions of this Court are still relevant and as such there being no change in the situation, any fresh look or reconsideration thereof is not warranted. This Court, the learned counsel urged that having framed a scheme in *Dr. Pradeep Jain's* case (supra) which is binding on all concerned in view of the provisions contained in Articles 141, 142, 143 and 144 of the Constitution of India, may not depart therefrom in view of the fact that this Court in *Magan Mehrotra's* case (supra) upon issuance of notice to all States had clearly directed that the law relating to institutional preference laid down in *Dr. Pradeep Jain's* case (supra) should be followed and in particular directed that the States of Assam, Karnataka, Tamil Nadu and Goa to follow reservation by way of institutional preference alone.

23. The learned counsel contended that all the States have since amended their rules so as to consider the candidature of those students who had studied in any of the institutions situated in that State on 15% all-India quota and in that view of the matter the said students do not require a further indulgence. According to the learned counsel apart from the fact that the students who had gone to pursue their MBBS courses outside the State are entitled to take part in all-India open competition, they having regard to the amendments made in the rules framed by the States of Karnataka, Assam and others being entitled to institutional preference in the State where they had studied, may not be held to be entitled to a further indulgence of competing with the students of Delhi University in 75% quota on the ground that they are residents of Delhi and thereby bringing back the concept of reservation on domicile indirectly again.

24. Shri Sanjay Hegde, learned counsel appearing on behalf of the State of Karnataka, Shri A. Phukan, learned counsel appearing for the State of Assam and Shri R.S. Suri, learned counsel appearing for the State of Punjab, however, submitted that the States should be allowed to set apart some seats for the local candidates. It was pointed out that unlike other studies Post-Graduate Medical Courses involve practical training and the students are required to work in the hospitals wherein they are paid stipends by the States. It was urged that the States have been finding it extremely difficult to get good number of local doctors to serve the rural population and, thus, such a criteria, according to the learned counsel, cannot be said to be unconstitutional.

25. Before we embark upon the questions raised at the Bar, we may notice that the States before the decision of this Court in *Dr. Parag Gupta's* case (supra) had been following different criteria as regard grant of preference *i.e.,* either on institution basis or on residence basis or both. The positions prevailing in different States before and after *Dr. Parag Gupta's* case (*supra*) and at present are given as under:

POSITION BEFORE PARAG GUPTA

Sl.	State	Nature of Preference	
1.	U.P.	Institutional	
2.	Delhi	Institutional	
3.	Maharashtra	Institutional	
4.	Gujarat	Institutional	
5.	West Bengal	Institutional	
6.	Assam		Residence
7.	Tamil Nadu		Residence
8.	Goa		Residence (10 years)
9.	Karnataka		Residence
10.	Madhya Pradesh	Institutional OR Residence	
11.	Haryana	Institutional OR Residence	
12.	Punjab	Institutional OR Residence	
13.	Rajasthan	Institutional OR Residence	
14.	Kerala	Institutional OR Residence	
15.	Orissa	Institutional OR Residence	
16.	Himachal Pradesh	Institutional OR Residence	
17.	Bihar	Institutional OR Residence	
18.	Pondicherry	25% all-India quota + 37.5% Institutional available seats + 37. 5% of available open for all	

POSITION AFTER PARAG OUPTA

Sl.	State	Nature of Preference	
1.	U.P.	Institutional	Residence (15%)
2.	Delhi	Institutional	Residence (15%)
3.	Maharashtra	Institutional	
4.	Gujarat	Institutional	
5.	West Bengal	Institutional	
6.	Assam		Residence
7.	Tamil Nadu		Residence
8.	Goa		Residence (10 years)
9.	Karnataka		Residence
10.	Madhya Pradesh	Institutional OR Residence	
11.	Haryana	Institutional OR Residence	

Sl.	State	Nature of Preference	
12.	Punjab	Institutional OR Residence	
13.	Rajasthan	Institutional OR Residence	
14.	Kerala	Institutional OR Residence	
15.	Orissa	Institutional OR Residence	
16.	Himachal Pradesh	Institutional OR Residence	
17.	Bihar	Institutional OR Residence	
18.	Pondicherry	25% all-India quota + 37.5% Institutional of available seats + 37.5% of available seats open for all	

PRESENT POSITION

Sl.	State	Nature of Preference	
1.	U.P.	Institutional	
2.	Delhi	Institutional	
3.	Maharashtra	Institutional	
4.	Gujarat	Institutional	
5.	West Bengal	Institutional	
6.	Assam		Residence
7.	Tamil Nadu		Residence
8.	Goa		Residence (10 years]
9.	Karnataka		Residence (10 years)
10.	Madhya Pradesh	Institutional OR Residence	
11.	Haryana	Institutional OR Residence	
12.	Punjab		Residence
13.	Rajasthan	Institutional OR Residence	
14.	Kerala	Institutional OR Residence	
15.	Orissa	Institutional OR Residence	
16.	Himachal Pradesh	Institutional OR Residence	
17.	Bihar	Institutional OR Residence	
18.	Pondicherry	25% all-India quota + 37.5% Institutional of available seats + 37.5% of available seats open for all	

26. It is neither in doubt nor in dispute that before the scheme was evolved in *Dr. Pradeep Jain's* case (supra), notices had been issued to all the States and all of them were fully heard. But despite the same, the orders passed by this Court in *Dr. Pradeep Jain's* case (*supra*) had been flouted with impunity, *inter alia,* by the States of Assam, Karnataka, Goa and Tamil Nadu. Now it transpires that even the State of Punjab has also not been following the said decision.

27. The necessity of issuing notices by this Court again in *Magan Mehrotra's* case (*supra*) must be considered from that angle. In *Magan Mehrota's* case (supra), this Court not only reiterated that the reservation by way of institutional preference be maintained but also directed the aforementioned States to follow the same.

28. The questions must, therefore, be considered in the aforementioned factual backdrop.

29. The first question that arises for consideration is, **whether the reservation on the basis of domicile is impermissible in terms of Clause (1) of Article 15 of the Constitution of India ?** The term 'place of birth' occurs in Clause (1) of Article 15 but not 'domicile'. If a comparison is made between Article 15(1) and Article 16(2) of the Constitution of India, it would appear that whereas the former refers to 'place of birth' alone, the latter refers to both 'domicile' and 'residence' apart from place of birth. A distinction, therefore, has been made by the makers of the Constitution themselves to the effect that the expression 'place of birth' is not synonymous to the expression "domicile" and they reflect two different concepts. It may be true, as has been pointed out by Shri Salve and pursued by Mr. Nariman, that both the expressions appeared to be synonymous to some of the members of the Constituent Assembly but the same, in our opinion, cannot be a guiding factor. In *D.P. Joshi's* case (supra), a Constitution Bench held so in no uncertain terms.

30. This Bench is bound by the said decision.

31. In *State of Uttar Pradesh* v. *Pradip Tandon,* MANU/SC/0086/1974, this Court observed:

> "The reservation for rural areas cannot be sustained on the ground that the rural areas represent socially and educationally backward classes of citizens. This reservation appears to be made for the majority population of the State. Eighty per cent. of the population of the State cannot be a homogeneous class. Poverty in rural areas cannot be the basis of classification to support reservation for rural areas. Poverty, is found in all parts of India, In the instructions for reservation of seats it is provided that in the application form a candidate for reserved seats from rural areas must submit a certificate of the District Magistrate of the District to which he belonged that he was born in rural areas and had a permanent home there, and is residing there or that he was born in India and his parents and guardians are still living there and earn their livelihood there. The incident of birth in rural areas is made the basic qualification. No reservation can be made on the basis of place of birth, as this would offend Article 15."

32. Answer to the said question must, therefore, be rendered in the negative.

33. The second question that arises for our consideration is, **whether reservation by way of institutional preference comes within suspected classification warranting strict scrutiny test ?**

34. Once it is held that clause (1) of Article 15 of the Constitution of India is not attracted, the only question which survives is as to whether the same attracts the wrath of Article 14 of the Constitution of India. Article 14 forbids class legislation but permits reasonable classification subject to the conditions that it is based on an intelligible differentia and that the differentia must have a rational relation to the object sought to be achieved.

35. In *Shri Ram Krishna Dalmia's* case (*supra*), this Court categorically held:

> "...It is now well-established that while Article 14 forbids class legislation, it does not forbid reasonable classification for the purposes of legislation. In order, however, to pass the test of permissible classification two conditions must be fulfilled, namely, (i) that the classification must be founded on an intelligible *differentia* which distinguishes persons or things that are grouped together from others left out of the group and, (ii) that that *differentia* must have a rational relation to the object sought to be achieved by the statute in question. The classification may be founded on different bases, namely, geographical, or according to objects or occupations or the like. What is necessary is that there must be a nexus between the basis of classification and the object of the Act under consideration. It is also well-established by the decisions of this Court that article 14 condemns discrimination not only by a substantive law but also by a law of procedure."

The principle enunciated above has been consistently adopted and applied in subsequent cases. The decisions of this Court further establish

(a) that a law may be constitutional even though it relates to a single individual if, on account of some special circumstances or reasons applicable to him and not applicable to others, that single individual may be treated as a class by himself;

(b) that there is always a presumption in favour of the constitutionality of an enactment and the burden is upon him who attacks it to show that there has been a clear transgression of the constitutional principles;

(c) that it must be presumed that the legislature understands and corruptly appreciates the need of (sic) problems made manifest by experience and that its discrimination's are based on adequate grounds;

(d) that the legislature is free to recognise degrees of harm and may confine its restrictions to those cases where the need is deemed to be the clearest;

(e) that in order to sustain the presumption of constitutionality the court may take into consideration matters of common knowledge, matters of common report, the history of the times and may assume every state of facts which can be conceived existing at the time of legislation; and

(f) that while good faith and knowledge of the existing conditions on the part of a legislature are to he presumed, if there is nothing on the face of the law or the surrounding circumstances brought to the notice of the court on which the classification may reasonably be regarded as based, the presumption of constitutionally cannot be carried to the extent of always holding that there must be some undisclosed and unknown reasons for subjecting certain individuals or corporations to hostile or discriminating legislation.

The above principles will have to be constantly borne in mind by the court when it is called upon to adjudge the constitutionality of any particular law attacked as discriminatory and violative of the equal protection of the laws."

36. The strict scrutiny test or the intermediate scrutiny test applicable in the United States of America as argued by Shri Salve cannot be applied in this case. Such a test is not applied in Indian Courts. In any event, such a test may be applied in a case where a legislation *ex facie* is found to be unreasonable. Such a test may also be applied in a case where by reason of a statute the life and liberty of a citizen is put in jeopardy. This Court since its inception apart from a few cases where the legislation was found to be *ex facie* wholly unreasonable proceeded on the doctrine that constitutionality of a statute is to be presumed and the burden to prove contra is on him who asserts the same. The courts always lean against a construction which reduces the statute to a futility. A statute or any enacting provision therein must be so construed as to make it effective and operative "on the principle expressed in the maxim: *ut res magis valeat quam pereat*". [See *CIT* v. *Teja Singh,* MANU/SC/0062/1958 and *Tinsukhia Electric Supply Co. Ltd.* v. *State of Assam,* MANU/SC/0027/1990].

37. Applying the test of presumption of constitutionality no case has been made out for invoking the doctrine of strict construction or intermediate construction.

38. The third question that arises for our consideration is, whether the reservation by institutional preference is valid? India is one country and all its citizens should equally be treated. The essence of equality is enshrined in Article 14 of the Constitution of India. But does it mean that equality clause must be applied to all citizens to all situations? It is true that the country should strive to achieve a goal of excellence which in turn would mean that meritorious students should not be denied pursuit of higher studies. This itself brings us the question, who is to judge the merit and what are the standards therefor? It is extremely difficult to lay down a fool-proof criteria. Success or failure of a candidate in one examination or the other may not lead to infallible conclusion as regard the merit of a candidate so as to achieve excellence. The larger question, therefore, would be how to and to what extent balance should be struck.

39. Ideal situation, although it might have been to see that only meritorious students irrespective of caste, creed, sex, place of birth, domicile/residence are treated equally but history is replete with situations to show that India is not ready therefore. Sociological condition prevailing in India compelled the makers of the Constitution to bring in Articles 15 and 16 in the Constitution. The said Articles for all intent and purport are species of Article 14 which is the genies in a sense that they provide for exception to the equality clause also. Preference to a class of persons whether based on caste, creed, religion, place of birth, domicile or residence is embedded incur constitutional scheme. Whereas larger interest of the country must be perceived, the law makers cannot shut their eyes to the local needs also. Such local needs must receive due consideration keeping in view the duties of the State contained in Articles 41 and 47 of the Constitution of India.

(Emphasis mine)

40. For the last five decades this Court times without number had adopted the efficacy of one catena or the other for giving preference to a section of students.

41. Constitutional interpretation is a difficult task. Its concept varies from statute to statute, fact to fact, situation to situation and subject-matter to subject-matter. Perceptions are yet to be perceived by the court which would moot all situations while laying down emphasis for achieving excellence in all spheres of life keeping in view Chapter IV-A of the Constitution of India which provide for fundamental duties, circumstances and compulsions faced by the State in this behalf led the courts to uphold a statute providing for reservation for a special class of people. Mostly they suffer from disability either being belonging to an oppressed community or by way of economical, cultural or social imbalances. The courts shall all along strive hard for maintaining a balance. While interpreting the Constitution, we must notice the following view of Justice Holmes expressed in *Missouri* v. *Holland,* [252 US 416 (433)]:

> "When we are dealing with words that also are a constituent act, like the Constitution of the United States, we must realise that they have called into life a being the development of which could not have been foreseen completely by the most gifted of its begetters. It was enough for them to realise or to hope that they had created an organism, it has taken a century and has cost their successors must sweat and blood to prove that they created a nation. The case before us must be considered in the light of our whole experience and not merely in that of what was said a hundred years ago."

[Emphasis supplied]

42. Equally important is an elucidation of Justice Frankfurter contained in an article "Some Reflections on the Reading of Statutes". This Court also in *Jagadish Saran* v. *Union of India,* MANU/SC/0067/1980, a decision which is applicable in the fact situation of this case, stated the law thus:

> "Law, constitutional law, is not an omnipotent abstraction or distant idealization but a principled, yet pragmatic, value-laden and resulted-oriented, set of propositions applicable to and conditioned by a concrete stage of social development of the nation and aspirational imperatives of the people. India Today — that is the inarticulate major premise of our constitutional law and life."

43. In *D.P. Joshi's* case (supra) advantage given to local residents as regard payment of capitation fee was upheld. A Constitution Bench of this Court in *Km. Chitra Ghosh* v. *Union of India,* MANU/SC/0042/1969 stated the law thus:

> "It is the Central Government which bear's the financial burden of running the medical college. It is for it to lay down the criteria for eligibility. From the very nature of things it is not possible to throw the admission open to students from all over the country. The Government cannot be denied the right to decide from what sources the admission will be made. That essentially is a question of policy and depends *inter alia* on an overall assessment and survey of the requirements of residents of

particular territories and other categories of persons for whom it is necessary to provide facilities for medical education. If the sources are properly classified whether on territorial, geographical or other reasonable basis it is not for the courts to interfere with the manner and method of making the classification."

[Emphasis supplied]

44. The matter came up for consideration again in *D.N. Chanchala* v. *State of Mysore*, MANU/SC/0040/1971; *M.R. Mini (Minor) represented by her Guardian and Father M.P. Rajappan* v. *State of Kerala*, MANU/SC/0073/1980, wherein a similar note was struck.

45. In *Dr. Jagadish Saran's* case (*supra*) this Court had an occasion to consider the question as to whether grant of institutional preference was a valid basis for admission. This case dealt with admission in Post-Graduate Courses of the Delhi University, Krishna Iyer, J. with whom Pathak, J. concurred in no uncertain terms upheld such preference.

46. A large number of decisions on the point were taken into consideration by this Court in *Dr. Pradeep Jain's* case (*supra*). Upon a detailed analysis of the constitutional provisions, case laws as also the practical difficulties faced by the States, students as also the institutions, it was held:

> "...What is, therefore, necessary is to set up proper and adequate structures in rural areas where competent medical services can be provided by doctors and some motivation must be provided to the doctors servicing those areas. But, as the position stands today, there is considerable paucity of seats in medical colleges to satisfy the increasing demand of students for admission and some principle has, therefore, to be evolved for making selection of students for admission to the medical colleges and such principle has to be in conformity with the requirement of Article 14. Now, the primary imperative of Article 14 is equal opportunity for all across the nation for education and advancement and, as pointed out by Krishna Iyer, J. in *Jagdish Saran* v. *Union of India* "this has burning relevance to our times when the country is gradually being 'broken up into fragments by narrow' domestic walls' by surrender to narrow parochial loyalties". What is fundamental, as an enduring value of our polity, is guarantee to each of equal opportunity to unfold the full potential of his personality. Anyone anywhere, humble or high agrestic or urban, man or women, whatever be his language or religion, place of birth or residence, is entitled to be afforded equal chance for admission to any secular educational course for cultural growth, training facility, speciality or employment. It would run counter to the basic principle of equality before the law and equal protection of the law if a citizen by reason of his residence in State A, which ordinarily in the commonality of cases, would be the result of his birth in a place situate within that State, should have opportunity for education or advancement which is denied to another citizen because he happens to be resident in State B. It is axiomatic that talent is not the monopoly of the residents of any particular

State; it is more or less evenly distributed and given proper opportunity and environment, everyone has a prospect of rising to the peak. What is necessary is equality of opportunity and that cannot be made dependent upon where a citizen resides. If every citizen is afforded equal opportunity, genetically and environmentally, to develop his potential, he will be able in his own way to manifest his faculties fully leading to all round improvement in excellence. The philosophy and pragmatism of universal excellence through equality of opportunity for education and advancement across the nation is part of our founding faith and constitutional creed. The effort must, therefore, always be to select the best and most meritorious students for admission to technical institutions and medical colleges by providing equal opportunity to all citizens in the country and no citizen can legitimately, without serious detriment to the unity and integrity of the nation, be regarded as an outsider in our constitutional set-up. Moreover, it would be against national interest to admit in medical colleges or other institutions giving instruction in specialties, less meritorious students when more meritorious students are available, simply because the former are permanent residents or residents for a certain number of years in the State while the latter are not, though both categories are citizens of India. Exclusion of more meritorious students on the ground that they are not resident within the State would be likely to promote substandard candidates and bring about fall in medical competence, injurious in the long run to the very region. "It is no blessing to inflict quacks and medical midgets on people by wholesale sacrifice of talent at the threshold. Nor can the very best be rejected from admission because that will be a national loss and the interests of no region can be higher than those of the nation." The primary consideration in selection of candidates for admission to the medical colleges must, therefore, be merit. The object of any rules which may be made for regulating admissions to the medical colleges must be to secure the best and most meritorious students.'"

47. But it was observed:

"...Whether consistently with the constitutional values, admissions to a medical college or any other institution of higher learning situate in a State can be confined to those who have their 'domicile' within the State or who are residents within the State for a specified number of years or can any reservation in admission be made for them so as to give them precedence over those who do not possess 'domicile' or residential qualification within the State, irrespective of merit..."

48. The right of development in a developing country is acknowledged in International Treaties, Charters and Conventions.

49. Referring to the State mentality and pointing out to the law that there does not exist any separate State domicile in India, this Court specifically banished the residential requirement for the purpose of admission into Post-Graduate Medical Courses for all times. It directed:

"So much for admission to the MBBS course, but different consideration must prevail when, we come to consider the question of reservation based on residence requirement within the State or on institutional preference for admission to the post-graduate courses, such as, MD, MS and the like. There we cannot allow excellence to be compromised by any other considerations because that would be detrimental to the interest of the nation. It was rightly pointed out by Krishna Iyer, J. in *Jagdish Saran* case, and we wholly endorse what he has said:

The basic medical needs of a region or the preferential push justified for a handicapped group cannot prevail in the same measure at the highest scales of specialty where the best skill or talent, must be handpicked by selecting according to capability. At the level of PhD, MD, or levels of higher proficiency, where intentional measure of talent is made, where losing one great scientist or technologist in-the-making is a national loss, the considerations we have expanded upon as important lose their potency. Here equality, measured by matching excellence, has more meaning and cannot be diluted much without grave risk.

* * *

If equality of opportunity for every person in the country is the constitutional guarantee, a candidate who gets more marks than another is entitled to preference for admission. Merit must be the test when choosing the best, according to this rule of equal chance for equal marks. This proposition has greater importance when we reach the higher levels of education like post-graduate courses. After all, top technological expertise in any vital field like medicine is a nation's human asset without which its advance and development will be stunted. The role of high grade skill or special talent may be less at the lesser levels of education, jobs and disciplines of social inconsequence, but more at the higher levels of sophisticated skills and strategic employment. To devalue merit at the summit is to temporise with the country's development in the vital areas of professional expertise. In science and technology and other specialised fields of developmental significance, to relax lazily or easily in regard to exacting standards of performance may be running a grave national risk because in advanced medicine and other critical departments of higher knowledge, crucial to material progress, the people of India should not be denied the best the nation's talent lying latent can produce. If the best potential in these fields is cold-shouldered for populist considerations garbed as reservations, the victims, in the long run, may be the people themselves. Of course, this unrelenting strictness in selecting the best may not be so imperative at other levels where a broad measure of efficiency may be good enough and what is needed is merely to weed out the worthless.

* * *

Secondly, and more importantly, it is difficult to denounce or renounce the merit criterion when the selection is for post-graduate or post-doctoral courses in specialised subjects. There is no substitute for sheer flair, for creative talent, for fine-tuned performance at the difficult heights of some disciplines where the best alone is likely to blossom as the best. To sympathise mawkishly with the weaker sections by selecting sub-standard candidates, is to punish society as a whole by denying the prospect of excellence say in hospital sendee. Even the poorest, when stricken by critical illness, needs the attention of super-skilled specialists, not humdrum second-rates. So it is that relaxation on merit, by overruling equality and quality altogether, is a social risk where the stage is post-graduate or post-doctoral.

These passages from the judgment of Krishna Iyer, J. clearly and forcibly express the same view which we have independently reached on our own and indeed that view has been so ably expressed in these passages that we do not think we can usefully add anything to what has already been said there. We may point out that the Indian Medical Council has also emphasized that playing with merit so far as admissions to post-graduate courses are concerned, for pampering local feeling, will boomerang. We may with advantage reproduce the recommendation of the Indian medical Council on this point which may not be the last word in social wisdom but is certainly worthy of consideration:

Students for post-graduate training should be selected strictly on merit judged on the basis of academic record in the under graduate course. All selection for post-graduate studies should be conduced by the Universities.

The Medical Education Review Committee has also expressed the opinion that "all admissions to the post-graduate courses in any institution should be open to candidates on an all-India basis and there should be no restriction regarding domicile in the State/Union Territory in which the institution is located". So also in the policy statement filed by the learned Attorney-General, the Government of India has categorically expressed the view that:

So far as admission to the institutions of post-graduate colleges and special professional colleges is concerned, it should be entirely on the basis of all-India merit subject to constitutional reservations in favour of Scheduled Castes and Scheduled Tribes.

We are therefore of the view that so far as admissions to post- graduate courses, such as MS, MD and the like are concerned, it would be eminently desirable not to provide for any reservation based on residence requirement within the State or on institutional preference. But, having regard to broader considerations of equality of opportunity and institutional continuity in education which has its own importance and value, we would direct that though residence requirement within the State shall not be a ground for reservation in admissions to post-graduate courses, a certain percentage of seats may in the present circumstances, be reserved on the basis of institutional preference in the sense that a

> student who has passed MBBS course from a medical college or university, may be given preference for admission to the post-graduate course in the same medical college or university but such reservation on the basis of institutional preference should not in any event exceed 50 per cent. of the total number of open seats available for admission to the Post-Graduate course. This outer limit which we are fixing will also be subject to revision on the lower side by the Indian Medical Council in the same manner as directed by us in the case of admission to the MBBS course. But, even in regard to admissions to the Post-Graduate course, we would direct that so far as super specialties such as neuron-surgery and cardiology are concerned, there should be no reservation at all even on the basis of institutional preference and admissions should be granted purely on merit on all-India basis."

50. It in no uncertain terms directed:

> "The decisions reached by us in these writ petitions will bind the Union of India, the State Governments and Administrations of Union territories because it lays down the law for the entire country and moreover we have reached this decision after giving notice to the Union of India and all the State Governments and Union territories..."

51. A scheme, thus, came to be framed by this Court which is a law within the meaning of Article 141 of the Constitution of India and is binding-on all the States in terms of Article 144 of the Constitution of India. The principal considerations which weighed with the court for arriving at the aforementioned conclusion were:

> "...There can be no doubt that the policy of ensuring admissions to the MBBS Course on all-India basis is a highly desirable policy, based as it is on the postulate - that India is one nation and every citizen of India is entitled to have equal opportunity for education and advancement, but it is an ideal to be aimed at and it may not be realistically possible, in the present circumstances, to adopt it, for it cannot produce real equality of opportunity unless, there is complete absence of disparities and inequalities — a situation which simply does not exist in the country today. There are massive social and economic disparities and inequalities not only between State and State but also between region and region within a State and even between citizens and citizens within the same region. There is a yawning gap between the rich and the poor and there are so many disabilities and injustices from which the poor suffer as a class that they cannot avail themselves of any opportunities which may in law be open to them. They do not have the social and material resources to take advantage of these opportunities which remain merely on paper recognized by law but nonexistent in fact. Students from backward States or regions will hardly be able to compete with those from advanced States or regions because, though possessing an intelligent mind, they would have had no adequate opportunities for development so as to be in a position to compete with others. So also students belonging

to the weaker sections who have not, by reason of their socially or economically disadvantaged position, been able to secure education in good schools would be at a disadvantage compared to students belonging to the affluent or well-to-do families who have had the best of school education and in open all-India competition, they would be likely to be worsted..."

52. A distinction was made therefore between the Undergraduate Course *i.e.,* MBBS Course and Post-Graduate Medical Course as also super speciality courses. The Court, therefore, sought to strike a balance of rights and interests of all concerned.

53. However, the percentage of seats to be allotted on all-India basis, however, came to be modified in *Dr. Dinesh Kumar* v. *Motilal Nehru Medical College, Allahabad,* MANU/SC/0028/1985 in the following terms:—

"We would also like to clear up one misunderstanding which seems to prevail with some State Governments and universities in regard to the true import of our Judgment dated June 22, 1984. They have misinterpreted our Judgment to mean that 30% of the total number of seats available for admission to MBBS course in a medical college should be kept free from reservation on the basis of residence requirement or institutional preference. That is a total misreading of our Judgment. What we have said in our Judgment is that after providing for reservation validly made, whatever seats remain available for non-reserved categories, 30% of such seats at the least, should be left free for open competition and admission to such 30% open seats should not be based on residence requirement or institutional preference but students from all over the country should be able to compete for admissions to such 30% open seats. To take an example, suppose there are 100 seats in a medical college or university and 30% of the seats are validly reserved for candidates belonging to Scheduled Castes and Scheduled Tribes. That would leave 70 seats available for others belonging to non-reserved categories. According to our Judgment, 30% of 70 seats, that is, 21 seats out of 70 and not 30% of the total number of 100 seats, namely, 30 seats, must be filled up by open competition regardless of residence requirement or institutional preference."

54. Changes were made in the formula in *Dr. Dinesh Kumar (II)* v. *Motilal Nehru Medical College, Allahabad,* MANU/SC/0073/1986. This Court thereafter times without number issued directions from time-to-time regulating admissions in different courses of studies, meticulous supervisions and conduct of examinations by the Universities as also all-India tests in the following:

1. *Dr. Dinesh Kumar (III),* MANU/SC/0105/1987
2. *Dr. Dinesh Kumar (IV),* MANU/SC/0106/1987
3. *Dr. Dinseh Kumar (V),* (1989) Supp 2 SCC 428]
4. *Dr. Dinseh Kumar (VI),* (1987) 1 SCALE 1232
5. *Dr. Dinseh Kumar (VII),* (1987) 2 SCALE 22

6. *Dr. Dinseh Kumar (VIII),* (1988) 1 SCALE 428

7. *Dr. Dinseh Kumar (IX),* MANU/SC/0353/1990.

55. The State of Assam, it appears, was specifically directed to follow institutional preference by this Court by an order dated 2.2.1996 in Writ Petition (Civil) No. 625 of 1995.

56. A deviation to the said dicta, however, was sought to be made by a two-Judge Bench of this Court in *Dr. Parag Gupta's* case (supra). In the said decision some of the students complained that whereas the students who had undergone studies in other Universities were entitled to reservation by way of domicile or institutional preference, but they, although had successfully completed in All India Entrance Test in MBBS Course, are not being permitted to compete with their fellow students of Delhi University on the ground of institutional preference, although they belong to the same class of students.

57. This Court in *Dr. Parag Gupta* (*supra*) did not lay down any law. It dealt with the situation on equitable and humanitarian grounds but while doing so it indisputably deviated from the law laid down in *Dr. Pradeep Jain's* case (*supra*) only by way of an interim arrangement. It inadvertently created reservation on domicile which was forbidden in *Dr. Pradeep Jain's* case (*supra*). The said provisional directions being binding on Delhi University came to be followed in subsequent years. The sympathetic consideration shown by this Court in *Dr. Parag Gupta's* case (*supra*) came to be misapplied by the Allahabad High Court in *Vineet Singh's* case wherein the High Court directed consideration of cases of the students who belonged to the State of U.P. irrespective of the fact that whether they had gone out of their home State on 15% all-India quota or not. This Court in *State of U.P.* v. *Vineet Singh,* MANU/SC/0546/2000 clarified the position holding that the High Court was wrong in extending the benefit in *Dr. Parag Gupta's* case (*supra*) to other students and reiterated that *Dr. Parag Gupta's* decision was confined to the students who had gone to other States under 15% all-India quota. The ratio of the judgment in *Dr. Parag Gupta's* case (*supra*) came to be reiterated in *Abhinav Aggarwal* v. *Union of India,* (2001) 3 SCC 425.

58. In *Dr. Prachi Almeida* v. *Dean, Goa Medical College,* MANU/SC/0524/2001, a problem was faced by a student from Delhi who was admitted into Goa Medical College under the 15% all-India quota. She was denied admission in Goa on the ground that she was not resident of the said State. She, however, was married in Goa. This Court followed *Dr. Pradeep Jain's* case (*supra*) and directed that the student cannot be denied admission on the basis of residence requirement holding that if the candidate has done MBBS Course in that State such a candidate would be eligible for admission in Post-Graduate Medical Course therein.

59. Some students of the Delhi University, thereafter filed a writ petition questioning the residential reservation in *Magan Mehrotra* v. *Union of India* since reported in (2003) 3 SCALE 101. A Bench of this Court therein by an order dated 11.09.2002 noticing the conflict between the decisions in *Dr. Pradeep Jain* (supra) on the one hand and *Dr. Parag Gupta* (supra) on the other, issued notices to all the States excepting the States of Jammu & Kashmir and Andhra Pradesh and referred the matter to a three-Judge Bench. In *Magan Mehrotra* (*supra*), this Court held that the decision in *Dr. Parag Gupta* (*supra*) is contrary to the decision in *Dr. Pradeep Jain* (*supra*) stating:

> "...A bare look at the judgment of the 3-JudgeBench in *Pradeep Jain's* case and two-Judge Bench in *Parag Gupta's* case in relation to the question of preference in the post-graduate course it cannot but be held that the *Parag Gupta's* case took a different view by upholding the residential preference, in essence, which was contrary to the judgment of the three-Judge Bench in *Pradeep Jain's* case. Independently on examining the 7 issue of preference, we are also of the considered opinion that the decision rendered by this Court in *Pradeep Jain's* case had taken a correct criteria into consideration and we therefore, agree with the principles evolved and the ratio given in *Pradeep Jain's* case so far as it relates to admission into the post-graduate courses and the question of institutional preference to be given to those who had studied their under-graduate courses in the very institutions against the 15% quota on the All India basis. In this view of the matter, the impugned Bulletin of Information issued by the Delhi University in relation to the Post-doctoral (D.M./M.Ch.) Post-Graduate Degree must be held to be contrary to the direction of this Court in *Pradeep Jain's* case and the same is accordingly quashed. However, this order shall be made effective from the next academic session. We, however, direct the Sates of Assam, Tamil Nadu, Goa and Karnataka to follow the pattern of institutional preference as has been indicated by this Court in *Pradeep Jain's* case and reiterated by us today..."

60. We may, however, notice that this Court in *K. Duraisamy* v. *State of Tamil Nadu*, MANU/SC/0044/2001 upheld the sources for admission by giving preference to the doctors working in the hospitals in the Post-Graduate Courses on the ground that the same constitutes a valid classification.

61. The discussions on this topic would remain incomplete if we fail to notice a recent decision of this Court in *All India Institute of Medical Sciences Students' Union* (*supra*) rendered by one of us, Hon'ble Lahoti, J. wherein this Court, keeping in view the peculiar situation obtaining in the case of AIMS, held institutional reservation to be unconstitutional. It, however, keeping in view the necessity of giving institutional preference to students who had studied from AIIMS, directed that such preference be given to the extent of 25% of students instead of 33%. However, keeping in view the fact that there were 40 seats in MBBS Course whereas 132 seats in Post-Graduate Courses, the institutional preference to be given to the students of AIIMS came to about 82.5%.

62. In this context it is relevant to examine the **relevance of an entry in the State List or Concurrent List.**

63. 'Education' appears both in Union List as also in the Concurrent List. The relevant entries in the Constitution are as under:

> "66. List I - Co-ordination and determination of standards in institutions for higher education or research and scientific and technical institutions."

> "25. List III - Education, including technical education, medical education and universities, subject to the provisions of entries 63, 64, 65 and 66 of List I; vocational and technical training of labour."

64. An argument has been advanced that different interpretation is needed having regard to the shift of constitutional entry from List II to List III. One of us in *T.M.A. Pai Foundation* v. *State of Karnataka*, MANU/SC/1050/2002, had to say the following:

> "Further, under clause (2) of Article 246 Parliament and subject to clause (1) the legislature of any State are empowered to make law with respect to any of the matters enumerated in List III Seventh Schedule and under clause (3) of Article 246, the legislature of any State is empowered to enact law with respect to any of the matters enumerated in List II in the Seventh Schedule subject to clauses (1) and (2). From the aforesaid provisions it is clear that it is Article 246 and other articles which either empower Parliament or the State Legislature to enact law and not the entries finding place in three lists of the Seventh Schedule, Thus the function of entries in three lists of the Seventh Schedule is to demarcate the area over which the appropriate legislatures can enact laws but do not confer power either on Parliament or the State Legislatures to enact laws. It may be remembered, by transfer of the entries, the character of the entries is not lost or destroyed. In this view of the matter by transfer of contents of Entry 11 of List II to List III as Entry 25 has not denuded the power of the State Legislature to enact law on the subject "Education" but has also conferred power on Parliament to enact law on the subject "Education"."

65. Shifting of the entry from the State List to the Concurrent List is not, thus, relevant inasmuch the State in absence of any Parliamentary act has the legislative competence to enact a statute laying down reservation for entry in any course of studies including the medical courses.

66. The sole question, therefore, is as to whether reservation by way of institutional preference is *ultra vires* Article 14 of the Constitution of India. We think not. Article 14, it will bear repetition to state, forbids class legislation but does not forbid reasonable classification, which means - (1) must be based on reasonable and intelligible differentia; and (2) such differentia must be on rational basis.

67. Hence, we may also notice the argument, whether institutional reservation fulfils the aforementioned criteria or not must be judged on the following:—

1. There is a presumption of constitutionality;
2. The burden of proof is upon the writ petitioners as they have questioned the constitutionality of the provisions;
3. There is a presumption as regard the State's power on extent of its legislative competence;
4. Hardship of few cannot be the basis for determining the validity of any statute.

68. The court while adjudicating upon the constitutionality of the provisions of the statute may notice all relevant facts whether existing or conceived.

This Court may therefore notice the following:

(i) The State runs the Universities.

(ii) It has to spend a lot of money in imparting medical education to the students of the State.

(iii) Those who get admission in Post-Graduate Courses are also required to be paid stipends. Reservation of some seats to a reasonable extent, thus, would not violate the equality clause.

(iv) The criteria for institutional preference has now come to stay. It has worked out satisfactorily in most of the States for last about two decades.

(v) Even those States which defied the decision of this Court in *Dr. Pradeep Jain's* case (*supra*) had realized the need for institutional preference.

(vi) No sufficient material has been brought on record for departing from this well-established admission criteria.

(vii) It goes beyond any cavil of doubt that institutional preference is based on a reasonable and identifiable classification. It may be that while working out the percentage of reservation invariably some local students will have preference having regard to the fact that domicile/residence was one of the criteria for admission in MBBS Course. But together with the local students 15%, students who had competed in all-India Entrance Examination would also be getting the same benefit. The percentage of students who were to get the benefit of reservation by way of institutional preference would further go down if the decision of this Court in *Dr. Pradeep Jain's* case (*supra*) is scrupulously followed.

(viii) Giving of such a preference is a matter of State policy which can be invalidated only in the event of being violative of Article 14 of the Constitution of India.

(ix) The students who would get the benefit of institutional preference being on identifiable ground, there is hardly any scope for manipulation.

69. In *Km. N. Vasundara* v. *State of Mysore*, (1971) 1 Supp SCR 381, it was observed:

> "But cases of hardship are likely to arise in the working of almost any rule which may be framed for selecting a limited number of candidates for admission out of a long list. This, however, would not render the rule unconstitutional."

70. As noticed hereinbefore, in *D.N. Chanchala's* case (*supra*), *M.R. Mini's* case (*supra*) and *Jagadish Saran's* case (*supra*) institutional preference has been preferred. It has been reiterated in the law laid down by way of a scheme evolved in *Dr. Pradeep Jain* (supra) and reiterated in *Magan Mehrotra* (supra).

71. We, therefore, do not find any reason to depart from the ratio laid down by this Court in *Dr. Pradeep Jain* (*supra*). The logical corollary of our finding is that reservation by way of institutional preference must be held to be not offending Article 14 of the Constitution of India.

72. However, the test to uphold the validity of a statute on equality must be judged on the touch-stone of reasonableness. It was noticed in *Dr. Pradeep's Jain's* case (supra) that reservation to the extent of 50% was held to be reasonable. Although subsequently in *Dr. Dinesh Kumar's* case (supra) it was reduced to 25% of the total seats. The said percentage of reservation was fixed keeping in view the situation as then existing. The situation has now changed to a great extent. Twenty years have passed. The country has during this time have produced a large number of Post-Graduate doctors. Our Constitution is organic in nature. Being a living organ, it is ongoing and with the passage of time, law must change. Horizons of constitutional law are expanding.

73. Having regard to the facts and circumstances of the case, we are of the opinion that the original scheme as framed in *Dr. Pradeep Jain's* case (*supra*) should be reiterated in preference to *Dr. Dinesh Kumar's* case (supra). Reservation by way of institutional preference, therefore, should be confined to 50% of the seats since it is in public interest.

74. For the purpose of selecting the candidates, it is necessary to hold an All India Entrance Examination by an impartial and reputed body. We must, therefore, lay down the criteria therefore. AIIMS in terms of an order passed by this Court has been conducting the said examination. It may continue to do so unless a competent body is created by the Central Government in terms of a Parliamentary Act or otherwise. All expenses for conducting such examination shall be borne by the Central Government which would also provide the requisite infrastructure therefore. One test shall be held for all the students taking admission throughout the country. This order is passed keeping in view the fact that now one common entrance test is held for admission against 25% of all India quota and other tests are being held by the respective Universities. Disparities in such tests should be done away with and merit of the students should be judged on the basis of one test held therefore.

75. AIIMS is an institution of excellence. It is a class by itself and pride. We are, therefore, of the opinion that in the AIIMS and the medical colleges of the Central University, merit should have primacy subject of course to institutional preference to the extent of 50% of the total seats in the MBBS Course. In all other respects the decision of this Court in *All India Institute of Medical Sciences Students' Union's* case (*supra*) shall operate.

76. Our directions aforementioned, however, are interim in nature. The Parliament having regard to Entry 66, List I of the Seventh Schedule of the Constitution of India has the legislative competence which would take care of the country as a whole. While making such a legislation, the Parliament undoubtedly would take into consideration the special needs of some small States, having regard to their backwardness economic, social and educational as also geographical conditions.

77. The Parliament has also the legislative competence in terms of Entry 25, List III of the Seventh Schedule of the Constitution. It for education and particularly higher education where excellence is required, while enacting law must also foresee that in the era of liberalisation and globalisation, Indian citizens must compete with their counter-parts of the developed countries. Merit, thus, must be allowed to explore to the fullest extent. Genius hidden in the citizens must be allowed to blossom. Despite 55 years of India's existence as an independent nation, a National policy on higher education has not come into being. Its significance and importance was highlighted in *Dr. Pradeep Jain's* case (*supra*); but the Parliament did not pay any heed thereto.

78. The courts are normally reluctant to issue any direction to the Central Government for making law. Following our practice, we refrain ourselves to issue any direction in this regard. We hope and trust that the Central Government expeditiously consider of making legislation or taking such steps as are necessary in this behalf keeping in view the requirement of coordination in higher education in terms of Entry 66, List I of the Seventh Schedule of the Constitution of India.

79. For the aforesaid reasons, we do not find any merit in the contentions advanced on behalf of the petitioners. The petitioners are not entitled to any relief. With the aforesaid directions, these writ petitions and the appeal are disposed of.

80. There shall be no order as to costs.

S.N. Sinha, J.

81. I have had the advantage of reading the draft opinion of Hon'ble the Chief Justice of India. While concurring with the said judgment, I would like to add a few rods of mine.

82. The core question involved in these appeals is as to whether by providing for institutional reservation, the equality clause is violated.

83. Article 14 of the Constitution of India prohibits discrimination in any form. Discrimination at its worst form would be violative of the basic and essential feature of the Constitution. It is trite that even the fundamental rights of a citizen must conform to the basic feature of the Constitution. Preamble of the Constitution in no uncertain terms lays emphasis on equality.

84. In *Kesavananda Bharati* v. *State of Kerala,* MANU/SC/0445/1973 Shelat and Grover, JJ. stated that:

> "582.....(5) The dignity of the individual secured by the various freedoms and basic rights in Part III and the mandate to build a welfare State contained in Part IV would be violative of basic feature of the Constitution of India.'

85. Further, Hegde and Mukherjea, JJ stated the law thus:

> "661.....The broad contours the basic elements or fundamental features of our Constitution are clearly delineated in the Preamble. Unlike in most of the other Constitution, it is comparatively easy in the case of our Constitution to discern and determine the basic elements or the fundamental features of our Constitution. For doing so, one has only to look to the Preamble."

86. *Keshavananda Bharati* (*supra*) has been followed in *L. Chandra Kumar* v. *Union of India*, MANU/SC/0261/1997.

87. In *Maharao Sahib Shri Bhim Singhji* v. *Union of India*, MANU/SC/0509/1980 Krishna Iyer, J., however, in his characteristic style opined:

> "20... The question of basic structure being breached cannot arise when we examine the vires of an ordinary legislation as distinguished from a constitutional amendment. Kesavananda Bharati cannot be the last refuge of the Proprietariat when benign legislation takes away their 'excess' for societal weal. Nor, indeed, can every breach of equality spell disaster as a lethal violation of the basic structure. Peripheral inequality is inevitable when large-scale equalization processes are put into action. If all the judges of the Supreme Court in solemn session sit and deliberate for half a year to produce a legislation for reducing glaring economic inequality their genius will let them down if the essay is to avoid even peripheral inequalities. Every large cause claims some martyr, as sociologists will know. Therefore, what is a betrayal of the basic feature is not a mere violation of Article 14 but a shocking, unconscionable or unscrupulous travesty of the quintessence of equal justice. If a legislation does go that far it shakes the democratic foundation and must suffer the death penalty."

88. Recently a question came up before the US Supreme Court in *Jennifer Gratz and Patrick Hamacher* v. *Lee Bollinger* decided on 23rd June, 2003 likely to be reported in (2003) 539 U.S. wherein the guidelines providing for selection method under which every applicant from an under represented racial or ethnic minority groups was to be automatically awarded 20 points out of 100 points needed to guarantee admission, was struck down as has been violative of equality protection clause. It was observed:

> "The very nature of a college's permissible practice of awarding value to racial diversity means that race must be considered in a way that increases some applicants' chances for admission. Since college admission is not left entirely to inarticulate intuition, it is hard to see what is inappropriate in association some stated value to a relevant characteristic, whether it be reasoning ability, writing style, running speed, or minority race. Justice Powell's plus factors necessarily are assigned some values. The college simply does by a numbered scale what the law school accomplish in its "holistic review", Grutter, Post, at 26; the distinction does not imply that applicants to the undergraduate college are denied individualized consideration or a fair chance to compete on the basis of all the various merits their applications may disclose."

89. Delivering his minority opinion on his own behalf as also on behalf of Justice Souter, Justice Ginsburg, however, held:

> "Our jurisprudence ranks race a "suspect" category, "not because (race) is inevitably an impermissible classification, but because it is one which usually, to our national shame has been drawn for the purpose of maintaining racial inequality." *Norwalk Core* v. *Norwalk Redevelopment*

Agency, 395 F. 2d 920, 931-932 (CA2 1968) (footnote omitted). But where race is considered "for the purpose of achieving equality." id. at 932, no automatic prescription is in order. For as insightfully explained, "the Constitution is both color blind and color conscious. To avoid conflict with the equal protection clause, a classification that denies a benefit causes harm or imposes a burden must not be based on race in that sense, the Constitution is color blind. But the Constitution is color conscious to prevent discrimination being perpetuated and to undo the effects of past discrimination, "*United States* v. *Jefferson County Bd. of Ed.,* 372 F.2d 836, 876 (CA5 1966) (Wisdom, J.)' see Wechsler, *The Nationalization of Civil Liberties and Civil Rights* Supp. To 12 Tex. Q.10, 23 (1968) (Brown may be seen as disallowing racial classifications that "imply an invidious assessment" while allowing such classifications when "not invidious in implication" but advanced to "correct inequalities"). Contemporary human rights documents draw just this line, they distinguish between policies of oppression and measures designed to accelerate *de facto* equality. See Grutter, post, at 1 (Ginsburg, J. concurring) (citing the United Nations - initiated Conventions on the Elimination of All Forms of Racial Discrimination and on the Elimination of All Forms of Discrimination against Women)."

90. The validity of institutional reservation must be judged on the touchstone of equality clause.

91. While considering the reasonableness of the institutional reservation, we have taken into consideration the effect of equality clause contained in Article 14 and 15 of the Constitution of India.

92. The question as regard merit of the students *vis-a-vis* right of development and human rights angle had been considered at some length in *Islamic Academy of Education* v. *State of Karnataka,* JT 2003 (7) SC 1 and following *Pradeep Jain* v. *Union of India,* MANU/SC/0047/1984 it has been held:

For the purpose of achieving excellence in a professional institution, merit indisputably should be a relevant criterion. Merit, as has been noticed in the judgment may be determined in various ways (Para 59). There cannot be, however, any fool-proof method whereby and whereunder the merit of a student for all times to come may be judged. Only, however, because a student may fare differently in a different situation and at different point of time by itself cannot be a ground to adopt different standards for judging his merit at different points of time. Merit for any purpose and in particular for the purpose of admission in a professional college should be judged as far as possible on the basis of same or similar examination. In other words, *inter se* merit amongst the students similarly situated should be judged applying the same norm or standard. Different types of examinations, different sets of questions, different ways of evaluating the answer books may yield different results in the case of the same student.

Selection of students, however, by the minority institutions even for the members of their community cannot be bereft of merit. Only in a given situation less meritorious candidates from the minority community can be admitted *vis-a-vis* the general category; but therefore the modality has to be worked out. For the said purpose *de facto* equality doctrine may be applied instead of *de jure* equality as every kind of discrimination may not be violative of the equality clause. (See *Pradeep Jain* v. *Union of India,* MANU/SC/0047/1984).

93. Even applying the said tests, institutional reservation cannot be held to be unconstitutional.

94. Mr. Nariman contended that provision for reservation being a suspect legislation the strict scrutiny test should be applied. Even applying such a test, we do not think that the institutional reservation should be done away with having regard to the present day scenario. We may notice that such a test has been applied for upholding a statute recently in *Balram Kumawat* v. *Union of India,* (2003) 7 SCC 626.

AR. Lakshmanan, J.

95. While concurring with the conclusion arrived at by Hon'ble the Chief Justice, I would like to add the following few lines for streamlining the policies and processes for admission to Medical Courses and other Professional Courses. The issues and options are discussed below:

96. Every year during the admission season several lakhs of students undergo immense suffering and harassment in seeking admission to Professional Courses caused by uncertain policies, ambiguous procedures and inadequate information. The miseries of students and parents are escalating year after year due to boundless expansion in the number of professional institutions and their intake capacity, emergence of a large variety of newer disciplines and mobility of students seeking admissions beyond the boundaries of States. The students who are about to complete their high school education go through a period of acute anxiety caused by the uncertain situation about their chances for further education. The number of qualified students wanting to go for higher studies has been swelling largely motivated by hopes of better economic security and partly by a desire to attain greater upward social mobility. Then begins their trauma due to many prevailing unfair practices in admissions and devious ways of fee collections exploiting the anxiety of students and uncertainty of procedures. Most of the efforts to deal with these problems are *ad hoc* in nature often decided under judicial orders. Different State and Central authorities take many different actions often leading to severe inconsistencies. There is substantial scope for streamlining the admission process, even within the regulatory powers of the authorities, provided these issues are not dealt with on an emergency basis during the admission season but done in a co-ordinated and comprehensive manner ahead of time.

ISSUE NUMBER ONE:

ENTRY QUALIFICATION:

97. For admissions to under-graduate programmes, there are **several different eligibility norms** among the different categories of institutions and among the various States. Some are based on Twelfth Standard marks or grades only, some are based on the Entrance Examination only, and some are determined by a combination of these with different weightages. There is endless number of justifications for each of the above, confusing the students from different parts of the country.

98. The preferred option, in my view, should be for a designated agency or the University concerned to conduct the entrance examination for professional as well as non-professional institutions in the specified subjects, (an option suggested by this Court). The marks awarded in those subjects should be the basis for determining the merits of the students for admission to the institutions to which they apply.

ISSUE NUMBER TWO:

UNPLANNED GROWTH OF INSTITUTIONS

99. The growth of the Professional Institutions has been at an geometrical rate during the last five years. During recent years the expansion of educational facilities for higher education has been nearly exclusively in the private unaided sector due to the financial incapacity of Governments.

100. Those who have ventured to start the new institutions are motivated by commercial interests and not by educational and social interests. Political considerations have become paramount in sanctioning of colleges. There has been a high level of exploitation of students in certain disciplines through unethical and illegal collection of unauthorized payments. The discontent among the meritorious students is simmering also because only those, even with poor competence, but who could pay high illegal amounts can get into many institutions.

OPTIONS:

1. The country needs to evolve urgently a predictable pattern of growth for the High Education system in Technical, Managerial, and other Professional disciplines as well in Science and Humanities at least for the next five years. The present level of *ad hoc* approach and stampede should be eliminated.

2. The national blue print and the road map for the development of professional education should be based on maintaining credible level of quality standards and anticipated demand structure in economic and social sectors.

ISSUE NUMBER THREE:

FEE STRUCTURE:

101. This Court states: "A rational fee structure should be adopted by the Management, which would not be entitled to charge a capitation fee. Appropriate machinery can be devised by the State or University to ensure that no capitation fee is charged and that there is no profiteering."

OPTIONS:

102. One possible remedy is to make a rule under the Prevention of the Capitation Fee Act that collecting any fee that was not previously announced in the college publications and any fee collected without a formal receipt should be punishable offences. This rule should be strictly enforced.

ISSUE NUMBER FOUR:

CERTIFICATES HASSLES:

103. When we consider the size of our country and the large number of institutions and huge volume of applicants, the man hour and money lost in running around for getting the certificates during the admission seasons must run into equivalent of several crores of rupees. A more hassle-free system for authenticating the required information from students should be evolved.

OPTIONS:

104. Every student be provided with a basic identity certificate while he/she is in the higher secondary stage (10th to 12th std). This should provide all essential information such as date of birth, community, domicile, photo identity etc., authenticated by a designated official. This should be acceptable for admission requirements in any institution and in any State in India.

Super speciality institutions and institutions where highly skilled Training/ Education is imparted:

105. On the issue whether there can be Article 15(4) reservation in Super specialty courses, this Court was categorical when it declared that there could not be any reservation at the level of super-specialization in medicine because any dilution of merit at the level would adversely affect the national interest in having the best possible at the highest level of professional and educational training."

106. Similar view was already taken by this Court in *Pradeep Jain* v. *Union of India,* MANU/SC/0047/1984.

107. In similar vein, in *Jagdish Saran* v. *Union of India,* MANU/SC/0067/ 1980, this Court observed that Merit must be the test when choosing the best, according to this rule of equal chance for equal marks. This proposition has greater importance when we reach the higher levels of education for postgraduate courses. This Court further observed that the host of variables influence the qualification of the reservation as one factor deserves great emphasis, the higher the level of the speciality the lesser the role of reservation.

108. In the case of Article 15(4) reservations, this Court has made it clear that the claims of national interest demands that these reservations can never exceed 50% of the available seats in the concerned educational institutions.

109. The view was approved by this Court in the case of *India Sawhney* v. *Union of India.* If one looks at this issue in the light of the spirit of the ratios laid down in *Preeti Srivastava* v. *State of M.P.,* MANU/SC/1021/1999 and in *AIIMS Students Union* v. *A.I.I.M.S.,* MANU/SC/0480/2001, one would come to the inevitable conclusions that the constitutional reservations contemplated under Article 15(4) should be kept at the minimal level so that national interest in the achievement of the goal of excellence in all fields is not unduly affected.

110. Of course, as between the reserved category candidates, there should be *inter se* merit observed. This has been emphasised by this Court in several cases.

111. As regards the constitutional validity of institutional/regional/ university wise reservation/preference, in view of this court's emphasis on the need to strive for excellence which alone is in the national interest, it may not be possible to sustain its constitutional validity. However, the presently available decisional law is in support of institutional preference to the extent of 50% of the total available seats in the concerned educational institutions.

Conclusions:

(1) In the case of Central educational institutions and other institutions of excellence in the country the judicial thinking has veered around the dominant idea of national interest with its limiting effect on the constitutional prescription of reservations. The result is that in the case of these institutions the scope for reservations is minimal.

(2) As regards the feasibility of constitutional reservations at the level of superspecialities, the position is that the judiciary has adopted the dominant norm, *i.e.,* "the higher the level of the speciality the lesser the role of reservation". At the level of super-specialties the rule of "equal chance for equal marks" dominates. This view equally applies to all super-speciality institutions.

(3) As regards the scope of reservation of seats in educational institutions affiliated and recognised by State Universities, the constitutional prescription of reservation of 50% of the available seats has to be respected and enforced.

(4) The institutional preference should be limited to 50% and the rest being left for open competition based purely on merits on an All-India basis.

(5) As regards private non-minority educational institutions distinction between government aided and unaided institutions. While government/State can prescribe guidelines as to the process of selection and admission of students, the government/State while issuing guidelines has to take into consideration the constitutional mandate of the requirement of protective discrimination in matters of reservation of seats as ordained by the decisional law in the country. Accordingly, the extent of reservation in no case can exceed 50% of the seats. The *inter se* merit may be assessed on the basis of a common All-India Entrance Test or on the basis of marks at the level of qualifying examination.

(6) The position with respect to minority aided institutions is that they are bound by the requirement of constitutional reservation along with other regulatory controls. However, the right to admit students of their choice being part of the right of religious and linguistic minorities, to establish and administer educational institutions of their choice, the managements of these educational institutions can reserve seats to a reasonable extent. not necessarily 50% as laid down in Stephans College case. Out of the seats left after the deduction of management quota, the State can require the observance of the requirement of Constitutional reservation.

(7) As regards the unaided institutions, they have large measure of autonomy even in matters of admission of students as they are not bound by the constraints of the demands of Article 29(2). Nor are they bound by the constraints of the obligatory requirements of Constitutional reservation.

112. Before parting with this case, I am of the opinion that *the younger generation in our society nurturing fond hopes and aspiration for their future* *professional careers should feel it as a pleasurable experience to explore the available options in higher education.* They should be spread from the mental torture due hassles and unsavoury experiences in getting to the first base. To the extent possible they should be made to feel that they are part of one nation. Tensions and frustrations at their impressionable age will surely result in a society with distorted and negative values damaging the foundations of a healthy society. The policies and procedures for admissions should be viewed from the larger impact on the future of India.

Atyant Pichhara Barg Chhatra Sangh v. *Jharkhand State Vaishya Federation*

AIR 2006 SC 2814: 2006 (3) AWC 2944 (SC): 2006 (4) JCR 67 (SC): JT 2006 (7) SC 514: (2006) 7 SCALE 579: (2006) 6 SCC 718: 2006 (2) UJ 1190 (SC)
Civil Appeal No. 3430 of 2006
(Arising out of S.L.P. (C) No. 23559 of 2003)
Decided on 08-08-2006

Coram: **Hon'ble Mr. Justice Lokeshwar Singh Panta**
Hon'ble Dr. Justice AR. Lakshmanan

Judgment by: **Hon'ble Dr. Justice AR. Lakshmanan**

FACTS: The State of Jharkhand had given 73% reservation for appointments in Government services. The process of reservations to 73% was challenged before the High Court of Jharkhand on the ground that it was *ultra vires* the Constitution in a number of writ petitions. The High Court subsequently ordered that the reservation to be reduced to 50%. Accordingly, the State of Jharkhand issued a notification amalgamating two classes namely, 'Backward Classes' and 'Extremely Backward Classes' together.

ISSUE: Whether amalgamation of 'Extremely Backward Class' and 'Backward Class Categories' into one group for the purpose of reservation for appointments in Government services is violative of article 14 of the Constitution of India?

HELD: The amalgamation of two classes of people for reservation would be unreasonable as two different classes are treated similarly which is in violation of the mandate of article 14 of the Constitution of India which is to "treat similar similarly and to treat different differently."

JUDGMENT

Dr. AR. Lakshmanan, J.

1. Leave granted.

2. The above appeal is directed against the impugned common final judgment and order dated 16.8.2003 of the Division Bench of the High Court of Judicature at Jharkhand, Ranchi passed in L.P.A. No. 176 of 2003, whereby the High Court allowed the said appeal of respondent No. 1 - Jharkhand State Vaishya Page 3840 Federation and set aside the common judgment and order dated 3.3.2003 of the learned single Judge of the High Court and thus upheld the validity of Resolution No. 5800 dated 10.10.2002 of the State Government and thus affirmed the decision of the State Government to amalgamate the two classes *i.e.,* Extremely Backward Class and Backward Class and the reduction of reservation from 12% and 9% respectively to 14% only for the purpose of admission in professional educational institutions.

3. This appeal raises important questions of law with respect to reservation in professional educational institutions for the Extremely Backward Classes in the State of Jharkhand. The State of Jharkhand had given 73% reservation for appointments in Government services adopting the Bihar (Scheduled Castes, Scheduled Tribes and Backward Classes) Reservation Act (Bihar Act No. 3 of 1992) with certain modifications vide Notification No. 3465 of 2001 issued on 3.10.2001. Similarly through Notification No. 3884 of 2001 issued on 5.11.2001, there were four specific categories that were entitled to reservation in professional/technical colleges:

Scheduled Caste	-	14%
Scheduled Tribe	-	32%
Extremely Backward Classes	-	18%
Backward Classes	-	09%
Total	-	73%

4. The process of reservations to 73% was challenged before the High Court of Jharkhand on the ground that it was *ultra vires* the Constitution in a number of writ petitions. Keeping in mind the fact that a similar petition was pending before this Court (*VOICE* v. *State of Tamil Nadu,* S.L.P.(C) No. 13526 of 1993), the Full Bench of the High Court deferred the hearing to await the judgment of this Court. But as an interim measure, the High Court on 22.8.2002 reduced the reservation to 50% with specific directions to be given that any appointment to Government service made in the open category would be subject to the decision of this Court and also directed that the same reservations would *mutatis mutandis* apply to reservation in educational institutions as well. The Court clarified this order on 30.9.2002 which reads as under:

The appointments thus to be made in the said 50% categories (as would now correspondingly stand reduced from 73% to 50%) shall, be on proportionate basis, with due reference and regard being had to the percentage of the categories as constituted the sum-total of the original impugned 73%.

Accordingly, the State of Jharkhand issued Notification No. 5800 of 2002 on 10.10.2002 superseding the earlier Notification of 5.11.2001 whereby quotas were reduced to 50% in consonance with the High Court's orders. This action by the Government through Notification No. 5800 of 2002 dated 10.10.2002 of amalgamating two classes namely, Backward Classes and Extremely Backward Classes was challenged by the appellants before the High Court of Jharkhand through W.P.(C) Nos. 6220, 6332 and 6545 of 2002. The learned single Judge quashed the Notification. On appeal by the State, the Division Bench allowed the appeal.

5. In response to a number of writ petitions (W.P. Nos. 3696/2002, 4706/2001, 4637/2001 etc.) challenging the validity of 73% reservations with respect to appointments, Full Bench of the High Court through an interim order mandated that the reservation should be limited to only 50% and that the reduction should be done on a proportionate basis with due reference and regard being had to the percentage of categories as constituted the sum total of the impugned order. It also noted that the observations would *mutatis mutandis* apply to the admission process. This order of Full Bench (Five Judges) is marked as Annexure P-2. On a petition seeking clarification of the said order at the instance of the State of Jharkhand, the High Court made modifications whereby it clarified that it would be open to the State to fix appropriate percentage quotas with respect to each individual, class and category, as it may objectively and fairly decide, constituting the sum total of 50% (Annexure P-3).

6. Resolution contained in Memo No. 5 - Reservation 3/ 2001-5800/Ranchi was issued by the State Government superceding the earlier Notification of 5.11.2001 whereby quotas were reduced to 50% in consonance with the High Court orders. But the quotas were now fixed amalgamating the categories of Backward Classes and Extremely Backward Classes in the following manner:

Scheduled Caste	-	10%
Scheduled Tribe	-	26%
Other Backward Category	-	14%
Total	-	50%

Writ Petition No. 6220 of 2002 was filed by the appellant herein in the High Court of Jharkhand at Ranchi challenging the validity of the Government's Resolution contained in Memo No. 5800/2002 which did not fix the quotas in terms of the order of the Full Bench of the High Court but amalgamated the Backward Classes and Extremely Backward Classes quotas and provided consolidated reservation.

7. The learned single Judge by his judgment and order dated 3.3.2003 allowed the writ petitions and came to the conclusion that the original Resolution No. 3884/Ranchi dated 5.11.2001 being still in existence so far as it relates to the "Reserved Categories", the respondents cannot club together the Extremely Backward. Category and Backward Category for the purpose of interim arrangement. Consequently, he set aside Resolution No. 5800/Ranchi dated 10.10.2002 to the extent it clubbed together the Extremely Backward Category and Backward Category. The matter was remitted to the State to determine separately as to what will be the percentage of Extremely Backward Category and Backward Category for the purpose of interim arrangement and for admission in professional/technical and equivalent training. The Court also took note of the fact that the High Court on earlier occasion, had merely brought down the percentage of reservation and it did not permit the State to club together one or other category or interfere with the reservation given in favour of the Extremely Backward Category.

8. Being aggrieved, the State Government filed L.P.A. No. 237 of 2003 and the Intervener-Jharkhand State Vaishya Federation filed L.P.A. No. 176 of 2003 with the leave of the Court against the common judgment and order of the learned single Judge in W.P.(C) No. 6332 86 6220 of 2002 respectively. However, no appeal was preferred against the said judgment and order of the learned single Judge passed in W.P.(C) No. 6545 of 2003 and the said judgment and order was allowed to become final.

9. The Division Bench of the High Court by its final judgment and order allowed the appeals and set aside the judgment and order of the learned single Judge and thus upheld the validity of Resolution No. 5800 dated 10.10.2002 of the State Government and thus affirmed the decision of the State Government to amalgamate the two classes *i.e.,* Extremely Backward Classes and Backward Classes and the reduction of percentage of reservation from 18% and 9% respectively to 14% only.

10. The Division Bench came to the conclusion that even though, a sub-categorization of a particular category may not be interfered with by the Court, the Court cannot direct that the State should make a sub-categorization of a reserved category, that was really a matter of policy. It also came to the conclusion that the earlier order of the Full Bench cannot be understood as confined to altering the proportion and not the category or as preventing it bringing together two categories into one common category. It further came to the conclusion that Resolution No. 5800 dated 10.10.2002 passed by the Government cannot be called in question either on the ground that it is beyond the power of the Government generally or on the ground that it is against the terms of the interim order of the Full Bench as modified. In view of the aforesaid conclusion, it also set aside the direction of the learned single Judge remitting the matter to the State Government to determine separately the percentage of seats for the Extremely Backward Categories and Backward Categories. Aggrieved by the said order, the above appeal is filed by way of special leave before this Court.

11. We heard Dr. Rajeev Dhawan, learned senior counsel assisted by Mr. Lakshmi Raman Singh, learned Counsel appearing for the appellants and Mr. Anil K. Jha, learned Counsel appearing for the respondents. We have gone through the papers, records and documents placed before us including the order impugned in this appeal and also the order passed by the Full Bench of the High Court. Dr. Rajeev, Dhawan, learned senior counsel appearing for the appellants, submitted that the Government was not justified in ordering amalgamation of two classes *i.e.,* Extremely Backward Classes and Backward Classes based on different sets of relevant materials and also ordering amalgamation without there being any study, data and materials to justify the amalgamation and, therefore, the decision of the Government is vitiated on account of non-consideration of the relevant facts and materials and consideration of irrelevant materials. He further contended that the decision of the State Government to amalgamate two classes does suffer from the vice of discrimination as the two unequals have been treated as equals and thus two different classes of people have been treated as similar.

12. Our attention was drawn to Notification No. 5800 of 2002 dated 10.10.2002 passed by the State of Jharkhand which, according to the learned senior counsel, was not in terms of the order of the Full Bench of the High Court dated 22.8.2002 read with the clarificatory order dated Page 3843 30.9.2002 which was passed during the pendency of the writ petitions before the Full Bench. It was further submitted that the Division Bench ought to have noticed that after being given Statehood, the State of Jharkhand had specifically adopted the Bihar Act and also issued Notifications giving 73% reservation to four categories, but in the gap of a year after the High Court orders, the State had issued Notification amalgamating the categories of Extremely Backward Classes and Backward Classes into one without application of mind and without taking into account all the relevant facts which have got an important bearing on the issue. Our attention was also drawn to the decision of this Court in the case of *Mandal Commission, Indira Sawhney* v. *Union of India,* 1992 Supp (3) SCC 217. Our attention was drawn to certain passages in the said judgment.

13. Mr. Anil K. Jha, learned Counsel appearing for the respondents, submitted that the State Government superseded the earlier Resolution No. 3884 dated 5.11.2001 regarding extension of reservation in admission in specified professional and technical institutions and issued a fresh Resolution No. 5800 dated 10.1.2002 in its place to make it consistent with the directions of the High Court and that in accordance with the directions of the High Court. It was further contended that no separate percentage was fixed for Backward Classes and Extremely Backward Classes and the same was done after careful application of mind and due deliberation by the highest policy making body of the Government *i.e.,* the Council of Ministers and that the decision was taken in view of the fact that the categorization of other Backward Classes between Extremely Backward Classes and Backward Classes was done by the undivided Government of Bihar and was not found exactly relevant in the context of the State of Jharkhand. It was contended that this new policy of the State Government of allocating reservation of other Backward Classes as one block is also similar to and consistent with the policy of the Central Government in this regard.

14. We have given our thoughtful consideration to the rival submissions made by the learned Counsel appearing for either side. In our opinion, the Division Bench did not appreciate that the Full Bench had given the Government the limited liberty to bring down the percentage of reservation from 73% to 50% for an interim purpose and did not give any direction with respect to the amalgamation of categories. In our opinion, the amalgamation of two classes of people for reservation would be unreasonable as two different classes are treated similarly which is in violation of the mandate of Article 14 of the Constitution of India which is to *"treat similar similarly and to treat different differently."* It is well settled that to treat unequals as equals also violates Article 14 of the Constitution.

15. The State has failed to show any new circumstances except for a bald statement that the same was done after careful application of mind and due deliberation by the highest policy making body *i.e.,* the Council of Ministers. There are no materials or empirical data to indicate that the circumstances had been changed and the State has not undertaken any study, research or work. In such circumstances to merely suggest that the council of Ministers had applied their minds and had reached a decision is arbitrary and unreasonable.

16. *Mandal Commission's* decision (supra) has specifically noted that there is no constitutional bar to a state categorizing the backward classes as backward and more backward class. State of Jharkhand by its actions seeks to disempower communities that have been extended the benefits of reservation after a conscious adoption of the Bihar Act. What the G.O. 5800 seeks to do by combining the Extremely Backward Class and Backward Class into one group is to treat unequals as equals thus violating the notion of substantive equality and Article 14 of the Constitution of India bringing it within the purview of judicial review by Court. It is also to be noticed that while the Bihar Act applied only to the appointment to posts in services, it had been extended to the admissions in educational institutions in the State by the operation of the Court's order dated 22.8.2002 which enabled the *mutatis mutandis* application of the reservations in employment to educational institutions as well.

17. *Mandal Commission's* case notes that the actions of the State Government while including or excluding classes to the List is subject to the judicial review. Paragraphs 229 and 422 of the judgment of the *Mandal Commission* note that a community that has been included in the List can be taken out only after the State has reached a conclusion that the community is adequately represented in the services of the State. Paragraphs 229 and 422 of the *Mandal Commission's* decision are as under:

> 229... There cannot be any controversy indeed there is none - that the Government which is certainly interested in the maintenance of standards of its administration, possesses and retains its sovereign authority to adopt general regulatory measures within the constitutional framework by reviewing any of its schemes or policies. The interval of the period at

which the review is to be held is within the authority and discretion of the Government, but of course subject to the constitutional parameters and well settled principles of judicial review. Therefore, it is for the Government to review the lists at any point of time and take a decision for the exclusion of any pseudo community or caste smuggled into the backward class or for inclusion of any other community which in the opinion of the Government suffers from social backwardness.

> 422. Under the Constitution, the reservations in employment in favour of backward classes are not intended either to be indiscriminate or permanent. Article 16(4) which provides for reservations, also at the same time prescribes their limits and conditions. In the first place, the reservations are not to be kept in favour of every backward class of citizens. It is only that backward class of citizens which, in the opinion of the State, is "not adequately represented" in the services under the State, which is entitled to the benefit of the reservations. Secondly, and this follows from the first, even that backward class of citizens would cease to be the beneficiary of the reservation policy, the moment the State comes to the conclusion that it is adequately represented in the services.

This apart, *Mandal Commission's* case went on to note the importance of setting up of a Backward Commission. It was observed by this Court in Paragraph 847 as under:

> We are of the considered view that there ought to be a permanent body, in the nature of a Commission or Tribunal, to which complaints of wrong inclusion or non-inclusion of groups, classes and sections in the lists of Other Backward Classes can be made. Such body must be empowered to examine complaints of the said nature and pass appropriate orders. Its advice/opinion should ordinarily be binding upon the Government. Where, however, the Government does not agree with its recommendation, it must record its reasons therefore. Even if any new class/group is proposed to be included among the other backward classes, such matter must also be referred to the said body in the first instance and action taken on the basis of its recommendation. The body must be composed of experts in the field, both official and non-official, and must be vested with the necessary powers to make a proper and effective inquiry. It is equally desirable that each State constitutes such a body, which step would go a long way in redressing genuine grievances. Such a body can be created under clause (4) of Article 16 itself - or under Article 16(4) read with Article 340 - as a concomitant of the power to identify and specify backward class of citizens, in whose favour reservations are to be provided. We direct that such a body be constituted both at Central level and at the level of the States within four months from today. They should become immediately operational and be in a position to entertain and examine forthwith complaints and matters of the nature aforementioned, if any, received. It should be open to the Government of India and the respective State Governments to devise the procedure to be followed by such body. The body or bodies so created can also be consulted in the

matter of periodic revision of lists, of O.B.Cs. As suggested by Chandrachud, CJ. in Vasant Kumar, there should be a periodic revision of these lists to exclude those who have ceased to be backward or for inclusion of new classes, as the case may be.

18. The communities which are included in the List of Backward Classes and most Backward Classes have been receiving the benefit of reservation after a conscious adoption of the Bihar legislation and categorization by the State of Jharkhand. To say that there has been a complete change in their circumstances in two years so as to exclude them from their special status without any reference to the Backward Castes Commission or a Special Commission which has been specifically appointed for the purpose would be in violation of the guidelines laid down in the *Mandal Commission's* case. Such a stand has been taken by the Andhra Pradesh High Court in a Muslim reservation's case, *T. Murlidhar Rao* v. *State of Andhra Pradesh* W.P. M.P. No. 15546 of 2004 in W.P. No. 12239 of 2004 which has noted that consultation with the Commission is a mandatory requirement.

19. It was argued by the learned Counsel appearing for the respondents that the Central Government is following the policy of clubbing the Extremely Backward Classes with the Backward Classes. In our opinion, it does not justify Jharkhand following the same policy. Jharkhand Government will look into the facts and circumstances that are peculiar to it by appointing an Expert Commission or a Body as has been provided for in the *Mandal Commission's* case which can inquire into the Page 3846 representations/complaints made over under inclusion and over-inclusion and make binding recommendations. As rightly pointed out by the learned senior counsel appearing for the appellants, the Division Bench failed to notice that the Government did not provide any material on record which would have justified amalgamation of the two classes of people nor were any documents, relevant materials or any reports produced to show a change in circumstances as was alleged by the Government. Before taking the decision to amalgamate two classes, the relevant factors were not taken into account. In fact, the specific reservation for Extremely Backward Classes had been granted on the recommendation of the Backward Commission headed by Shri Mungeri Lal constituted for the said purpose. The said Committee before making recommendation to make reservation separately for Backward Classes and Extremely Backward Classes had kept in mind the economic and social situation as also the necessity for separate reservation. The recommendation is based after a detailed survey. On the other hand, when the amalgamation of the categories took place, there were no material or empirical data to indicate that the circumstances had been changed other than a mere bald statement to the effect. It is settled law that even policy matters have to be tested at the touchstone of arbitrariness and that the present policy is discriminatory and arbitrary. As already noticed, the State of Jharkhand has specifically adopted the Bihar Act and also issued Notifications giving 73% reservation to four categories. This apart, the Full Bench had allowed the State Government only the liberty to reduce the percentage of reservation and not the categories or classes to whom the reservation could be extended to.

20. For the aforesaid reasons, we hold that the order dated 16.8.2003 passed by the Division Bench in L.P.A. No. 176 of 2003 is set aside and the matter is remitted to the State Government for undertaking a deep study and research by a special Committee of Experts constituted for the purpose or by appointing an Expert Commission headed by a Retired High Court Judge or body as has been provided for in the *Mandal Commission's* case to enquire into the recommendations/complaints made over under-inclusion and over-inclusion and make binding recommendations. The State Government is directed to constitute an Expert Commission of a Body within three months from the date of the receipt of this order. In the result, the appeal is allowed and the order dated 16.8.2003 passed in L.P.A. No. 176 of 2003 is set aside. However, there shall be no order as to costs.

Ajay Goswami v. *Union of India*

AIR 2007 SC 493: (2007) 1 SCC 143
Writ Petition (civil) 384 of 2005
Decided on 12-12-2006

Coram: **Hon'ble Mr. Justice Tarun Chatterjee**
Hon'ble Dr. Justice AR. Lakshmanan

Judgment by: **Hon'ble Dr. Justice AR. Lakshmanan**

FACTS: The petitioner's grievance in this case was that the freedom of speech and expression enjoyed by the newspaper industry was not keeping balance with the protection of children from harmful and disturbing obscene materials. Article 19(1)(a) guarantees freedom of speech and expression of individual as well as press. It acknowledges that the press is free to express its ideas but on the same hand, individual also has right to their own space and right not to be exposed against their will to other's expressions of ideas and actions.

ISSUE: Publication of obscene materials and articles in newspaper.

HELD: Blanket ban cannot be imposed on the publication of obscene materials and articles in order to shield juvenile innocence. An imposition of a blanket ban on the publication of

certain photographs and news items etc., will lead to a situation where the newspaper will be publishing material which caters only to children and adolescents and the adults will be deprived of reading their share of the entertainment which can be permissible under the normal norms of decency in any society.

JUDGMENT

Dr. AR. Lakshmanan, J.

The Petitioner is a lawyer by profession. Respondent No. 1 is Union of India, respondent No. 2 is a statutory body, respondent Nos. 3 & 4 are the leading national daily newspapers and respondent No.5 & 6 are news agencies. The present petition involves a substantial question of law and public importance on the fundamental right of the citizens, regarding the freedom of speech and expression as enshrined under Article 19(1)(a) of the Constitution of India.

The petitioner's grievance is that the freedom of speech and expression enjoyed by the newspaper industry is not keeping balance with the protection of children from harmful and disturbing materials. Article 19(1)(a) guarantees freedom of speech and expression of individual as well as press. It acknowledges that the press is free to express its ideas but on the same hand, individual also has right to their own space and right not to be exposed against their will to other's expressions of ideas and actions.

By way of this petition, the petitioner requested the Court to direct the authorities to strike a reasonable balance between the fundamental right of freedom of speech and expression enjoyed by the press and the duty of the Government, being signatory of United Nations Convention on the Rights of the Child, 1989 and Universal Declaration of Human Rights, to protect the vulnerable minors from abuse, exploitation and harmful effects of such expression. The petitioner requested the Court to direct the concerned authorities to provide for classification or introduction of a regulatory system for facilitating climate of reciprocal tolerance which may include:—

(a) an acceptance of other people's rights to express and receive certain ideas and actions; and

(b) accepting that other people have the right not to be exposed against their will to one's expression of ideas and actions.

The reciprocal tolerance is further necessary considering the growing tendency among youngsters and minors in indulging in X-rated jokes, SMS and MMS.

We heard Mr. Ajay Goswami, petitioner-in-person and Mr. Harish Chandra, learned senior counsel, Mr. P.H. Parekh, Mr. Sanjay Kumar, Mr. A.K. Seth, Mr. Gopal Jain, Mr. Vimal Chandra, Mr. S. Dave, learned counsel appearing for the respondents and the entire documents placed before us. The Lawyer Petitioner who appeared in person submitted that he filed this petition to seek protection from this Court to ensure that minors are not exposed to sexually exploitative materials, whether or not the same is obscene or is within the law. The real objective is that the nature and extent of the material having sexual contents should not be exposed to the minors indiscriminately and without regard to the age of minor. The discretion in this regard should vest with parents, guardians, teachers or experts on sex education. The petitioner is not in any way seeking restrain on the freedom of press or any censorship prior to the publication of article or other material. The petitioner is only seeking for the regulation at the receiving end and not at the source. Whatever is obscene is not protected by any law and there are numerous avenues for the redressal of grievance for the publication of any obscene material. However, all sex oriented material are not always obscene or even indecent or immoral. The effect of words or written material should always judged from the standards of reasonable strong minded, firm and courageous man *i.e.*, an average adult human being. No attempt has been made till date to define any yardstick for the minors whose tender minds are open for being polluted and are like plain state on which any painting can be drawn.

1. Is the material in newspaper really harmful for the minors? These articles etc., may not be obscene within the four corners of law but certainly have tendencies to deprave and corrupt the minds of young and adolescent who by reasons of their physical and mental immaturity needs special safeguards and care. He invited our attention to some of the clippings annexed along with the petition. These clipping are only examples and such examples not only confine to newspapers mentioned herein but is of general nature. The double meaning jokes cannot in any way leave healthy impact on the tender minds of the teenagers. The photographs certainly are part of news from around the world and India. However, the tone and tenor of the article as a whole and the way some of the photographs are published and described may not be in the interest of the minors. The photographs annexed at page 24 of the paper book and the caption below them such as "the center of attention", "double jeopardy" "butt of course" leave much for the thoughts of minors. If the minor is of an age where he/she cannot understand the meaning, he/she would like to know from others and if the minor has come to an age where he/she is able to understand this would certainly energize his grey cells in the brain and would titillate him/her. What kind of culture and message the article titled "moan for more" or "get that zing bag into your sex life" convey. Is it really necessary for a child to read at a very early stage the concept of masturbation, ejaculation, penetration etc., as is normally discussed by so called sex experts in columns of newspapers. At what age should we start telling our children where to have sex and how to break their monotony. News item on MMS clipping is certainly not obscene but do we really need to show the nude photographs with only small black stripes on the private parts to our children without even bothering of its effect. In Times of India dated 1.8.2005 an article titled "Porn In potter VI" was published, copy of which is annexed with the petition. The author has tried to read and suggest sexual messages in these lines. Children who were reading the book might not have any such inclination.

However, after reading newspaper their mind would certainly wander to an area which the author might not have even conceived.

No doubt, we are not living an era of Gandhari but certainly we have culture and respect for elders and some decorum and decency towards children. Undoubtedly, such kind of stuff is available freely on internet, movies; televisions etc. but are the families and the community environment really ready to accept it *in toto* or are they passive receiver of the same without any control or check. Are these articles really making our children morally healthy? Moral values should not be allowed to be sacrificed in the guise of social change or cultural assimilation.

2. Whether the minors have got any independent right enforceable under Article 32 of the Constitution? The right of the minor flows from Article 19(1)(a), Article 21 read with Article 39(f) of the Constitution of India and United Nation Convention on the Rights of the Child. In a recent judgment delivered by this court in the matter of *Director General, Directorate General of Doordarshan* v. *Anand Patwardhan* (C.A.No. 613 of 2005), to which one of us was a member, Dr. Justice AR. Lakshmanan, observed as under:

> "..one of the most controversial issue is balancing the need to protect society against the potential harm that may flow from obscene material, and the need to ensure respect for freedom of expression and to preserve a free flow of information and idea."

It was further observed by this Court:

> "...The Indian Penal Code on obscenity grew out of the English Law, which made court the guardian of public morals. It is important that where bodies exercise discretion, which may interfere in the enjoyment of constitutional rights, that discretion must be subject to adequate law."
>
> "The judge should thereafter place himself in the position of a reader of every age group in whose hands the book is likely to fall and should try to appreciate what kind of possible influence the book is likely to have in the minds of the readers."

It was observed by this Court in the matter of *Lakshmikant Pandey* v. *Union of India*, (1984) 2 SCC 244 as follows:

> "It is obvious that in a civilized society the importance of child welfare cannot be over-emphasized, because the welfare of the entire community, its growth and development, depend on the health and well-being of its children. Children are a "supremely important national asset" and the future well being of the nation depends on how its children grow and develop. The great poet Milton put it admirably when he said: "Child shows the man as morning shows the day" and the Study Team on Social Welfare said much to the same effect when it observed that "the physical and mental health of the nation is determined largely by the manner in which it is shaped in the early stages". The child is a soul with a being, a nature and capacities of its own, who must be helped to find them, to grow into their maturity, into fulness of physical and vital energy and the

utmost breadth, depth and height of its emotional, intellectual and spiritual being; otherwise there cannot be a healthy growth of the nation. Now obviously children need special protection because of their tender age and physique mental immaturity and incapacity to look-after themselves. That is why there is a growing realisation in every part of the globe that children must be brought up in an atmosphere of love and affection and under the tender care and attention of parents so that they may be able to attain full emotional, intellectual and spiritual stability and maturity and acquire self-confidence and self-respect and a balanced view of life with full appreciation and realisation of the role which they have to play in the nation building process without which the nation cannot develop and attain real prosperity because a large segment of the society would then be left out of the developmental process. In India this consciousness is reflected in the provisions enacted in the Constitution. Clause (3) of Article 15 enables the State to make special provisions *inter alia* for children and Article 24 provides that no child below the age of fourteen years shall be employed to work in any factory or mine or engaged in any other hazardous employment. Clauses (e) and (f) of Article 39 provide that the State shall direct its policy towards securing *inter alia* that the tender age of children is not abused, that citizens are not forced by economic necessity to enter avocations unsuited to their age and strength and that children are given facility to develop in a healthy manner and in conditions of freedom and dignity and that childhood and youth are protected against exploitation and against moral and material abandonment.

These constitutional provisions reflect the great anxiety of the constitution makers to protect and safeguard the interest and welfare of children in the country. The Government of India has also in pursuance of these constitutional provisions evolved a National Policy for the Welfare of Children. This Policy starts with a goal-oriented perambulatory introduction:

The nation's children are a supremely important asset. Their nurture and solicitude are our responsibility. Children's programme should find a prominent part in our national plans for the development of human resources, so that our children grow up to become robust citizens, physically fit, mentally alert and morally healthy, endowed with the skills and motivations needed by society. Equal opportunities for development to all children during the period of growth should be our aim, for this would serve our larger purpose of reducing inequality and ensuring social justice.

The National Policy sets out the measures which the Government of India proposes to adopt towards attainment of the objectives set out in the perambulatory introduction and they include measures designed to protect children against neglect, cruelty and exploitation and to strengthen family ties "so that full potentialities of growth of children are realised within the normal family neighbourhood and community environment.."

Further this Court in *Unnikrishnan, J.P* v. *State of Andhra Pradesh,* (1993) 1 SCC 645 upheld the right to education for children of age of 14 as fundamental right. In para 165, this Court observed as follows:

> "It is thus well established by the decisions of this Court that the provisions of Parts III and IV are supplementary and complementary to each other and that Fundamental Rights are but a means to achieve the goal indicated in Part IV. It is also held that the fundamental Rights must be construed in the light of the Directive Principles. It is from the above stand-point that Question No. 1 has to be approached".

This judgment to that extent was not overruled even by larger Bench. This Court in the case of *Unnikrishnan* (*supra*) relied upon numerous judgments.

In *His Holiness Kesavananda Bharati Sripadagalvaru* v. *State of Kerala,* (1973) 4 SCC 225, this court observed as follows:

> "..The fundamental rights and the directive principles constitute the 'conscience' of our Constitution.To ignore Part IV is to ignore the sustenance provided for in the Constitution, the hopes held out to the Nation and the very ideals on which our Constitution is built here is no anti-thesis between the fundamental rights and the directive principles. One supplements the other.
>
> ..Both Parts III and IV–have to be balanced and harmonized.then alone the dignity of the individual can be achieved..They (fundamental rights and directive principles) were meant to supplement each other.
>
> Mathew,J. while adopting the same approach remarked: (SCC pp. 875-76, para 1700)
>
> The object of the people in establishing the Constitution was to promote justice, social and economic, liberty and equality. The modus operandi to achieve these objectives is set out in Part III and IV of the Constitution. Both parts III and IV enumerate certain moral rights. Each of these parts represent in the main the statements in one sense of certain aspirations whose fulfillment was regarded as essential to the kind of society which the Constitution makers wanted to build. Many of the articles, whether in Part III or IV, represents moral rights which they have recognized as inherent in every human being in this country. The tasks of protecting and realizing these rights is imposed upon all organs of the state, namely, legislative, executive and judicial. What then is the importance to be attached to the fact that the provisions of Part III are enforceable in a court and the provisions in Part IV are not? Is it that the rights reflected in the provisions of Part III are somehow superior to the moral claims and aspirations reflected in the provisions of Part IV or not? I think not. Free and compulsory education under Article 25, Freedom from starvation is as important as right to life. Nor are the provisions in Part III absolute in the sense that the rights represented by them can always be given full implementation.."

This Court also cited observation in *Brown* v. *Board of Education,* 347 US 483 (1954) wherein it was emphasized in the following words:

> "...Today, education is perhaps the most important function of State and a local government.It is required in the performance of our most basic responsibilities, even service in the armed forces. It is the very foundation of good citizenship. Today, it is the principal instrument in awakening the child to cultural values, in preparing him for later professional training, and in helping him to adjust normally to his environment. In these days, it is doubtful any child may reasonably be expected to succeed in life if he is denied the opportunity of education."

This Court in the case of *M.C. Mehta* v. *State of T.N.*, (1996) 6 SCC 756 observed that:

> "Of the aforesaid provisions, the one finding place in Article 24 has been a fundamental right ever since 28th January, 1950. Article 45 too has been raised to high pedestal by *Unnikrishnan*, which was decided on 4th February, 1993. Though other articles are part of directive principles, they are fundamental in the governance of our country and it is the duty of all the organs of the State (a la Article 37) to apply these principles. Judiciary, being also one of the three principal organs of the State, has to keep the same in mind when called upon to decide matters of great public importance. Abolition of child labour is definitely a matter of great public concern and significance.
>
> It would be apposite to apprise ourselves also about our commitment to world community. For the case at hand it would be enough to note that India has accepted the convention on the Rights of the Child, which was concluded by the UN General Assembly on 20th November, 1989. This Convention affirms that children's right require special protection and it aims, not only to provide such protection, but also to ensure the continuous improvement in the situation of children all over the world, as well as their development and education in conditions of peace and security. Thus, the Convention not only protects the child's civil and political right, but also extends protection to child's economic, social, cultural and humanitarian rights."

3. Maintainability of Petition

In view of the above facts and circumstances and legal proposition, Mr. Ajay Goswami, the petitioner-in-person submitted that:

(i) Newspapers are publishing sex oriented material which may not be obscene otherwise but still caters to prurient interest of the minor.

(ii) Minors have got fundamental right under Article 19(1)(a), Article 21 read with Article 39(f) of the Constitution and United Nation Convention on the Rights of the Child. As freedom of speech and expression also includes the expressions of the minors which need care as the minor due to their tender age and mental immaturity are not capable of deciding themselves as to what is in the interest of their growth morally & culturally, so that they can assume their responsibility within the community.

(iii) The right also flows from Article 21 as the right to live shall also includes right to education as pronounced in the judgments of this Court. By necessary corollary, it shall also mean right to proper education which may be decided by the parents, teachers and other experts and newspapers cannot be allowed to disturb that by their indeterminately access of the offending article to the minors regardless of their age.

(iv) The State which has the duty to protect the minors by appropriate legislation or executive orders has failed in its duty. The Press Council of India which was constituted for preserving the freedom of press and maintaining and improving the standards of newspapers and news agency is a powerless body. No guidelines have been framed for the minors and adolescents in particular, which can be enforced in Court of law. The Council itself feel the necessity of some strong and effective measure to correct it.

(v) The citizens of this country can only pray to this Court to prevent injustice being done to them. This Court under Article 32 read with Article 142 can issue guidelines to ensure the growth of the children in a healthy and moral atmosphere which is exploited by the newspapers.

Mr. Ajay Goswami relied on two judgments of this Court. In *Comptroller & Auditor-General of India* v. *K.S. Jagnathan*, (1986) 2 SCC 679, this Court held as under:

> "...In order to prevent injustice resulting to the concerned parties, the Court may itself pass an order to give directions which the government or the public authority should have passed or given had it properly and lawfully exercised its discretion."

Similarly in *Vineet Narain* v. *U.O.I.*, (1998) 1 SCC 226, this Court held as under:

> "There are ample powers conferred by Article 32 read with Article 142 to make orders which have the effect of law by virtue of Article 141 and there is mandate to all authorities to act in aid of the orders of this Court as provided in Article 144 of the Constitution. In a catena of decisions of this Court, this power has been recognized and exercised, if need be, by issuing necessary directions to fill the vacuum till such time the legislature steps in to cover the gap or the executive discharges its role."
>
> "Where there is inaction by the legislature it is the duty of executive to fill the vacuum and where there is inaction even by executive for whatever reasons judiciary must step in."

Concluding his arguments, Mr. Ajay Goswamy, petitioner-in-person made the following proposals:

(i) Guidelines in detail may be issued to all the newspapers regarding the matter which may not be suitable for the reading of minors or which may require parents or teachers discretion.

(ii) Newspapers should have self regulatory system to access the publication in view of those guidelines.

(iii) In case the newspapers publish any material which is categorized in the guidelines the newspaper be packed in some different form and should convey in bold in front of newspapers of the existence of such material.

(iv) This would give discretion to the parents to instruct the news vendor whether to deliver such newspaper or not.

OR

In the alternative, he suggested a Committee be appointed to suggest ways and means for regulating the access of minors to adult oriented sexual, titillating or prurient material.

Mr. Harish Chandra, learned senior counsel appearing for Union of India - respondent No.1 in reply to the arguments of the petitioner submitted that publishing as well as circulating of obscene and nude/semi-nude photographs of women already constitutes a penal offence under the provisions of the Indecent Representation of Women (Prohibition) Act, 1986, administered by the Department of Women & Child Development, Ministry of Human Resources Development. Relevant sections 3 & 4 of the Indecent Representation of Women (Prohibition) Act, 1986 are reproduced hereunder for ready reference:

> "3. Prohibition of advertisements containing indecent representation of woman:—No person shall publish, or cause to be published or arrange or take part in the publication or exhibition or, any advertisement which contains indecent representation of women in any form.
>
> 4. Prohibition of publication or sending by post of books, pamphlets etc. containing indecent representation of women No person shall produce or cause to be produced, sell, let to hire, distribute or circulate or send by post any book, pamphlet, paper, slide, film, writing drawing, painting, photographs, representation or figure of women in any form, provided that nothing in this section shall apply to:
>
> (a) any book, pamphlet, paper, slide, film, writing, drawing, painting, photograph, representation or figure:—
>
> (i) the publication of which is proved to be justified as being for the public good on the ground that such book, pamphlet, paper, slide, film, writing, drawing, painting, photograph, representation or figure is in the interest of science, literature, art or learning or other object of general concern; or
>
> (ii) which is kept or used *bona fide* for religious purposes;
>
> (b) any representation sculptured, engraved, painted or otherwise represented on or in—
>
> (i) any ancient monument within the meaning of the Ancient Monument and Archaeological Sites and Remains Act, 1958 (24 of 1958)
>
> (ii) any temple, or on any car used for the conveyance of idols, or kept or used for any religious purposes;

(c) any film in respect of which the provisions of Part II of the Cinematograph Act, 1952 (37 of 1952), will be applicable."

Section 6 of the Indecent Representation of Women (Prohibition) Act, 1986 provides the penalty for committing such offences in contravention of sections 3 & 4 of the said Act. Section 6 reads as follows:

"6. *Penalty.*—Any person who contravenes the provisions of Sections 3 & 4 shall be punishable on first conviction with imprisonment of either description for a term which may extend to two years, and with fine which may extend to two thousand rupees, and in the event of a second or subsequent conviction with imprisonment for a term of not less than six months but which may extend to five years and also with a fine not less than ten thousand rupees but which may extend to one lac rupees."

It was further submitted that sale, letting, hiring, distributing, exhibiting, circulating of obscene books and objects of young persons under the age of twenty years also constitutes a penal offence under Sections 292 and 293 of the Indian Penal Code and is punishable on first conviction with imprisonment of either description for a term which may extend to two thousand rupees and in the event of a second or subsequent conviction, with imprisonment of either description for a term which may extend to seven years, and also with fine which may extend to five thousand rupees. Concluding his submissions, he submitted that there are laws in existence which prohibit publishing, circulating and selling obscene books and objects to young persons and it is the responsibility of the "Press" to adhere to and comply with these laws and not to abuse the freedom of speech and expression (freedom of press) guaranteed under Article 19(1)(a) of the Constitution of India.

Mr. P.H. Parekh, learned counsel appearing for respondent No. 2 – Press Council of India, submitted that the Press Council enjoys only limited authority, with its power limited to giving directions, censure etc. to the parties arraigned before it, to publish particulars relating to its enquiry and adjudication etc. The powers of the Council in so far its authority over the press is concerned are enumerated under section 14 of the Press Council Act, 1978. However, it has no further authority to ensure that its directions are complied with and its observations implemented by the erring parties. Lack of punitive powers with Press Council has tied its hands in exercising control over the erring publications.

Learned counsel further submitted that despite various requests to the Central Government from the year 1999 to amend the Press Council Act, 1978, the same has not been amended. Recently, on 1.6.2006, under clause 18(d), an advertisement policy was issued by the Directorate of Audio Visual Publicity under the Central Government Advertisement Policy stating that the newspapers will be suspended from empanelment by DG, DAVP with immediate effect if it indulged in unethical practices or anti-national activities as found by the Press Council of India.

Learned counsel further submitted that as the issue which arise in the present petition requires urgent action, it will be appropriate that this Court may formulate certain guidelines as suggested by the Press Council *vide* its letter dated 6.1.2002 for amendment by way of incorporation of two provisions *viz.*, section 14(2)(a) and section 14(2)(b) in the Press Council Act, 1978 till the law made by the legislature amending the Press Council Act, 1978 as per the various judgments passed by this Court which are as follows:

1. *Vishaka* v. *State of Rajasthan*, (1997) 6 SCC 241
2. *Vineet Narain* v. *U.O.I.*, (1998) 1 SCC 226
3. *Union of India* v. *Association for Democratic Reforms*, (2002) 5 SCC 294.

Learned counsel submitted that this Court may consider to issue appropriate guidelines.

Learned counsel appearing for respondent No. 3 (Times of India) contented that legislations, rules and regulations already exists within the Indian legal framework to check publication of obscene materials and articles. Section 292 of the Indian Penal Code prohibits and punishes selling, hiring, exhibition, circulation, possession, importation, exportation of obscene material.

Sections 3 and 4 of the Indecent Representation of Women Act also imposes a prohibition on the publication or sending by post of books, pamphlets etc., selling, hiring, distributing and circulating any material that contains indecent representation of women in any form. Section 6 of the said Act, also provides for punishment in the case of non-compliance to sections 3 and 4 of the Act.

Further he submitted that the Press Council of India is constituted duly under the Constitution of India for regulating the functions and activities of the Press. Sections 13(2)(c), 14(1) and 14(2) of the Press Council of India Act empowers the Press Council to impose serious checks on the Newspaper, News Agency, an editor or a journalist who flouts the norms as formulated by the Press Council and is against societal norms of decency.

Learned Counsel also submitted that the Indian Constitution under Article 19(1)(a) guarantees every citizen the right to freedom of speech and expression and respondent being a leading Newspaper has the right to express its views and various news of National and International relevance in its edition and any kind of unreasonable restriction on this right will amount to the violation of the right guaranteed by the Indian Constitution. Learned Counsel referred to a recent judgment of this Court, *Director-General of Doordarshan* v. *Anand Patwardhan* (Supra), it was observed that the basic test for obscenity would be:

"(a) whether the average person applying contemporary community standards would find that the work, taken as a whole appeal to the prurient interest"

(b) whether the work depicts or describes, in a patently offensive way, sexual conduct specifically, defined by the applicable State law,

(c) whether the work taken as a whole, lacks serious literary, artistic, political or scientific value."

In *Shri Chandrakant Kalyandas Kakodkar* v. *The State of Maharashtra*, (1962) 2 SCC 687, this Court observed that:

> "12. The concept of obscenity would differ from country to country depending on the standards of morals of contemporary society. What is considered as a piece of literature in France may be obscene in England and what is considered in both countries as not harmful to public order and morals may be obscene in our country. But to insist that the standard should always be for the writer to see that the adolescent ought not to be brought into contact with sex or that if they read any references to sex in what is written whether that is the dominant theme or not they would be affected, would be to require authors to write books only for the adolescent and not for the adults."

Learned counsel referred to the case of *Samaresh Bose* v. *Amal Mitra,* (1985) 4 SCC 289, this court observed that:

> "The decision of the Court must necessarily be on an objective assessment of the book or story or article as a whole and with particular reference to the passages complained of in the book, story or article. The Court must take an overall view of the matter complained of as obscene in the setting of the whole work, but the matter charged as obscene must also be considered by itself and separately to find out whether it is so gross and its obscenity so pronounced that it is likely to deprave and corrupt those whose minds are open to influence of this sort and into whose hands the book is likely to fall."

> Learned counsel also referred to American jurisprudence and stated that even nudity *per se* is not obscenity. In 50 Am Jur 2 d, para 22 at page 23, "Articles and pictures in a newspaper must meet the Miller's test's Constitutional standard of obscenity in order for the publisher or distributor to be prosecuted for obscenity. Nudity alone is not enough to make a material legally obscene"

In *Alfred E Butler* v. *State of Michigan,* 1 Led 2d 412, the U.S. Supreme Court has held that: "The state insists that, by thus quarantining the general reading public against books not too rugged for grown men and women in order to shield juvenile innocence, it is exercising its power to promote the general welfare. Surely, this is to burn the house to roast the pig."

Further the learned counsel submitted that, the Times of India, respondent No. 3, is one of the leading newspapers and its popularity only stands to show that the pictures published in it are not objectionable and also that respondent while publishing any news article has any intention to cater to the prurient interest of anybody. Also the respondent No. 3 has an internal regulatory system to ensure that no objectionable photograph or matter gets published.

Mr. Gopal Jain, learned counsel appearing for Hindustan Times respondent No. 4, practically adopted the arguments put forth by respondent No. 3. In addition, respondent No. 4 drew our attention to the Guidelines under the "Norms of Journalistic Conduct" which lays down guidelines for newspapers/ journalists to maintain standards with regard to obscenity and vulgarity.

Norm 17 reads as follows:

"Obscenity and vulgarity to be eschewed

(i) Newspapers/journalists shall not publish anything which is obscene, vulgar or offensive to public good taste.

(ii) Newspapers shall not display advertisements which are vulgar or which, through depiction of a woman in nude or lewd posture, provoke lecherous attention of males as if she herself was a commercial commodity for sale.

(iii) Whether a picture is obscene or not, is to be judged in relation to three tests: namely

(a) Is it vulgar and indecent?

(b) Is it a piece of mere pornography?

(c) Is its publication meant merely to make money by titillating the sex feelings of adolescents and among whom it is intended to circulate? In other words, does it constitute an unwholesome exploitation for commercial gain.

Other relevant considerations are whether the picture is relevant to the subject-matter of the magazine. That is to say, whether its publication serves any preponderating social or public purpose, in relation to art, painting, medicine, research or reform of sex.

(iv) The globalisation and liberalization does not give licence to the media to misuse freedom of the Press and to lower the values of the society. The media performs a distinct role and public purpose which require it to rise above commercial consideration guiding other industries and businesses. So far as that role is concerned, one of the duties of the media is to preserve and promote our cultural heritage and social values.

(v) Columns such as 'Very Personal' in a newspaper replying to personal queries of the readers must not become grossly offensive presentations, which either outrage public decency or corrupt public moral."

Learned Counsel contented that, the test of judging should be that of an ordinary man of common sense and prudence and not an "out of the ordinary hypersensitive man".

In the case of *K.A. Abbas* , Hidayatullah, C.J. opined: "If the depraved begins to see in these things more than what an average person would, in much the same way, as it is wrongly said, a Frenchman sees a woman's legs in everything, it cannot be helped."

Learned counsel further explained the procedure followed by Hindustan Times before the publication of any advertisement, "Advertisements are scrutinized by the advertising department and in the event the advertising department is in doubt, the assistance of the legal department is resorted to. The departments are manned by qualified persons who are well acquainted with the Norms and Guidelines issued by the Press Council."

Further the learned counsel submitted that, keeping in mind special educational needs of the school-going students a supplement called "HT Next-

School Times" is published by Hindustan Times. The respondent does not send any other supplement other than this to educational institutions along with the main paper. Thus, it was stated that respondent realizes its responsibility towards children and at the same time it would be inappropriate to deprive the adult population of the entertainment which is well within the acceptable levels on the ground that it may not be appropriate for the children. In conclusion, it was urged that any step to ban publishing of certain news-pieces or pictures would fetter the independence of free-press.

Learned Counsel appearing for respondent No. 5 and Learned Counsel Dr. Kailash Chand appearing for respondent No. 6, submitted that the relief sought by the petitioner does not relate to them and accordingly they are not giving any reply.

We have given our careful consideration to the entire material placed before us and the rival submissions made by learned counsel appearing for the respective parties. Maintainability of Writ Petition:

Before proceeding further, we feel better to reproduce the prayers made in the writ petition which read as follows:

"(1) Issue writ in the nature of writ of mandamus/order or direction to the respondent Nos. 1 & 2 for laying down rules/regulations to ensure that minor is not exposed to sexually explicit material whether or not the same is obscene or is within the law without express consent of the parents, guardians or the experts on sex education.

(2) Respondent Nos. 1 & 2 be directed to constitute an expert committee to look into the problem of unwanted exposure to the minor through press and to lay down appropriate rules and regulations for the same."

The maintainability of the writ petition was also raised as a preliminary issue by learned counsel appearing for some of the respondents and, in particular, respondent Nos. 3 and 4. Learned counsel for respondent No. 3 pointed out that there can be no *mandamus* for legislation and in support of the said submission, he relied on the judgment of this Court in *Networking of Rivers: In Re,* (2004) 11 SCC 360 wherein this Court held

> "It is not open to this Court to issue any direction to Parliament to legislate but the Attorney-General submits that the Government will consider this aspect and, if so advised, will bring an appropriate legislation."

He also cited *Common Cause* v. *Union of India,* (2003) 8 SCC 250. This Court held:

> "From the facts placed before us it cannot be said that the Government is not alive to the problem or is desirous of ignoring the will of Parliament. When the legislature itself had vested the power in the Central Government to notify the date from which the Act would come into force, then the Central Government is entitled to take into consideration various facts including the facts set out above while considering whether the Act should be brought into force or not. No

mandamus can be issued to the Central Government to issue the notification contemplated under section 1(3) of the Act to bring the Act into force, keeping in view the facts brought on record and the consistent view of this Court.

We have already noticed the prayer in the present writ petition. In our view, the prayer No. 1 cannot at all be countenanced inasmuch as sufficient protection in the form of legislations, rules, regulations and norms have already been laid down under the Press Council Act, 1978, I.P.C. etc., Prayer No. 2 equally is vague and no case has been made out for constituting an Expert Committee.

LEGISLATIONS AGAINST OBSCENITY:

Section 13 of the Press Council Act, 1978 specifies the objects and functions of the council.

Section 13(2)(c) states:

"to ensure on the part of newspapers, news agencies and journalists, the maintenance of high standards of public taste and foster a due sense of both the rights and responsibilities of citizenship;

Section 14(1) states:

"Where, on receipt of a complaint made to it or otherwise, the Council has reason to believe that a newspaper or news agency has offended against the standards of journalistic ethics or public taste or that an editor or working journalist has committed any professional misconduct, the Council may, after giving the newspaper, or news agency, the editor or journalist concerned an opportunity of being heard, hold an inquiry in such manner as may be provided by regulations made under this Act and, if it is satisfied that it is necessary so to do, it may, for reasons to be recorded in writing, warn, admonish or censure the newspaper, the news agency, the editor or the journalist or disapprove the conduct of the editor or the journalist, as the case may be:

Provided that the Council may not take cognizance of a complaint if in the opinion of the Chairman, there is no sufficient ground for holding an inquiry.

Section 14(2) states:—

"If the Council is of the opinion that it is necessary or expedient in public interest so to do, it may require any newspaper to publish therein in such manner as the Council thinks fit, any particulars relating to any inquiry under this section against a newspaper or news agency, an editor or a journalist working therein, including the name of such newspaper, news agency, editor or journalist.

Section 292 of the Indian Penal Code reads:—

"Sale, etc., of obscene books, etc.—(1) For the purposes of sub-section (2), a book, pamphlet, paper, writing, drawing, painting, representation, figure or any other object, shall be deemed to be obscene if it is lascivious or appeals to the prurient interest or if its effect, or (where it comprises two or more distinct items) the effect of any one of its items, is, if taken as a whole, such as to tend to deprave and corrupt person, who are likely, having regard to all relevant circumstances, to read, see or hear the matter contained or embodied in it].

[(2)] Whoever—

(a) sells, lets to hire, distributes, publicly exhibits or in any manner puts into circulation, or for purposes of sale, hire, distribution, public exhibition or circulation, makes, produces or has in his possession any obscene book, pamphlet, paper, drawing, painting, representation or figure or any other obscene object whatsoever, or

(b) imports, exports or conveys any obscene object for any of the purposes aforesaid, or knowing or having reason to believe that such object will be sold, let to hire, distributed or publicly exhibited or in any manner put into circulation, or

(c) takes part in or receives profits from any business in the course of which he knows or has reason to believe that any such obscene objects are for any of the purposes aforesaid, made, produced, purchased, kept, imported, exported, conveyed, publicly exhibited or in any manner put into circulation, or

(d) advertises or makes known by any means whatsoever that any person is engaged or is ready to engage in any act which is an offence under this section, or that any such obscene object can be procured from or through any person, or

(e) offers or attempts to do any act which is an offence under this section,

shall be punished on first conviction with imprisonment of either description for a term which may extend to two years, and with fine which may extend to two thousand rupees, and, in the event of a second or subsequent conviction, with imprisonment of either description for a term which may extend to five years, and also with fine which may extend to five thousand rupees.

[*Exception.*—This section does not extend to—

(a) any book, pamphlet, paper, writing, drawing, painting, representation or figure—

(i) the publication of which is proved to be justified as being for the public good on the ground that such book, pamphlet, paper, writing, drawing, painting, representation or figure is in the interest of science, literature, art of learning or other objects of general concern, or

(ii) which is kept or used *bona fide* for religious purposes;

(b) any representation sculptured, engraved, painted or otherwise represented on or in—

(i) any ancient monument within the meaning of the Ancient Monuments and Archaeological Sites and Remains Act, 1958 (24 of 1958), or

(ii) any temple, or on any car used for the conveyance of idols, or kept or used for any religious purpose.]"

Sections 4 and 6 of the Indecent Representation of Women Act, 1986 are also in existence.

In view of the availability of sufficient safeguards in terms of various legislations, norms and rules and regulations to protect the society in general and children, in particular, from obscene and prurient contents, we are of the opinion that the writ at the instance of the petitioner is not maintainable.

Article 19(1)(a) deals with freedom of speech and expression. In the matter of *Virendra* v. *State of Punjab*, AIR 1957 SC 896 this Court held:

> "It is certainly a serious encroachment on the valuable and cherished right to freedom of speech and expression if a newspaper is prevented from publishing its own views or the views of its correspondents relating to or concerning what may be the burning topic of the day. Our social interest ordinarily demands the free propagation and interchange of views but circumstances may arise when the social interest in public order may require a reasonable subordination of the social interest in free speech and expression to the needs of our social interest in public order. Our Constitution recognises this necessity and has attempte to strike a balance between the two social interests. It permits the imposition of reasonable restrictions on the freedom of speech and expression in the interest of public order and on the freedom of carrying on trade or business in the interest of the general public.
>
> Therefore, the crucial question must always be: Are the restrictions imposed on the exercise of the rights under Arts. 19(1)(a) and 19(1)(g) reasonable in view of all the surrounding circumstances ? In other words are the restrictions reasonably necessary in the interest of public order under Art. 19(2) or in the interest of the general public under Art. 19(6)?"

Test of obscenity:

This Court has time and again dealt with the issue of obscenity and laid down law after considering the right of freedom and expression enshrined in Article 19(1)(a) of the Constitution of India, its purport and intent, and laid down the broad principles to determine/judge obscenity. In a recent judgment *Director-General, Directorate General of Doordarshan* v. *Anand Patwardhan* reported in JT 2006 (8) SC 255 (Dr. AR. Lakshmanan and L.S. Panta, JJ) This Court has referred to the Hicklin test laid down in (1868) 3 QB 360 and observed:

"(a) whether the average person applying contemporary community standards would find that the work, taken as a whole appeal to the prurient interest"

(b) whether the work depicts or describes, in a patently offensive way, sexual conduct specifically, defined by the applicable State law,

(c) whether the work taken as a whole, lacks serious literary, artistic, political or scientific value."

In *Shri Chandrakant Kalyandas Kakodkar* v. *The State of Maharashtra*, (1969) 2 SCC 687. This Court has held:

> "In early English writings authors wrote only with unmarried girls in view but society has changed since then to allow litterateurs and artists to give expression to their ideas, emotions and objectives with full freedom except that is should not fall within the definition of 'obscene' having regard to the standards of contemporary society in which it is read. The standards of contemporary society in India are also fast changing. The adults and adolescents have available to them a large number of classics, novels, stories and pieces of literature which have a content of sex, love and romance. As observed in *Udeshi's* case (Supra) if a reference to sex by itself is considered obscene, no books can be sold except those which are purely religious. In the field of art and cinema also the adolescent is shown situations which even a quarter of a century ago would be considered derogatory to public morality, but having regard to changed conditions are more taken for granted without in anyway tending to debase or debauch the mind. What we have to see is that whether a class, not an isolated case, into whose hands the book, article or story falls suffer in their moral outlook or become depraved by reading it or might have impure and lecherous thought aroused in their minds. The charge of obscenity must, therefore, be judged from this aspect"

In *Samaresh Bose* v. *Amal Mitra* (Supra), this Court held as under:

> "In England, as we have earlier noticed, the decision on the question of obscenity rests with the jury who on the basis of the summing up of the legal principles governing such action by the learned Judge decides whether any particular novel, story or writing is obscene or not. In India, however, the responsibility of the decision rests essentially on the Court. As laid down in both the decisions of this Court earlier referred to, "the question whether a particular article or story or book is obscene or not does not altogether depend on oral evidence, because it is the duty of the Court to ascertain whether the book or story or any passage or passages therein offend the provisions of section 292, I.P.C." In deciding the question of obscenity of any book, story or article the Court whose responsibility it is to adjudge the question may, if the Court considers it necessary, rely to an extent on evidence and views of leading literary personage, if available, for its own appreciation and assessment and for satisfaction of its own conscience. The decision of the Court must necessarily be on an objective assessment of the book or story or article as a whole and with particular reference to the passages complained of in the book, story or article. The Court must take an overall view of the matter complained of as obscene in the setting of the whole work, but the matter charged as obscene must also be considered by itself and separately to find out whether it is so gross and its obscenity so pronounced that it is likely to deprave and corrupt those whose minds are open to influence of this sort and into whose hands the book is likely to fall. Though the Court must consider the question objectively with an

open mind, yet in the matter of objective assessment the subjective attitude of the Judge hearing the matter is likely to influence, even though unconsciously, his mind and his decision on the question. A Judge with a puritan and prudish outlook may on the basis of an objective assessment of any book or story or article, consider the same to be obscene. It is possible that another Judge with a different kind of outlook may not consider the same book to be obscene on his objective assessment of the very same book. The concept of obscenity is moulded to a very great extent by the social outlook of the people who are generally expected to read the book. It is beyond dispute that the concept of obscenity usually differs from country to country depending on the standards of morality of contemporary society in different countries. In our opinion, in judging the question of obscenity, the Judge in the first place should try to place himself in the position of the author and from the view point of the author the judge should try to understand what is it that the author seeks to convey and whether what the author conveys has any literary and artistic value. The Judge should thereafter place himself in the position of a reader of every age group in whose hands the book is likely to fall and should try to appreciate what kind of possible influence the book is likely to have in the minds of the readers. A Judge should thereafter apply his judicial mind dispassionately to decide whether the book in question can be said to be obscene within the meaning of section 292, I.P.C. by an objective assessment of the book as a whole and also of the passages complained of as obscene separately. In appropriate cases, the Court, for eliminating any subjective element or personal preference which may remain hidden in the sub-conscious mind and may unconsciously affect a proper objective assessment, may draw upon the evidence on record and also consider the views expressed by reputed or recognised authors of literature on such questions if there be any for his own consideration and satisfaction to enable the Court to discharge the duty of making a proper assessment".

Per se nudity is not obscenity:

The American Courts, from time-to-time, have dealt with the issues of obscenity and laid down parameters to test obscenity. It was further submitted that while determining whether a picture is obscene or not it is essential to first determine as to quality and nature of material published and the category of readers.

In 50 Am Jur 2 d, para 22 at page 23 reads as under:

> "Articles and pictures in a newspaper must meet the Miller test's constitutional standard of obscenity in order for the publisher or distributor to be prosecuted for obscenity. Nudity alone is not enough to make material legally obscene.
>
> The possession in the home of obscene newspaper is constitutionally protected, except where the such materials constitute child pornography."

Contemporary Society:

It was also submitted that in order to shield minors and children the State should not forget that the same content might not be offensive to the sensibilities of adult men and women. The incidence of shielding the minors should not be that the adult population is restricted to read and see what is fit for children.

In *Alfred E Butler* v. *State of Michigan,* 1 Led 2d 412, U.S. Supreme Court held as under:

> "The State insists that, by thus quarantining the general reading public against books not too rugged for grown men and women in order to shield juvenile innocence, it is exercising its power to promote the general welfare. Surely, this is to burn the house to roast the pig."

There should be no suppression of speech and expression in protecting children from harmful materials: In *Janet Reno* v. *American Civil Liberties Union,* 138 Led 2d 874, it has been held that:

> "The Federal Government's interest in protecting children from harmful materials does not justify an unnecessarily broad suppression of speech addressed to adults, in violation of the Federal Constitution's First Amendment; the Government may not reduce the adult population to only what is fit for children, and thus the mere fact that a statutory regulation of speech was enacted for the important purpose of protecting children from exposure to sexually explicit material does not foreclose inquiry into the statute's validity under the First Amendment, such inquiry embodies an overarching commitment to make sure that Congress has designed its statute to accomplish its purpose without imposing an unnecessarily great restriction on speech."

In 146 Led 2d 865, *United States* v. *Playboy Entertainment Group Inc.,* it has been held that:

> "In order for the State – to justify prohibition of a particular expression of opinion, it must be able to show that its action was caused by something more than a mere desire to avoid the discomfort and unpleasantness that always accompany an unpopular viewpoint. What the Constitution says is that these judgments are for the individual to make, not for the government of decree, even with the mandate or approval of a majority. Technology expands the capacity to choose; and it denies the potential of this revolution if we assume the Government is best positioned to make these choices for us."

Literary merit and "prepondering social purpose"

Where art and obscenity are mixed, what must be seen is whether the artistic, literary or social merit of the work in question outweighs its "obscene" content. This view was accepted by this Court in *Ranjit D. Udeshi* v. *State of Maharashtra,* AIR 1965 SC case:

> "Where there is propagation of ideas, opinions and information of public interest or profit the approach to the problem may become different because then the interest of society may tilt the scales in favour of free

speech and expression. It is thus that books on medical science with intimate illustrations and photographs, though in a sense immodest, are not considered to be obscene but the same illustrations and photographs collected in book form without the medical text would certainly be considered to be obscene.

Where art and obscenity are mixed, the element of art must be so prepondering as to overshadow the obscenity or make it so trivial/ inconsequential that it can be ignored; Obscenity without a preponderating social purpose or profit cannot have the constitutional protection of free speech"

Contemporary Standards

In judging as to whether a particular work is obscene, regard must be had to contemporary mores and national standards. While the Supreme Court in India held Lady Chatterley's Lover to be obscene, in England the jury acquitted the publishers finding that the publication did not fall foul of the obscenity test. This was heralded as a turning point in the fight for literary freedom in UK. Perhaps "community mores and standards" played a part in the Indian Supreme Court taking a different view from the English jury. The test has become somewhat outdated in the context of the internet age which has broken down traditional barriers and made publications from across the globe available with the click of a mouse.

Judging the work as a whole

It is necessary that publication must be judged as a whole and the impugned should also separately be examined so as to judge whether the impugned passages are so grossly obscene and are likely to deprave and corrupt.

Opinion of literary/artistic experts

In *Ranjit Udeshi* (*Supra*) this Court held that the delicate task of deciding what is artistic and what is obscene has to be performed by courts and as a last resort by the Supreme Court and therefore, the evidence of men of literature or others on the question of obscenity is not relevant. However, in *Samresh Bose* v. *Amal Mitra* (*Supra*) this Court observed:

"In appropriate cases, the court, for eliminating any subjective element or personal preference which may remain hidden in the subconscious mind and may unconsciously affect a proper objective assessment, may draw upon the evidence on record and also consider the views expressed by reputed or recognized authors of literature on such questions as if there by any of his own consideration and satisfaction to enable the court to discharge the duty of making a proper assessment."

Clear and Present Danger

In *S. Ragarajan* v. *P. Jagjivan Ram*, while interpreting Article 19(2), this Court borrowed from the American test of clear and present danger and observed:

"the commitment to freedom demands that it cannot be suppressed unless the situations created by allowing the freedom are pressing and the community interest is endangered. The anticipated danger should not be remote, conjectural or far-fetched. It should have a proximate and direct nexus with the expression. The expression of thought should be intrinsically dangerous to the public interest. In other words, the expression should be inseparably like the equivalent of a 'spark in a power keg'."

Test of Ordinary Man

The test for judging a work should be that of an ordinary man of common sense and prudence and not an "out of the ordinary or hypersensitive man." As Hidayatullah, C.J. remarked in *K.A. Abbas*:

> "If the depraved begins to see in these things more than what an average person would, in much the same way, as it is wrongly said, a Frenchman sees a woman's legs in everything, it cannot be helped."

An additional affidavit was filed on behalf of the Press Council of India on 7.8.2006. Inviting our attention to the said affidavit, Mr. P.H. Parekh submitted that Section 14 of the Press Council Act, 1978 empowers the Press Council only to warn, admonish or censure newspapers or news agencies and that it has no jurisdiction over the electronic media and that the Press Council enjoys only the authority of declaratory adjudication with its power limited to giving directions to the answering respondents arraigned before it to publish particulars relating to its enquiry and adjudication. It, however, has no further authority to ensure that its directions are complied with and its observations implemented by the erring parties. Lack of punitive powers with the Press Council of India has tied its hands in exercising control over the erring publications.

Mr. P.H. Parekh further submitted that prompted by the continued flouting of its observation/directions by some of the Press of the country, the Press Council has recommended to the Government between 1999-2003 to amend the provisions of Section 14(1) of the Press Council Act, 1978 to arm the Council with the authority to recommend to the Government de-recognition of newspapers for Government advertisement or withdrawal of the accreditation granted to a journalist which facilitates performance of his function and also entitles him to claim concession in railways etc. or to recommend de-recognition of a newspaper for the period deemed appropriate for the proposals made. The Press Council of India is yet to receive any response from the Government. The counsel has also filed the copies of the letters written by Justice K. Jayachandra Reddy dated 17.12.2002 and 06.12.2003 issued by the Press Council to the Government of India for extending punitive powers and the amendments proposed by the Council have been annexed to the main writ petition. In our opinion, the present scenario provides for a regulatory framework under which punishment is prescribed for flouting the standards set by the Press Council of India by newspapers/print media. Further, respondent Nos. 3 & 4 have a self-regulatory mechanism in place and they have to strictly adhere to the standards set by the Press Council Act, 1978. According to them, the advertisement, news articles and photographs are scrutinized by the advertising department and in the event the advertising department is in doubt, the assistance of the legal department is resorted to. It is also their case that the said departments are manned by qualified persons who are well acquainted with the Norms and Guidelines issued by the press Council. It was also submitted that respondent No. 4, as among others, consistently rejected the publication of liquor and sexually exploitative advertisements, which may offend the sensibilities of families and in contravention it was further submitted that respondent No. 4, keeping in mind, special educational needs of school going children publishes a supplement called "HT Next School Times" every Monday and the respondent does not send any supplement to schools other than "HT Next School Times" along with the main paper. Further, the respondent publishes "HT Next" which is a newspaper positioned mainly for the youth. This paper too keeps in mind the special needs of the youth of today. The market segment that the respondent's paper wishes to cater and caters to sections of society interested in business and is keen on gathering information on all fronts of life. It was further submitted that the newspaper intends to give a holistic perspective of the world to an individual. It was submitted that the respondent's paper has consistently over the last few decades had a large circulation and consistent increase in its circulation each year has not been due to publishing of its supplement "HT City".

In view of the foregoing legal propositions the pictures in dispute had been published by the respondents with the intent to inform readers of the current entertainment news from around the world and India. The respondent's newspaper seeks to provide a wholesome reading experience offering current affairs, sports, politics as well as entertainment news to keep its readers abreast of all the latest happenings in the world. The pictures that have been published should not be viewed in isolation rather they have to be read with the news reports next to them. In the event, that a particular news items or picture offends any person they may avail of the remedies available to them under the present legal framework. Any steps to impose a blanket ban on publishing of such photographs, in our opinion, would amount to prejudging the matter as has been held in the matter of *Fraser* v. *Evans*, 1969 (1) QB 549.

The definition of obscenity differs from culture to culture, between communities within a single culture, and also between individuals within those communities. Many cultures have produced laws to define what is considered to be obscene, and censorship is often used to try to suppress or control materials that are obscene under these definitions.

The term obscenity is most often used in a legal context to describe expressions (words, images, actions) that offend the prevalent sexual morality. On the other hand the Constitution of India guarantees the right of freedom to speech and expression to every citizen. This right will encompass an individuals take on any issue. However, this right is not absolute, if such speech and expression is immensely gross and will badly violate the standards of morality of a society. Therefore, any expression is subject to reasonable restriction. Freedom of expression has contributed much to the development and well-being of our free society.

This right conferred by the Constitution has triggered various issues. One of the most controversial issues is balancing the need to protect society against the potential harm that may flow from obscene material, and the need to ensure respect for freedom of expression and to preserve a free flow of information and idea.

Be that as it may, the respondents are leading newspapers in India they have to respect the freedom of speech and expression as is guaranteed by our constitution and in fact reaches out to its readers any responsible and decent manner. In our view, any steps to ban publishing of certain news pieces or pictures would fetter the independence of free press which is one of the hallmarks of our democratic setup. In our opinion, the submissions and the propositions of law made by the respective counsel for the respondents clearly established that the present petition is liable to be dismissed as the petitioner has failed to establish the need and requirement to curtail the freedom of speech and expression. The Times of India and Hindustan Times are leading newspapers in Delhi having substantial subscribers from all sections. It has been made clear by learned counsel appearing for the leading newspapers that it is not their intention to publish photographs which cater to the prurient interest. As already stated, they have an internal regulatory system to ensure no objectionable photographs or matters gets published. We are able to see that respondent Nos. 3 & 4 are conscious of their responsibility towards children but at the same time it would be inappropriate to deprive the adult population of the entertainment which is well within the acceptable levels of decency on the ground that it may not be appropriate for the children. An imposition of a blanket ban on the publication of certain photographs and news items etc., will lead to a situation where the newspaper will be publishing material which caters only to children and adolescents and the adults will be deprived of reading their share of their entertainment which can be permissible under the normal norms of decency in any society.

We are also of the view that a culture of 'responsible reading' should be inculcated among the readers of any news article. No news item should be viewed or read in isolation. It is necessary that publication must be judged as a whole and news items, advertisements or passages should not be read without the accompanying message that is purported to be conveyed to the public. Also the members of the public and readers should not look for meanings in a picture or written article, which is not conceived to be conveyed through the picture or the news item.

We observe that, as decided by the American Supreme Court in *United States* v. *Playboy Entertainment Group Inc*, 146 L ed 2d 865, that, "in order for the Stateto justify prohibition of a particular expression of opinion, it must be able to show that its action was caused by something more than a mere desire to avoid the discomfort and unpleasantness that always accompany an unpopular viewpoint." Therefore, in our view, in the present matter, the petitioner has failed to establish his case clearly. The petitioner only states that the pictures and the news items that are published by the respondents 3 and 4 'leave much for the thoughts of minors'.

Therefore, we believe that fertile imagination of anybody especially of minors should not be a matter that should be agitated in the court of law. In addition we also hold that news is not limited to Times of India and Hindustan Times. Any hypersensitive person can subscribe to many other Newspaper of their choice, which might not be against the standards of morality of the concerned person.

We, therefore, dismiss the writ petition but however observed that the request made by the Press Council of India to amend the Section should be seriously looked into by the Government of India and appropriate amendments be made in public interest. No costs.

Ramchandra Mahadev Jagpat

V.

Chief Executive Officer

AIR 2007 SC 650: JT 2007 (3) SC 413: (2006) 12 SCALE 33: (2006) 11 SCC 661
Special Leave Petition (civil) No. 10281 of 2006, I.A. Nos. 2-5 and 8 in Special Leave Petition (C) No. 10281/2006 and I.A. No. 1 in S.L.P. (C) No. ... of 2006 (CC 5527)
Decided on 07-11-2006

AND

Sigtia Construction Company Private Ltd.

V.

Ram Chandra Mahadev Jagpat

Coram: **Hon'ble Mr. Justice Tarun Chatterjee**
Hon'ble Dr. Justice AR. Lakshmanan

Judgment by: **Hon'ble Dr. Justice AR. Lakshmanan**

FACTS: The applicant was appointed as a developer by the Slum Dwellers Co-operative Housing Society. A writ petition challenging appointment of the applicant was dismissed with

directions to Slum Rehabilitation Authority (SRA) to put additional conditions on the applicant. Subsequently the society terminated the agreement with the applicant and appointed a new developer. Some of the slum dwellers initiated proceedings before the High Court and the Supreme Court by way of Special Leave Petition where termination of agreement with the applicant and replacement of the applicant by a new developer was the subject-matter. An interim order was made directing SRA to issue Letter of Intent in favour of the replaced developer. The interim order was obtained in an SLP without impleading the applicant.

ISSUE: Impleadment of proper and necessary parties.

HELD: Interim order directing SRA to issue Letter of Intent in favour of replaced developer obtained in S.L.P. without impleading applicant is liable to be recalled. The Authority was directed to decide matter after hearing both the developers.

JUDGMENT

Dr. AR. Lakshmanan, J.

1. I.A. No. 1 for impleadment is ordered on 10.07.2006. M/s Sigtia Construction Company Private Limited was impleaded as respondent No. 5 in Special Leave Petition No. 10281 of 2006.

2. I.A. No. 3 of 2006 was filed by the applicant - M/s Sigtia Construction Company Private Limited to recall the order dated 27.06.2006 passed by this Court in Special Leave Petition No. 10281 of 2006. The order passed by this Court in Special Leave Petition No. 10281/2006 dated 27.06.2006 reads thus:

ORDER

Heard Mr. L.N. Rao, senior advocate for the petitioners. Mr. Sanjay V. Khande, Mr. B.S. Rao and Ms. Indra Sawhney, advocates accepts notice on behalf of respondent Nos. 1 to 3. We also heard their submissions.

By a prayer for interim relief, the petitioners seek direction directing the Slum Rehabilitation Authority to issue a letter of intent in favour of M/s Keya Developers and Construction Company (P) Ltd. For undertaking re- development work in the slum situated at Irla Tank, S.V. Road, Vile Parle (West) Mumbai.

The grievance of the petitioners is that despite no legal impediment, the Slum Rehabilitation Authority was not issuing the letter of intent in favour of M/s Keya Developers and Construction Company (P) Ltd. despite a request made by the Society. According to them, it was merely a case of replacement of previous developers M/s Sigtia Construction Company Pvt. Ltd. who had not even started the project even after almost eight years and whose agreement with the Society had come to an end by efflux of time.

Mr. Sunil K. Varma, advocate, appears for the Chief Executive Officer, Slum Rehabilitation Authority, Bandra (E), Mumbai (respondent No. 1). The learned

Counsel submits that the Slum Rehabilitation Authority will issue proper orders within two weeks from today. In view of the submission made by the learned Counsel for respondent No. 1, we direct the Slum Rehabilitation Authority to issue the letter of intent in favour of M/s Keya Developers and Construction Company (P) Ltd. which is also represented by Mr. Jaideep Gupta, learned senior counsel and the Society is represented by Mr. P.K. Ghosh, learned senior counsel.

The Special Leave Petition is disposed of accordingly.

3. The reasons for recalling the order as stated in I.A.No. 3 of 2006 are as under:

The applicant Sigtia Construction Company Private Limited (in short "Sigtia") was appointed as developer by the Vile Parle Prem Nagar Co-operative Housing Society Limited (hereinafter called "Society" the respondent No. 2). The applicant who is directly affected by an order appointing M/s Keya Developers and Construction Private Limited (in short "Keya") as Developer was not made a party respondent in Writ Petition No. 1277 of 2006 and also in the Special Leave Petition No. 10281 of 2006 although the applicant was a party in the previous proceedings, namely, Writ Petition No. 988 of 2004 which was filed before the High Court and the Special Leave Petition No. 11318 of 2005 and 19848 of 2005. According to the applicant, the respondents in the Special Leave Petition No. 10281 are not contesting respondents and particularly respondent No. 1 - the Slum Rehabilitation Authority (in short "SRA") had taken a stand before this Court in earlier round in Special Leave Petition No. 19848 of 2005 by way of an affidavit that they will abide by any orders which may be passed by this Court. Nobody appeared for Bombay Municipal Corporation on 27.06.2006. Therefore, there was nobody present who could have opposed the passing of the order. The applicant, against whom allegations were made, was not made a party to the special leave petition. It was the duty of the petitioner in the special leave petition, to make the applicant - Sigtia, who is directly affected, a party to the special leave petition. However, instead of doing that this Court was given the impression that all the affected parties were before this Court.

4. Mr. Arun Jaitley, learned senior counsel appearing for the applicant Sigtia made the following submissions as to why the order dated 27.06.2006 in special leave petition No. 10281 of 2006 should be recalled.

(a) M/s Sigtia was appointed as developers in respect of Slum Rehabilitation Scheme of the property in the sub-urban district of Mumbai at Irla Tank by the general body of the proposed Prem Nagar Housing Society;

(b) Sigtia submitted the proposal for re-development of the slum known as Prem Nagar situated at Vile Parle (W), CTS No. 439-442; 446-448; 451-1-15, 452, 453, 454A under Slum Rehabilitation Scheme on 11.09.2002 with the consent of 1054 hutment dwellers;

(c) In all 1054 individual agreements and consent affidavits were filed by slum dwellers in favour of Sigtia before the SRA and approved by the Additional Collector (Encroachment) by its order dated 23.01.2003;

(d) When the applicant was about to get the Letter of Intent, the Writ Petition No. 988 of 2004 was filed on 31.03.2004 before the High Court of Bombay by Mr. Nazir Khan Yakub Khan and 8 others slum dwellers challenging the appointment of Sigtia as developer to undertake the re-development of the slum area on the ground that Sigtia was having neither technical expertise nor financial capability to complete the project.

(e) In the above writ petition, the Chief Promoter of the Society filed two affidavits before the High Court dated 07.06.2004 and 29.06.2004 expressing confidence and faith in the technical and financial capability of Sigtia to execute the project. The Chief Executive Officer, SRA also filed additional affidavit on 11.02.2005 supporting the scheme in totality.

(f) The High Court, while dismissing the Writ Petition No. 988 of 2004 on 11.03.2005 directed the SRA to put additional conditions as follows:

a. Obtaining security deposit of Rs. 2.5 crores from the developer to safeguard the interests of the Slum Dwellers.

b. Supervision by the Senior Engineer of Bombay Municipal Corporation at the cost of the developer.

c. No construction of sale component till all the slum dwellers are rehabilitated in the new buildings, and

d. Undertaking/ indemnity from the developer for fulfilling the above three conditions.

5. Out of 9 petitioners in Writ Petition No. 988 of 2004, one Nazir Khan Yakub Khan alone filed a Special Leave Petition No. 11318 of 2005 challenging the order of the High Court passed in Writ Petition No. 988 of 2004. Sigtia was impleaded in the special leave petition as Respondent No. 7. The Special Leave Petition was withdrawn by the petitioner on 26.09.2005. 4 other petitioners out of original 9 filed Special Leave Petition No. 19848 of 2005 challenging the order in Writ Petition No. 988 of 2004 and obtained interim stay on 19.09.2005 from this Court. Due to the above said stay order, Sigtia could not take any further steps towards the implementation of the project. The stay order continued till 13.04.2006 on which date this Court dismissed the Special Leave Petition No. 19848 of 2005 as withdrawn.

6. During the pendency of the Special Leave Petition No. 19848 of 2005, counsel of Prem Nagar Co-operative Housing Society gave notices dated 26.04.2005 and 06.06.2005 purporting to revoke the development agreement and the Power of Attorney executed in favour of Sigtia. By letter dated 15.06.2005, Sigtia gave reply questioning the authority of the persons purporting to terminate and revoke the said development agreement and Power-of-Attorney. A public notice dated 05.09.2005 was issued by the Vile Parle Society referring to the termination of the development agreement and power-of-attorney by the Society. The Management of the society also decided to appoint one M/s Keya Developers (in short "Keya") to execute the project and intimation to this effect was sent to SRA by way of an application.

7. In the above special leave petition, certain interlocutory applications were filed by some hutment dwellers praying for directions to SRA to examine and consider the proposed scheme for rehabilitation submitted by M/s Keya. These IAs were dismissed along with the special leave petition. The very same slum dwellers filed Writ Petition No. 1277 of 2006 seeking the same prayer alleging that Sigtia did not commenced re-development of the properties in terms of the agreement entered into with SRA and was never interested in re-development of the said property for the benefit of slum dwellers. Sigtia was not made a party to this writ petition. Sigtia wrote a letter to the CEO, SRA on 25.04.2006 stating that Sigtia was keenly interested in developing the Vile Parle Slum and would take immediate steps to deposit Rs. 2.5 crores by SRA in the matter and also would furnish indemnity as required by SRA. On 04.05.2006, the High Court passed an order in Writ Petition No. 1277 of 2006 directing the SRA to call the parties in terms of the judgment of the Court. On 02.06.2006, Sigtia wrote a letter to the SRA stating that Keya had obtained the order dated 04.05.2006 from the High Court in writ petition No. 1277 of 2006 and that the applicant was not made a party to the writ petition and, therefore, they were not heard at all and requested the SRA to postpone the hearing fixed on 03.06.2006 to enable Sigtia to move the High Court. However, there was no response from the SRA.

8. On 02.06.2006, Sigtia wrote a letter to SRA enclosing a cheque for a sum of Rs. 2.5 crores towards the interest free deposit with SRA as the performance related guarantee as directed by the High Court in its judgment dated 11.03.2005. The Law Officer of SRA conveyed to Sigtia that the cheque for Rs. 2.5 crores could not be accepted by SRA as there was no specific order of the High Court to accept Rs. 2.5 crores from Sigtia. The Principal Secretary, Housing Department in compliance with the order dated 11.03.2005 issued clear directions to SRA to issue Letter of Intent in favour of Sigtia. On 21.06.2006, the petitioners in the Writ Petition No. 1277 of 2006 filed special leave petition before this Court against the order dated 04.05.2005 and by way of interim relief prayed that SRA be directed to issue Letter of Intent in favour of Keya. Sigtia was again not made a party in the special leave petition. This Court, on 27.06.2006, passed an order directing SRA to issue Letter of Intent in favour of Keya within two weeks.

9. Mr. Arun Jaitley, learned senior counsel strenuously contended that before issuance of the Letter of Intent certain conditions ought to be fulfilled by a developer as per the rules and regulations of SRA and as per the guidelines and regulations of SRA, a developer needs to obtain Annexure-II and Annexure-III from SRA. Annexure II is issued when the developer shows that he has consent from atleast 70% eligible hutment dwellers and Annexure III is issued when SRA is satisfied about the financial and technical capability of the developer. It is not disputed that the applicant has obtained both the Annexures and therefore there is no reason for not issuing LOI to the applicant. It is submitted that the Keya Developer does not have consent of atleast 70% hutment dwellers and therefore is not entitled to get LOI issued in its favour for the said project. Moreover SRA having been set up by the State in exercise of its powers under the Slum Act, it is ultimately for it to decide as to who should be permitted to undertake the redevelopment of slum and the SRA has shown confidence in the applicant by filing affidavits before the Bombay High Court in Writ Petition No. 988 of 2004.

10. According to Mr. Arun Jaitley, the purported termination of the development agreement with Sigtia by the society is illegal, without authority of law as the society has no authority to do so. It is further submitted that 1054 slum dwellers filed consent affidavits in favour of the applicant in the year 2002 itself and therefore the Chief Promoter and few Committee members of the Society cannot terminate the appointment of the developer. In fact the original Writ Petitioner who filed Writ Petition No. 988/2004, namely, Nazir Khan Yakub Khan and others made serious allegations against the Chief Promoter - Shri Vichare and few Managing Committee members that they have manipulated the records and got the extra units to their family members.

He would further submit that as per section 3(k) of the Maharashtra Slum Area (Improvement, Clearance and Re-development) Act, 1971, the SRA is bound to follow the directions given by the Government of Maharashtra for the implementation of provisions under the Act and that the Government issued directions to SRA to issue letter of intent to Sigtia way back on 20.06.2005 but those directions have not been complied with. Mr. Jaitley further submitted that the main grievance of the slum dwellers in the I.As filed in this Court and in the Writ Petition No. 1277 of 2006 is that no steps have been taken by Sigtia Constructions towards the completion of the project. It is submitted that after obtaining Annexure II and Annexure III from SRA, when the applicant was about to get LOI the writ petition No. 988 of 2005 was filed on 31.3.2004 challenging the technical and financial capability of the applicant. After the said Writ Petition was dismissed, the applicant approached SRA many times to get LOI but it received no response and this fact has been recorded by the Principal Secretary, Housing in its order dated 20.06.2005. Thereafter, stay order was passed by this Court in SLP(C) No. 19848 of 2005 staying the order of the High Court dated 11.03.2005 passed in Writ Petition No. 988 of 2004. After the said SLP was dismissed by this Court on 13.04.2006 the applicant has written several letters to SRA to issue LOI and also sent a cheque of Rs. 2.51 crores but the same was not accepted by SRA. That there has been no delay on the part of the applicant in the implementation of the development work but it is due to frivolous litigations filed by some slum dwellers who were put up by rival developers that the project was stalled.

11. Mr. Arun Jaitley further submitted that the applicant was a necessary party in the Writ Petition No. 1277 of 2006 and also to the above special leave petition as it was appointed as developer by the society and is at having consent of more than 70% of the slum dwellers in the area and therefore, any order passed issuing Letter of Intent to some other developer gravely injures the applicant and therefore no such order can be passed without giving an opportunity to the applicant to be heard. Concluding his arguments, Mr. Jaitley submitted that the order has been obtained behind the back of the applicant Sigtia and that the order is contrary to the order of the High Court dated 11.03.2005 passed in writ petition No. 988 of 2004 which has become final with the dismissal of Special Leave Petition No. 11318 of 2005 and 19848 of 2005. In this context, Mr. Arun Jaitley invited our attention to the order dated 11.03.2005 passed in Writ Petition No. 988 of 2004.

12. At the time of hearing, Mr. Jaitley also invited our attention to the order passed by the High Court in Writ Petition No. 1277 of 2006 dated 04.05.2006. It is useful to reproduce the said short order which reads thus:

CORAM: F.I. REBELLO & ANOOP V. MOHTA, JJ.

DATE: 4th May, 2006.

P.C.:

In the ordinary course, we would not have entertained this petition when there is a society who is responsible for the development. However, on behalf of respondent No. 2, their learned Counsel makes a statement that they had already communicated to Respondent No. 1 to appoint respondent No. 3 as a developer and that the application is pending before the Respondent No. 1 pursuant to the termination of the first developer by Respondent No. 2. The respondent No. 1 to call the parties in terms of the judgment of this Court and after hearing the parties, dispose of the application of Respondent No. 2 according to law within the period of six weeks from today.

(F.I. Rebello, J.)

(Anoop V. Mohta, J.)

He also drew our attention to para 12 of the order in Writ Petition No. 988 of 2004 passed by the High Court which reads thus:

The SRA having been set up by the State in exercise of its power under the Slum Act, it is ultimately, for it to decide as to who should be permitted to undertake the redevelopment of slum. In this behalf, perusal of the relevant statutory provisions including Section 13 would make it abundantly clear that the SRA is empowered to permit land holders of occupants of an area which is declared as slum rehabilitation area to undertake scheme of development of such land and if they do not come forward with a scheme for redevelopment within a reasonable time, the SRA may decide to redevelop such land by entrusting it to any other Agency. In the instant case, respondent No. 7 has been selected by respondent No. 6. The SRA is satisfied that the requisite 70% numbers/ occupiers of slum area have come forward and reposed confidence in respondent No. 7. Since petitioners raised objections to the capacity and capability of respondent No. 7, this Court issued directions that these aspects be scrutinized and verified once again. Even that exercise is now complete and a report is submitted by the CEO of SRA. In such circumstances, we are of the view that all aspects have been considered by the SRA and its decision cannot be faulted. More so, when the proposal is at a primary stage.

Our attention has also been drawn to the order of this Court in Special Leave Petition No. 19848 of 2005 dated 13.04.2006 dismissing the writ petition as withdrawn filed by Mr. Nilesh Wakadey and Ors. preferred against the judgment and order dated 11.03.2005 in Writ Petition No. 988 of 2004. Likewise, Special Leave Petition No. 11318 of 2005 filed against the very same order in writ petition No. 988 of 2004 was also dismissed as withdrawn.

13. We may also usefully refer to the letter dated 02.06.2006 of Sigtia addressed to SRA, the relevant portion of which reads thus:

In this connection, we wish to submit that M/s. Sigtia Construction Pvt. Limited is bound by the directive and conditions in the High Court Judgment dt. 11.3.2005 and also by the guidelines of the SRA for the development of the Vile-Parle (W) Slum project. As such, the company will be complying with all the conditions recommended by the SRA and accepted by the Hon'ble High Court.

In pursuance of the said High Court order dt. 11.3.2005, M/s. Sigtia Construction Pvt. Ltd. is hereby depositing a sum of Rs. 2,50,00,000 (Rupees Two Crores Fifty Lakhs only) drawn on Standard Chartered Bank, Santacruz (W) Branch, Mumbai *vide* Cheque No. 991396 dt. 2.6.2006 towards the interest free deposit with SRA as the performance related guarantee as directed by the Hon'ble High Court in its landmark judgment dt. 11.3.2005. The SRA may put it in its fixed deposit account, as it may deem fit.

Besides interest free deposit of Rs. 2.5 crocres, M/s. Sigtia Construction Pvt. Ltd. will comply with and abide other conditions such as—

(a) First we will construct Rehab portion in all respect and then ask permission of sale portion.

(b) We accept the Supervision of B.M.C. Engineer who will monitor the project.

(c) We will give required undertaking/indemnity bond etc., as directed by Hon'ble High Court and as desired by SRA.

We may also refer to the proceedings of the Principal Secretary, Housing Department, Government of Maharashtra on the representation received from Sigtia and the orders passed thereunder. The relevant portion reads thus:

In view of the above, I, N. Rama Rao, Principal Secretary, Housing Department, Government of Maharashtra, in the capacity of the Administrative Head of the Department, direct that

(1) LOI be issued in favour of Sigtia Constructions Pvt. Ltd. who have a joint venture agreement with Spark Developers as stated above and who had completed all the formalities to ensure the implementation of the project without permitting any further delay.

(2) The CEO, SRA is further directed to comply with the other directions and suggestions given by the Hon'ble High Court in its order dated 11.03.2005.

(3) The Developer also, hereby directed to comply with the conditions imposed by the Hon'ble High Court in the said order.

It is to be noted that this order was not challenged before any forum.

14. Our attention was also drawn to the notice dated 26.04.2005 issued by Mr. Suresh P. Chaugule to Sigtia and the further notice dated 06.06.2005 by the very same advocate to the Chief Officer, Slum Rehabilitation Authority on termination of appointment of developer. A copy of the same was also marked to Sigtia Constructions. Our attention was also drawn to the IA No. Nil of 2006 filed by Nilesh Wakade and Ors. in Special Leave Petition (C) No. 19848 of 2005 in which Babita Baliram Tambe & Ors. as applicants made the following prayer in the above I.A.:

PRAYER

Thus, in the facts and circumstances, it is most respectfully prayed that this Hon'ble Court may be pleased to:

(a) Direct that the rehabilitation of the slum area in question is carried out at the earliest;

(b) Direct M/s. Keya Developers & Construction Pvt. Ltd. Developers & Construction (P) Ltd., Tardeo Air-conditioned Market, Tardeo, Mumbai-34 to produce its proposed Scheme for Rehabilitation;

(c) Direct the Respondent Authorities to forthwith examine and consider the said proposed Scheme for Rehabilitation submitted by M/s Keya Developers & Construction Pvt. Ltd. Developers (P) Ltd; and

(d) If the above scheme is approved by the Respondent No. 2, then the Respondent Authorities and the developer be directed to forthwith implement the Scheme in a time bound manner subject to such terms and conditions as this Hon'ble Court may deem fit and proper.

15. It was also brought to our notice about the undertaking given on the stamp paper by the Chief Promoter and Members of the Managing Committee of Vile Parle Prem Nagar Cooperative Housing Society who declared as under:

(1) That the General Body of the Vile Parle Prem Nagar Co-operative Housing Society (Proposed) in their meeting held on 8.9.2001 has confirmed the appointment of M/s. Sigtia Construction Pvt. Ltd. as our Developer and Shri Bipin Khatri as Architect of the S.R.A. project to be undertaken by our society.

(2) That in pursuance to the above appointments of the Developer and the Architect, both agencies have carried out voluminous work in connection with the formulation of S.R.A proposal and to submit the same to the office of S.R.A. For doing this they had to obtain, the necessary undertakings from over 1000 hutment dwellers on Rs. 20 stamps paper, surveying the area by appointing Surveyor, preparation of plans and other relevant documents for obtaining Annexure-II. The developer has obtained Annexure-II and submitted the required information in Annexure - I & III to the office of S.R.A. for issuance of Letter of Intent to our S.R.A. proposal in shortest possible time with active support from the society and we are satisfied with their performance in this regard.

(3) That we have not engaged any other Developers or the Architect. This question did not arise since the present Developer and the Architect have done their duties to the expectation of the Society. While carrying out the job by the Developer and the Architect they have carried out the job with due consultation with the Society and have kept us informed of the progress of the work from time-to-time.

(4) That the Society hereby confirm and undertake to continue the Developer M/s. Sigtia Construction Pvt. Ltd. and the Architect Mr. Bipin Khatri as our Developer and Architect respectively till the completion of the S.R.A. project under D.C. Regulation 33(10) undertaken by our Vile Parle Prem Nagar Co-operative Housing Society (Proposed)

For Vile-Parle Premnagar Co-operative Housing Society. (Proposed)

Sd/-

Shamrao A. Vichare

Chief Promoter

Date: 26.2.2004

16. Mr. Goolam E. Vahanvati, learned Solicitor-General appeared for the Slum Rehabilitation Authority. He placed before us the Maharashtra Slum Areas (Improvement, Clearance and Re-development) Act, 1971. He also invited our attention to the procedure for submission, processing and approval of Slum Rehabilitation Schemes which reads thus:

1. All slums and pavements whose inhabitants' names and structures appear in the electoral roll prepared with reference to 1st January, 1995 or a date prior thereto and who are actual occupants of the hutments are eligible for the slum rehabilitation scheme.
2. 70% or more of the eligible hutment-dwellers in a slum or pavement in a viable stretch at one place have to show their willingness to join slum rehabilitation scheme and come together to form a co-operative housing society of all eligible hutment-dwellers through a resolution to that effect. The following resolution should be adopted:
   (a) Resolution electing a chief Promoter.
   (b) Resolution giving the chief promoter authority to apply for reservation of name for co-operative housing society.
   (c) To collect share capital (Rs. 50 per member for slum societies) and Re. 1 as entrance fee and to open account in Mumbai District Central Co-operative/Maharashtra State Co-operative Bank Ltd (any branch)
3. The chief promoter, office bearers and the members of the proposed society should collect the documents such as 7/12 extract and the PR card of the plot on which the slum is situate. They should then get the plot surveyed/measured and prepare map of the plot showing slum structures therein with the help of surveyors attached to the office of Additional Collector (Encroachment) or the Deputy Collector (Encroachment) or the Deputy Collector (Encroachment of the zone.
4. While undertaking the survey, they should collect the information of the proposed members/slum-dwellers and fill up land occupied by the slum-dwellers, number and type of structures such as residential, industrial, commercial, amenity structures etc., and the list of eligible and ineligible occupants and consent of the slum-dwellers to join the scheme. Earlier the promoter/co-operative housing society had to first approach the different

Competent Authorities namely Additional Collector for the slums on government and private lands and the land owning authorities for the slums on different public authority lands, for obtaining certified Annexure-II, before they could put in application for slum rehabilitation scheme SRA. As a simplification measure, this procedure is now discontinued and Annexure-II format is now required to be filled by the promoter/co-operative housing society itself for submitting building proposal to SRA, so that the scrutiny of the proposal and certification of Annexure-II can start simultaneously. Annexure-II needs to be submitted in duplicate. As a measure of further simplification, Additional Collector (Encroachment) is being designated as the sole Competent Authority for deciding eligibility and for taking eviction action against non-participants in slum rehabilitation schemes."

5. The chief promoter and the office bearers of the proposed society should then apply for name reservation of the proposed co-operative housing society along with the self- prepared Annexure-II and the required resolutions to the Assistant Registrar of Co-operative Societies. To facilitate this, office of the Assistant Registrar has been started in SRA itself. It is no longer necessary to approach different offices of the Co-operation Department for this purpose. The assistant Registrar/SRA will issue a letter reserving the name for the proposed co-operative housing society and permission to open a bank account in the proposed society's name.
6. While the above steps are being taken, the decision to search a competent developer to act as a promoter has to be taken up by the proposed co-operative housing society of slum-dwellers. The society itself or an NGO/ developer/owner can take up slum rehabilitation scheme as a promoter.
7. The promoter so chosen has to enter into agreement with every eligible slum-dweller while putting up slum rehabilitation proposal to SRA for approval. SRA is in the process of trying to evolve standard formats for the following four types of agreements required in the scheme, with the approval of the State Government.
   (a) Consent-cum-agreement between the promoter and the slum-dwellers.
   (b) Development rights/Agreement to lease between the promoter and the land owning authority.
   (c) Lease agreement between the land owning authority and the co-operative society of slum-dwellers.
   (d) Lease agreement between the land owning authority and the co-operative society of free-sale tenement buyers.
8. The promoter has also to appoint an architect in consultation with the proposed co-operative housing society of slum-dwellers to prepare the plans of development of the slum area as per the DCR-33(10). It is expected that the architect ensures community participation in preparation of the building plans. All required documents such as

building plan, layout plan, PR Card etc., along with Annexure-I, Annexure-II and Annexure-III are to be submitted to SRA by the architect alongwith an application for the slum rehabilitation scheme. A checklist of all such documents required for submission is available in SRA office.

10. Annexure-III is prescribed to asses the financial capability of the promoter. The items contained in Annexure-III are self explanatory. Keeping in view the sensitivity of this information, it is kept strictly confidential by SRA.

11. After a pre-security by a designated engineer of SRA, to ensure completeness of the proposal submitted, so far as documents are concerned, proposals are accepted. Then a computerized file number is allotted to the scheme on payment of scrutiny fees which are charged at half file number is allotted to the scheme on payment of scrutiny fees which are charged bat half the rate of the Municipal Corporation's general building permission fees. Upon acceptance, the scrutiny of Annexures, I, II and III start simultaneously in the building permission Wing, Eligibility Certification Wing and Accounts & Finance Wing respectively.

17. He also invited our attention to para 18 of the order in Writ Petition No. 988 of 2004 dated 11.03.2005

In the affidavit filed on 11th February, 2005 the SRA has further pointed out that the Slum Rehabilitation Scheme proposal is at primary scrutiny stage and not yet approved. They have pointed out that eligibility of the members of Managing Committee of respondent No. 6 shall be thoroughly scrutinized by the Slum Rehabilitation Authority before issuing LOI and in any case within eight weeks from the date of this affidavit. Mr. Singh appearing for 7th respondent makes a statement that the developer will file necessary undertaking as per para No. 7 of the affidavit dated 11th February 2005 of SRA, within such time as is stipulated by it. He has also agreed to file an undertaking in terms of para 7 of this affidavit in this Court in case the Letter of intent is issued in favour of respondent No. 7. He has also agreed to furnish indemnity as insisted by SRA.

He also specifically drew our attention to the order dated 11.03.2005 in Writ Petition No. 988 of 2004 and the order dated 04.05.2006 in Writ Petition No. 1277 of 2006 and also the application for direction filed by Babita Baliram Tambey on the prayer made by him in the IA in special leave petition No. 19848 of 2005. The said Babita Baliram was also petitioner No. 10 in Writ Petition No. 1277 of 2006 which was verified in April, 2006 whereas the final order in the said writ petition was made on 04.05.2006. Concluding his arguments, the learned Solicitor General submitted that as per the guidelines there are several conditions to be fulfilled by the slum dwellers/proposed society as well as by the proposed developer and remarks required to be obtained on the proposal from concerned authorities before issuing Letter of Intent. The SRA also to verify the resolution passed by the general body of the slum dwellers, proposed society by majority for appointing or replacing the developer for the development of the scheme. It is also necessary to verify by the SRA to see whether the plot under the development is not affected by any reservation such as playground or recreation ground in view of the interim stay order in writ Petition No. 1152 of 2002 of the High Court. The SRA has to verify whether the proposed appointed developer has the financial capacity to undertake and complete the same. Therefore, in the context of the submissions made above by the learned Solicitor-General further directions with regard to this Court's order dated 27.06.2006 should be given to SRA. As already noticed, the writ petition No. 1277 of 2006 was filed by the very same petitioner in SLP No. 10281 of 2006 Sigtia was not made a party to the writ petition No. 1277 of 2006. However, the High Court, by order dated 04.05.2006 in writ petition No. 1277 of 2006 has directed the SRA to call the parties in terms of the judgment of the High Court dated 11.03.2005 in writ petition No. 988 of 2004 and after hearing the parties disposed of the application of the society respondent No. 2 according to law within 6 weeks from 04.03.2006. It is also useful to refer to the direction given in the order dated 11.03.2005 in para 20 in writ petition No. 988 of 2004. The High Court, by the said order, has observed that it is not necessary to quash or set aside the Scheme or issue further directions as sought and that final approval have not been granted by SRA and if SRA decides not to issue the Letter of Intent in favour of respondent No. 7 (Sigtia), it will always be open for the parties to submit a fresh development scheme. In view of the order dated 11.03.2005 and 04.05.2006 of the High Court, the learned Solicitor-General submitted that the SRA has to call both Sigtia and Keya in order to dispose of the application of the society according to law.

18. Mr. Harish Salve appearing for the petitioner in special leave petition Shri Ramchandra Mahadev Jagpat submitted that SRA cannot decide any contractual dispute and that the order dated 11.03.2005 put certain obligations on Sigtia and that the Society in its general body meeting dated 29.05.2005 terminated the agreement with Sigtia and decided to invite other builders. In this context, he drew our attention to the unanimous resolution passed by the Society in regard to the appellant of Keya for the development of slum property at Premnagar dated 10.06.2005. This letter dated 10.06.2005 was addressed to Keya Developer and Construction Company, Mumbai. The letter reads as follows:

We are informing hereof that the Managing Committee had decided in the meeting held on 6th June, 2005 Monday at 8.00 p.m. *vide* Resolution No. 6 to develop the property bearing C.S. Nos. 439,439-1 & 2,440-1 to 6,441, 441-1 to 3,442,442-1 to 3,443,443-1 to 15,444,444-1 to 6,446,447,447-1 to 3,448,448-1 to 5,451-1 to 3,452-1 to 24,453, 453-1 to 5,454(A), Irla, Vile-parle (West) in the District of Mumbai, the area is 28200 sq. mtrs. And the owner is the Mumbai Municipal Corporation. This land be declared Slum as per Slum Act, 1971 sub-section 4(1). You are appointed to re-develop the said property as per Maharashtra Government Rules and Regulations. In the subject-matter we are enclosing herewith the true certified copy to you. You are requested to intimate your consent in this regards and co-operation.

True Extract of Resolution No. 6 of General Body meeting held on 8th June, 2005 at 8.00 p.m. Committee Office RESOLUTION NO. 6.

Resolved that M/s Keya Developer and Construction Pvt. Ltd. Having its office at 302, Tardeo Air Condition Market, Tardeo Road, Mumbai-400024 is and be appointed as Developer to develop the slum property by providing permanent alternate accommodation of 225 sq.ft. Carpet Area to all eligible Slum dwellers and to sell balance from sale component in open market as per O.C.R. 33(10) of 1991. Also power care given to said developer to enable him to exercise the powers for the development of the said property. This appointment will remaining in force and valid till entire Project is successfully completed in all respect as tenant are handed over to all slum dwellers. No any Managing Committee, existing or forth coming, shall have any right to change the developer under any circumstances whatsoever may be the nature.

Proposed By: Mrs.Sandhaya Ketemkar

Seconded By: Mr. Sanjay Kadam

RESOLUTION UNANIMOUSLY PASSED

Sd/-

(Mr. Shamrao Vicharee)

Chief Promoter

He also drew our attention to the subsequent events in the appointment of Keya Developers and the letter dated 10.06.2005 issued to Keya Developers made in the I.A. in 19848 of 2005 filed by Babita Baliram. He also invited our attention to the second round of litigation on the non-deposit of the amount by Sigtia. He also submitted that Sigtia have acted on termination and have not challenged the termination of the agreement.

19. Mr. Salve also submitted that there is no question of fraud having played upon by this Court as alleged or told and that the applicant Sigita has conveniently not mentioned that his agreement with the society had come to an end by efflux of time and stood cancelled on 24.04.2005 and that the society had also unanimously terminated the appointment of Sigtia as the developer and that the prayer in writ petition No. 1277 of 2006 was directed against the SRA and that there was no prayer or relief sought against the Sigtia and, therefore, Sigtia was not arrayed as a party in the said writ petition and that there was also no reason to make Sigtia as a party as they had been replaced by a new developer as far back as June, 2005 of which the Sigtia had notice. Mr. Salve further submitted that it is incorrect to say that the parties before this Court in special leave petition (C) No. 10281 of 2006 were not the affected parties. In fact all the parties are affected parties excepting the Sigtia who has undertaken no development work from 1997 and even after agreement dated 2002 was entered into with the society and therefore, Sigtia has no subsisting legal or other rights whatsoever and the present I.A. to recall the order deserves to be dismissed.

I.A.No. 9 of 2006

20. Mr. Dushyant Dave, learned senior counsel filed an application for impleadment in I.A. No. 9 of 2006 on behalf of Nazeer Khan Yakub Khan who is also slum dweller. Learned senior counsel submitted even that in 1997 Sigtia was appointed by the Society as a developer for the slum and the appointment was approved by SRA. However, no efforts were taken by Sigtia for development. As per the agreement Sigtia the agreement has to complete the entire development work within 3 years and if the development work was not so completed the agreement was to be treated as cancelled automatically. It is further argued that Sigtia had taken no efforts for development of the slum and in fact had no financial or technical capability to carry out the development. Sigtia had also not deposited the 2.5 crores as interest free deposit and, therefore, the applicant in I.A. No. 9 of 2006 filed special leave petition No. 11318 of 2005 before this Court challenging the order dated 11.03.2005 and in the meantime, the agreement of Sigtia with the society to develop the slum itself came to an end on the expiry of 3 years from the date of agreement and, thereafter, the Society at a general body meeting dated 29.05.2005 resolved to terminate the appointment of Sigtia as the developer and the SRA was also informed of such decision since the appointment of Sigtia stood terminated and a new developer had been appointed the applicant Nazeer Khan Yakub Khan had no further grievance as it was apparent that the development work of the slum would finally commence and in these circumstances the applicant withdraw special leave petition (C) No. 11318 of 2005 on 26.09.2005.

Mr. Dave further submitted that the applicant in IA No. 9 of 2006 had always opposed the appointment of Sigtia as developers as they had no technical capability to carry out the development work and in fact undertook no work whatsoever for over 8 years to the department of the slum dwellers and other similar situate slum dwellers. It is further submitted the order in special leave petition No. 10281 of 2006 is fair and just and in the interest of the slum dwellers who will finally be able to see the development work of their slum being undertaken and that the Sigtia have no legal right for undertaking the development of the slum in view of the termination and automatic cancellation of their agreement with the Society.

I.A. No. 8 of 2006

21. The applicant is a Zuveriya Developer. Their application for intervention is allowed and Mr. Shekhar Naphade, advocate was heard on his behalf. I.A. No. 8 of 2006 was filed to recall the order dated 27.06.2006 in special leave petition No. 10281 of 2006 and allow the applicant to file a reply to the above special leave petition. We have perused the intervention application. The applicant was not a party to the earlier writ petition. The applicant put up a proposal to the Municipal Corporation of Greater Bombay being the competent authority under the act expressing its willingness to re-accommodate the hutment dwellers and offered to give certain portion of plot of land to Municipal Corporation free from encumbrances as per the Slum Rehabilitation Scheme. The Managing Committee of the original society have executed an agreement dated 16.07.1997 that the applicant and gave development rights in favour of the applicant for the development of the property. They have also issued general Power of Attorney in favour of the applicant. The Addl. Collector (Encroachment) has fixed the hearing for the purpose of issuance of Annexure- 2 when one M/ s Sigtia Construction Pvt. Ltd. intervened in the matter by representing that another society by name Ville Parle Premnagar Cooperative Society (proposed) had appointed the said Sigtia as developer. The applicant was not a party to the writ petition No. 988 of 2004 filed by some of the hutment dwellers not to issue annexure-3 and Letter of Intent in favour of Sigtia. The applicant or the original society was not a party to the said writ petition upon knowledge the applicant has taken out chamber summons in the petition to intervene in the matter. The High Court dismissed the writ petition and also the chamber summons as it was too late for the applicant to apply to joint as party to the said writ petition. The applicant again made a representation to the SRA. The applicants are agreeable to obtain similar agreement from slum dwellers in support of the said proposal with a view to develop the property.

22. Writ petition No. 1277 of 2006 was also filed by the petitioners without impleading the applicant before the High Court. It is submitted without making the applicant a party the petitioner has obtained an order dated 27.06.2006 whereby this Court has directed the SRA to issue a Letter of Intent in favour of Keya Developers. Hence the applicant is making the present intervention application for recalling the said order dated 27.06.2006. In our opinion, the above I.A. has no merits and is belated. No relief can, therefore, be granted to the applicant. I.A. No. 8 of 2006 stands dismissed.

23. Dr. Abhishek Singhvi, learned senior counsel appearing for Keya Developers submitted that Sigtia did not take any recourse to any legal proceedings to challenge the termination and by letter dated 10.06.2005 Keya was informed of the resolution appointing it as developer to develop the property on the terms and conditions mentioned therein. In view of the termination of Sigtia as developer two groups of slum dwellers who had filed special leave petition before this Court against the order of the High Court dated 11.03.2005 withdrew the special leave petition on 26.09.2005 and 13.04.2005 respectively. Sigtia was represented in the proceedings and did not represent the factum of expiry/termination of the agreement between Sigtia and the society. Keyes since the intimation of the resolution of the society has been taking all steps within its power to prepare for the development of the property including the appointment of M/s Anil Chawla and Associates as architects and made arrangements for a transit camp for residence of the members of the society during the period of re-development. The Keya's has also made arrangements with HDFC Bank Ltd. for provision of loan of over Rs. 12 crores towards the implementation of the project and is also ready and willing to deposit such amount as this Court may determine by way of security deposit. Keyas has also approached the SRA for grant of Letter of Intent in its favour for the purpose of transit accommodation and has also already incurred an expenditure of Rs. 45,56,720 Keyas has also not been served with any notice or order of any Court with respect to any challenge to the termination of the Sigtia or appointment of the Keyas as developer of the property. In these circumstances, Dr. Singhvi submitted that the SRA was bound to consider the application for issue of Letter of Intent to Keyas and Keyas has also been approached from time to time by the society and its members for taking further steps to commence the actual work of re-development of the property. However, Keyas was unable to commence the actual work of re-development for want of Letter of Intent from the authority in the present special leave petition No. 10281 of 2006. This Court passed the order in the presence of the counsel for all the parties and deny that any fraud has been played upon this Court as alleged. It is further submitted Sigtia has been terminated as developer of the property long before the writ petition was filed in the High Court. According to learned senior counsel Sigtia is not a necessary party to the special leave petition and that it had the consent of more than 70% of the slum dwellers and that the same is in any event irrelevant after the termination of the contract with the society. Concluding his submission, learned senior counsel submitted that the applicant has failed to make out any good ground for the recall of the order dated 27.06.2006 and, therefore, the said application is liable to be dismissed.

Mr. T.L. Nageswara Rao, learned senior counsel appearing for Vile Parle Premnagar Society submitted that in view of the termination of the agreement given to Sigtia, Sigtia is not a necessary party to the special leave petition 10281 and that the SRA should be directed to consider only the application made by Keyes.

24. We have given our anxious and careful consideration to the lengthy submissions made by all the learned senior counsel appearing for the respective parties with reference to the pleadings, annexures etc. The applicant Sigtia have explained to this Court as to how the deposit of Rs. 2.5 crores was not be deposited with SRA. It also denied that the agreement entered into between Sigtia and the society came to an end on 25.04.2005 by efflux of time. In this context, Clause 22 of the agreement must be read as a whole and when so read, it would be clear that the developer was to start the actual construction after the issuance of the commencement certificate by the authority. Therefore, the period of 3 years must be construed to begin from the date when commencement certificate is issued and not from the date of execution of the agreement. It was also submitted that the letters dated 25.04.2005 and 06.06.2005 were issued by 2 or 3 members of the society who were acting with ulterior motive and in collusion with the rival developer. Even the SRA to whom the letter dated 06.06.2005 was addressed in its counter-affidavit filed before this Court in the present proceedings has stated that they did not take notice of the said letter of termination as the letter was not supported by the relevant resolution of the society. After 11.03.2005, Sigtia approached the SRA on several occasions requesting for the issuance of the Letter of Intent but since no response was coming from the Housing Department of Government of Maharashtra on 10.06.1995. In our view after the dismissal of the special leave petition No. 19848 of 2005, the order of the High Court dated 11.03.2005 attained finality and there was no proposal of M/s Keya Developers before the SRA on 13.04.2006 and, therefore, there was no question of SRA considering the proposal made by the new developer. In our view, Sigtia was a necessary party to the writ petition and to the special leave petition No. 10281 of 2006 as it directly affected by any order appointing Keya as developer. The society has also entered into an agreement and also executed an irrevocable general Power-of-Attorney dated 19.03.2004 wherein expressed its satisfaction with the progress in the work made by the

Sigtia and also by the undertaking dated 26.02.2004 where the society undertook to continue with Sigtia as developer till the completion of the SRA project.

Though it is contended by Sigtia that the termination by the society on 29.04.2005 was illegal and without authority, the Sigtia has not so far challenged the order of termination by the society. This important factor has also to be taken note off by the SRA at the time of considering the case of Sigtia along with Keya Developers. It is also stated that the consent affidavits of more than 70% of the slum dwellers had already been obtained by Sigtia. It is also submitted in the rejoinder affidavit that Sigtia did have the technical expertise and financial capability to complete the work and that all these issues were decided in favour of Sigita by the High Court in writ petition No. 988 of 2004 by order dated 11.03.2005 which order has attained finality in view of the dismissal of special leave petition Nos. 11318 of 2005 and 19848 of 2005. Sigtia, after receiving the copy of the letters dated 24.05.2006 and 06.06.2005 sent a reply dated 15.06.2005 wherein the Sigtia submitted that the purported termination is illegal and without any authority and no further reply was sent by the society to the said letter. Moreover, in the hearing held before the Principal Secretary dated 20.06.2005, the representative of the society made no arguments with regard to the purported termination of the agreement. Therefore, it is contended that the society has not acted on the letter of termination and that the matter has come to an end and, therefore, Sigtia did not file any petition to challenge the purported termination. It is also argued that the prayer in the writ petition No. 1277 of 2006 adversely affects the interests of the Sigtia. It is stated that with the dismissal of special leave petition No. 19848 of 2005 all the applications filed in the said petition also stood dismissed and, therefore, the petitioners in the special leave petition had no right to approach this Court by way of writ petition making the same prayer which was made in the application for directions filed in special leave petition No. 19848 of 2005 and that the effect of the order dated 13.04.2006 is that the order of the High Court dated 11.03.2005 which was not challenged in the special leave petition attained finality and that in the application for directions filed in the special leave petition No. 19848 of 2005 the society had raised the issue of termination of agreement of Sigtia and appointment of Keya developers and the same stood dismissed with the dismissal of the said special leave petition. Therefore, as rightly pointed out by Mr. Arun Jaitley in any subsequent proceedings where the termination of the agreement of applicant Sigtia with the society and replacement of Sigtia a new developer is a subject-matter, Sigtia is a proper and necessary party to it. We see much force and substance in the said argument. In our view, the applicant Sigtia has also the right to have a hearing before the SRA along with Keya Developers, the new appointee. It must also be seen that the relief sought in the special leave petition No. 10281 of 2006 though only against SRA but in effect against the applicant Sigtia and, therefore, Sigtia is the necessary party to any proceedings wherein the replacement of the Sigtia with a new developer and the termination of the agreement with the Sigtia is in issue and, therefore, Sigtia should have been made a party respondent in the writ petition No. 1277 of 2004 as well as special leave petition No. 10281 of 2006. It is also not in dispute that Sigtia was impleaded as party respondent No. 7 in the special leave petition which came to be withdrawn by the petitioner therein on 26.09.2005 on which date Sigtia appeared through their advocate in this Court. As rightly submitted by the learned Solicitor General after the withdrawal of special leave petition No. 11318 of 2005 by the petitioner Nazeer Khan Yakub Khan both the developers i.e. M/s Sigtia and Keya Developers kept on submitting applications with the SRA. However, due to pendency of the special leave petition in this Court, SRA was not able to take any decision on the representations of the developers as well as the society. At the time of hearing, our attention was also drawn to the guidelines and the several conditions to be fulfilled by the slum dwellers/the society/ as well as the developers and the remarks required to be obtained on the proposal from the concerned authorities before issuing Letter of Intent. The SRA has also to verify the resolution as passed by the general body of the slum dwellers proposed society by majority for appointing or replacing the developers for the development of the scheme. It is also necessary for SRA to verify and to see whether the plot under the development is not affected by any reservation such as playground or recreation ground in view of the stay granted by the High Court in writ petition No. 1152 of 2002 and also to verify whether the proposed appointed developer has the financial capacity to undertake and complete the scheme. Therefore, for the foregoing reasons, we hold that Sigtia is a necessary and proper party to the special leave petition No. 10281 of 2006 filed by Ramchandra Mahadev Jagpat & Ors. We say that the order dated 27.06.2006 was passed in S.L.P. No. 10281/2006 on the basis of representation made by all the respective senior counsel appearing at that time. The order was not obtained as playing fraud on Court as alleged by the applicant herein. Now, it is brought to our notice and made out a clear case as to why Sigtia was a necessary party to the special leave petition No. 10281 of 2006 and in the light of the directions given by the High Court dated 11.03.2005 in writ petition No. 988 of 2004 and of the order dated 04.05.2006 in writ petition No. 77 of 2006. We have, therefore, no hesitation to recall our order dated 27.06.2006 in special leave petition No. 10281 of 2006. Since the entire matter was argued at length now by all the respective senior counsel, there is no necessity to rehear special leave petition No. 10281 of 2006. This apart in the concluding portion of our order dated 27.06.2006 in special leave petition No. 10281 of 2006, this Court directed the SRA to issue proper orders within two weeks from 27.06.2006. The said direction is also not correct. This Court ought to have directed the SRA, if at all, to consider issuing of the Letter of Intent in favour of Keya Developers in view of the replacement of previous Developers M/s Sigtia.

25. We, therefore, allow the application I.A. No. 3 of 2006 filed by the applicant Sigtia and recall our order dated 27.06.2006 passed in special leave petition No. 10281 of 2006 and pass the following order:

As directed by the order in writ petition No. 988 of 2004 dated 11.03.2005 and order dated 04.05.2006 in writ petition No. 1277 of 2006 the SRA is directed to call the two developers, namely, M/s Keya and M/s Sigtia and dispose of their application for issuing the Letter of Intent and to pass appropriate orders and in accordance with the Maharashtra Slum Areas Improvement, Clearance and Re-development Act, 1971 and also strictly following the procedure for submission processing and approval of Slum Rehabilitation Scheme and to Award the Letter of Intent to the developer who satisfies the required qualifications and conditions and regulations and the provision of the Act, 1971.

The SRA is also directed to consider as to whether the guidelines and other conditions are fulfilled by the slum dwellers/the society/as well by the developers and issue notice to the society also and hear them and pass appropriate speaking order within 3 months from today. The above direction is issued in the larger interest of the slum dwellers and in order to rehabilitate the poor slum dwellers and needy slum dwellers at the earliest. We place on record the very valuable assistance and guidance of all the learned senior counsel rendered to this Court and, in particular, the learned Solicitor General inviting our attention to the proper procedure, guidelines and conditions to be followed by SRA while granting the Letter of Intent to the Developer. All the IAs are disposed off as above. No costs.

T.N. Rajasekhar v. *Kasiviswanathan*

2005 (5) SCJ 640: JT 2005 (6) SC 536
Appeal (civil) 4561-4564 of 2005
(Arising out of S.L.P.(C) Nos. 14332-14335 of 2003)
Decided on 28/07/2005

Coram: **Hon'ble Mr. Justice Ruma Pal**
Hon'ble Dr. Justice AR. Lakshmanan
Judgment by: **Hon'ble Dr. Justice AR. Lakshmanan**

FACTS: This case relates to a partition suit. On the application of the respondents for seeking specific direction for allotment of properties, the single Judge ordered *inter alia* that the plaintiff's 1/5th share was allotted to him and that the owelty amount of Rs. 90,24,086 being the excess value allotted to the petitioner has to be paid by the plaintiff to the defendants as owelty. Aggrieved by this judgment and order the respondents filed OSA. The appellant filed Cross Objections for the Commissioner's Report and also reply affidavit to the OSA. The Division Bench of the Madras High Court allowed the appeals filed by the respondent partly by setting aside the direction issued by the learned single Judge to adjust the owelty amount from out of the land acquisition

compensation proceedings. The Bench directed that the parties can get the compensation amount independently according to their shares as and when the amounts are deposited by the State Government. In other respects, the decree of the learned single Judge was confirmed and the cross-objections were dismissed.

Against the above judgment the appellant preferred the Special Leave Petition before the Supreme Court.

ISSUE: Veracity of the decision of the Division Bench.

HELD: The judgment of the Division Bench of the Madras High Court was confirmed with certain directions.

JUDGMENT

Dr. AR. Lakshmanan, J.

Leave granted.

The above appeals were preferred by the appellant/plaintiff against the final judgment dated 11.03.2003 passed by the High Court of Judicature at Madras in O.S.A. Nos. 23 and 24 of 2003 and Cross Objection Nos. 4 and 5 of 2003. Respondent Nos. 1-3 T.N. Kasiviswanathan, T.N. Natarajan and T.N. Shanmughavel and the appellant T.N. Rajasekar are brothers. The fourth respondent Kalyani Gopalan is the sister of the appellant. The appellant's brother T.N. Ganapathi was sick and died on 06.05.1997 leaving the appellant and the respondents herein as his legal representatives of Class-II heir as per the Hindu Succession Act.

The suit property is the absolute property of T.N. Ganapthi. He died unmarried and issueless. The appellant and the respondents have succeeded to his estate.

During the pendency of the appeal, the appellant T.N. Rajasekar and the first respondent T.N. Kasiviswanathan died. Their legal representatives were brought on record in I.A.No. 1 of 2005 and I.A.Nos. 5-8 of 2004 respectively.

The appellant filed C.S. No. 110 of 1999 on the original side of the High Court for a preliminary decree for partition claiming 1/5th share for himself and for other incidental and ancillary reliefs. The respondents have not filed any written statement. The learned single Judge passed the preliminary decree on 11.09.2000. The single Judge directed the respondents herein to remit a sum of Rs. 37,68,000 into the Court and render accounts. Aggrieved by this order, the respondents herein preferred O.S.A. No. 78 of 2001. The Division Bench of the High Court directed the respondents to deposit only 1/5th share of Rs. 37,68,000 *i.e.,* Rs. 7,53,000 which is the due share of the appellant and that there was no question of rendering accounts from the date of Power-of-Attorney given by late T.N. Ganapathi. The Division Bench by judgment dated 04.04.2001 directed that the properties of late T.N. Ganapthi which existed on the date of his death alone should be divided.

The appellant herein filed application No. 204 of 2001 for passing a final decree and for appointment of an Advocate Commissioner. On 05.08.2002, the learned single Judge passed the final decree assessing the value of the properties of Rs. 2,98,79,569 out of which the appellant's 1/5th share was Rs. 59,75,914. Towards the share of the appellant, he was allotted item No. 6 of the schedule mentioned property *i.e.,* House bearing Door No. 16, Dr. Vasudevan Street, Kilpauk, Chennai 10 and the value of the house was assessed at Rs. 1,50,00,000. Thus it is evident that the appellant was allotted the house in excess of his share of Rs. 59,75,914, the difference of which *i.e.,* value of the house allotted deducting value of his share has to go to the other four legal representatives *i.e.,* Rs. 90,24,086. The learned single Judge also ordered that this amount of owelty to be adjusted from the land acquisition compensation amount due to the appellant/plaintiff herein.

As there was no specific direction in the judgment of the learned single Judge regarding the allotment of properties to the respondents, the respondents filed application No. 4307 of 2002 for specific order on other items of the properties to them. On the application of the respondents for seeking specific direction for allotment of properties, the learned single Judge ordered in the following terms on 22.11.2002.

(i) Item No. 6 was allotted to the plaintiff towards his 1/5th share;

(ii) The owelty amount of Rs. 90,24,086 being the excess value of Item No. 6 allotted to the petitioner has to be paid by the plaintiff to the defendants as owelty;

(iii) Item Nos. 1 to 5, 7 as well as owelty amount in relation to Item No. 6 allotted to the respondents representing their 4/5th share of the schedule mentioned property;

(iv) The defendants should pay 4/5th share of Rs. 28,681 to the plaintiff. This has already paid to the Advocate Commissioner by the plaintiff.

Aggrieved by this judgment and order both in the application Nos. 204 of 2001 and 4307 of 2002, the respondents filed OSA 23 of 2003 and 24 of 2003 respectively. The appellant filed Cross Objections for the Commissioner's Report and also reply affidavit to OSA Nos. 23 and 24. These appeals have been disposed of by the Division Bench of the High Court on 11.3.2003 allowing the appeals filed by the respondent partly by setting aside the direction issued by the learned single Judge to adjust the owelty amount from out of the land acquisition compensation proceedings. The Bench directed that the parties can get the compensation amount independently according to their shares as and when the amounts are deposited by the State Government. In other respects, the decree of the learned single Judge was confirmed and the cross-objections were dismissed. It is now seen from the rejoinder affidavit that all the sharers have withdrawn their respective land acquisition compensation amounts.

Against the above judgment, the appellant preferred the Special Leave Petition Nos. 14332-14335 of 2003.

We heard Mr. S.D.N. Vimalanathan, learned counsel for the appellant and Mr. A.T.M. Sampath, learned counsel for the respondents. Mr. S.D.N. Vimalanathan made the following submissions:—

(a) The order of the learned trial Judge and of the Division Bench is not correct in stating the rough value given by the appellant/plaintiff in the plaint as Rs. 1,50,00,000 for the purposes of valuation in the plaint as the valuation given in the plaint is tentative and not based on the market value of the site and building on the date of filing of the plaint;

(b) All the immovable properties are valued by the approved engineer who was the retired Chief Engineer for which no objections were raised by either parties;

(c) There cannot be any estoppel against the statute as the non-judicial stamp papers to be supplied cannot be on the value stated in the plaint.

Concluding his arguments, the learned counsel submitted that this Court should accept the value of Item No. 6 as stated by the Commissioner and the owelty amount be arrived at and as the appellant has deposited over and above their value to the tune of Rs. 60 lacs, suitable directions may be passed for adjustment. The learned counsel also submitted that the learned Judges of the Division Bench have not answered many of the contentions raised before them and, therefore, such an omission by the learned Judges of the Division Bench amounts violation of the principles laid down under Order XXVI, rule 13 of C.P.C. and Order XXXXI, rule 31 and rule 33 and the original side rules of the High Court and since there is an apparent omission to answer the questions raised in the OSAs and the cross objections except Item No. 6 and the said infirmities is not legally sustainable, the matter may be remitted for a fresh consideration before the Division Bench except Item No. 6 of the plaint schedule.

Per contra, Mr. A.T.M. Sampath, learned counsel for the contesting respondent submitted that the appellant himself valued Item No.6 at Rs. 1,50,00,000 both in the plaint as well as in the final decree application and that the Court appointed Commissioner recorded the same in his report with reference to Item No. 6 of the suit item. He would also further submit that since the learned Judges of the Division Bench have elaborately dealt with all the submissions made by both the parties there is no need or necessity to remit the matter for fresh consideration insofar as other items of the plaint schedule properties are concerned.

We have perused the entire pleadings and all the annexures filed along with the appeals. We have also carefully perused the judgment under appeal. We are of the opinion that there is no infirmity in the judgment passed by the learned Judges of the Division Bench. The learned Judges in paragraphs 16 and 17 have elaborately considered the valuation arrived at by the advocate Commissioner and the valuation of Item No. 6 suggested by the appellant and the respondent and the decisions arrived at by the learned single Judge and ultimately held that there is no infirmity in the determination and value of Item No. 6 as made by the learned single Judge.

As already noticed, the learned single Judge passed the final decree assessing the value of the properties at Rs. 2,98,79,569 out of which the appellant's 1/5th share was Rs. 59,75,914 and towards the share of the appellant he was allotted Item No. 6 the house property situated at Kilpauk,

Chennai, the value of which was assessed at Rs. 1,50,00,000. The appellant's 1/5th share comes to Rs. 59,75,914. The appellant, pursuant to the directions of this Court, have deposited Rs. 60,00,000 in this Court which is now deposited in short term fixed deposit with the UCO Bank, Supreme Court Compound, New, Delhi. Deducting the value of the house allotted to the share of the appellant, the balance sum of Rs. 90,24,086 has to come to the other four legal representatives. Deducting the sum of Rs. 60,00,000 which was deposited by the appellant earlier, the appellant is now directed to pay the balance of Rs. 30,24,086 with interest to the respondents as owelty amount as has been directed in the lower Court's order. The appellant wants three weeks time to deposit the same in this Court. We, therefore, grant three weeks' time from today to deposit the balance of Rs. 30,24,086 in the UCO Bank towards the credit of the present proceedings in this Court. The respondents are at liberty to withdraw the entire sum deposited with accrued interest from the UCO Bank, Supreme Court Compound, New Delhi on production of the copy of this judgment. On deposit of the balance amount of Rs. 30,24,086, the respondents shall hand over the peaceful vacant possession of the suit Item No. 6 *i.e.,* House bearing No. 16, Dr. Vasudevan Street, Kilpauk, Chennai 600 010 to the appellant herein/plaintiff within one week thereafter. The above directions shall be complied with punctually by both parties.

In the result, the judgment of the Division Bench of the Madras High Court is confirmed subject to the directions mentioned in paragraphs *supra.* The appeals stand disposed of accordingly. There would be no order as to costs.

Intellectuals Forum, Tirupathi

v.

State of A.P.

AIR 2006 SC 1350: (2006) 3 SCC 549
Appeal (civil) 1251 of 2006
(Arising out of S.L.P. (Civil) Nos. 7196-7197 oF 2001)
Decided on 23-02-2006

Coram: **Hon'ble Mr. Justice Ruma Pal**
Hon'ble Dr. Justice AR. Lakshmanan

Judgment by: **Hon'ble Dr. Justice AR. Lakshmanan**

FACTS: This case relates to the preservation of and restoration of *status quo* ante of two tanks, historical in nature being in existence since the time of Srikrishnadevaraya, 1500 A.D. The grievance of the appellants was the systematic destruction of percolation, irrigation and drinking water tanks in Tirupathi Town, namely, Avilala and Peruru Tank and alienation of the Avilala Tank bed land to Tirupathi Urban Development Authority and A.P. Housing Board and the Peruru Tank bed land to Tirumala Tirupathi Devasthanam for housing purposes by the State Government.

ISSUE: Protection and preservation of historical tanks.

HELD: Merely asserting an intention for development will not be enough to sanction the destruction of local ecological resources. The Court passed certain directions for the revival of Peruru and Avivala Tank in Tirupathi and prohibits further housing constructions.

JUDGMENT

Dr. AR. Lakshmanan, J.

Leave granted.

The present matter raises two kinds of questions. Firstly, at a jurisprudential level, it falls on this court to lay down the law regarding the use of public lands or natural resources, which have a direct link to the environment of a particular area, by the Government. Secondly, this court should decide, on the facts of the present case, the order to be passed with respect to two tanks in the Tirupathi area Peruru, and Avilala.

The above two appeals were filed by a registered society called, the Intellectuals Forum, against the respondents herein. The contesting parties are the State of Andhra Pradesh represented by its Chief Secretary, Tirupathi Urban Development Authority represented by its Vice-Chairman and the A.P. Housing Board represented by its Vice-Chairman and Housing Commissioner.

The present case relates to the preservation of and restoration of *status quo* ante of two tanks, historical in nature being in existence since the time of Srikrishnadevaraya, 1500 A.D.

The tanks are called 'Avilala Tank' and 'Peruru Tank' which are situated in suburbs of Tirupathi Town which is a world renowned popular pilgrim centre having every day in-flow of tourists between one lakh to two lakhs.

GRIEVANCE:

Systematic destruction of percolation, irrigation and drinking water tanks in Tirupathi Town, namely, Avilala and Peruru Tank and alienation of the Avilala Tank bed land to Tirupathi Urban Development Authority (In short, TUDA) and A.P. Housing Board under G.O. Ms. No. 84 Rev. dated 28.1.1994 and Peruru

Tank bed land to Tirumala Tirupathi Devasthanam (In short, TTD) for housing purposes under G.O. Ms. No. 181 Rev. dated 15.3.1991, which are impugned in Writ Petition Nos. 8650 of 1994 and 7955 of 1994 respectively.

According to the appellant, the cry of socially spirited citizens calling for judicial remedy was not considered in the right perspective by the Division Bench of the High Court of Andhra Pradesh despite there being over-whelming evidence of the tanks being in existence and were being put to use not only for irrigation purpose but also as lakes which were furthering percolation to improve the ground water table, thus serving the needs of the people in and around these tanks. It was submitted that the High Court has given precedence to the economic growth by completely ignoring the importance and primacy attached to the protection of environment and protection of valuable and most cherished fresh water resources. The Government without considering the well planned development of Tirupathi town alienated the Tank bed lands in favour of some governmental agencies for valuable consideration. It was further submitted that since Tirupathi is in the draught prone region called Rayala Seema, there is always shortage of water and the District machinery is constantly put on alert for devising schemes for the purpose of improving the existing water resources. An Engineering Team which is assigned such a task had visited in and around the foot-hills of Tirupathi and Tirumala for the purpose of identifying sources of fresh water and suggestions to be given for their improvement. Apart from suggestions, the team of Engineers, in the minutes of the meeting held on 26.5.1990, suggested that improvement of feeder channels (Vagus) for Peruru tank and Avilala tank would improve the percolation of all the surrounding areas and that there is enough potential for the tanks to get enough water if the feeder channels are improved. It was also submitted by representation that the Commissioner of Land Revenue to retain Peruru tank and Avilala tank, since retention of water in the said tanks would improve the water table which is already very low in the surrounding wells and also to the east of the tanks before of gradients. In the meantime, the Government passed G.O.Ms. No. 181 Revenue dated 15.3.1991 alienating an extent of 150 acres of land which belongs to the tank bed area of Peruru tank to Tirumala Tirupathi Devasthanam (In short, TTD). The members of the appellant's forum as also the various other socially spirited citizens have written letters to various authorities of the Government requesting the said authorities including the Chief Minister not to alienate the tank bed areas of both the tanks for housing or for any other activity except for the purpose for which it is meant. However, the Government issued G.O. Ms. No. 84 Revenue dated 28.1.1994 authorizing the District Collector, Chittoor to alienate 90 acres of land belonging to Avilala tank bed area to A.P. Housing Board. This Government order further directed that the TUDA should provide a Master plan for the entire area of 170 acres so as to ensure integrated development of Avilala tank area.

Since, there was no response to the representations made, the appellant filed two writ petitions in the High Court challenging the Government Orders passed by the Government of Andhra Pradesh by which the District Collector, Chittoor was directed to hand over the tank bed areas of Avilala tank and Peruru tank to TTD and to A.P. Housing Board.

Writ Petition No. 7955 of 1994 was filed assailing G.O. Ms. No. 181 dated 15.3.1991, in respect of alienation of Peruru tank bed land to TTD and Writ Petition No. 8650 of 1994 was filed assailing G.O. Ms. No. 84 dated 28.1.1994 alienating Avilala tank bed area land to A.P. Housing Board. The respondents filed their counter-affidavits opposing the writ petitions. The Indian Medical Association also made a similar plea that the Government should immediately withdraw its G.Os. alienating Avilala tank and Peruru tank and restore them urgently as percolation tanks, to improve the ground water table. This prayer was made by the Indian Medical Association due to alarming increase of the toxic contents like Fluorides and other salts in the underground water due to steep fall in the underground water table level. A feasibility report on Peruru tank was prepared by Sri Venkateswara University College of Engineering, Department of Civil Engineering, Tirupathi. Several other individuals filed affidavits supporting the cause of the appellant.

A counter affidavit was filed by the Government, Revenue Department, in Writ Petition No. 8650 of 1994 whereby the said respondent justified the issuance of G.O. Ms. No. 84-Revenue Dept. dated 28.1.1994 stating that the same was in public interest. A counter affidavit was also filed by respondent No. 3, the Law Officer of the Housing Board stating that the Housing Board has invested Rs. 88.43 lakhs towards development of land and thus the Board has invested in all a sum of Rs. 1,78,43,000 and prayed for dismissal of the writ petition. An additional counter affidavit was also filed by respondent No. 3 stating that the area is fully developed. Likewise, Shri P. Krishnaiah, the Executive Officer of the TTD filed affidavit stating that a number of dwelling have come up in the entire area and the prayer in the writ petition could not be granted and prayed for dismissal of the writ petition.

By the impugned and common judgment dated 28.9.2000, the Division Bench of the High Court finding no illegality or irregularity in the action of the respondents dismissed both the writ petitions. Aggrieved by the dismissal of the writ petitions, the appellant has filed these appeals by way of special leave petitions.

We heard Mr. G. Ramakrishna Prasad, learned counsel appearing for the appellant-Forum, Mr. V.R. Reddy, learned senior counsel appearing for the TTD, Mr. P.P. Rao, learned senior counsel Mr. Jaideep Gupta, Mr. D. Ramakrishna Reddy, Mr. P.S. Narasimha, learned counsel and Mr. Anoop G. Chaudhary, learned senior counsel for the respective parties.

Elaborate arguments were advanced by the respective counsel appearing for the parties to this action. We have been taken through the entire pleadings, documents and annexures filed along with the appeals and also the report submitted by the Expert Committee and the objections filed by the parties to the said report.

Mr. G. Ramakrishna Prasad, learned counsel appearing for the appellant made the following submissions:

1. The High Court has failed to appreciate that in the light of over-whelming evidence with regard to the Tank beds being put in use for irrigation,

drinking purpose, and being used as percolation tanks to improve the groundwater table and quality of underground water in the neighbouring areas and many villages including Tirupathi town, the High Court committed error in holding that the water tanks in issue are now non-existent.

2. The High Court committed an error in coming to the conclusion that the urban development could be given primacy over and above the need to protect the environment and valuable fresh water resources.
3. The High Court is not correct in holding that if the Government is not permitted to use the lands in question properly it will ultimately go into the hands of land grabbers and anti-social elements and they will be converted into slums and that such lands will be used as dumping grounds.
4. The High Court has failed to notice the fact that the need for sustainable development cannot be ignored, could not do away with and could not cause harm to the environment in the name of urban development and that certain acts of omissions and commissions on the part of the respondents in not taking proper measures for the preservation of the Peruru tank, the flow of water into the tank is reduced every year as most of its feeder channels are either spoiled or closed by unauthorised encroachers.
5. The respondents have failed to take necessary measures to remove the encroachments and repair the feeder channels and as a result, the natural flow of water into the tank during the rainy season is reduced. On account of reduction in the water catchment area due to encroachments, the quantity of water collected in the tank is getting drastically depleted year by year and that the water table in the neighbouring area of the tank including a colony is going down and even the ground water available is becoming more and more saline with high fluoride content every year and becoming unfit for drinking purposes.
6. It was submitted that the respondents are under constitutional obligation to protect the environment. The tanks in question is a public property in which each and every ayacutdar has got a property right and this right cannot be taken away by the Government to their detriment and that the communal property cannot be diverted for the purpose of construction of houses to section of people.

Mr. V.R. Reddy, learned senior counsel, appearing for TTD submitted that TTD gave its own land to Sri Padmavathi Mahila Viswavidyalayam and in lieu of the land so given by it, the State Government under G.O. Ms. No. 181 Revenue dated 15.3.1991 has given Ac.150 m Perur tank to TTD. TTD took possession of the said land on 19.3.1993. In 1984 itself, the tank bed became barren and there is no water supply to the tank. The agricultural lands which were dependent on the tank water which was used only for agricultural purposes, therefore, became housing colonies. There is no source of water now to the tank and it is not possible to store water in the tank. Tirupathi is a growing town whose population is going up constantly demanding more and more house sites and housing accommodation for the growing town population. The pilgrim inflow is also steadily growing requiring more facilities. An agricultural tank which has become dry by 1984 itself and which is no longer capable of being used for agricultural irrigation purposes as it gets no water any more being surrounded by the expanding town, roads and built up areas cannot anymore be maintained as a tank in its original form. There are other tanks and dams and water supply schemes being undertaken in Tirupathi having regard to their feasibility. The High Court has considered these aspects also, he submitted.

TTD is one of the well-known Devasthanams in the country which is undertaking projects of general public welfare consistent with its policy. It is doing everything possible in Tirupathi and in Tirumala where the World famous Sri Venkateswara Swami Temple is situated, to preserve and improve the natural environment. The tank in question *i.e.,* Peruru tank cannot be maintained as a tank in the present situation and it has ceased to be a tank long ago except in name. It has been obtained by it in lieu of its own land it has given for a public purpose of a women's university and requires it for its own optimum use. The objection sought to be taken by the appellant as a public interest objection is without any merit or substance as far as Peruru tank is concerned on the facts and circumstances of the case.

Mr. P.S. Narasimha, learned counsel appearing for A.P. Housing Board, submitted that S.No. 18/1 of Avilala village is on the outskirts of Tirupathi town measuring about 187 acres was classified as Avilala tank Poramboke. The said tank was abandoned as far back as in the year 1992. The Tank area was bulldozed and the entire land was levelled. The cultivation particulars of the Ayacut in this tank reveals that no lands were being irrigated from the water derived from this tank right from the year 1395 F *i.e.,* the year 1984 A.D. The feeder source for Avilala tank namely (i) Ramayapalli Kasarkaluwa (ii) Kasarkaluwa of Vedantpuram Agraharam and (iii) drainage water of Timlagunta wet fields (iv) Nadinvaka all these sources got defaced and there has been no scope for accumulation of water in the tank. It was also observed that even after sinking that well to a depth of about 60 feet, the land was not receiving any water from any ground resources after construction of Kalyani Reservoir. Therefore, proposal for abandonment of tank was submitted by the Revenue Divisional Officer, Tirupathi to the District Collector in the years 1988 and 1992. Thereafter, public notices were issued inviting objections but no objections were filed by anyone.

Thereafter a technical opinion was given by the Executive Engineer of the Irrigation Department in favour of the alienation of the said land to an extent of 98 acres. Even the Gram Panchayat had passed resolution on 14.8.1988 proposing to alienate 98 acres in S.No. 18/3 carved out S.No. 18/1 of Avilala Village in favour of A.P. Housing Board. The Government have issued orders in G.O. Ms. No. 691 dated 18.7.1989 alienating 98 acres of land for the purpose of constructions of house under the rental housing scheme for the Government employees. The said land has been levelled in the year 1992 after taking possession. The Housing Board has undertaken infrastructural facilities by laying of B.T. Roads, electrical lines, digging bore wells apart from levelling and plotting the land and a sub-station 33 K.V. capacity has been established by the A.P. Electricity Board.

It was submitted that the A.P. Housing Board paid Rs. 90 lakhs towards the cost of the land @ Rs.1 lakh for each acre to the Government and also spent a sum of Rs. 88.43 lakhs towards development of the land so far. Thus, in all A.P. Housing Board has invested a sum of Rs. 1,78,43,000 and the further development was stopped in view of the pendency of the writ petition.

The A.P. Dairy Development Corporation has established Balaji Dairy in a portion of the land under reference by spending over Rs. 8 crores. All these amounts were spent by the Government from its own expenditure from out of public funds. Apart from the above, the Land Acquisition proceedings were initiated for laying of approach road and compensation thereafter has been paid by the Revenue Department. Mr. P.S. Narasimha further submitted that the laudable objective of maintenance of ecology, environment and preservation of water resources are subject to the vagaries of nature and in the realm of technical matter, there cannot be judicially manageable standard for granting any relief.

Arguing further, he submitted that there are many factors and reasons attributing to depletion of ground water table due to the expanding urbanization and increasing the non-agricultural activities. All such activities have not the sanction of the law supported by legislative mandate under the A.P. Urban Areas Development Act. The administration has been entrusted with the responsibility of ensuring equitable urban growth by balancing ecological and environmental interest and in the instant case, the administration has taken all the proceedings and attending precautions to act in larger public interest in general for which the appellant cannot have any grievance. Mr. Jaideep Gupta, learned senior counsel, appearing for TUDA filed a detailed reply to the appeal. He invited our attention to the elaborate and detailed reply affidavit filed by them. It is seen from the affidavit that the proposals for abandonment of the erstwhile tank were submitted by the Revenue Divisional Officer, Tirupathi with reference to the Collector's letter No. B-1/7089/88 dated 17.9.1988. A notice for public response to the said proposal was published in the village but no objections were received. As the land was in the past classified as a tank poramboke, technical opinion had already been obtained and the Irrigation Department opined that there was no objection for alienation of the said land. As per the report of the Revenue Divisional Officer, Tirupathi submitted in his letter No. Roc. No. G/2016/88, dated 6.9.1988 that the Avilala Gram Panchayat in its resolution dated 14.8.1988 had resolved to alienate an extent of 90.00 acres in Sy. No. 18/3 (carved out from 18/1) of Avilala village in favour of A.P. Housing Board.

In the above circumstances, the Government have alienated 90 acres of land in Sy. No. 18/3 carved out from Sy. No. 18/1 in favour of A.P. Housing Board for construction of houses under rental housing scheme for Government employees *vide* G.O. Ms. No. 691 dated 10.7.1989 of the Revenue (Assn. IV) Department. The District Collector, Chittoor in his letter No. B1/15246/90 dated

14.7.1992 addressed to the Secretary to the Government, Revenue Department has informed that the Ayacutdars have also given their consent for abandonment of the erstwhile tank and to treat the Ayacut as dry land since the tank does not have any water source.

After the Government have alienated an extent of 90 acres of land to A.P. Housing Board and 1.12 acres to A.P.S.E.B. and 5 acres towards compensation for private lands acquired for approach road, there remains a balance of 96 acres of land. Accordingly the Revenue Divisional Officer, Tirupathi in his letter G/5234/92 dated 16.9.1992 addressed the District Collector that the balance land available can be better utilized by handing it over to various agencies for developmental purposes, because of its proximity to Tirupathi town and adjoining residential colonies like Vaikuntapuram, Bairagipatteda etc. There has been a substantial growth in population of Tirupathi town coupled with physical expansion of the town and consequent conversion of agricultural lands into pucca residential area and layouts. The population of Tirupathi is growing day by day and to cater to the growing demand for housing this authority had requested the Government for alienation of 90 acres of land for sites and services programmes.

Accordingly, the Government in G.O. Ms. No. 84 Revenue (Assn.IV) Department, dated 28.1.1994 alienated 90 acres of land in Sy. No. 17/1 of Avilala in favour of this authority. Based on the Government Orders and proceedings of the District Collector, Chittoor in D.O. Toc. No. B/1/15246/92 dated 3.3.1994, the Mandal Revenue Officer, Tirupathi Rural Mandal has handed over the possession of 65.19 acres of land on 18.4.1994 to this authority.

Mr. Gupta further submitted that the Urban Development Authorities are bound to regulate the massive urban growth and migration of people with appropriate development plans to prevent formation of slums and consequent urban decay.

Accordingly, the TUDA has taken up development of new Satellite townships around Tirupathi to relieve congestion of the existing township and one such satellite town is Rajiv Nagar being developed in the land many years back was under the then existing Avilala tank in Sy. No. 18/1.

As it is evident from the joint inspection of the Joint Collector, Chittoor, Superintending Engineer, Irrigation, Chittoor, etc., on dated 4.4.1992, there has been no source of the supply channel for maintenance of the Avilala tank and it has not been practicable either to restore it as irrigation tank or even as a percolation tank any longer. However, as a part of the development of a satellite township, it is proposed to provide lung spaces, water harvesting structures in an extent of 18 acres of land benefiting the people in Sy. No. 18/1 of Avilala village and Rajiv Nagar area by TUDA and A.P. Housing Board.

After obtaining approval from the State Government, TUDA announced the scheme to the public on 18.3.2001, 26.3.2001 and 30.3.2001 by giving wide publicity in the newspaper and inviting applications for participating in the auction. The plots were allotted to the public in a public auction as per the orders of the Government *vide* G.O. Ms. No. 84 Revenue (Assn.IV) Deptt. Dated

28.1.1994. The auction was conducted on 13th, 14th and 15th April, 2001 and plots were allotted to the successful bidders immediately *i.e.,* before the issue of *status quo* order of this Court. TUDA has already taken up plans of action to provide in the new township partly with the amounts received from open auction:

It is also seen from the reply affidavit filed by TUDA that a comprehensive scheme name "HARITA" has been jointly promoted by Forest Department, TTD and TUDA at a cost of Rs. 24.83 crores to be implemented in five years from 2000 to 2005. The scheme had already commenced and massive plantation programme was taken up by planting 16 lakhs trees during the year 2000-2001 apart from other schemes that have been envisaged in the plan.

The National Remote Sensing Agency, Department of Space, Government of India in their report titled "Land use Land cover monitoring in TUDA area with special reference to Avilala tank and environs Tirupathi, Andhra Pradesh" has conducted detailed study with the help of satellite imageries on Avilala tank over a period of time. In its report, it is stated that the tank in earlier days *i.e.* earlier to 1970 was drained mostly by natural springs located in the head of the region of the catchment. Over a period of time, the spring got dried up due to various geological factors with no source of surface flow. Also the small streams which were draining to the tank were disturbed and occupied, with the result the tank remained dry with part of it covered with scrub since 1976 onwards.

It is also stated in the report that as per the satellite image of February, 2001 there are about 232 tanks identified in TUDA area. Most of the tanks are located along the foot hills of Tirumala hills and plains of Swarnamukhi river. Kalyani reservoir is the major one in the area. Considering the location as well as distribution about 20 tanks are identified for conservation and future development to meet the urban water requirement. However, other existing tanks may also be fenced and preserved to meet the future requirement.

The TUDA along with the support of other Government Departments have been making conscious efforts for conserving and preserving potential tanks in TUDA region as per the recommendations of National Remote Sensing Agency and other experts in the field. In this direction, the TUDA has already initiated action in developing Tiruchanoor tank in Sy. No. 253 of Tiruchanoor at a cost of Rs. 30 lakhs under Phase I Scheme which includes desilting, strengthening of bunds, landscaping of bunds and tree plantation. However, there is no possibility at all of restoring the abandoned Avilala tank as per the scientific data available with TUDA which can be at best developed as a satellite township with all facilities thus contributing to the planned urban growth of Tirupathi and decongesting the main township.

Mr. Anoop G. Chaudhary, learned senior counsel appearing for the State of Andhra Pradesh drew our attention to the detailed counter affidavit filed by the State of A.P. through its Joint Secretary to the Government Revenue Department wherein the Government has explained to this Court as to how the impugned G.O.'s alienating the lands in favour of TTD, TUDA and Andhra Pradesh Housing Board for public purposes were issued. According to Mr. Anoop

Chaudhary, there is nothing illegal in issuing in G.Os. It is not violating anybody's fundamental rights. An extent of 180 acres of land was tank bed land of Avilala tank. This tank was an abandoned tank ever since 1984 as the channel source of this tank was closed due to construction of Kalyani dam and because of lack of water this tank was no longer used for storage of water. As it was an abandoned tank and was no longer in existence and the land became plain and considering the matter and report of the District Collector, the Government issued orders in G.O. Ms. No. 691 Revenue Department dated 10.7.1989 for alienating an extent of 90 acres of land to A.P. Housing Board for the purpose of rental Housing scheme for Government employees on payment of Rs. 1 lakh per acre by the Housing Board and before this land was alienated a notice was published in the village calling for objections by the Revenue authorities and no objections were received in pursuance of the said notice. The Ayacutdars have also consented for the alienation of the land. Thereafter, after obtaining the opinion of the concerned Executive Engineer of the Irrigation Department and the report of the District Collector, the above Government Order was issued.

Concluding his arguments, he submitted that there is ample material on record showing that these tanks were abandoned long back and they were no longer serving as water storage tanks more particularly, as their supply channels have been dried up. On 5.12.2003, this Court passed the following order:

> "The Secretary, Ministry of Water Resources, Government of India is directed to constitute a committee of experts for the purpose of submitting a report on the question whether the two tanks, namely, the Peruru and Avilala or either of them can be utilized for water harvesting. The report shall be submitted to this Court within a period of six weeks from the date of the communication of this order. The Registry is directed to forward a set of the documents, which have been filed before this Court to the Secretary for being placed before and considered by such Committee. The committee will hold local inspection. Before it does so it shall give notice to the concerned advocate-on-record. The State respondent will provide such documents as may be required by the Committee for the purpose of submitting the report.

List the matter thereafter."

The Government of India constituted a Committee for the purpose of submitting its report to this Court:

The term of reference of the Committee was to submit a report on the question whether the two tanks namely, the Peruru and Avilala or either of them can be utilized for water harvesting. Pursuant to this, the Committee visited Tirupathi on 19th and 20th January, 2004 for local inspection and necessary investigations. During the visit, a detailed discussion was held with the representatives of TUDA, TTD and members of the Intellectual Forum.

The Committee submitted its detailed inspection report on 21.1.2004.

The appellants submitted its objections to the report of the Committee and the respondents supported the inspection report.

In the above background, the following questions of law arise for consideration by this Court:—

1. Whether the Urban Development could be given primacy over and above the need to protect the environment and valuable fresh water resources?
2. Whether the action of the A.P. state in issuing the impugned G.Os could be permitted in derogation of Articles 14 and 21 of the Constitution of India as also the Directive Principles of State Policy and fundamental duties enshrined in the Constitution of India?
3. Whether the need for sustainable development can be ignored, do away with and cause harm to the environment in the name of urban development?
4. Whether there are any competing public interests and if so how the conflict is to be adjudicated/reconciled?

We have already referred to the directions issued to the Government of India to constitute a Committee of Experts for the purpose of submitting a report on the question whether the two tanks namely, the Peruru and Avilala or either of them can be utilised for water harvesting. The Expert Committee took into account the factors that had led to the depletion of influx of water to Peruru Tank in the report and observed in paragraphs 3 & 4 of the Report.

According to the learned counsel appearing for the TTD, Peruru tank as a water body had three main sources of influx of water which were as follows:

1. Overflow of water through feeder channel from the combined Kalyani River Swarnamukhi river The Kalyani river joins Swarnmukhi river near Agasteeswara Temple. At that point, the overflow of water in the combined rivers as going to peruru tank through a feeder channel of about 1.6 Km. Length. After the construction of the Kalyani Dam on Kalyani River in the year 1974, the flow of water from Kalyani river into Swarnamukhi river considerably reduced. As a result, there was no overflow of water going to the feeder channel, which over the years has become defunct due to its bed level being at a higher level than the riverbed. Since the feeder channel has become defunct and abandoned, a road has been constructed for the temple by filling up the channel.The Expert Committee, after observing the above, in paragraph 3 of its report under Peruru tank has opined as follows:

   "The revival of old feeder channel which involves deepening of the existing channel and restoring the channel in the initial reaches is not considered cost effective in view of the meagre quantity of river water availability for a very short period."

2. Catchment area of 42.9 sq.Kms. TTD under "Neeru Meeru" programme, constructed 22 check dams, 9 percolation tanks, 437 rock fill dams and contour trench on a length of 1.22 km for improving the water table and water conservation and efficient use of rain water without wastage in the catchment area falling under S.V. Zoological Park. The Expert Committee, after observing the above in para 4 of its report has stated that the inflow

of water into Peruru tank has been reduced considerably due to the construction of check dams etc. While it is so, it is also to be noted in this context, that on account of Kalyani Dam a water body has come into existence in the form of Reservoir is spread over an area of 31065 acres and holds 910 mc. Ft. Water when filled to capacity. Similarly, Dalavai Tank, which is created in the Catchment area, is also a water body occupying 66.70 acres and holds 15.79 mc. Ft. of water when full. It is pertinent to submit in this context that under the "Neeru Meeru" programme vigorously pursued by the Government in the entire State, construction of such check dams, percolation tanks etc., was conceived and executed for improving the water table and water conservation and efficient use of rain water without wastage at considerable cost.

3. Nakkala vanka and Bodeddulu Vanka : prior to the construction of Dalavai tank in the catchment area, water used to flow downstream to peruru tank through Nakkalavanka and Bnodeddula Vanka. After the construction of Dalavai Tank, the flow of water through Nakkalavanka and Bnodeddula Vanka has considerably reduced.

The Expert Committee after observing the above facts in paragraphs 4 & 5 of its report opined that the flow of water through Bodeddulla Vanka to the Peruru tank can be restored by removing a small check dam at Malapalli which it is submitted might be considered a retrograde step affecting other projects for water conservation. Learned counsel further submitted that in view of the aforesaid recommendation of the Expert Committee that instead of 20 acres as presently assigned a minimum of 50 acres may be utilised for a water body in the tank area may not be a practicable proposal.

However, the TTD would willingly and earnestly endeavour to implement the proposal if this Court accepts and approves the Report of the Expert Committee. In our opinion, the Expert Committee's report should be accepted by TTD. Learned counsel appearing for the TTD at the time of argument, has also brought to our notice some of the programmes launched by TTD for sustainable improvement of the living environment. Mr. P.S. Narasimha, learned counsel, submitted that no competing or conflicting public interests arise in this case inasmuch as the very subject of the environment issue has ceased to be a resource as it were.

The enquiry is, therefore, upon the very basic question *i.e.,* whether there exist at all a natural resource. The research is empirical and not adjudication or prioritisation of conflicting public interest. A further question can also be raised *i.e.* even if the said resource has deteriorated, is it possible to revive its resource. The adjudication in both the appeals is confined to an empirical enquiry based on scientific data. The enquiry as indicated above has already been done in this case. It is in two stages.

STAGE ONE Till the judgment of the High Court of Andhra Pradesh, which dismissed the writ petitions.

STAGE TWO Enquiry at the instance of this Court pending disposal of the special leave petitions.

STAGE ONE—

Our attention was drawn to the counter-affidavit dated 7.9.1994 of TUDA in W.P.No. 8650 of 1994 which reads as under:

> "The tank in question as could be seen from the permanent `A' Register (Re-settlement Registrar) was to be fed by (1) Ramayapalli Kasam Kalva (2) Kasam Kalva of Vedan thapuram Agraharam (3) Drainage water of Thummalapetta wet fields and (4) by Nadim Kalva which are almost defaced and as such there is no scope for accumulation of water in the tank. It is also observed from a well about 60 feet depth located on South-West corner of the land that no water exists in the well. The foreshore of the tank is almost plain. It is an abandoned tank and the tank is also not receiving any supply of water due to closure of supply channels after the construction of Kalyani Dam Reservoir."

STAGE TWO

The Inspection report of the Committee constituted under the directions of this Court considered various issues. It is stated in the report as follows:

1. There is no tank existing in the area at present. Remains of the original demolished bund were seen. The area upstream was plain with no indications of any water storage.
2. reported feeder channels to the tank are in fact localized drainage lines which do not have any direct source of surface water from the nearby Tirumala hills. The tank might have receive water as over flow from Peruru tank located on west of Avilala tank.

As per the Respondents contention, the Tank in dispute has been shown in Resettlement Register 'A'. For the purpose of change of classification from tank poramboke to ayan, 'A' notice was published in the Avilala Village displaying the said notices at the conspicuous places which is statutory and no objections were received and as stated already, consent letters were given by the individual ayacutdars for the abandonment of the tank.

Proposals for abandonment of the erstwhile tank were submitted by the Revenue Divisional Officer, Tirupathi with reference to the Collector's letter No. B-1/7089/88 dated 17.9.1988. A notice for public response to the said proposal was published in the village but no objections were received. As the land was in the past classified as a tank poramboke, technical opinion had already been obtained and the Irrigation Department opined that there was no objection for alienation of the said land. The opinion is in Collectorate reference No. B-1/14157/85. As per the report of the Revenue Divisional Officer, Tirupathi submitted in his letter No. Roc. No. G/2016/88 dated 6.9.1988 that the Avilala Gram Panchayat in its Resolution dated 14.8.1988 had resolved to alienate an extent of 90 acres in Sy. No. 18/3 of Avilala village in favour of Andhra Pradesh Housing Board. The materials placed before us and the report of the Expert Committee and the stand taken by the public bodies and the rapid change in the demographic feature of the Tirupathi town and its surrounding suburbs have necessitated the process of urbanization.

The TUDA in its additional counter-affidavit filed on 21.2.2002 stated that the Tirupathi urban agglomeration as notified consists of 849 sq. Kms. with one Municipality and 89 villages. The total population of TUDA area is 4,88,248 according to 2001 census and the projected population by 2021 is 9,60,000. 49% of the urban agglomeration is covered by Tirumala hills and forest area and the remaining area is going to be developed into a Metropolis over the next 20 years, according to the present decadal population growth of 32% for TUDA region, compared to 13% of A.P. population growth rate as per 2001 census. The growth of population of Tirupathi Municipal area was highest during the decades of 1971 (83.68%) and in 1981 (75.10%) but now stabilized at nearly 30% (2001). But in respect of the suburbs surroundings Tirupathi, which are fast growing recording very high population growth rates, are an indication that TUDA area is one of the very fast developing urban agglomerations in the country. Akkarampale (v) one of the suburbs with a population of 20,325 recorded 250% of decadal growth between 1991-2001. Similarly Avilala (v) another suburb of Tirupathi, where "Rajivnagar", the land in question in the present appeals, is situated, the decadal growth rate between 1991 and 2001 was above 150%. The population of Avilala (v) which was 1141 in 1971, has grown to 12,058 by the year 2001, while converting most of the agricultural lands into residential plots. According to the report of NRSA, Hyderabad in July 2001 on "Land Use-Land Cover Monitoring in TUDA area with special reference to Avilala Tank and Environs, Tirupathi, A.P." the Avilala (v) along with the tank area which has a total extent of 942.47 hectares of which residential area was 32.91 hectares in 1976-77 has now increased to 349.28 hectares in the year 2001, which also includes institutional and industrial areas. In respect of agricultural lands, which was 677.78 hectares in 1976-77 has been diminished into 204.22 hectares in 2001. The high population growth rates of Avilala (v) combined with increase in the residential area (961%) is a clear indication that the original purpose of Avilala tank as irrigation tank, is no more relevant in the present scenario of fast urban development in this area.

It has been further stated in the additional affidavit filed by TUDA on 21.2.2002 that the TUDA has taken up revision of its master plan with digitisation of land use along with a comprehensive development plan of the urban agglomeration up to 2021, with public participation. According to the said Master plan prepared by TUDA in 1981, the said lands of Avilala (v) are earmarked under residential zone and development of satellite township to ease the congestion on the main city and the purpose of retaining irrigation tank in an extent of 150 acres at Avilala near Tirupathi is no longer useful to the public under the circumstances explained.

In the counter-affidavit filed by A.P. Housing Board on 26.6.2000, it is submitted that the A.P. Housing Board paid Rs. 90 lakhs towards the cost of the land @ Rs.1 lakh for each acre to the Government and also spent a sum of Rs. 88.43 lakhs towards development of the land so far. Thus, in all APHB has invested a sum of Rs. 1,78,43,000 and the further development was stopped in view of the pendency of the writ petition.

The area around the property in question is fully developed. There is a weaver's colony, PR Engineers Colony, Judicial Employees Plots and Colony and Balai Dairy (in 10 acres of land APDDCF). Thus, the area around the land in question is already developed and several colonies have come up and in any event the land cannot be used as reservoir.

As per the notification, APHB has proposed about 342 HIG design, 497 MIG-2 design and 283 MIG-1 design houses with the details mentioned therein totalling about 1126 houses in the said proposed colony. The details of number of houses to be allotted under different categories and modes like outright sale, allotment on payment of 50%, 30% amount etc., are also mentioned in the said notification. It also provided reservation for various categories like 5% of houses to Legislators, 5% to defence people, 14% for SC, 4% for ST, 9% for OBC, 10% for retired Government employees, 1% for physically handicapped, 1% for freedom fighters and 51% for other categories. The applicants under the above-referred notifications are the persons having no plot or no house for their residence in Tirupathi or nearby places and as such they are in dire need of a place of residence which is sought to be fulfilled under the above scheme by the APHB.

It is also seen from the additional counter-affidavit dated 21.2.2002 filed by TUDA that they have taken up revision of its Master plan with digitisation of land use along with a comprehensive development plan of the urban agglomeration up to 2021, with public participation. According to the Master plan prepared by TUDA in 1981, the said lands of Avilala (v) are earmarked under residential zone and development of satellite township to ease the congestion on the main city.

It was also submitted that subsequent to the filing of the present appeals, substantial developments have taken place which can be summed up here. As stated in the counter-affidavit filed by TUDA on dt. 29.11.2001, after the dismissal of Writ Petition No.8650 of 1994 by the High Court on dated 28.9.2000, TUDA submitted the entire scheme of sites and services to be taken up at Rajiv Nagar at a cost of Rs. 600 lakhs to the State Government for approval vide its letter No.2148/G1/99 dated 3.12.1999. The State Government *vide* G.. Rt. No. 124 M.A. dated 15.2.2001 had approved the proposal of TUDA.

Mr. Jaideep Gupta, learned senior counsel appearing for the TUDA, has placed before us a report on Land Use Land Cover Monitoring in TUDA area with special reference to Avilala Tank and Environs Tirupathi. The main objective of this study was:

1. To map and estimate the water bodies and drainage pattern within the TUDA limits and to suggest the water conservation plan, on a scale of 1:50,000 using satellite and other collateral data.
2. To monitor the changes in and around the Avilala Tank over a period from 1976-2001 and carry out the change analysis.

The report contains all meticulous details about the study area, data base, advantages and limitations of satellite data, methodology, analysis and observations, water resources analysis of TUDA area, land use/land cover analysis of Avilala tank and its environs. The report has been prepared in a meticulous manner with reference to various plans. Another report was also submitted with regard to the Revitalisation of Lakes in TUDA Region which also contains many details about the land use of TUDA Region and the conservation and preservation of water bodies and the identification of potential tanks for conservation and the salient proposals for revitalisation of identified tanks. The Salient proposals for revitalisation of tanks are as under:

On realizing the importance of restoration of tank basins towards conservation of water and recharging of ground water, increase the storage capacity of tanks, renovating the tank bunds as well as feeder channels, TUDA has taken over 30 tanks in its operational area for taking up the improvements. Proposals include removal or eviction of encroachments, desilting of tank basins, clearing of jungle, strengthening of tank bunds, excavation of boundary trenches, widening and excavation of feeder channels, construction of boundary pillars and compound walls along the tank boundary. Block plantation, programmes for development as landscaped parks and water based entertainment units for the benefit of the public in off shore areas of the tanks have been proposed wherever feasible and viable.

Towards protection of environment, provision for treatment system is also made in the project to take care of entry of drainage/sullage into the tank storages. Block plantation on all on-shore areas of tank have been taken up as a part of Neeru Meeru programme to prevent erosion of soils and entry of encroachments which will have long term positive environment results.

As per the estimates prepared, the total cost of the scheme works out to Rs. 993.64 lakhs for taking up the above programmes in 32 tanks spread over 32 settlements around Tirupathi town and in TUDA region. The abstract statement showing the details of tanks proposed for revitalization and the cost of development is given below:

(Rs. In lakhs)

S.No.	Mandal	No. of tanks	Cost of development	Cost of greening/ landscaping Programme	Total
1.	Tirupati(U) Mandal	10	387.84	82.50	470.34
2.	Tirupati(R)Mandal	10	203.10	64.90	268.00
3.	Reningunta Mandal	9	129.50	47.60	177.10
4.	Chandragir Mandal	3	71.70	6.50	78.20
	Total	32	792.14	201.50	993.64

As already noticed, the Expert Committee in its Inspection Report, has gone into various technical details about the cause for gradual reduction of inflow of water to the Peruru tank, which is a rain-fed tank, over the last 50 years. The Committee has observed in its report that the reduction in the inflow of water to the tank was due to the construction of 22 check dams, 8 percolation tanks, 437 rock fill dams and contour trench on a length of 1.22 km for water conservation and efficient use of rain water without wastage. The Committee has also observed in its Report that the main supply channel to the Peruru tank was affected due to the revival of Dalavai Tank situated at a distance of about 2 Kms upstream in the catchment area.

The Expert Committee in its report has suggested some additional measures for rain water harvesting by providing for a percolation tank in an area of 50 acres instead of 20 acres already earmarked for the said purpose by the Revenue authorities with roof top rain water harvesting and artificial recharge.

The Expert Committee has gone into various technical and cost aspects about the feasibility of reviving the Peruru tank. Only after the Committee found that the tank could not be revived in its original form, it suggested in its report for construction of percolation tank and roof top rain water harvesting and artificial recharge for increasing the ground water level.

A careful perusal of the report would clearly reveal that the Committee has given its suggestions only after taking into account various possibilities in recharging the ground water level. It is not proper in doubting the correctness of the Committee's report as contended by the appellants. The Committee, in our view, has gone into the details about the revival of the feeder channel to the Peruru tank from Swarnamukhi river and having regard to the impracticability of restoring the same as feeder channel had suggested an alternative which in their view, is feasible and beneficial.

It is evident from the report of the Expert Committee that the Members of the Expert Committee have taken technical aspects as contained therein and the objections of the appellant in this regard are untenable. The Government of Andhra Pradesh has also taken various steps pursuant to the directions given by this Court which could be seen from the additional affidavit dated 25.3.2005 filed by the State of Andhra Pradesh.

We have given our thoughtful and careful consideration to the sensitive issues raised in the appeals by the appellants and countered by the respective respondents with reference to the pleadings, the documents, annexures filed and judgment of the High Court. We have also carefully perused the report submitted by the Expert Committee and also considered the rival submissions made by the respective counsel.

In our opinion, the nature of the question in this case is twofold. Firstly, the jurisprudential issues. In the event of conflict between the competing interests of protecting the environment and social development, this Court in the case of *M.C. Mehta* v. *Kamal Nath*, (1997) 1 SCC 388, in paragraph 35 held as under:

> "The issues presented in this case illustrate the classic struggle between those members of the public who would preserve our rivers, forests, parks and open lands in their pristine purity and those charged with administrative responsibility, who under the pressures of the changing needs of an increasingly complex society find it necessary to encroach to some extent upon open lands heretofore considered inviolate to change. The resolution of this conflict in any given case is for the legislature and not for the Courts. If there is a law made by Parliament or the State Legislatures, the Courts can serve as an instrument for determining

legislative intent in the exercise of powers of judicial review under the Constitution. But, in the absence of any legislation, the executive acting under the doctrine of public trust cannot abdicate the natural resource and convert them into private ownership or commercial use. The aesthetic use and the pristine glory of the natural resources, the environment and the ecosystems of our country cannot be permitted to be eroded for private, commercial or any other use unless the Courts find it necessary, in good faith, for the public and in public interest to encroach upon the said recourses."

The responsibility of the state to protect the environment is now a well-accepted notion in all countries. It is this notion that, in international law, gave rise to the principle of "State responsibility" for pollution emanating within one's own territories [Corfu Channel Case, ICJ Reports (1949) 4]. This responsibility is clearly enunciated in the United Nations Conference on the Human Environment, Stockholm 1972 (Stockholm Convention), to which India was a party. The relevant Clause of this Declaration in the present context is Paragraph 2, which states:

> "The natural resources of the earth, including the air, water, land, flora and fauna and especially representative samples of natural ecosystems, must be safeguarded for the benefit of present and future generations through careful planning or management, as appropriate."

Thus, there is no doubt about the fact that there is a responsibility bestowed upon the Government to protect and preserve the tanks, which are an important part of the environment of the area.

Sustainable Development

The respondents, however, have taken the plea that the actions taken by the Government were in pursuance of urgent needs of development. The debate between the developmental and economic needs and that of the environment is an enduring one, since if environment is destroyed for any purpose without a compelling developmental cause, it will most probably run foul of the executive and judicial safeguards. However, this court has often faced situations where the needs of environmental protection have been pitched against the demands of economic development. In response to this difficulty, policy makers and judicial bodies across the world have produced the concept of "sustainable development". This concept, as defined in the 1987 report of the World Commission on Environment and Development (Brundtland Report) defines it as "Development that meets the needs of the present without compromising the ability of the future generations to meet their own needs".

Returning to the Stockholm Convention, a support of such a notion can be found in Paragraph 13, which states:

> "In order to achieve a more rational management of resources and thus to improve the environment, States should adopt an integrated and coordinated approach to their development planning so as to ensure that development is compatible with the need to protect and improve environment for the benefit of their population."

Subsequently the Rio Declaration on Environment and Development, passed during the Earth Summit at 1992, to which also India is a party, adopts the notion of sustainable development. Principle 4 of the declaration states:

> "In order to achieve sustainable development, environmental protection shall constitute an integral part of the development process and cannot be considered in isolation from it. "

This court in the case of *Essar Oil* v. *Halar Utkarsh Samiti*, (2004) 2 SCC 392, Para 27] was pleased to expound on this. Their Lordships held:

> "This, therefore, is the sole aim, namely, to balance economic and social needs on the one hand with environmental considerations on the other. But in a sense all development is an environmental threat. Indeed, the very existence of humanity and the rapid increase in population together with the consequential demands to sustain the population has resulted in the concreting of open lands, cutting down of forests, filling up of lakes and the pollution of water resources and the very air that we breathe. However there need not necessarily be a deadlock between development on the one hand and the environment on the other. The objective of all laws on environment should be to create harmony between the two since neither one can be sacrificed at the altar of the other. "

A similar view was taken by this Court in Indian Council for *Enviro-Legal Action* v. *Union of India*, (1996) 5 SCC 281, Para 31] where their Lordships said:

> "While economic development should not be allowed to take place at the cost of ecology or by causing widespread environmental destruction and violation; at the same time the necessity to preserve ecology and environment should not hamper economic and other developments. Both development and environment should go hand in hand, in other words, there should not be development at the cost of environment and vice versa, but there should be development while taking due care and ensuring the protection of the environment."

The concept of sustainable development also finds support in the decisions of this court in the cases *M.C. Mehta* v. *Union of India* (*Taj Trapezium* Case), (1997) 2 SCC 653; *State of Himachal Pradesh* v. *Ganesh Wood Products*, (1995) 3 SCC 363 and *Narmada Bachao Andolan* v. *Union of India*, (2002) 10 SCC 664.

In light of the above discussions, it seems fit to hold that merely asserting an intention for development will not be enough to sanction the destruction of local ecological resources. What this Court should follow is a principle of sustainable development and find a balance between the developmental needs which the respondents assert, and the environmental degradation, that the appellants allege.

Public Trust Doctrine

Another legal doctrine that is relevant to this matter is the Doctrine of Public Trust. This doctrine, though in existence from Roman times, was enunciated in its modern form by the US Supreme Court in *Illinois Central Railroad Company* v. *People of the State of Illinois*, [146 US 537 (1892)] where the Court held:

The bed or soil of navigable waters is held by the people of the State in their character as sovereign, in trust for public uses for which they are adapted.

[–] the state holds the title to the bed of navigable waters upon a public trust, and no alienation or disposition of such property by the State, which does not recognize and is not in execution of this trust is permissible.

What this doctrine says therefore is that natural resources, which includes lakes, are held by the State as a "trustee" of the public, and can be disposed of only in a manner that is consistent with the nature of such a trust. Though this doctrine existed in the Roman and English Law, it related to specific types of resources. The US Courts have expanded and given the doctrine its contemporary shape whereby it encompasses the entire spectrum of the environment.

The doctrine, in its present form, was incorporated as a part of Indian law by this Court in the case of *M.C. Mehta* v. *Kamal Nath*, (*supra*) and also in *M.I. Builders* v. *Radhey Shyam Sahu*, (1999) 6 SCC 464. In M.C. Mehta, Kuldip Singh J., writing for the majority held:

[our legal system] includes the public trust doctrine as part of its jurisprudence. The state is the trustee of all natural resources which are by nature meant for public use and enjoyment. [–] The state as a trustee is under the legal duty to protect the natural resources. [Para 22]

The Supreme Court of California, in the case of *National Audubon Society* v. *Superior Court of Alpine Country*, 33 Cal 419 also known as the *Mono Lake* case summed up the substance of the doctrine. The Court said:

Thus the public trust is more than an affirmation of State power to use public property for public purposes. It is an affirmation of the duty of the State to protect the people's common heritage of streams, lakes, marshlands and tidelands, surrendering the right only in those rare cases when the abandonment of the right is consistent with the purposes of the trust.

This is an articulation of the doctrine from the angle of the affirmative duties of the State with regard to public trust. Formulated from a negatory angle, the doctrine does not exactly prohibit the alienation of the property held as a public trust. However, when the State holds a resource that is freely available for the use of the public, it provides for a high degree of judicial scrutiny upon any action of the Government, no matter how consistent with the existing legislations, that attempts to restrict such free use. To properly scrutinize such actions of the Government, the Courts must make a distinction between the government's general obligation to act for the public benefit, and the special, more demanding obligation which it may have as a trustee of certain public resources, [Joseph L. Sax "The public Trust Doctrine in Natural Resource Law: Effective Judicial Intervention", Michigan Law Review, Vol. 68 No. 3 (Jan. 1970) PP 471-566)]. According to Prof. Sax, whose article on this subject is considered to be an authority, three types of restrictions on governmental authority are often thought to imposed by the public trust doctrine [*ibid*]:

1. the property subject to the trust must not only be used for a public purpose, but it must be held available for use by the general public;

2. the property may not be sold, even for fair cash equivalent
3. the property must be maintained for particular types of use. (i) either traditional uses, or (ii) some uses particular to that form of resources.

In the instant case, it seems, that the Government Orders, as they stand now, are violative of principles 1 and 3, even if we overlook principle 2 on the basis of the fact that the Government is itself developing it rather than transferring it to a third party for value.

Therefore, our order should try to rectify these defects along with following the principle of sustainable development as discussed above.

Further the principle of "Inter-Generational Equity" has also been adopted while determining cases involving environmental issues. This Court in the case of *A.P. Pollution Control Board* v. *Prof. M.V. Nayudu*, (1999) 2 SCC 718 in paragraph 53 held as under:

> "The principle of inter-generational equity is of recent origin. The 1972 Stockholm Declaration refers to it in principles 1 and 2. In this context, the environment is viewed more as a resource basis for the survival of the present and future generations.
>
> Principle 1 - Man has the fundamental right to freedom, equality and adequate conditions of life, in an environment of quality that permits a life of dignity and well-being, and he bears a solemn responsibility to protect and improve the environment for the present and future generations—
>
> Principle 2 – The natural resources of the earth, including the air, water, lands, flora and fauna and especially representative samples of natural ecosystems, must be safeguarded for the benefit of the present and future generations through careful planning or management, as appropriate."

Several international conventions and treaties have recognized the above principles and, in fact, several imaginative proposals have been submitted including the *locus standi* of individuals or groups to take out actions as representatives of future generations, or appointing an ombudsman to take care of the rights of the future against the present (proposals of Sands and Brown Weiss referred to by Dr. Sreenivas Rao Permmaraju, Special Rapporteur, paras 97 and 98 of his report).

The principles mentioned above wholly apply for adjudicating matters concerning environment and ecology. These principles must, therefore, be applied in full force for protecting the natural resources of this country.

Art. 48A of the Constitution of India mandates that the State shall endeavour to protect and improve the environment to safeguard the forests and wild-life of the country.

Art. 51A of the Constitution of India, enjoins that it shall be the duty of every citizen of India, *inter alia*, to protect and improve national environment including forests, lakes, rivers, wild life and to have compassion for living creatures. These two Articles are not only fundamental in the governance of the country but also it shall be the duty of the State to apply these principles in making laws and further these two articles are to be kept in mind in understanding the scope and purport of the fundamental rights guaranteed by the Constitution including Articles 14, 19 and 21 of the Constitution of India and also the various laws enacted by the Parliament and the State Legislature.

On the other hand, we cannot also shut our eyes that shelter is one of the basic human needs just next to food and clothing. Need for a National Housing and Habitat Policy emerges from the growing requirements of shelter and related infrastructure.

These requirements are growing in the context of rapid pace of urbanization, increasing migration from rural to urban centres in search of livelihood, mismatch between demand and supply of sites and services at affordable cost and inability of most new and poorer urban settlers to access formal land markets in urban areas due to high costs and their own lower incomes, leading to a non-sustainable situation. This policy intends to promote sustainable development of habitat in the country, with a view to ensure equitable supply of land, shelter and services at affordable prices.

The World has reached a level of growth in the 21st Century as never before envisaged. While the crisis of economic growth is still on, the key question which often arises and the Courts are asked to adjudicate upon is whether economic growth can supersede the concern for environmental protection and whether sustainable development which can be achieved only by way of protecting the environment and conserving the natural resources for the benefit of the humanity and future generations could be ignored in the garb of economic growth or compelling human necessity. The growth and development process are terms without any content, without an inkling as to the substance of their end results. This inevitably leaves us to the conception of growth and development which sustains from one generation to the next in order to secure 'our common future'. In pursuit of development, focus has to be on sustainability of development and policies towards that end have to be earnestly formulated and sincerely observed. As Prof. Weiss puts it, "conservation, however, always takes a back seat in times of economic stress." It is now an accepted social principle that all human beings have a fundamental right to a healthy environment, commensurate with their well being, coupled with a corresponding duty of ensuring that resources are conserved and preserved in such a way that present as well as the future generations are aware of them equally.

The Parliament has considerably responded to the call of the Nations for conservation of environment and natural resources and enacted suitable laws.

The Judicial Wing of the country, more particularly, this Court has laid down a plethora of decisions asserting the need for environmental protection and conservation of natural resources. The environmental protection and conservation of natural resources has been given a status of a fundamental right and brought under Art. 21 of the Constitution of India. This apart, the Directive Principles of State Policy as also the fundamental duties enshrined in Part IV and Part IVA of the Constitution of India respectively also stresses the need to protect and improve the natural environment including the forests, lakes, rivers and wild-life and to have compassion for living creatures.

This Court in *Dahanu Taluka Environmental Protection Group* v. *Bombay Suburban Electricity Supply Co. Ltd.,* (1991) 2 SCC 539 held that the concerned Government should "consider the importance of public projects for the betterment of the conditions of living people on one hand and the necessity for preservation of social and ecological balance and avoidance of deforestation and maintenance of purity of the atmosphere and water free from pollution on the other in the light of various factual, technical and other aspects that may be brought to its notice by various bodies of laymen, experts and public workers and strike a balance between the two conflicting objectives."

However, some of the environmental activists, as noted in the 'The Environmental Activities Hand Book' authored by Gayatri Singh, Kerban Ankleswaria and Colins Gonsalves, that the Judges are carried away by the money spent on projects and that mega projects, that harm the environment are not condemned. However, this criticism seems to be baseless since in *Virender Gaur* v. *State of Haryana,* (1995) 2 SCC 577, this Court insisted on the demolition of structure which have been constructed on the lands reserved for common purposes and that this Court did not allow its decision to be frustrated by the actions of a party. This Court followed the said decision in several cases issuing directions and ensuring its enforcement by nothing short of demolition or restoration of status quo ante. The fact that crores of rupees was spent already on development projects did not convince this Court while being in a zeal to jealously safeguarding the environment and in preventing the abuse of the environment by a group of humans or the authorities under the State for that matter.

The set of facts in the present case relates to the preservation of and restoration of *status quo* ante of two tanks, historical in nature being in existence since the time of Srikrishnadevaraya, The Great, 1500 A.D., where the cry of socially spirited citizens calling for judicial remedy was not considered in the right perspective by the Division Bench of the High Court of Andhra Pradesh despite there being overwhelming evidence of the tanks being in existence and were being put to use not only for irrigation purpose but also as lakes which were furthering percolation to improve the ground water lavele, thus serving the needs of the people in and around these tanks. The Division Bench of the High Court, in the impugned order, has given precedence to the economic growth by completely ignoring the importance and primacy attached to the protection of environment and protection of valuable and most cherished fresh water resources.

No doubt, the wishful thinking and the desire of the appellant-forum, that the Tanks should be there, and the old glory of the tanks should be continued, is laudable.

But the ground realities are otherwise. We have already noticed the ground realities as pointed out by the Government of Andhra Pradesh, TUDA and TTD in their reply to the Civil appeals by furnishing details, datas and particulars. Now a days because of the poverty and lack of employment avenues, migration of people from rural areas to urban areas is a common phenomenon. Because of the limited infrastructure of the towns, the towns are becoming slums. We, therefore, cannot countenance the submissions made by the appellant in regard to the complete restoration and revival of two tanks in the peculiar facts and circumstances of this case. We cannot, at the same time, prevent the Government from proceeding with the proper development of Tirupathi town. The two Government Orders which are impugned have been issued long before and pursuant to the issuance of the Government Orders, several other developments have taken place.

Constructions and improvements have been made in a vast measure. Because of spending crores and crores of rupees by various authorities, the only option now left to the appellant and the respondents is to see that the report submitted by the Expert Committee is implemented in its letter and spirit and all the respondents shall cooperate in giving effect to the Committee's report. It is true that the tank is a communal property and the State authorities are trustees to hold and manage such properties for the benefits of the community and they cannot be allowed to commit any act or omission which will infringe the right of the Community and alienate the property to any other person or body.

Taking into account all these principles of law, and after considering the competing claims of environment and the need for housing, this Court holds the following as per the facts of this case.

The Respondents have claimed that the valuable right to shelter will be violated if the impugned Government Orders are revoked. On the facts of the present case, it seems that the respondents intend to build residential blocks of flat for High and Middle income families, institutions as well as infrastructure for the TTDS. If the proposed constructions are not carried on, it seems unlikely that anyone will be left homeless or without their basic need for shelter. Therefore, one feels that the right to shelter does not seem to be so pressing under the present circumstances so as to outweigh all environmental considerations.

Another plea repeatedly taken by the respondents correspond to the money already spent on developing the land. However, the decision of this case cannot be based solely upon the investments committed by any party. Since, otherwise, it would seem that once any party makes certain investment in a project, it would be a fait accompli and this Court will not have any option but to deem it legal.

Therefore, under the present circumstances, the Court should do the most it can to safeguard the two tanks in question. However, due to the persistent developmental activities over a long time, much of the natural resources of the lakes has been lost, and considered irreparable. This, though regrettable, is beyond the power of this court to rectify.

One particular feature of this case was the competing nature of claims by both the parties on the present State of the two tanks and the feasibility of their revival. We thought that it would be best, therefore, if we place reliance on the findings of the expert committee appointed by us which has considered the factual situation and the feasibility of revival of the two tanks. Thus in pursuance of a study of that committee, this Court passes the following orders.

The appeals are disposed of with the following directions:

With regard to Peruru tank:

(i) No further constructions to be made.

(ii) The supply channel of Bodeddula Vanka needs to be cleared and revitalized. A small check dam at Malapali to be removed to ensure the free flow and supply to the tank.

(iii) Percolation tank to be constructed and artificial recharge to be done to ensure the revival of the tank, keeping in mind its advantage at being situated at the foot hills.

(iv) The area allotted by Mandal Revenue Office for construction of the tank to be increased to a minimum of 50 acres. Percolation tank with sufficient number of recharge shafts to be developed to recharge the unsaturated horizons up to 20 m. The design of the shafts etc., to be prepared in consultation with the CGWB. The proposed percolation tank to be suitably located along the bund keeping in view the inlets, irrigation sluices and surplus water.

(v) Feasibility and cost estimation for the revival of the old feeder channel for Swarnamukhi River should be carried and a report to be submitted to the Court.

(vi) Each house already constructed by the TTD must provide for roof top rain water harvesting. Abstraction from ground water to be completely banned. No borewell/tubewell for any purpose to be allowed in the area.

(vii) Piezometers to be set up at selected locations, in consultation with the CGWB to observe the impact of rain water harvesting in the area on ground water regime.

With regard to Avilala tank:

(i) No further construction to be allowed in the area.

(ii) Each house already constructed by the APHB/TUDA must provide structure for roof top rain water harvesting. All the storm water in the already built colonies to be recharged to ground water. Structures for such purposes to be designed in consultation with the CGWB.

(iii) No borewell/tubewell for any purpose to be allowed in the area.

(iv) An area of 40 acres presently reserved for the Government should not be developed in any way that may lead to concretization of the ground surface. Recharge structures to be constructed for rainwater harvesting.

(v) Piezometers to be set up at selected locations, in consultation with the CGWB to observe the impact of rain water harvesting in the area on ground water regime.

We place on record our deep appreciation for the valuable assistance rendered by all the counsel appearing in this case which made our job easier.

The appeals are disposed of accordingly no costs.

Director-General, Directorate General of Doordarshan v. A. Patwardhan

AIR 2006 SC 3346: (2006) 8 SCC 433
Appeal (Civil) 613 of 2005
Decided on 25-08-2006

Coram: **Hon'ble Mr. Justice Lokeshwar Singh Panta**
Hon'ble Dr. Justice AR. Lakshmanan

Judgment by: **Hon'ble Dr. Justice AR. Lakshmanan**

FACTS: The respondent made a film which was submitted to Doordarshan for telecast. But Doordarshan refused to telecast the film. On a writ petition filed before the High Court, the Court directed Doordarshan to telecast the film. Aggrieved by the order of the High Court Doordarshan preferred an appeal before the Supreme Court.

ISSUE: Restriction on the freedom of speech and expression.

HELD: Doordarshan being a State controlled agency funded by public funds could not have denied access to screen the respondent's documentary except on specified valid grounds. Doordarshan was directed to exhibit the entire film of the respondent.

JUDGMENT

Dr. AR. Lakshmanan, J.

The appellant in the present matter is Doordarshan who have decided not to telecast the documentary film made by the respondent titled "Father, son and Holy War". The respondent is a filmmaker. The respondent No. 1 in 1995 submitted his documentary film, "Father, son and Holy War", to the appellant for telecast on National network Doordarshan. Respondent No. 1 was to provide a U-matic Certificate for the same to be aired by Doordarshan.

The documentary film was in two parts, the film dealt with social realities and issues such as patriarchy, violence, fundamentalism, suppression of women etc. Part-I was given 'U' Certificate and Part-II was given 'A' Certificate by the Censor Board.

A few lines about the film and the producer: – Father, Son and Holy War is the third part of a trilogy of documentary films against communal violence that the author made from the mid 1980's to the mid 1990's. His two earlier films In Memory of Friends (1990) (on building communal peace in strife torn Punjab) and Ram Ke Naam/In the Name of God (1992) (on the Ayodhya crisis) looked at the question of class and caste. Both films won National Awards but both were rejected by Doordarshan on the grounds that they would create law and order problems. In the end, the author won the cases in the High Court and the films were finally telecast by Doordarshan. No law and order problems resulted and the telecasts were well received.

Father, Son and Holy War (1995) was also shot during this period. It looks at the question of gender along with the issue of religious violence. What triggered this way of looking was the incident of Sati in Deorala and that fact that thousands of young men were celebrating the death of Roop Kanwar. This led the author to examine the male psyche behind violence and the idea that women were property.It is common knowledge that very often sexual violence against women accompanies communal riots. This may be because the "enemy's" women are seen as his property and so, worthy of abduction or destruction.

The first part of Father, Son and Holy War ("Trial by Fire") looks at the problems faced by Hindu and Muslim women within their own religions. Part 2 (Hero Pharmacy) examines the construction of the values of "manhood". As the film proceeds we become privy to the inner psyche of men and begin to learn how men are socialized into believing that violence is desirable. The film looks at the rhetoric of street sellers of aphrodisiac who create feelings of male insecurity and impotence in their audience and then offer their cheap medicine as a cure. It then looks at the rhetoric of communal politicians (both Hindus and Muslims) and see that they too are appealing largely to their male audiences, they too are taunting them for their impotence, but the medicine they offer for the creation of "real men" is hatred against the other community.

On 14.8.1996, the appellant issued a circular which stated that Doordarshan will not telecast any 'A' certified adult or U/A feature film on it. On 28.2.1997, the respondent handed over a copy of the U-matic Certificate of the documentary film to the appellant. However, Doordarshan still refused to telecast the documentary film.

On 22.9.1998, the respondent No. 1, filed a writ petition before the Bombay High Court against the refusal of Doordarshan to telecast the documentary film, which was disposed off by the Division Bench by directing Doordarshan to take a decision on the application of respondent No. 1 within a period of six weeks.

A selection Committee was constituted on 10.8.1998 by the appellant to preview the documentary film produced by respondent No. 1. The selection Committee observed that, "The documentary entitled 'Father, Son & Holy War' depicts the rise of Hindu fundamentalism and male chauvinism without giving any solution how it could be checked. The violence and hatred which is depicted in the whole documentary will have an adverse effect on the minds of the viewers". This decision of the Selection Committee was communicated to the respondents on 20.8.1998.

Against this the respondent No. 1 approached Bombay High Court. A Division Bench of the Bombay High Court allowed the writ and directed the appellant to telecast the respondent No. 1 documentary film "Father, son and the Holy War" within a period of six weeks in the evening slot. This decision by the High Court was challenged by the appellant by way of a Special Leave Petition in this Court. This Court observed that, the Committee which was constituted to consider the proposal of the respondent was not validly constituted as required under the guidelines of Doordarshan and therefore the decision taken by the Committee was without jurisdiction. This court went ahead to order on 12.12.2001 the constitution of a new Committee in accordance with para 5(ii) of the Guidelines of Doordarshan to consider the proposal of the respondent within three months of the constitution of such Committee.

A Committee was duly constituted and on 6.8.2002, the committee viewed the documentary film and was of the opinion that, "the film has a secular message relevant to our times and our society however, the film contains scenes and speeches, which can influence negative passions and the committee would like a larger committee with representatives of religion and politics also to see the film and form an opinion before it is open to public viewing."

A larger committee was constituted and viewed the documentary film. The said committee on 5.6.2003 recommended the screening of this documentary film on Doordarshan while observing that, "it may alienate sections of Indian society and screening may lead to reactions by organized groups."

On 11.7.2003, the Prasar Bharati Board pre-viewed the documentary film and was of the opinion that the documentary film contained scenes which could promote violence, its production quality was unsatisfactory and its telecast would be violative of the policy of the Doordarshan of not screening "A" certified movies. This decision of Doordarshan was communicated to the respondent No. 1 on 18.7.2003.

A contempt petition was filed by respondent No. 1 alleging the disobedience of the order of the High Court dated 12.12.2001. The High Court disposed off the petition by holding that the respondent was aggrieved of the decision of Prasar Bharati Board, and it was open to him to challenge the same before an appropriate forum.

The respondent filed a writ petition in the Bombay High Court and directed Doordarshan to exhibit the documentary film of the respondent No. 1, "Father, son and Holy War" on channel I or II within 12 weeks from the date of the judgment on a convenient day and time as fixed by Doordarshan. It is against this decision of the High Court of Bombay the Doordarshan has come on appeal to this Court.

We heard Mr. Rajeev Sharma, learned counsel appearing for the appellants and Mr. Prashant Bhushan, learned counsel appearing for the respondent. We have viewed the screening of the documentary film titled "Father, son and the Holy War" which is the subject-matter of the present case before us. We have also carefully perused all the documents presented by both the parties before us.

Mr. Rajeev Sharma, learned counsel appearing for the Doordarshan submitted that the decision not to telecast the film of the respondent is based on valid and germane considerations and no film maker can claim that he has a vested right that a film made by him must be telecast on Doordarshan. He submitted that as a matter of policy the Doordarshan do not telecast films which are certified as "A" or "UA". Admittedly Part one of the film in question has been certified as "U" and Part two as "A". The policy of Doordarshan of not telecasting "A" or "UA" films has not been challenged by the respondent here. Therefore, the Doordarshan cannot be directed to telecast the film contrary to its policy. Learned counsel also submitted that the telecast of the film is likely to give rise to communal violence and riots and that Doordarshan has reached the remote corners of the country. It has a wide audience which mainly consists of illiterate and average persons who will be largely affected due to screening of the film.

Mr. Prashant Bhushan, learned counsel appearing on behalf of the respondent submitted that the refusal by Prasar bharti to telecast the film is a clear violation of the respondent's fundamental right under Article 19(1)(a) of the Constitution. He urged that the film carries a strong message for unity and secular India and there is no justification to prevent its telecast on Doordarshan. It is submitted that the Doordarshan has a policy of telecasting award winning films and documentaries and the action of the Doordarshan in refusing to screen the film contrary to the said policy is totally unfair, unjust and arbitrary. Learned counsel further submitted that the Censor Board has approved the film and the guidelines of Doordarshan in telecasting the film cannot be substantially different from the guidelines laid down under the Cinematographic Act, 1952. In any event, according to the learned counsel unless the said guidelines are read down they would be liable to be strucked down as grossly violating the fundamental rights guaranteed by Article 19(1)(a) of the Constitution.

In view of the rival submissions, the following substantial questions of law arise for adjudication by this Court.

(a) Whether any film producer has a right to insist that his film must be shown on Doordarshan?

(b) Whether the High Court was justified in directing the screening of the film certified as U/A. Notwithstanding the fact as a matter of policy, Doordarshan does not telecast adult film?

(c) Whether the policy of Doordarshan of not telecasting adult movies can be said to be violative of Article 19(1)(a) of the Constitution of India as has been held by the High Court?

(d) Whether or not it is open to the High Court to substitute its opinion for that of the competent authority as to whether a film is fit for being telecast on a public medium such as Doordarshan?

In the instant case, the documentary of the respondent has been cleared by the Central Board for Film Certification, the Film Certification Board, which is a body of experts was obviously not of the view that the film promotes communal violence, otherwise, the film would not have been certified by the Board for public exhibition. In view of this background, we are unable to appreciate the view taken by the Prasarbharti Board.

The film of the respondent no doubt deals with the communal violence. At the same time, we also listen to a stirring speech made by a woman activist on a street who exhorts people to "remember their neighbours" during communal riots. The film contains a narrative of a muslim woman, a social worker who has been raped by the communal murderers of her husband and that of a Hindu mill worker whose children were killed in the bomb blast which occurred in the aftermath of the communal riots. The attempt of the film maker is to portray the miseries of the innocent victims of the communal riots. These sequences convey an obvious message of communal harmony as an ordinary muslim slum dweller is seen in the closing sequences of the film re-building the destroyed home of his Hindu neighbour. The message of the filmmaker cannot be gathered by viewing only certain portions of the film in isolation but one has to view it as a whole. There are scenes of violence, social injustices but the film by no stretch of imagination can be said to subscribe to the same. They are meant to convey that such social evils are evil. There cannot be any apprehension that it is likely to affect public order or it is likely to incite commission of an offence. We are shocked at the observation of the Prasar Bharati Board that the film is not suitable due to unsatisfactory production quality and that the film has nothing specific to convey in public interest. The documentary was given two awards in 42nd National Film Festival of 1995 conducted by the Ministry of Information and Broadcasting, Government of India as Best Investigative Film and Best film on social issues. It is, therefore, highly irrational and incorrect to say that the documentary which was selected as best investigative film and best film on social issues promote violence and its production quality was unsatisfactory and that the film has no specific message to convey. The documentary has won several awards in the International film festivals. However, the Prasar Bharati Board strangely comments that the film had nothing specific to convey in public interest. This view of the Prasar Bharati is in contrast with the opinion expressed by the two committees constituted by the appellants. The first committee held that the film had a secular message relevant to our times and our society and it was a critique of the current concept of masculinity and the violence it legitimises. The second committee said that it was a very good film and must be shown. Ordinarily the decision of the selection committee in all cases shall be final as per para 5(viii) of the guidelines laid down by the Ministry of Information and Broadcasting for telecasting films. However, it appears that the appellants were bent upon rejecting the film and the decision of the committee was overruled by the Prasar Bharati Board under the pretext that the guidelines prohibit Doordarshan from exhibiting any film which is granted 'A' certificate and since part II *i.e.,* Hero Pharmacy has been granted 'A' certificate telecast of the said film is not permitted under the guidelines framed by the Ministry of Information and Broadcasting.

In the instant case, the guidelines relied upon by the Doordarshan are not even framed under the Cinematograph Act but they are merely internal guidelines for the guidance of the officials of the Doordarshan. Therefore, in our view, it would not be proper to deny telecast of an award winning documentary merely on the ground that part II of the said documentary is certified as "A" by the Censor Board. In our view, a documentary cannot be denied exhibition on Doordarshan simply on account of its "A" certification or "UA" certification. Mr. Rajeev Sharma made an attempt to object to certain scenes in the documentary especially one scene where a person is seen selling aphrodisciacs on the road and while doing so is making certain remarks on the sexuality of males.

As indicated in paragraphs supra, a film must be judged from an average, healthy and common sense point of view. If the said yardstick is applied and the film is judged in its entirety and keeping in view the manner in which the filmmaker has handled the theme, it is impossible to agree that those scenes are offended by vulgarity and obscenity. It is interesting to note that these objections were not even raised by any of the committees constituted for the purpose of assessing the film.

OBSERVATIONS:

One of the most controversial issues is balancing the need to protect society against the potential harm that may flow from obscene material, and the need to ensure respect for freedom of expression and to preserve a free flow of information and idea. The Constitution guarantees freedom of expression but in Article 19(2) it also makes it clear that the State may impose reasonable restriction in the interest of public decency and morality.

The crucial question therefore, is, 'what is obscenity?'

The law relating to obscenity is laid down in section 292 of the Indian Penal Code, which came about, by Act 36 of 1969.

Under the present section 292 and section 293 of the Indian Penal Code, there is a danger of publication meant for public good or for *bona fide* purpose of science, literature, art or any other branch of learning being declared as obscene literature as there is no specific provision in the act for exempting them from operations of those sections.

The present provision is so vague that it becomes difficult to apply it. The purposeful omission of the definition of obscenity has led to attack of section 292 of the Indian penal Code as being too vague to qualify as a penal provision. It is quite unclear what the provisions mean. This unacceptably large 'grey area', common in laws restricting sexual material, would appear to result not from a lack of capacity or effort on the part of drafters or legislators.

The Indian Penal Code on obscenity grew out of the English Law, which made court the guardian of public morals. It is important that where bodies exercise discretion, which may interfere in the enjoyment of constitutional rights, that discretion must be subject to adequate law. The effect of provisions granting broad discretionary regulatory powers is unforeseeable and they are open to arbitrary abuse.

In *Samaresh Bose* v. *Amal Mitra,* (1985) 4 SCC 284 it was observed by this Court: "The concept of obscenity is moulded to a very great extent by the social outlook of the people who are generally expected to read the book. It is beyond dispute that the concept of obscenity usually differs from country to country depending on the standards of morality of contemporary society in different countries. In our opinion, in judging the question of obscenity, the Judge in the first place should try to place himself in the position of the author and from the viewpoint of the author.

The judge should thereafter place himself in the position of a reader of every age group in whose hands the book is likely to fall and should try to appreciate what kind of possible influence the book is likely to have in the minds of the readers.

The judge should thereafter apply his judicial mind dispassionately to decide whether the book in question can be said to be obscene within the meaning of section 292, IPC by an objective assessment of the book as a whole and also of the passages complained of as obscene separately."

This is one of the few liberal judgments the courts have given. The point to worry about is the power given to the judge to decide what he/she thinks is obscene. This essentially deposits on the Supreme Court of India, the responsibility to define obscenity and classify matters coming on media as obscene or otherwise. This Court has time and again adopted the test of obscenity laid down by Cockburn CJ. The test of obscenity is, 'whether the tendency of the matter charged as obscenity is to deprave and corrupt those whose minds are open to such immoral influences, and in whose hands a publication in media of this sort may fall.'

Interestingly, this test of obscenity, which was laid down in the *Hicklin* case in 1869, is the only test in India to determine obscenity.

The Encyclopedia definition of obscenity states, 'By English law it is an indictable misdemeanor to show an obscene exhibition or to publish any obscene matter, whether it be writing or by pictures, effigy or otherwise.' The precise meaning of "obscene" is, however, decidedly ambiguous. It has been defined as something offensive to modesty or decency, or expressing or suggesting unchaste or lustful ideas or being impure, indecent or lewd".

In the United States, obscene material is any material or performance, if: the average person applying contemporary community standards would find that the subject-matter taken as a whole appeals to the prurient interest; the subject-matter depicts or describes in a patently offensive way, sexual conduct of a type described in this section; and the subject matter, taken as a whole, lacks serious literary, artistic, political, educational or scientific value.

Therefore, one can observe that, the basic guidelines for the tier of fact must be:

(a) whether "the average person, applying contemporary community standards" would find that the work, taken as a whole, appeals to the prurient interest.;

(b) whether the work depicts or describes, in a patently offensive way, sexual conduct specifically defined by the applicable State law; and

(c) whether the work, taken as a whole, lacks serious literary, artistic political, or scientific value.

The Constitution of India guarantees everyone the right to freedom of expression. India is also a party to the International Covenant on Civil and Political Rights and therefore bound to respect the right to freedom of expression guaranteed by Article 19 thereof, which states:

1. Everyone shall have the right to hold opinions without interference.
2. Everyone shall have the right to freedom of expression; this right shall include freedom to seek, receive and impart information and ideas of all kinds regardless of frontiers, either orally, in writing or in print, in form of art, or through any other media of his choice.

This right guaranteed by the Indian constitution is subject to various restrictions. Like, respect of the rights or reputation of others; protection of national security or of public order, or of public health or morals etc.

The catchword here is 'reasonable restriction' which corresponds to the societal norms of decency. In the present matter, the documentary film Father, Son and Holy War depicts social vices that are eating into the very foundation of our Constitutional. Communal riots, caste and class issues and violence against women are issues that require every citizen's attention for a feasible solution. Only the citizens especially the youth of our Nation who are correctly informed can arrive at a correct solution. This documentary film in our considered opinion showcases a real picture of crime and violence against women and members of various religious groups perpetrated by politically motivated leaders for political, social and personal gains.

This film so far as our opinion goes does not violate any Constitutional provision nor will create any law and order problems as the Doordarshan fears. This movie falls well within the limits prescribed by our Constitution and does not appeal to the prurient interests in an average person, applying contemporary community standards while taking the work as a whole, the work is not patently offensive and does not proceed to deprave and corrupt any average Indian citizen's mind.

In addition we are emphasizing here on the fact that many Committees have screened this documentary film including a committee set up by the appellants themselves involving media experts, representatives of various religions and politics, who have opined that, "It is a very good film and must be shown. It may alienate sections of Indian society and screening may lead to reactions by organized groups. In the unanimous view of the committee that protest is an important part of Indian democracy and was a part of its fight for independence, which is also a compelling reason for the film to be shown. Keeping these in mind the committee recommends that the screening of the film be preceded by a discussion in which alternative views are given by persons with different views." As we see, only Doordarshan has an opposition with airing the documentary film stating policy related difficulties. To this we are of the view that, since the Central Board of Film Certification has already cleared the documentary film in question by award of U/A certificate, the policy of

Doordarshan of non-telecast of 'A' certified films will not stand on the way of this film being aired. A blanket ban as this one will be in violation of Article 19(2) of the Constitution which guarantees right of a citizen to express himself/ herself. The Supreme Court has clarified on this regard way back in 1970, in the case of *K.A. Abbas* v. *The Union of India,* (1970) 2 SCC 780 where this Court held that, "Sex and obscenity are not always synonymous and it is wrong to classify sex as essentially obscene or even indecent or immoral." In yet another case of *Ramesh* v. *Union of India,* (1988) 1 SCC 668 this court has observed that, "that the effect of the words must be judged from the standards of reasonable, strong minded, firm and courageous men, and not those of weak and vacillating minds, nor of those who scent danger in every hostile point of view. This, in our opinion, is the correct approach in judging the effect of exhibition of a film or of reading a book. It is the standard of ordinary reasonable man or as they say in English law "the man on the top of Claapham omnibus."

Hence, in our view, the correct approach to be taken here is to look at the documentary film as a whole and not in bits, as any message that is purported to be conveyed by way of a film cannot be conveyed just by watching certain bits of the film. In the present situation the documentary film is seeking to portray certain evils prevalent in our society and is not seeking to cater to the prurient interests in any person.

Therefore, we have no hesitation in saying that this documentary film if judged in its entirety has a theme and message to convey and the view taken by the appellants that the film is not suitable for telecast is erroneous.

In this regard, the guidelines issued by the Central Government to evaluate films gain importance and can be referred to. Clause 3 of the Guidelines reads as follows:

> "Clause 3: The Board of Film Certification shall also ensure that the film:
>
> (i) is judged in its entirety from the point of the overall impact; and
>
> (ii) is examined in the light of the period depicted in the film and the contemporary standards of the country and the people to which the film relates, provided that the film does not deprave the morality of the audience."

It was held in *Bobby Art International* v. *Om Pal Singh Hoon,* (1996) 4 SCC 1, *K.A. Abbas* (*Supra*) that a film was required to be viewed as a whole, and in the context of the message that the filmmaker desired to communicate. In this film too, scenes must be seen in the context of the message of exploitation of women through insecurities created in men and the film must be evaluated in its entirety.

In *LIC of India* v. *Prof. Manubhai D. Shah* with *UOI* v. *Cinemart Foundation,* (1992) 3 SCC 637, it was held that merely because a film was critical of the State Government, DD could not deny selection and publication of the film. This film was an award winning film about the Bhopal Gas Tragedy. Likewise, in *S. Rangarajan* v. *P. Jagjivan Ram,* (1989) 2 SCC 574, it has been observed that Censors should not have an orthodox or conservative outlook, but must be responsive to change and must go with the current climate. The State cannot prevent open discussion, however hateful to its policies. This was about a film that criticized the existing reservation policy and proposed an alternative system based on economic deprivation.

We also are aware that the documentary film made by respondent No. 1 has won many National and International awards. The documentary film won National Awards in two categories *viz.*, "Best Investigative Film" and "Best Film on Social Issues" in the 42nd National Film Festival 1995, conducted by the Ministry of Information and Broadcasting. The documentary film also won Special Jury Award in Israel, Japan and Canada. Keeping these facts in view we find it absurd that a documentary film that has won the National award is facing problems for it being screened on the National Television.

CONCLUSION:

In our opinion, the respondent has a right to convey his perception on the oppression of women, flawed understanding of manhood and evils of communal violence through the documentary film produced by him. As already noticed, this film has won awards for best investigative film and best film on social issues at the national level. The documentary film has won several awards at the international level as well. The freedom of expression, which is legitimate and constitutionally protected, cannot be held to ransom on a mere fall of a hat.

The film in its entirety has a serious message to convey and is relevant in the present context. Doordarshan being a State controlled agency funded by public funds could not have denied access to screen the respondent's documentary except on specified valid grounds.

The refusal of the appellants to telecast the film in the current case in the face of unanimous recommendations by their own Committees set up in accordance to the direction of this Court is an issue to be addressed apart. The High Court of Bombay has not substituted its discretion for that of the authorities. On the contrary, the High Court has ruled that when the decision making process has itself resulted in the recommendations to telecast; it is not open to the Doordarshan to find other means just to circumvent this recommendation. The High Court has only corrected the failure of Doordarshan to follow through with their own decision making process on the pretext of a Circular which being non-statutory cannot be used to limit right of expression. Besides the Circular, in terms, applies only to feature films and not to documentaries. Before ruling thus, the High Court viewed the film for itself which is a process followed innumerable times before even by this Court in cases concerning the official media to satisfy itself the recommendations of the Expert Committee was not patently absurd. Thus, it is not a case where the High Court has substituted its judgment for that of the decision-making authority but one where the decision made by due process has been upheld by the High Court. In our view, the Doordarshan being a National Channel controls airwaves, which are public property. The right of the people to be informed calls for channelizing and streamlining Doordarshan's control over the national telecast media vehicle.

We also are of the view that, Doordarshan all through the present matter has been displaying a sad reluctance in telecasting this film, which was made almost ten years ago. We can trace a history of Doordarshan not telecasting many films in spite of them being award winning films at the national and international level, this can be seen in the case of films like "In Memory of Friends", "Ram ke Naam" etc. In addition an interesting observation that can be arrived is that Doordarshan has been finding flimsy excuses time and again as clear from the facts in not telecasting the documentary film in question every time the film was sought to be aired either at the instance of the respondent or due to the orders of the court. This in our view in highly irrational and is blatant violation of the right guaranteed under Article 19(1)(a) of the Constitution. This behavior of Doordarshan would justify us in stating that Doordarshan is being dictated by rules of malafides and arbitrariness in taking decisions with regard to In light of the above, the instant appeal at the instance of Doordarshan is devoid of any merits. Thus, the impugned judgment deserves to be upheld and sustained by this Court.

In the result, the appeal is dismissed and the orders passed by the learned Judges of the Division Bench are affirmed. However, there will be no order as to costs.

The appellant-Doordarshan is directed to exhibit the entire documentary film of the respondent Father, Son and Holy War on Channel No. 1 or 2 within 8 weeks from today on such convenient date and time as may be fixed by Doordarshan.

Kansing Kalusing Thakore
v.
Rabari Maganbhai Vashrambhai

2006 AIR SCW 6206: (2006) 12 SCALE 414
Civil Appeal No. 5089 of 2006
(Arising out of SLP (C) Nos. 124-125/2006)
Decided on 20-11-2006

Coram: **Hon'ble Mr. Justice Altamas Kabir**
Hon'ble Dr. Justice AR. Lakshmanan

Judgment by: **Hon'ble Dr. Justice AR. Lakshmanan**

FACTS: The appellants' lands were acquired by the State Government for establishing an agricultural university. As per the government policy, lands of such persons affected by the take

over, allotment and/or reservation of separate land had been made by the competent authority in the adjacent villages. Three villagers had filed a petition before the High Court contending that lands allocated was reserved for grazing of cattle *i.e., Gauchar* lands the allotment/settlement of which would affect the breeding of cattle in the village. Such lands also serve as the water needs of the village. The High Court arrived at a conclusion that there was hardly any material to indicate that the land in question was pasture land and that such land was in fact reserved for the rehabilitation of persons who were adversely affected by the acquisition of their lands for the establishment of the agricultural university. Aggrieved thereby, the appellants preferred apppeal before the Supreme Court by way of special leave.

ISSUE: Whether the High Court failed to appreciate that the process for rehabilitation was under a policy-decision of the Government of Gujarat and the lands being allotted to the appellants as an administrative act, which allotments was in lieu of the lands of the appellants acquired by the Government decades earlier, the judicial interference in the decision making process and policy of the Government not warranted in the facts of the case.

HELD: The writ petition filed by the respondents is an abuse of the process of the Court. By this PIL the respondents sought to ventilate/redress their personal grievances inasmuch as they are able to holding clout in their village and were enjoying illegal possession in several lands. The appellants herein were deliberately not made parties to the writ petition allegedly filed in public interest. It is a matter of record that the writ petitioners are the people who encroached upon the land sought to be granted to the appellants herein and hence having no legal right to continue their illegal occupancy, devised means to approach the High Court in alleged public interest. The maintainability of the PIL which was in issue was unfortunately not decided by the High Court. The High Court ought to have decided the maintainability of the PIL maintained at the instance of the encroachers and land grabbers and rejected the writ petitions at the threshold. Only a person acting *bona fide* and having sufficient interest in the proceeding of PIL will alone have *locus standi* and can approach the Court to wipe out the tears of the poor and needy suffering from violation of their fundamental rights but not a person for personal gain or private profit or political or any oblique consideration.

JUDGMENT

Dr. AR. Lakshmanan, J.

1. Leave granted.

2. This is a Public Interest Litigation (in short 'PIL') by the villagers of Rasana Nana in Gujarat. The appellants 1-6, who are the respondents in the public interest litigations before the High Court, are the appellants in these appeals who also belong to the same village.

3. In this PIL, the following question of law of great public importance arise for consideration of this Court which is, "whether the High Court failed to appreciate that the process for rehabilitation was under a policy decision of the Government of Gujarat and the lands being allotted to the appellants as an administrative act, which allotments was in lieu of the lands of the appellants acquired by the Government decades earlier, the judicial interference in the decision making process and policy of the Government not warranted in the facts of the case."

4. The appellants' lands were acquired by the State Government in the year 1954. This was in terms of section 8 of the Bombay Merged Territory and Areas (Jagir Abolition Act) of 1953. The reason for the acquirement of the lands of the appellants by the State Government was for the establishment of the Dantiwada Agricultural University. As per the Government Policy, lands of such persons affected by the take over, allotment and/or reservation of separate land had been made by the competent authority in the adjacent villages, including village Rasana Nana. The appellants herein are challenging only that part of the impugned order which affects their absolute right over the land given to them in lieu of their land which was surrendered by them for the purpose of establishment of the Agricultural University.

5. Land in survey Nos. 125 and 126 in village Rasana Nana though earmarked for rehabilitation was however not handed over to the persons affected by the take over of the lands for the purpose of establishment of the University. Several correspondences were made to the competent authority but for one reason or another, the land in the said survey Nos. could not be handed over. In the year 2003, some of the appellants approached the High Court through 3 separate applications contending that although most of the persons affected had been given lands as per Government allotment policy dated 18.07.1973 and 11.02.1997 the appellants had been subjected to inequitable treatment. Three orders on different dates, *i.e.*, on 20.09.2003, 14.10.2003 and 26.04.2004 were passed in the aforesaid 3 applications by the High Court. Directions were given to the competent authorities to consider and examine the case of each appellant and to take appropriate decision thereafter in terms of the policy framed by the State Government.

6. On 09.08.2004, the Deputy Collector passed 3 separate orders. He verified individual cases and took a final decision after consultation with the Collector whereby the reserved lands at survey Nos. 125 and 126 of village Rasana Nana were directed to be granted over to the appellants who also paid the occupancy price subsequently. It is stated that the order of the Deputy Collector was in furtherance of the policy decision of the State and was part of an Administrative Act. The appellants' claims were based upon the principles of legitimate expectation and the reliefs claimed by them were equitable in nature.

7. In October, 2004, five persons of the said village filed a petition before the High Court purportedly under public interest. They claimed themselves to be "public spirited individuals". In this petition, the challenge was to the 3 orders passed by the Deputy Collector allotting land from survey Nos. 125 and 126 of Village Rasana Nana and no challenge was made to the other allotments of the said village. It was contended that the lands allocated by this order was reserved for grazing of cattle *i.e.,* Gauche lands the allotment/settlement of which would affect the breeding of cattle in the village, such lands also serve as the water needs of the village. The appellants were deliberately not made parties in the writ petitions filed allegedly in public interest. According to the appellants, the petitioners in the alleged PIL are people holding clout in the village Rasana Nana and who were all along enjoying illegal possession of the lands contained in survey Nos. 125 and 126.

8. In December, 2004, an application was filed by the present appellants before the High Court and impleaded as respondents in the alleged PIL. This application was allowed by the High Court. The Sarpanch of the village filed an affidavit-in-reply opposing the relief prayed for in the writ petition. It was stated that the lands in survey Nos. 125 and 126 were deemed to be Government lands w.e.f. 01.08.1954 and were never Gauchar lands or vested in the Panchayat body. The appellants herein also filed an affidavit in reply contending that:

(a) There had been no violation of legal rights so as to maintain a petition under Article 226 of the Constitution of India.

(b) The petitioners in the alleged PIL had made false statements in as much as they were headstrong persons of the village having political clout.

(c) The petitioners in the PIL had suppressed material facts including resolutions taken by Panchayat Authority.

(d) The petitioners in the PIL had acted with *mala fide* intentions by not making necessary and appropriate parties.

9. By virtue of the impugned order dated 04.08.2005, the High Court arrived at a conclusion that there was hardly any material to indicate that the land in question was pasture land and that such land was in fact reserved for the rehabilitation of persons who were adversely affected by the acquisition of their lands for the establishment of the agricultural university and that the appellants herein had an existing right in terms of the Government policy and hence entitled to equitable relief. The High Court did not find any infirmity in the order of the Deputy Collector dated 09.08.2004. However, an argument was advanced on behalf of the public interest litigants contending that the grantees *i.e.,* the appellants herein would not use the land for agricultural purposes and would sell it away. The High Court imposed the following conditions:

I. The respondent Nos. 4 to 53 will not convert the land into N.A. But they will use the land only for agricultural purpose.

II. The respondent Nos. 4 to 53 shall not transfer the land either by sale or in any other manner directly or indirectly by executing power of attorney, to any other party and even if such power-of-attorney is already given in favour of the third party, the concerned respondents shall revoke the same before receiving the possession.

The aforesaid conditions imposed by the High Court will remain in force for a period of 15 years from the date of possession of the land.

10. The Deputy Collector, Palanpur was directed to see that these respondents give undertaking in writing to comply with the aforesaid conditions imposed by the High Court. Unless such undertaking is given, the possession shall not be granted to such respondents. The Deputy Collector was further directed to ensure before giving possession of land that no need of Power-of-Attorney to be executed by any of the respondents in favour of any other party. If it is found to be so, he shall forthwith call upon the said respondent to revoke it and render it ineffective. He is further directed that unless there is strict compliance of the aforesaid terms and conditions by the said respondents, he shall not put them into possession of the land in question.

11. The High Court, thereafter, directed the Deputy Collector to give possession to the appellants only after taking written undertakings of compliance of the aforesaid conditions. It is this portion of the order which the appellants have challenged. The appellants preferred a revision petition before the High Court which, on 11.10.2005, was also dismissed. Aggrieved by the orders passed by the High Court, the appellants have preferred the above civil appeals. We heard Mr. U.U. Lalit, learned senior counsel for the appellants and Ms. Hemantika Wahi, Mr. Rajiv Mehta and Mr. Gaurav Agarwal assisted by Mr. Siddhartha Chowdhury, learned Counsel for the respective respondents.

12. We have perused the resolution passed by the Government of Gujarat dated 18.07.1973, 11.02.1997 and the PIL filed by the respondents herein and the counter affidavit and reply filed by the respective parties and also the various orders passed by the High Court of Gujarat including the judgment in appeal.

13. Mr. U.U. Lalit, learned senior counsel took us through the relevant pleadings and also the judgments and other records. He contended that the High Court was not correct in its approach of imposing further conditions once it was evident that the lands to be allotted to the appellants was not pasture lands and reserved for allotment in terms of the Government policy. He further contended that the conditions imposed by the High Court was not within the ambit and scope of the PIL more particularly when the maintainability of the PIL was in issue and not decided. It was further urged that the appellants who were being allotted lands after about 30 years suffered inequity by imposition of such conditions by the High Court inasmuch as many persons (whose lands had also been taken and who were given/allotted lands decades earlier) were also subjected to such restrictions and conditions. He also submitted that the High Court was not correct in imposing a 15 year ban/restriction upon the appellants without any rationale, reason and without any material on record. According to Mr. Lalit, the stringent conditions imposed by the High Court are not sustainable in law inasmuch as the same amounts to judicial interference in purely administrative acts where there is no involvement of any *mala fide* and allocations sought to be made are only in lieu of lands acquired earlier by the Government, in furtherance of a policy decision aiming for rehabilitation. Arguing further, Mr. Lalit submitted that the High Court was also not correct in appreciating the fact that the only restriction in transferring the land was provided for in section 43 of the Bombay Tenancy and Agricultural Land Act and such restricted tenure land can also be transferred after obtaining permission from the Collector under the Bombay Land Revenue Code. In the instant case, by adding these two conditions, entire transfer to the appellants was given a discriminatory treatment. Concluding his argument, Mr. Lalit submitted that the High Court was not right in presuming without any material that the appellants/allotters will sell their land to the builders for constructing commercial complex.

14. Learned Counsel appearing for the State and for the Sarpanch invited our attention to the counter affidavit filed in the writ petition. The Deputy Collector stated that the petitioners in the PIL had personal interest involved and they were actually encroachers and had been removed therefrom and that the process of rehabilitation was a policy decision and that the public interest litigants does not deserve any relief in the writ petitions.

15. The Sarpanch of Village Rasana Nana filed an affidavit in reply opposing the relief prayed for in the writ petition. It was stated that the lands in survey Nos. 125 and 126 were deemed to be Government lands w.e.f. 01.08.1954 and were never gauchar lands and are vested in the Panchayat body. It was further submitted that after receipt of the notice from the High Court, the same was placed before the Panchayat in its meeting dated 16.02.2005 and the Panchayat after detailed deliberation and careful consideration taken the decision by resolving that the Panchayat had no objection in the land being granted to the ousted persons on account of setting up of Agricultural University.

Two panchnamas were made in furtherance of orders made by the Circle Officer and Surveyor of the Survey Department. It is recorded that all encroachments in the lands sought to be granted were unauthorized and possession was recovered. Mr. Gaurav Agarwal, learned Counsel for the contesting respondent, after reiterating the contentions raised in the writ petition, submitted that (a) the lands allocated by order dated 09.08.2004 was not available for any purpose other than to fulfill the water needs for the population of the village (b) lands so allotted were reserved for grazing *i.e.*, gauchar land (pasture) and (c) land allocated *vide* order dated 09.08.2004 would affect cattle breeding.

16. We have given our careful consideration for the rival submissions made by the respective counsel appearing for the respective parties. The writ petition filed by the respondents herein is an abuse of the process of the Court. By this PIL, the respondents sought to ventilate/redress their personal grievances inasmuch as they are able to holding clout in Village Rasana Nana and were enjoying illegal possession in several lands contained under said survey Nos. 125 and 126. The appellants herein were deliberately not made parties to the writ petition allegedly filed in public interest. It is a matter of record that the writ petitioners are the people who encroached upon the land sought to be granted to the appellants herein and hence having no legal right to continue their illegal occupancy, devised means to approach the High Court in alleged public interest. This would be evident from the affidavit of the Deputy Collector filed on 24.03. 2005. The maintainability of the writ petition at the instance of the respondents was specifically raised before the High Court. The maintainability of the PIL which was in issue was unfortunately not decided by the High Court. The High Court, in our opinion, ought to have decided the maintainability of the PIL maintained at the instance of the encroachers and land grabbers and rejected the writ petitions at the threshold. This Court in a catena of decisions held that only a person acting *bona fide* and having sufficient interest in the proceeding of PIL will alone have *locus standi* and can approach the Court to wipe out the tears of the poor and needy suffering from violation of their fundamental rights but not a person for personal gain or private profit or political or any oblique consideration. The High Court ought to have rejected the writ petition at the threshold as observed by this court in MANU/SC/0532/1992 *Janta Dal* v. *H.S. Chaudhary*. In our opinion, the writ petition filed by the respondents was not aimed at redressal of genuine public wrong or public injury but founded on personal vendetta. It is the duty of the High Court not to allow such process to be abused for oblique considerations and the petitions filed by such busy bodies deserves to be thrown out by rejection at the threshold and in appropriate cases with exemplary costs.

17. Even on merits, the respondents have absolutely no case. The records filed in this case clearly go to show that there had been no violation of legal rights so as to maintain a petition under Article 226 of the Constitution of India. The petitioners in the PIL had suppressed material facts including resolutions taken by *bona fide* authority and acted with *mala fide* intentions by not making necessary and appropriate parties. We have already reproduced the conditions/ restrictions imposed by the High Court against the appellants herein. In the instant case, the appellants lands were acquired by the State Government in the year 1954 and as per the government policy, lands of such persons affected by the take over allotment and/or reservation of separate land had been made by the competent authority in the adjacent villages. It is also evident that the lands to be allotted to the appellants was not pasture land and reserved for allotment in terms of government policy and that the appellants were allotted lands after about 30 years. Under such circumstances, the appellants are the ones who have suffered inequity for 30 years. The Court is not justified by the imposition of such stringent conditions and, in particular, imposing a 15 year ban upon the appellants without any rationale, reason and without any material on record. The stringent conditions imposed by the High Court are not sustainable in law and inasmuch as the same amounts to judicial interference in purely administrative acts when the allegation sought to be made are only in lieu of lands acquired earlier by the Government in furtherance of a policy decision aiming for rehabilitation. By imposing such conditions, the High Court has jeopardized the rights of the appellants who have been displaced and suffering for more than 3 decades. The High Court also failed to appreciate the legal provision of section 6 of the T.P. Act when the transfer of the property can be prohibited only by provision of the law and not by the judgment or direction referred in the writ petition under Article 226 of the Constitution of India. The only restriction in transferring the land is contained in section 43 of the Bombay Tenancy and Agricultural Land Act and such restricted tenure land can also be transferred after obtaining permission from the collector under the Bombay Land Revenue Code. In the instant case, by adding these two conditions the entire transfer of the appellants are given discriminatory treatment. The Government of Gujarat, by its resolution dated 18.07.1973, considered the question of granting the land to the affected account holders of these villagers in lieu of the land at the place possible was under consideration of the government and after consideration the government has resolved to adopt the policy to the affected account holders. It is resolved to grant the land to the account holders, whose lands shall be acquired for establishing the Head Quarter of the Agricultural University, including the Main Campus, as per the following norms in cases where the land shall be granted to them without the irrigation facility.

	LAND TO BE ACQUIRED/ LAND TO BE GRANTED	ACQUIRED LAND. IN EXCHANGE.
1.	Upto 4 Acres	Entire land.
2.	4 Acres upto 12 Acres	4 Acres.
3.	12 Acres to 15 Acres	1/3rd portion of the acquired land.
4.	Exceeding 15 Acres.	5 Acres.

If the land, which is likely to get the benefit of irrigation in near future, will be granted to the affected account holders, it is resolved to grant the land to them as per the following norms:

	LAND TO BE ACQUIRED/ ACQUIRED LAND	LAND TO BE GRANTED IN EXCHANGE.
1.	Upto 3 Acres	Entire land.
2.	Above 3 Acres and upto 9 Acres.	3 Acres.
3.	Above 9 Acres and upto 12 Acres.	1/3rd portion of acquired land.
4.	Above 12 Acres.	4 Acres.

18. In our opinion, none of the appellants have violated any of the rights guaranteed to the petitioners in the writ petition either under the Constitution or under any other law and hence the PIL filed by the respondents herein is not at all maintainable and is liable to be dismissed. Now that the civil appeals are allowed, we direct the respondent-authorities to grant possession of the land immediately to the appellants without insisting for any undertaking from the appellants as directed by the High Court in its impugned judgment. Since the patience of the appellants have been tested for so long by the State Government and other authorities and also the public interest litigant, it is not proper for the government and other appropriate authorities to ask the appellants to wait for any longer.

19. We direct the government and the other appropriate authorities to immediately handover possession of the land allotted to them by way of rehabilitation. Accordingly, we dismiss the writ petitions filed by the respondents and allow the above civil appeals and set aside the order impugned in these civil appeals passed by the High Court of Gujarat. However, we order no costs.

State of Maharashtra
v.
Public Concern for Governance Trust

AIR 2007 SC 777: (2007) 3 SCC 587
(Arising out of S.L.P. (Civil) No. 18965 of 2006)
Decided on 04-01-2007
Civil Appeal No. 15 oF 2007
(Arising out of S.L.P. (Civil) No. 2707 of 2006)
WITH

Vinay Mohan Lal
v.
State of Maharashtra

Civil Appeal No. 14 of 2007
(Arising out of S.L.P. (Civil) No. 18965 of 2006)

Coram: **Hon'ble Mr. Justice Altamas Kabir**
Hon'ble Dr. Justice AR. Lakshmanan

Judgment by: **Hon'ble Dr. Justice AR. Lakshmanan**

FACTS: On a dispute relating to allotment of land the Bombay High Court made certain adverse remarks about the Chief Minister of Maharashtra without giving him an opportunity of hearing. The appellant filed an appeal in the Supreme Court from the said judgment and order of the Bombay High Court only for the purpose of expunging certain remarks made by the High Court, inasmuch as the same may affect the working and functioning of the office of the Chief Minister of the State of Maharashtra.

ISSUE: Expunction of adverse remarks.

HELD: The observations/strictures and remarks made by the High Court against the appellant is totally uncalled for and not warranted which are liable to be expunged.

JUDGMENT

Dr. AR. Lakshmanan, J.

Leave granted.

The appellant State of Maharashtra has filed the above appeal from the judgment and order of the Bombay High Court dated 23.05.2005 only for the purpose of expunging certain remarks made by the High Court, inasmuch as the same may affect the working and functioning of the office of the Chief Minister of the State of Maharashtra.

BACKGROUND FACTS:

The City and Industrial Development Corporation (CIDCO) is an authority constituted under the Maharashtra Regional and Town Planning Act, 1966 (MRTP Act) for development of Navi Mumbai as a township.

CIDCO grants plots in Navi Mumbai for construction and development under the MRTP Act read with prevalent development control regulations for Navi Mumbai. There are detailed regulations and procedures for allotment of land by CIDCO to various entities.

Five different applications were made by respondent Nos. 5 to 10 to the then Chief Minister of Maharashtra who was also the Minister for Urban Development. All business of Urban Development Department was under the control of the Minister for urban development.

The then Chief Minister in turn noted on five of the said applications the words "please put up". Since the authority concerned *i.e.,* CIDCO was required to process the same, the said applications were forwarded to the new town development authority *i.e.,* CIDCO for further processing. No other or further endorsement of any nature whatsoever was made on any of the said files in relation to the said applications by the Chief Minister. Thus, except for the original noting "please put up", no other noting, direction or order had been made or passed on any of the said files by the Chief Minister. A 6th application though addressed to the Chief Minister, no endorsement whatsoever was made by the Chief Minister of Maharashtra on the said file. The said file at no stage reached the office of the Chief Minister of Maharashtra. The role of the Chief Minister ended on his endorsing five out of six files with the noting "please put up".

The said six applications were processed by CIDCO and CIDCO made allotments of land to the six cooperative housing societies.

Public Interest Litigation No. 43 of 2005 was filed in the Bombay High Court challenging the allotments to the six Co-operative Housing Societies.

The Bombay High Court, after calling the files of CIDCO relating to the allotment, by its judgment dated 23.11.2005 set aside the allotments. In the judgment dated 23.11.2005, the Bombay High Court on its own conclusions and interpretations of the file notations without calling for any explanation, made certain unwarranted observations as regards the making of the application to the then Chief Minister as also the notation "please put up" made by the then Chief Minister in the five applications. The High Court in fact made a complete factual error in observing that a notation on the application of respondent No. 10 "please process and pass by 12th April, 2004" was made by the then Chief Minister when in fact, no such endorsement was made by the then Chief Minister.

In the impugned order dated 23.11.2005, the Bombay High Court made the following observations against the then Chief Minister which, according to the appellant State of Maharashtra, are unwarranted:—

"(i) "When we look into these documents, what we find is that the letters of application titled "Request for allotment" by respondent Nos. 5 to 9 societies are computer print-outs. All the letters are undated. All of them are addressed to the then Chief Minister of Maharashtra Shri Sushil Kumar Shinde and not to CIDCO which as a statutory Corporation, is a separate competent legal entity. Each of them bears the endorsement of the Chief Minister "please put up" dated 21st February 2004" (para 23)

(ii) "It is seen that Co-operative Housing Societies stated to be having different names and different addresses in far off areas have all sought to apply for allotment by writing identical letters on the same day, not to CIDCO but to the then Chief Minister of Maharashtra" (para 25)

(iii) The application of respondent No. 10 has been made separately. It is also undated. It is received initially on 5th April 2004 and bears endorsement of the Chief Minister dated 5th April, 2004 "Please process and pass by 12th April, 2004" (para 27)

(iv) "Neither the then Chief Minister nor the Marketing Manager nor the Managing Director of CIDCO are seen to have made any query in spite of this astonishing similarity of approach of these six societies coming from different parts of the city. Strangely enough, their response to these identical applications is also astonishingly identical" (para 28)

(v) It is esoteric how promoters of societies of such members initially applied not to CIDCO but to the Chief Minister whose office finds no place in the MRTP Act or the aforesaid Rules filed for grant of any plot of CIDCO". (para 38)

(vi) "It is not known how he became the Chief Promoter of the said Society which applied later than the other societies and whose application was not only directed to be put up by the then Chief Minister but to be put up by a specific date within a week of the application having been made and even before its copy was received by the Managing Director of CIDCO" (para 79)

(vii) The Chief Minister endorsed on five of them to the Managing Director to "please put up" and on the sixth to process and pass by the specified date" (para 134)

(viii) "Would the Managing Directors and the officers of CIDCO have entertained these applicants who are principally slum dwellers for the prime plot known as "Marine Drive of Navi Mumbai". If they were to approach them without being led by these traders and supported by a builder and without the blessing of the Chief Minister? (para 139)"

Mr. G.E. Vahanvati, learned Solicitor General of India and Mr. Ravi Kadam, learned Advocate-General for the State of Maharashta have appeared and argued the matter on behalf of the appellant. Mr. Chander Uday Singh, learned senior counsel appeared and countered the argument of the appellant on behalf of the contesting Ist respondent. Mr. Altaf Ahmed, learned senior counsel appeared for the CIDCO.

The learned Solicitor-General argued the matter at length and invited our attention to the strictures and remarks made by the High Court against the then Chief Minister of Maharashtra Mr. Sushil Kumar Shinde and the documents at page Nos. 139, 141, 145, 147 and 149 and also the pleadings and other annexures.

Learned Solicitor-General submitted that the present appeal was filed only for the limited purpose of expunging certain remarks made by the High Court against the then Chief Minister who was not even a party to the case and without calling for an explanation. He also submitted that it is not correct on the part of the Court to call for the files, pursue the same and make observations on its own understanding and interpretation of the notings in the file without calling for any explanation from the person making the noting or the concerned department. He would further submit that it was not proper and correct on the part of the High Court to draw adverse inference on certain endorsement made by the then Chief Minister without any reference to the State or the then Chief Minister who was not even a party to the case and without calling for an explanation. According to the learned Solicitor-General, the file notings such as please put up are made in the usual day to day functioning of the office of the Chief Minister and various other offices and, therefore, the observation of the High Court against the then Chief Minister will affect the functioning of the Chief Minister and, therefore, it is not fair and justified.

Learned Solicitor-General also cited the following rulings of this Court in support of his contention. They are:—

1. *Dr. Dilip Kumar Deka* v. *State of Assam*, (1996) 6 SCC 234 (paras 6, 7 & 8).
2. *Rajiv Ranjan Singh 'Lalan' (VIII)* v. *Union of India*, (2006) 6 SCC 613 (645) (para 57)
3. *Dr. J.N. Banavalikar* v. *Municipal Corporation of Delhi*, 1995 Supp (4) SCC 89 (para 21).
4. *S. Pratap Singh* v. *The State of Punjab*, (1964) 4 SCR 733 (747) (para 2).
5. *A.K.K. Nambiar* v. *Union of India*, (1969) 3 SCC 864 (867) (para 8 & 9).

Mr. Chander Uday Singh, learned senior counsel for the first respondent (writ petitioner) submitted that the first respondent filed the writ petition by way of PIL in order to expose a massive and orchestrated scam by which CIDCO a special planning authority constituted under the Maharashtra Regional Town Planning Act, 1966 has diverted public lands intended for genuine cooperative housing societies to a small coterie of commercial builders/developers and thereby conferred massive commercial largesse upon such builders/developers while simultaneously causing losses to CIDCO and the members of the general public. According to him, small coteries of builders/developers approached the then Chief Minister of Maharashtra and by addressing applications directly to him in the name of societies on identical or suspiciously similar computer generated stationery/letter heads made specific requests for allotment of prime plots of land by expressly mentioning the plot or plots desired by them and that the Chief Minister endorsed each such application with the words "please put up" and thereupon these applications were hand delivered to CIDCO's Head Office at Nariman Point, Mumbai and that these applications were assigned inward numbers thereby signifying that they are recommended by the Chief Minister and on the very same date, when they were received by CIDCO at Nirmal, the Vice-Chairman and M.D. added their endorsements reading please process early or words to that effect. He would further submit that the Chief Minister's recommendation proved so compelling that CIDCO instantly allotted the chosen plots for residential user even though the classification and earmarking of these plots was commercial plus residential on the development plan of CIDCO thereby causing loss to CIDCO of the much higher premium available on C+R lands. It was submitted by learned senior counsel for the respondent that the High Court pronounced a detailed and well-reasoned judgment which dealt with the entire subterfuge resorted to in order to make such dummy allotments at the behest of the former Chief Minister of Maharashtra and have been dealt with in great detail by the Division Bench. He further submitted that the first respondent filed the writ petition in the High Court since there had been violations of law as well as of CIDCO's land allotment policy, *inter alia,* in making allotments to cooperative societies and that the first respondent had learnt that these allotments had been made on the basis of the recommendations by the then Chief Minister or other High functionaries acting at his behest and that all rules and norms had been disregarded by CIDCO as a consequence of such recommendations. Respondent No. 1 accordingly pleaded in para 4 and 14 of the writ petition that it appeared that these illegal allotments had been made at the behest of the Chief Minister or other Ministers of the Government of Maharashtra and in para 14 have specifically called upon CIDCO to confirm or deny this fact.

According to the first respondent, it is apparent from the documents produced before the High Court and the manner in which allotments were made by CIDCO that this was done only on the behest of the then Chief Minister. Learned senior counsel for the first respondent further submitted that the special leave petition was filed to seek expunction of certain adverse comments made against the former Chief Minister of Maharashtra was filed by the State of

Maharashtra and not by Shri Sushil Kumar Shinde. According to the learned counsel, it is not open to the State of Maharashtra to now file a special leave petition to challenge the said findings or remarks and that if at all anybody is aggrieved by the said finding or remarks, it would be the former Chief Minister and he had chosen not to file any special leave petition nor to question the same. Hence, the present special leave petition is not maintainable. While winding-up his argument, learned senior counsel for the first respondent made a prayer that he would now implead the then Chief Minister of Maharashtra - Shri Sushil Kumar Shinde as a party respondent and that permission in that regard may be granted to him in view of the importance of the public interest litigation.

We have given our anxious and careful consideration to the submissions made by both the learned senior counsel. We have also carefully perused the pleadings, documents, annexures and the rulings cited at the time of hearing.Various applications and representations on diverse subjects are received by the Chief Ministers of the States as the Head of the State and in respect of the Ministries under their control. Often such applications are directly addressed by members of the public to the Chief Minister. The Chief Minister then endorses the same to the concerned department so that the same my subsequently be followed up by the concerned department. When the Chief Minister is on tour in various parts of the State, representations and applications are given to him by various people who meet him. In the routine course, the Chief Minister endorses the same with a noting "please put up" and forward the same to the concerned department. Such notation merely means that the concerned department should process the applications and representations lawfully and in accordance with certain prescribed procedure. While making such notations on the representations/applications so received, the Chief Minister does not analyse each and every case since this is to be done at the level of the concerned department which then scrutinizes the same in accordance with law. In our view, the notation is not even treated as a determination of eligibility or the merit of the concerned application. It is a routine notation made in the normal course and is really an action of forwarding to the concerned department the representations/applications received by the Chief Minister.

The concerned department is then expected to examine the said representations/applications and decide the same on its own merits and in accordance with law. As rightly pointed out by learned Solicitor-General as to how he treats the file the nomenclature given to such matters are of matters of internal administration of the concerned department/corporation. It is pointed out to us that in the present case, the Chief Minister was heading the Urban Development Department. CIDCO comes under the administrative control of the said department. Since applications for allotment of land were received by the Chief Minister, he merely made a notation that the applications be put up before the concerned authority. No notation whatsoever was made that the applications be processed by any particular date. The words please put up, in our opinion, only meant that the applications should be processed and decided in accordance with law and on its own merits. CIDCO which is a Corporation had detailed rules which govern the allotment of land and are to be complied with by CIDCO before any allotment of land is made. The records placed before us indicates that the applications put up to CIDCO were processed at various levels including the marketing manager, assistant marketing officer, managing director and upto the stage of board of directors.

In our view, the observations and strictures made by the High Court and are extracted in paragraphs *supra* certainly reflects on the functioning of the office of the Chief Minister and day-to-day discharge of the duties of the Chief Minister. As rightly pointed out by learned Solicitor-General, after the endorsement 'please put up', is made the file may or may not be approved by the concerned department and it is clear that the said notations are not approval of the contents of the representation and in our view, no other meaning could be taken. The observations/strictures made and the inference drawn by the High Court from the notation 'please put up' made by the Chief Minister are not warranted and are required to be expunged as rightly contended by learned senior counsel for the State of Maharashtra. The High Court has, in our view, erred in holding that by making a notation 'please put up' the applicants had blessings of the then Chief Minister. In our opinion, the civil appeal at the instance of the State of Maharashtra is maintainable inasmuch as the observations and strictures made by the High Court shall affect the working and functioning of the office of the Chief Minister of the State of Maharashtra. The submission of learned senior counsel for the first respondent that the first respondent had learnt that these averments had been made on the basis of the recommendations by the Chief Minister or other high functionaries acting at his behest and that all the rules and norms had been disregarded by CIDCO as a consequence of such recommendations as absolutely no basis whatsoever. The grievances expressed against the then Chief Minister is nothing but imaginary. Except making the endorsement 'please put up' the Chief Minister has not played any other role. The observations and strictures passed by the High Court against the then Chief Minister behind his back and without calling for an explanation from him is wholly illegal, incorrect and unwarranted and that the remarks made by the High Court against the then Chief Minister was most uncharitable and not called for.

We have perused the documents at page Nos. 139, 141, 143, 145, 147 and 149 an application was made on behalf of Seaquan Co-operative Housing Society, Bombay requesting for allotment of residential plot for housing society at Sector-4, Plot No. 24-B, Nerul. The said application was addressed to Shri Sushil Kumar Shinde, the then Chief Minister of the Maharashtra State. It was stated in the said application that CIDCO may allot the plot for residential purposes as per prevailing rules and that the applicants are ready to pay the necessary lease premium as per the rules and regulations. Since the application was made directly to the Chief Minister, he made an endorsement please put up on the same. At page 141, another application was made by Amey Co-operative Housing Society, Bombay requesting for allotment of residential plot at Sector-4, Plot No. 24-A, Nerul addressed to the then Chief Minister. Similar endorsement 'please put up' was made by the Chief Minister on this application. At page 143, a similar application was made by Sagarika Co-operative Housing Society requesting for allotment of residential plot addressed to the Chief Minister who made an endorsement saying 'please put up'. At page 145, Sealink Co-operative Housing Society made an application requesting for allotment of residential plot addressed to the Chief Minister who made an endorsement 'please put up'. An application was made at page 147 by Sea-view Co-operative Housing Society addressed to the then Chief Minister who also made an endorsement saying 'please put up'. At page 149, an application made for allotment of developed land for residential purpose was made by Vinayak Co-operative Housing Society addressed to the then Chief Minister. The said application, though addressed to the Chief Minister, no endorsement whatsoever was made by the Chief Minister of Maharashtra on the said file. The said file at no stage reached the office of the Chief Minister of Maharashtra. The role of the Chief Minister ended on his endorsing 5 out of 6 files with the noting 'please put up'.

Thereafter, the said 6 applications as per the records made available at the time of hearing were processed by CIDCO and CIDCO made allotment of lands to the said 6 Co-operative Housing Societies. These allotments were challenged in PIL No.43 of 2005 on various grounds. The High Court, after calling for the file of CIDCO relating to the said 6 allotments and perusing the same, by its judgments and order dated 23.11.2005 set aside the same. Challenging the said judgment Amey Co-operative Housing Society Ltd. filed special leave petition No.336 of 2006 questioning the correctness of the said judgment and the allotments made by CIDCO with which we are not concerned in this Civil Appeal. Elaborate and lengthy submissions were made in that case by the Senior Counsel appearing for the respective parties. The said special leave petition No. 336 of 2006 will separately be dealt with on merits by a separate judgment.

We are of the opinion that the strictures/observations/remarks made by the High Court against the then Chief Minister Shri Sushil Kumar Shinde is not warranted in the facts and circumstances of this case as according to us the High Court has erred in making observations as regards notations made in files which observations are made on their own reading and interpretation of the files without any further reference to the petitions or the then Chief Minister who was not even a party to the case and without even calling for an explanation in that regard. The High Court has failed to notice that the Chief Minister was heading the Urban Development Department and CIDCO comes under the administrative control of the urban development and since the applications for allotment of land were received by the Chief Minister, who merely made a notation that the application be put up before the concerned authority. The High Court also erred in observing that the application made by respondent No. 10 had been received by the Chief Minister and bore his endorsement on 05.04.2005 to the effect please process and pass by 12.04.2004. We have perused the said document. The above endorsement is not written by the Chief Minister and in fact the said application did not even reach the office of the Chief Minister at any point of time.

LAW ON THE SUBJECT:

We shall now analyze and consider the rulings of this Court cited by learned Solicitor-General.

1. *Dr. Dilip Kumar Deka* v. *State of Assam*, (1996) 6 SCC 234 (paras 6, 7 & 8)

The above judgment relates to expunging adverse remarks. The above was a case of adverse remarks recorded by the High Court against the members of hospital allegedly for misleading the court and stalling process of the court by submitting manipulated report regarding condition of a person to justify his shifting from police remand to the hospital. The High Court made adverse remarks without giving any opportunity to the members of extending or defending themselves, without any evidence showing that their conduct justified such remarks and without any necessity of such remarks for the purpose of deciding the matter. This Court held on facts that adverse remarks were unwarranted and hence expunged. This Court also cautioned superior courts to use temporate and moderate language and also held that opportunity to be given to the affected party before recording of adverse remarks by the Court. This Court also held thus:

> "6. The tests to be applied while dealing with the question of expunction of disparaging remarks against a person or authorities whose conduct comes in for consideration before a Court of law in cases to be decided by it were succinctly laid down by this Court in *State of U.P.* v. *Mohd. Naim*, AIR 1964 SC 703. Those tests are:
>
> (a) Whether the party whose conduct is in question is before the court or has an opportunity of explaining or defending himself;
>
> (b) Whether there is evidence on record bearing on that conduct justifying the remarks; and
>
> (c) Whether it is necessary for the decision of the case, as an integral part thereof, to animadvert on that conduct.
>
> The above tests have been quoted with approval and applied by this Court in its subsequent judgments in *Jage Ram* v. *Hans Raj Midha,* (1972) 1 SCC 181; *R.K. Lakshmanan* v. *A.K. Srinivasan,* (1975) 2 SCC 466 and *Niranjan Patnaik* v. *Sashibhusan Kar,* (1986) 2 SCC 569.
>
> 7. We are surprised to find that in spite of the above catena of decisions of this Court, the learned Judge did not, before making the remarks, give any opportunity to the appellants, who were admittedly not parties to the revision petition, to defend themselves. It cannot be gainsaid that the nature of remarks the learned Judge has made, has cast a serious aspersion on the appellants affecting their character and reputation and may, ultimately affect their career also. Condemnation of the appellants without giving them an opportunity of being heard was a complete negation of the fundamental principle of natural justice.
>
> 8. Judged in the context of the first test laid down in *Mohd. Naim's* case (*supra*) the above discussion of ours is sufficient to quash the impugned remarks, but we find that the remarks are vulnerable also to the second test laid down therein. On perusal of the order dismissing the revision petition we find that the remarks of the learned Judge are based solely upon the fact that the report of the medical Board consisting of four

medical experts belied their report. Indeed, except the report of the Board we have also not found any other material on record from which the learned Judge could have legitimately and justifiably obtained satisfaction to pass the above remarks against the two appellants before us. We hasten to add that in making the above observation we have left out of our consideration the materials which prompted the learned Judge to make adverse comments against the IO."

2. *Rajiv Ranjan Singh 'Lalan' (VIII)* v. *Union of India*, (2006) 6 SCC 613 (645) (para 57)

In the above case, Dr. AR. Lakshmanan, J. concurring with the opinion expressed by Hon. K.G. Balakrishnan, J. has observed that public interest litigation is meant for the benefit of the lost and the lonely and it is meant for the benefit of those whose social backwardness is the reason for no access to the Court and that PILs are not meant to advance the political gain and also to settle personal scores under the guise of PIL and to fight a legal battle. In para 57, it has been observed as follows:—

"57. Certain allegations have been made against CBDT and the Public Prosecutors, Members of the Income-tax Tribunal, etc. None of them were made parties before us. Therefore, the allegations made against them are one-sided and cannot be looked into at all. We cannot also say that all these authorities have acted in a *mala fide* manner."

3. *Dr. J.N. Banavalikar* v. *Municipal Corporation of Delhi*, 1995 Supp (4) SCC 89

This Court, in the above case, in para 21, observed thus:

"In the facts and circumstances of this appeal, it is not possible to hold that the impugned action in removing the appellant and appointing Dr. Patnaik is unfair or unjust or irrational or arbitrary or tainted with any *mala fide* intention. The contention of the appellant that in order to accommodate a junior doctor as Medical Superintendent in I.D. Hospital, Dr. Patnaik had been moved out from the said hospital to replace the appellant as Medical Superintendent of RBTB Hospital, is not only vague but lacks in particulars forming the foundation of such contention. Further, in the absence of impleadment of the junior doctor who is alleged to have been favoured by the course of action leading to removal of the appellant and the person who had allegedly passed *mala fide* order in order to favour such junior doctor, any contention of *mala fide* action in fact i.e. 'malice in fact' should not be countenanced by the court. This appeal therefore, fails and is dismissed without any order as to costs."

4. *S. Pratap Singh* v. *The State of Punjab*, (1964) 4 SCR 733 (747, 748 & 749).

This Court in para 2 held thus:

"We shall first take up for consideration the several allegations that have been made and see whether they had been satisfactorily made out. Before proceeding further it is necessary to state that allegations of a personal character having been made against the Chief Minister, there could only be two ways in which they could be repelled. First, if the allegations were wholly irrelevant, and even if true, would not afford a basis upon which the appellant would be entitled to any relief, they need not have been answered and the appellant could derive no benefit from the respondents not answering them. We have already dealt with this matter and have made it clear that if they were true and made out by acceptable evidence, they could not be ignored as irrelevant; (2) If they were relevant, in the absence of their intrinsic improbability the allegations could be countered by documentary or affidavit evidence which would show their falsity. In the absence of such evidence they could be disproved only by the party against whom the allegations were made denying the same on oath. In the present case there were serious allegations made against the Chief Minister and there were several matters of which he alone could have personal knowledge therefore which he could deny, but what was, however, placed before the Court in answer to the charges made against the Chief Minister was an affidavit by the Secretary to Government in the Medical Department who could only speak from official records and obviously not from personal knowledge about the several matters which were alleged against the Chief Minister. In these circumstances we do not think it would be proper to brush aside the allegations made by the appellant, particularly in respect of those matters where they are supported by some evidence of a documentary nature seeing that there is no contradiction by those persons who alone could have contradicted them. In making this observation we have in mind the Chief Minister as well as Mrs. Kairon against whom allegations have been made but who have not chosen to state on oath the true facts according to them. Before passing on to a consideration of the details of the several allegations there is one matter to which we ought to make reference at this stage and that is the admissibility and evidentiary value of the tape-recorded talks which have been produced as part of his supporting evidence by the appellant. The learned Judges of the High Court without saying in so many terms that these were inadmissible in evidence, this being the contention raised by the respondent-State, have practically put them out of consideration for the reason that tape-recordings were capable of being tampered with. With respect we cannot agree. There are few documents and possibly no piece of evidence which could not be tampered with, but that would certainly not be a ground on which Courts could reject evidence as inadmissible or refuse to consider it. It was not contended before us the tape-recordings were inadmissible. In the ultimate analysis the factor mentioned would have a bearing only on the weight to be attached to the evidence and not on its admissibility. Doubtless, if in any particular case there is a well-grounded suspicion, not even say proof, that a tape-recording has been tampered with, that would be a good ground for the court to discount wholly its evidentiary value.

But in the present case we do not see any basis for any such suggestion. The tape-recordings were referred to by the appellant in his writ petition as part of the evidence on which he proposed to rely in support of his assertions as regards the substance of what passed between him and the Chief Minister and the members of the latter's family on the several matters which were the subject of allegations in the petition."

5. *A.K.K. Nambiar* v. *Union of India*, (1969) 3 SCC 864 (867). This Court in paras 8 & 9 held thus:

> "The appellant made allegations against the Chief Minister of Andhra Pradesh and other persons some of whose names were disclosed and some of whose names were not disclosed. Neither the Chief Minister nor any other person was made a party. The appellant filed an affidavit in support of the petition. Neither the petition nor the affidavit was verified. The affidavits which were filed in answer to the appellant's petition were also not verified. The reason for verification of affidavits are to enable the Court to find out which facts can be said to be proved on the affidavit evidence of rival parties.
>
> Allegations may be true to knowledge or allegations may be true to information received from persons or allegations may be based on records. The importance of verification is to test the genuineness and authenticity of allegations and also to make the deponent responsible for allegations. In essence verification is required to enable the Court to find out as to whether it will be safe to act on such affidavit evidence. In the present case, the affidavits of all the parties suffer from the mischief of lack of proper verification with the result that the affidavits should not be admissible in evidence.
>
> The affidavit evidence assumes importance in the present case because of allegations of *mala fide* acts on the part of the respondents. The appellant alleged that the Union of India made the order of suspension because of the pressure of the Chief Minister of the State of Andhra Pradesh. The appellant, however, did not name any person of the Union of India who acted in that manner and did not implead the Chief Minister as a party. In order to succeed on the proof of *mala fides* in relation to the order of suspension, the appellant has to prove either that the order of suspension was made *mala fide* or that the order was made for collateral purposes. In the present case, the appellant neither alleged nor established either of these features."

In the instant case, allegations have been made against the then Chief Minister, however, he was not made party before the Court. Therefore, the allegations made against him are one-sided and do not merit any consideration.

We are surprised to find that inspite of catena of decisions of this Court, the High Court did not, give an opportunity to the affected party, the then Chief Minister, before making remarks. It cannot be gainsaid that the nature of remarks made in this judgment will cast a serious aspersion on the Chief Minister affecting his reputation, career etc.

Condemnation of the then Chief Minister without affording opportunity of being heard was a complete negation of the basic principles of natural justice.

For the foregoing reasons, we have no hesitation in expunging the remarks/observations/strictures made against the then Chief Minister of Maharashtra - Shri Sushil Kumar Shinde and allow the appeal filed by the State of Maharashtra who, in our opinion, is competent to maintain this appeal and order expunction of the remarks and observations/strictures made against the then Chief Minister. The appeal stands allowed only to the above extent. We make it clear that we are not expressing any opinion on merits of the rival claims made in the other special leave petition filed by the cooperative societies in special leave petition No. 336 of 2006 which will be dealt with separately.

In the result, the civil appeal arising out of special leave petition No. 18965 of 2006 stands allowed. However, there will be no order as to costs.

CIVIL APPEAL No. 15 of 2007

(Arising out of S.L.P. (Civil) No. 2707 of 2006)

The above appeal was filed by Mr. Vinay Mohan Lal who is a member of the IAS, 1970 batch working in the grade of Principal Secretary in the Maharashtra Government appointed as M.D. CIDCO and presently serving as M.D. MAFCO. The High Court, while disposing off the writ petition filed by way of PIL, had made certain observations against the appellant. The appeal was argued by the appellant himself. He submitted that he was neither a party to the said proceedings nor was directed to be made a party to the PIL. The observations made by the High Court against him is quoted herein below for ready reference:

> "We are also amazed as to how the then Managing Director, who is an IAS officer, got persuaded that these are genuine Housing Societies satisfying all the requirements and capable of bearing the financial burden. (para 38)
>
> "It was a grand plan to take advantage of their poverty, lack of understanding and ignorance, and it could not be executed unless, the original chief promoters, the builders and the officers of CIDCO at the higher level such as the Managing Director were party to it. Would the Managing Directors and the officers of CIDCO have entertained these applicants who are principally slum dwellers for this prime plot known as "Marine Drive of Navi Mumbai", if they were to approach them without being led by these traders and supported by a builder and without the blessings of the Chief Minister? It is either a case of involvement in the design or of gross dereliction of duty. In either case, it is unjustifiable and highly objectionable and the consequences must follow (para 139).
>
> "Now suddenly it appears that this device has been invented and with the participation of the officers of CIDCO right from the Managing Director to who so ever are the persons below, all the conditions of allotment and scrutiny are given a go by and a prime plot sought to be handed over to a builder on a platter. A good scheme has been permitted to be misused with full connivance of the officers of CIDCO. (para 140)

> "What we find is that there is a complete dereliction of responsibilities on the part of the then Managing Director of CIDCO and who so ever were incharge of this project. Merely because the then CM had asked them to process early, they have given a complete go-by to scrutiny— In view of what is stated above, we expect the authorities of the State Government and CIDCO to take appropriate actions against the persons concerned so that this kind of deviation does not take place in future. (para 141)"

The party in person submitted that the said observation made by the High Court without hearing the appellant has now mis-interpreted by the government counsel in their submission before the CAT in O.A. No. 528 of 2005 wherein the charge sheet issued to the appellant on 11th July has been challenged due to which the government counsel pointed out to the tribunal stating that the government was now under obligation to initiate action against the appellant since the High Court has so directed.

According to Mr. V. Mohan Lal the impugned judgment is not only erroneous but is also passed on inferences and surmises which are not sustainable. According to him, the petitioners before the High Court, present respondent No. 11 has mis-interpreted the facts and have misled the High Court and that events which have happened after due allotment and which could not have been anticipated at the time of allotment have been considered to conclude that the allotment itself was improper. Therefore, the appellant filed the above appeal being aggrieved by the observations made by the High Court in the impugned judgment with that limited scope. According to the appellant, the High Court was not right in passing strictures against the appellant when the appellant when the appellant was not a party to the said proceedings. He further submitted that the High Court was not right to pass adverse comments against the appellant which are likely to affect the career of the appellant without giving an opportunity to the appellant of being heard. He therefore, submitted that the order of the High Court is in utter violation of principles of natural justice.

According to him, the comments made against the appellant were uncalled for in the facts and circumstances of the case and that the said comments which were made without the appellant being heard could at all have been referred to and relied on by the High Court in some other proceedings.

We see much force and substance in the contentions put forward by the party in person. In our opinion, the High Court was not right in passing comments/observations/strictures against the appellant when the appellant was not a party to the said proceedings nor was directed to be made a party. The High Court was also not right in passing the comments against the appellant without giving an opportunity to the appellant of being heard. The act of the High Court, in our opinion, is in gross violation of the principles of natural justice.

The party in person cited a ruling of the this court being *State of Bihar* v. *Lal Krishna Advani*, (2003) 8 SCC 361 (367) wherein it was observed that strictures cannot be passed against an individual without making him a party and without giving an opportunity to be heard since the right to reputation is an individual's fundamental right. In our opinion, the observations made by the High Court in paras 38, 139, 140 & 141 of the impugned order are absolutely uncalled for as the appellant was not a party to the said PIL and they are also based on complete misunderstanding of the facts. The observations made by the High Court as rightly pointed out by the party in person would have wide ramifications and adverse impact on the career of the appellant.

We have already dealt with the cases and the rulings on the subject in question in the earlier part of the judgment in the appeal filed by the State of Maharashtra which, in our opinion, squarely applies to the facts and circumstances of the case filed by the party in person. We, therefore, expunge the remarks/observations/strictures made against the appellant as the same has been made behind his back. We also make it clear that we are not expressing any opinion on the merits of the special leave petition No. 336 of 2006 filed by Amey Co-operative Society which will be dealt with absolutely on merits of the rival claims by a separate judgment.

The party in person has also pointed out certain findings in the judgment of the High Court. We do not propose to go into the merits of the other contentions which is the subject-matter of the special leave petition No. 336 of 2006. In our opinion, when an authority takes a decision which may have civil consequences and affects the rights of a person, the principles of natural justice would at once come into play. Reputation of an individual is an important part of ones life. It is observed in 1955 American LR 171 *DF Marion* v. *Minnie Davis* and reads as follows:—

> "The right to enjoyment of a private reputation, unassailed by malicious slander is of an ancient origin, and is necessary to human society. A good reputation is an element of personal security, and is protected by the Constitution equally with the right to the enjoyment of life, liberty and property."

This court also in *Board of Trustees of the Port of Bombay* v. *Dilip Kumar Raghavendranath Natkarni*, (1983) 1 SCC 124 has observed that right to reputation is a facet of right to life of a citizen under Article 21 of the Constitution.

It is thus amply clear that one is entitled to have and preserve ones reputation and one also has a right to protect it. In case any authority in discharge of its duties fastened upon it under the law, travels into the realm of personal reputation adversely affecting him, it must provide a chance to him to have his say in the matter. In such circumstances, right of an individual to have the safeguard of the principles of natural justice before being adversely commented upon is statutorily recognized and violation of the same will have to bear the scrutiny of judicial review.

For the aforesaid reasons, we hold that the observations/strictures and remarks made by the High Court against the appellant behind his back is totally uncalled for and not warranted. We, therefore, have no hesitation to order expunction of the remarks made in para Nos. 38, 139, 140 and 141 of the impugned judgment. The civil appeal is allowed only to the above extent. We order no costs.

M/s. Popcorn Entertainment
v.
City Industrial Development Corpn.

AIR 2007 SC (Supp) 152: (2007) 3 SCALE 465
Civil Appeal No. 940 of 2007
(Arising out of SLP (C) No. 11085 of 2006)
[Alongwith Civil Appeal No. 941 of 2007
(Arising out of SLP (C) No. 11087 of 2006)]
Decided on 23-02-2007

Coram: Hon'ble Mr. Justice Altamas Kabir
Hon'ble Dr. Justice AR. Lakshmanan
Judgment by: Hon'ble Dr. Justice AR. Lakshmanan

FACTS: Certain land was allotted to the appellant for construction of multiplex. However, subsequently the concluded contract was cancelled on the ground that it was made without calling tenders. The order was passed without hearing the appellants. The writ petition filed before the High Court was dismissed on the ground of alternative remedy.

ISSUE: Dismissal of writ petition on ground of alternative remedy.

HELD: The High Court has committed a grave mistake by relegating the appellant to the alternative remedy when clearly in terms of the law laid down by the Supreme Court, this was a fit case in which the High Court should have exercised its jurisdiction in order to consider and grant relief to the respective parties.

JUDGMENT

Dr. AR. Lakshmanan, J.

SLP (C) No. 11085 of 2006

1. Leave granted.

2. The above appeal was filed against the final judgment and order dated 30.06.2006 passed by the High Court of Judicature at Bombay in W.P. No. 9467 of 2005 whereby the High Court has rejected the writ petition filed by the appellants by holding that the appellants have an equally efficacious remedy of filing a civil suit and thus the writ jurisdiction cannot be invoked.

3. BACKGROUND FACTS:

The appellant made an application for allotment of a plot on 18.05.2004 for construction of a multiplex at Kharghar railway station. The first respondent, The City Industrial Development Corporation (in short, "CIDCO") asked the appellants to pay an EMD of Rs. 20 lacs being 10% of the tentative price of the plot in order to consider the application of the appellant. The appellant deposited the said amount of EMD immediately. CIDCO, *vide* its Board Resolution dated 03.06.2004, approved the allotment in favour of the appellant considering the fact that there were no multiplex in the area and the earlier effort of CIDCO to advertise for such plots had met with no response. CIDCO issued allotment letter in favour of the appellant asking the appellant to pay Rs. 1,80,00,000 lacs being the balance price of the plot. The appellant made two separate payments of Rs. 90 lacs each towards the balance price of the plot on 16.08.2004 and 19.08.2004. The appellant paid a sum of Rs. 20,00,600 being the other charges demanded by the respondent. The appellant was asked to pay a further sum of Rs. 65,096 which the appellant paid immediately. CIDCO unilaterally decided to ask the appellants to pay a further sum of Rs. 20 lacs by enhancing the rate at which the plot was to be allotted to the appellant from Rs. 2500 per sq. metre as demanded in the allotment letter to Rs. 2,750 per sq. metre because the plot of the appellant was on a 24 metre road. The appellant on 17.11.2004 paid a further payment of Rs. 20 lacs along with Rs. 2,96,078 plus Rs. 4,957 being the additional cost and the other charges. On 14.01.2005, the appellant paid a further sum of Rs. 19,828 being the sum demanded by the respondent. The appellant on 17.01.2005 entered into an agreement to lease with the respondent for the allotment of the plot. On 28.02.2005, CIDCO being the Development Authority of the area issued commencement certificate to the appellant permitting the appellant to start construction. On 14.07.2005, the appellant received a show cause notice seeking to cancel the allotment in favour of the appellant on the ground that the allotment was void in view of section 23 of the Contract Act as being opposed to public policy. The main ground in the show cause notice was that the allotment was without issuance of tender and was opposed to public policy. On 27.07.2005, the appellant submitted a detailed reply to the show cause notice. On 16.12.2005, CIDCO issued an order canceling the agreement to lease and sought to resume the possession of the plot. According to the appellant only the appellant was singled out for cancellation whereas hundreds of allotments made without issuance of tender were allowed to remain which is also a matter of record. In these facts, on 28.12.2005, the appellant approached the High Court by way of writ petition against the said cancellation order dated 16.12.2005. The writ petition was numbered as 9467 of 2005 on 02.01.2006 and the High Court granted stay of the order dated 16.12.2005 and fixed the matter for further hearing on 04.01.2006. The appellant, vide reference dated 08.03.2006 of CIDCO, under the Right to Information Act, 2005 has asked them to supply information regarding the allotments made by Social Service Department without any advertisement *i.e.,* by considering individual applications.

On 16.03.2006, the appellants filed their rejoinder before the High Court pointing out further information sought under the Right to Information Act which clearly proved that the allotment in favour of the appellant was completely in order and was made in terms of the Land Pricing and Land Disposal Policy and also that there was no loss caused to CIDCO in the said allotments. The appellant sought another information from the CIDCO Authorities regarding methodology for allotment of plots for service industries, warehousing, multiplexes, etc. Again on 04.04.2006, the appellant had sought for further information in respect of 15 cases similar to the case of the appellants regarding whether disposal was by tender or without tender, whether the pricing policy was adopted or not etc. Further information was sought on 13.04.2006 regarding allotment of social facility plots during April, 2003 to March, 2005. CIDCO, vide their letter dated 13.04.2006, has informed the appellant that during April, 2003 to March, 2005, 27 plots were allotted for the opening of schools, 9 plots were allotted for opening of colleges, 5 plots were allotted to charitable and religious institutions, 9 plots were allotted to cultural organizations, 2 plots was allotted for sports and 13 plots were allotted for social welfare. In all 65 plots were allotted under the category of social facility. CIDCO has also confirmed that all the allotments had been made without issuance of tender and that all the abovementioned allotments have been made as per Land Pricing and Land Disposal Policy of CIDCO *i.e.,* the same as was done in the case of the appellant. None of these allotments have been cancelled by CIDCO till date. In this view of the matter, it is clear that the entire basis for seeking to cancel the appellant's plots is illegal and the same cannot stand the test of judicial scrutiny.

On 20.04.2006, the appellant filed an additional affidavit before the High Court pointing out certain more information sought by the appellant. On 17.05.2006, the matter was listed before the High Court and was adjourned for 4 weeks to examine the judgment passed by the High Court in the case of Raja Bahadur Mills. The matter was again listed on 30.06.2006 for hearing. The matter was heard and dismissed and the Court indicated that the detailed judgment would be pronounced later. At that stage, counsel for the appellants made a specific prayer to grant interim protection to the appellant for a period of 4 weeks to enable the appellant to approach this Court, the said prayer was orally granted by the High Court. However, on 06.07.2006, the High Court, while issuing a copy of the order on 06.07.2006, dismissed the writ petition of the appellant on the ground of availability of alternative remedy. The High Court rejected the prayer for interim protection to the appellant despite having granted it orally.

4. Aggrieved by the said order, the appellants filed this appeal by way of special leave petition before this Court.

This Court on 24.07.2006 issued notice returnable within 6 weeks and also passed the following interim order:

The petitioners had the benefit of stay of dispossession. There will be stay of dispossession pending further orders. But the petitioners will be restrained from putting up any construction until further orders.

SLP (C) NO. 11087 OF 2006

5. Leave granted.

The above appeal was filed against the final judgment and order dated 30.06.2006 passed by the High Court of Judicature at Bombay in W.P. No. 9468 of 2005 whereby the High Court rejected the writ petition on the ground that the writ jurisdiction cannot be invoked when an equally efficacious remedy of filing a civil suit is available.

BACKGROUND FACTS:

6. The appellant made an application on 22.2.2004 requesting for allotment of plot reserved for multiplex. On 8.6.2004, the appellants made a request for allotment of the plot in Airoli for setting up multiplex-cum-auditorium-cum-entertainment center. CIDCO, in response to the said application, requested the appellant to submit a detailed project defining all built up activities. The appellant submitted the detailed project report. CIDCO, by their letter of intent, requested the appellant to pay an EMD of Rs. 20,77,000 within 15 days from the receipt of the letter to enable the Board to consider the allotment in favour of the appellant. The appellant accordingly made the EMD on 29.06.2004. On 29.7.2004, CIDCO approved the allotment of plot No. 2, Sector 11, Airoli in favour of the appellant as the Board had not got any response for similar plots in public tender. The total lease premium in respect of the plot was Rs. 2,07,70,000 and the appellants were directed to pay the balance amount of Rs. 1,86,93,000 by 14.9.2004. The allotment was made in terms of the New Bombay Land Disposal Rules, 1975 and also in terms of the Land Pricing and Disposal Policy of CIDCO under which the land could be allotted to any person by considering his individual application at the reserved price fixed by CIDCO. On 16.08.2004 and 13.9.2004, the appellants paid Rs. 1,86,93,000 as demanded. On 15.10.2004, CIDCO after inspection of the plot issued a corrigendum asking the appellants to pay a further sum of Rs. 53,236 being the additional amount due to the marginal increase in the demarcation of the plot. The appellant paid the balance amount of Rs. 53,236 thus making a total payment of Rs. 2,08,22,420 being the full and final payment in respect of allotment in favour of the appellant as demanded by CIDCO. An agreement to lease was entered into with CIDCO in respect of the plot allotted to the appellant. CIDCO, on 1.8.2005, issued a show cause notice to the appellants regarding the plot at Airoli seeking to cancel the agreement to lease executed in favour of the appellants. The appellant made a detailed reply to the show cause notice. The appellant also sought information from CIDCO under the Right to Information Act on 21.12.2005/3.4.2006/4.4.2006/13.4.2006/20.4.2006 regarding allotment to various parties and the details thereon. The appellant, on 28.10.2005, approached the High Court against the cancellation order dated 18.12.2005. The writ petition was listed for hearing on 2.1.2006 and the High Court granted stay of the operation of the order dated 18.12.2005. Parties were asked to file their reply and rejoinder etc. in the writ petition. The matter was listed on 17.05.2006 for hearing and was adjourned by 4 weeks and again listed before the High Court on 30.6.3006 for hearing and the matter was heard and dismissed and the Court indicated that the detailed judgment would be pronounced later. However, on 6.7.2006, the High Court dismissed the writ petition of the appellant on the ground of availability of alternative remedy and rejected the prayer for interim protection to the appellant despite having granted it orally. Aggrieved by the said order, the appellants preferred this appeal by way of special leave petition in this Court.

7. This Court on 24.7.2006 ordered stay of dis-possession pending further orders. In this Court, the appellant in addition to the special leave petition also filed additional affidavit and the counter affidavit filed by respondent No. 1 before the High Court of Bombay as annexure-P17.

8. A counter-affidavit in reply on behalf of respondent No. 1 CIDCO was also filed in the special leave petition specifically stating that in the present case the allotment was cancelled having regard to section 23 of the Indian Contract Act as the subject allotment was illegal and that as regards the merits of rival contentions, a detailed affidavit was filed before the High Court and for the sake of brevity a copy of the same was annexed as Annexure-R1. The appellant also filed a rejoinder to the counter-affidavit filed on behalf of respondent No. 1.

9. We heard the arguments of Mr. Vikas Singh, learned senior counsel for the appellant and Mr. Altaf Ahmed, learned senior counsel for the contesting respondent. We have carefully perused the entire pleadings, documents and annexures filed along with the special leave petitions.

10. Mr. Vikas Singh, learned senior counsel took us through the various pleadings and also other relevant records. Mr. Vikas Singh made the following submissions:

1. Maintainability of the writ petition: As regards non-maintainability of the writ petition, the appellant relied upon the following decisions of this Court wherein this Court has held that the writ petitions can be held to be maintainable under certain circumstances:
   - (i) *Smt. Gunwant Kaur* v. *Municipal Committee Bhatinda,* MANU/SC/0397/1969.
   - (ii) *Century Spinning & Manufacturing Company Ltd.* v. *The Ulhasnagar Municipal Council,* MANU/SC/0397/1970.
   - (iii) *Dr. Bal Krishna Agarwal* v. *State of U.P.,*. MANU/SC/0574/1995
   - (iv) *Whirlpool Corporation* v. *Registrar of Trademarks, Mumbai,* MANU/SC/0664/1998
   - (v) *Harbanslal Sahnia* v. *Indian Oil Ltd.,* MANU/SC/1199/2002
   - (vi) *Corporation of the City of Bangalore* v. *Bangalore Stock Exchange,* MANU/SC/2926/2000
   - (vii) *ABL International Ltd.* v. *Export Credit Guarantee Corporation of India Ltd.,* MANU/SC/1080/2003
   - (viii) *Sanjana M. Wig (Ms.)* v. *Hindustan Petroleum Corporation Ltd.,* MANU/SC/0563/2005

He invited our attention to the *Whirlpool Corporation* case (*supra*) wherein this Court has held that there are three clear-cut circumstances wherein a writ petition would be maintainable even in a contractual matter. Firstly, if the action of the respondent is illegal and without jurisdiction, Secondly, if the principles of natural justice have been violated and Thirdly, if the appellants' fundamental rights have been violated. According to the learned senior counsel, all the three principles as laid down in the case of *Whirlpool Corporation* have been made out in the instant case because the action of CIDCO is wholly without jurisdiction as it is seeking to resile from a concluded contract contrary to the express terms of the contract. Secondly, CIDCO, has violated the principles of natural justice as an order affecting the right of the appellant has been passed without giving an opportunity of hearing to the appellant and thirdly, the appellants' fundamental rights as guaranteed under Article 14 of the Constitution of India have been violated because similar allotments made without calling for tenders are not sought to be cancelled and the appellant is being singled out by CIDCO while seeking to cancel the allotment in favour of the appellant.

11. According to the appellant similar allotments as well as the allotment of the appellant are valid allotments as the same have been made in exercise of the statutory powers of CIDCO under the New Bombay Land Disposal Regulation, 1975 in terms of the Land Pricing and Land Disposal Policy and hence all allotments being valid, there is no justification for CIDCO to cancel the allotment of the appellant while not disturbing the other allotments made in favour of the other parties.

12. Learned senior counsel invited our attention to the details of other allotments made without calling for tender which are available at pages 177 and 187 of the SLP paper book in SLP No. 11085 of 2006. Thus it is submitted that the High Court committed grave error in rejecting the petition filed by the appellant as not maintainable. Learned senior counsel made certain submissions in regard to the show cause notice where according to him, there is mention of a report submitted by one Dr. D.K. Shankaran, the then Additional Chief Secretary of the Government of Maharashtra. It is submitted that the said report was made behind the back of the appellant and without his knowledge and that the said report is an *ex-parte* report and no benefit can be taken of the same by CIDCO as the report is based upon conjectures and surmises and there is no scientific basis of the findings in the report. He would also further submit that the CIDCO in the final termination order dated 16.12.2005 did not rightly make a mention of Sankaran Report because the same could not have been relied upon as having been made without any legal sanctity.

13. He invited our attention to the recent pronouncement of this Court in the case of *Amey Cooperative Housing Society Ltd.* v. *Public Concern for Governance Trust,* (2007) 2 SCALE 405. In that case, the Advocate-General of Maharashtra submitted regarding the status of the Shankaran Committee report that it was treated by the State Government to be a preliminary report only and not conclusive and that in the final cancellation order the only ground made was that the allotment had been made without calling for tenders and without resorting to the process of competitive bidding.

14. Much argument was also advanced in regard to the allegations which have been made out in the counter-affidavit before the High Court and in this Court. It is submitted that they were not made party in the show cause notice and were also not a part of the final order of cancellation which is impugned by the appellant in these proceedings. Mr. Vikas Singh further invited our attention to a Constitution Bench judgment of this Court in *Mohinder Singh Gill* v. *C.E.C, New Delhi* reported in MANU/SC/0209/1977 wherein this Court held in para 8 that where an order is passed on certain grounds, its validity must be judged by the reasons so mentioned and cannot be supplemented by fresh reasons in the shape of affidavit or otherwise. It is also argued that the said Constitution Bench judgment of this Court has been followed in *Union of India* v. *E.G. Nambudiri MANU/SC/0293/1991; State Govt. Houseless Harijan Employees'* v. *State of Karnataka,* (2001) 1 SCC 610; *Pavanendra Narayan Verma* v. *Sanjay Gandhi PGI Medical Sciences,* MANU/SC/0705/2001and in *Chandra Singh* v. *State of Rajasthan,* MANU/SC/0479/2003. Thus, the learned senior submitted that the CIDCO is trying to go beyond the terms of the show cause notice/final order of cancellation when admittedly CIDCO has affirmed other similar allotment and permitted them to continue construction inspite of the allotment being made to the other parties without inviting tenders.

15. Learned senior counsel further submitted that the allotment made by CIDCO are governed by New Bombay Disposal of Lands Regulations, 1975. Chapter 4 of the said Regulations provide for mode of disposal of the land. Regulation 4 of Chapter 4 provides as under:

Manner of disposal of land: The Corporation may dispose plots of land by public auction or tender or by considering individual applications as the Corporation may determine from time-to-time.

16. As per the Land Pricing and Land Disposal Policy of CIDCO, CIDCO has been authorized to dispose of various types of land as per the method of disposal prescribed under column 3 of the said policy. The method of disposal has been prescribed broadly in the following manner:

1. By Public Advertisement & at fixed rate
2. By tender
3. On request at fixed rate.

17. The Land Pricing and Land Disposal Policy has in all 12 sub-headings like No. 1 is residential, No. 2 is commercial and No. 12 is public utility. In the said policy, making allotment for multiplexes/auditorium/theatre complex to be developed in the private sector is in Clause 12 of the Chapter relating to allotment for public utility. CIDCO in their affidavit have made wrong statement on oath that the allotment is commercial because clearly under the Land Pricing and Land Disposal Policy such allotment is not commercial but is allotment for public utility. CIDCO to that extent has committed perjury and are liable as such for the same.

18. Thus, from a conjoint reading of the Regulation and the Land Pricing and Land Disposal Policy of CIDCO, it is clear that the allotment of land could be done by considering individual application *i.e.,* without inviting tenders. From the Land Pricing and Land Disposal Policy it is also clear that disposal of land under different category are to be considered differently. In the case of allotment of land for auditorium/multiplex, theatre complex to be developed in the private sector, it is prescribed that the land is to be allotted at reserved price and the method of disposal is on request at fixed rate failing which by competitive bidding thus, in the instant case there is no infirmity in the allotment because the same has been made on request at fixed rate at the reserved price. Such allotment is clearly permitted under Regulation and prescribed as the manner of allotment under the Land Pricing and Land Disposal Policy of CIDCO. Even CIDCO in their affidavit filed in the case of *Sanjay Damodar Surve* v. *State of Maharastra,* being PIL No. 140/2004 as well as in the case of *K. Raheja* PIL No. 45879/2003, 7637/2004 have stated on oath this very stand that they have the right to make allotment by considering individual applications in terms of the power vested on them under regulation 4 of the New Bombay Disposal of Lands Regulations, 1975 and it is not understood why CIDCO is seeking to take a different stand in this matter by singling out the appellant.

19. Mr. Vikas Singh further submitted that the reference to a judgment of this Court in *Hazi Mastan* v. *Kerala Financial Corporation* reported in MANU/SC/0516/1987 is misconceived because in the said case there were no statutory regulations providing for the manner of disposal of land and secondly even in that case the Court had approved the disposal of land by considering individual application as being justified in the facts and circumstances of that case. Therefore, learned senior counsel submitted that the reference to the said judgment can be of no help to CIDCO to justify the cancellation order.

20. Learned senior counsel further contended that this Court in the case of *Corporation of the City of Bangalore* v. *Bangalore Stock Exchange,* reported in MANU/SC/2926/2000 has held that even in the case wherein cancellation of a lease was for a public purpose *i.e.,* for a park and playground by a resolution of the corporation of the city of Bangalore, the same was set aside as there were no such rights reserved to the corporation to cancel the lease under the lease agreement. The appellant in the reply to show cause notice has also referred to judgments in *Printers (Mysore) Ltd.* v. *M.A. Rasheed,* MANU/SC/0307/2004 and *Chairman & MD.BPL. Ltd.* v. *S.P. Gururaja,* MANU/SC/0804/2003 wherein also the allotment had been challenged on the ground that the same had been made without inviting tenders and the High Court had cancelled the allotment and this Court while reversing the order has held that if the Regulations of the Corporation empower the corporation to make allotment without inviting tenders then such allotment was clearly valid and no challenge to the same would be entertained on the ground that other persons could have been interested in applying for the allotment and that they had not been given opportunity to apply for the same. Clearly in terms of the two judgments referred to above, it could not be said that allotment made without issuance of tenders *per se* can be said to be bad or being opposed to public policy.

21. Learned senior counsel for the appellants further submitted that the impugned order violates the fundamental rights as guaranteed under Article 14 of the Constitution because in the similar allotments wherein also Dr. D.K. Shankaran had reported that the same had been done without inviting tenders and CIDCO has suffered huge losses running into crores, CIDCO has taken no steps to cancel those allotments and in fact construction on the said plots are continuing without any objection from CIDCO.

Learned Counsel for the appellant submitted that the appellant is clearly entitled to the same treatment *i.e.*, of being allowed to take the advantage of allotment in his favour which according to the appellant is in accordance with the Regulations as well as Land Pricing and Land Disposal Policy as done in the case of others and that the hostile discrimination of singling out of the appellant in the matter clearly violates the fundamental rights of the appellant.

22. In fact, learned Counsel invited our attention to the similar allotments referred to by Dr. D.K. Shankaran where also huge losses have been reported by Dr. D.K. Shankaran and which allotments are being permitted to continue as under:

1. M/s K. Raheja whose allotment is in the commercial category and where Shankaran had reported Rs. 50 crores loss,
2. M/s Shakti Commercial Premises where the allotment is for the multiplex and the loss reported by Dr. D.K. Shankaran is Rs. 35 crores,
3. M/s Mohan Entertainment where the allotment was also for the multiplex and the loss reported is Rs. 23 crores and,
4. M/s Gurudev Industrial Premises Co-operative where the allotment is for service industry/ warehousing and the loss reported is Rs. 63.55 crores, are some of such allotments which have been allowed to continue and no steps for cancellation of those allotments are being done by CIDCO as is being done in the instant case of the appellants. Furthermore, CIDCO is taking no action for cancellation of other allotments made by CIDCO without inviting tenders.

23. It is submitted that the impugned order cannot be sustained also on the ground that there is gross violation of the principles of natural justice in the order. The first violation of natural justice took place when Dr. D.K. Shankaran started his enquiry. Dr. Shankaran conducted the enquiry without notice to the appellant and without hearing the appellant. The appellant while submitting their reply to the show cause notice specifically sought for an opportunity of hearing, the same was also not granted to the appellant before passing of the final order and on this ground also the impugned order is liable to be set aside. The appellant was not even given the copy of Dr. D.K. Shankaran report for effective reply of show cause notice.

The impugned order is also liable to be quashed as the same is wholly without jurisdiction. Once a concluded contract has been entered into between the parties, the parties cannot be permitted to resile from the same contrary to the express terms of the concluded contract. It has been held in the case of *Corporation of the City of Bangalore's* case (*supra*) to the effect that CIDCO has no such right to revoke the concluded agreement and hence any action taken by

CIDCO contrary to the express terms of the agreement is wholly without jurisdiction. CIDCO cannot take recourse of section 23 of the Contract Act alleging that the agreement is opposed to public policy because clearly such right is reserved only to the Courts and it is submitted that authorities themselves cannot take recourse to the said section in order to annul a concluded agreement.

24. As regards the allegations made against Shri V.M. Lal, the then MD, CIDCO questioning the allotment in the counter-affidavit, it is submitted that firstly the entire basis of such allegation does not survive because this Court has already expunged all the remarks against Shri V.M. Lal in regard to similar allotment made without issuance of tender during his tenure and the Anti Corruption Bureau of the State of Maharashtra as well as the State of Maharashtra in disciplinary proceedings initiated against Shri V.M. Lal as ge has also been given clean chit with regard to all allotments made by CIDCO during his tenure as CMD of the Board. It is also further contended that it was wrongly suggested by CIDCO that the appellant was not eligible for such allotment because the only criteria of eligibility in such allotment by CIDCO is the submission of the EMD and no other criteria is being taken into consideration before making such allotments. The appellant had also submitted the project report and upon being asked by CIDCO regarding the financial capabilities and expertise of the appellant, the appellant had on 26.5.2004, which was received by CIDCO office on 27.5.2004, submitted a clarificatory letter stating about their experience in the field of construction industry for several years. The appellant had also expressed their willingness to approach technical experts from Multiplex industry to provide the area of Navi Mumbai with excellent entertainment facility. In the said letter they had also stated about their financial standing and had attached a letter from the bank regarding their financial capability and that the Bank also gave a letter dated 27.5.2004 certifying the financial standing of the appellant.

25. At the time of hearing, it was suggested by learned senior counsel for the respondent that the allotment was made without any justification and that there was a huge demand for such plot, it is submitted by learned Counsel for the appellant that the appellant has sought information from CIDCO under the Right to Information Act as to whether there was no application pending with them for allotment of the said plot prior in time to the application of the appellant. CIDCO in reply has clearly stated that there was no application prior to the application to the appellant. Even the allotment in favour of the appellant was a reasoned allotment taking into consideration the lack of entertainment facilities in the area and the said issue was also discussed in the board meeting before the allotment and these facts are clear from the information provided to the appellant under the Right to Information Act. Our attention was also drawn to the noting in the file while considering the case of the appellant and before making the allotment that

(i) There is no cinema/multiplex facility available today for the residents of CBD Belapur, Kharghar and Kalamboli residents.

(ii) From accessibility and land use compatibility point of view, plot No. 1, Sector 2, Kharghar admeasuring about 8000 sq. mtrs is an ideal location for multiplex.

(iii) This building will be visible from highway and will add to the image of the city.

(iv) Adjoining plot No. 1 of sector 1 attached to railway station admeasuring 5600 m2 (not demanded yet) is earmarked for city mall.

It is also brought to our notice that in the Board's deliberation it was noted by the then Chairman Shri Javed Khan that promoting a Multiplex near railway station shall be adding value to the development of that node and was needed in view of shortage of entertainment facility in Navi Mumbai.

26. As regards the suggestion of irregularity in the allotment in favour of the appellant is concerned it is submitted that the Principal Secretary, Urban Development, Government of Maharashtra was present in the Board meeting in which decision was taken to allot the subject plot in favour of the appellant and the subsequent CMD also in his letter dated 09.03.2005 had justified the allotment by saying that there was no comparable data to fault the allotment on the ground that CIDCO has suffered losses in the same. It is also pertinent to point out that Dr. Shankaran was also a member of the Board of Directors of CIDCO in the year 1992-93 and during the said period CIDCO Board approved the allotment in favour of a society without issuing tender in which society Dr. Shankaran also owned a flat. Concluding his elaborate and lengthy submissions, Mr. Vikas Singh submitted that the allotment in favour of the appellant cannot be faulted because the grounds made out in the show cause notice/final order of cancellation are clearly not sustainable in law and the cancellation order needs to be quashed. It is further submitted that the allotment in favour of the appellant is completely legal and correct and the same has been made after duly complying with the Land Disposal and Land Pricing Policy and new Bombay Land Disposal Regulations, 1975. He would therefore submit that the impugned order dated 16.12.2005 and show cause notice dated 14.07.2005 be quashed and the respondents are directed to permit the appellant to go ahead with the construction of multiplex in terms of the lease agreement executed between the appellant and the CIDCO and also in terms of the commencement certificate issued by CIDCO in favour of the appellant.

Same argument was advanced by learned senior counsel in the other civil appeal arising out of SLP (C) No. 11087 of 2006 filed by M/s Platinum Entertainment & Anr.

27. Mr. Altaf Ahmed, learned senior counsel appearing for the contesting first respondent submitted that the High Court in passing the impugned order rejecting the writ petition filed by the appellant herein has done so principally on the consideration that the appellants had not availed of the available alternative efficacious remedy and as such could not invoke writ jurisdiction of the High Court to decide contractual matters on whatever ground. He would further submit that on this premises the High Court declined to exercise jurisdiction under Article 226 of the Constitution sought to be invoked by the appellant herein. Mr. Altaf Ahmed further submitted that this Court in its decision in *Kerala State Electricity Board* v. *Kurien E. Kelathil*, reported in MANU/SC/0435/2000 has categorically held that merely because a Corporation/Electricity Board can be termed as a limb or instrumentality of the Government and hence State within the meaning of Article 12 of the Constitution of India nonetheless in the matter of contract jurisdiction under Article 226 of the Constitution of India cannot be invoked and that this view is also affirmed in decisions in *National Highways Authority of India* v. *Ganga Enterprises* reported in MANU/SC/0665/2003 and *Rajureshwar Associates* v. *State of Maharashtra,* MANU/SC/0532/2004.

28. Mr. Altaf Ahmed further submitted that in the present case the allotment was cancelled having regard to section 23 of the Indian Contract Act as the subject allotment was illegal and that as regards the merits of rival contentions a detailed affidavit was filed before the High Court denying the contents of the special leave petition and its accompaniments and list of dates which are inconsistent with and contrary to what is stated hereinabove and as if the same has been expressly traversed and denied. He would, therefore, submit that the appeal is devoid of merits and hence deserves to be dismissed at the threshold in the interest of justice and prayed accordingly. It was further submitted that in case this Court were to remit the matter back to the High Court for fresh disposal, the same writ petition be restored to its original No along with the pleadings which were already complete with a direction to the High Court to decide the same in a time-bound manner preferably within a short period.

29. We have given our careful consideration to the rival submissions made by the respective counsel appearing on either side. In our opinion, the High Court has committed a grave mistake by relegating the appellant to the alternative remedy when clearly in terms of the law laid down by this Court, this was a fit case in which the High Court should have exercised its jurisdiction in order to consider and grant relief to the respective parties. In our opinion, in the instant case, 3 of the 4 grounds on which writ petitions can be entertained in contractual matter were made out and hence it was completely wrong by the High Court to dismiss the writ petitions. In the instant case, 3 grounds as referred to in *Whirlpool Corpn.* (*supra*) has been made out and accordingly the writ petition was clearly maintainable and the High Court has committed an error in relegating the appellant to the civil court.

30. It is also pertinent to notice when the allotment was made in favour of the appellant there was no entertainment facility available in the area and CIDCO in its endeavour to do proper planned development of the area was obliged to provide for entertainment for the residents. CIDCO in fact had put an advertisement for tender for various other plots for the said purpose and upon getting no response to the advertisement, CIDCO approved the allotment in favour of the appellant on first come first serve basis. It is not the case of CIDCO or by any other private party that any other application was made prior in time to the application made by the appellants for the same plot and hence the allotment in favour of the appellant cannot be faulted in any manner. It has been held by several decisions of this Court that while developing a new township the objective of the planning authorities is not to earn money but to provide for systematic and all-round development of the area so that the purpose of setting up the township is achieved by more and more people wanting to live in the area in view of the various amenities being provided in the area. Considering this objective in mind, we are of the view that the allotment made in favour of the appellants cannot be faulted with and this Court will accordingly set aside the orders of CIDCO seeking to resile from a concluded contract in favour of the appellants.

31. It is also pertinent to mention that CIDCO in the show cause notice has taken the ground of non-issuance of tender as the only basis for cancelling the allotment and CIDCO in the final order has also confined itself to the non-issuance of tender as the ground for cancellation but in the reply to the writ petition, CIDCO is seeking to add further grounds to justify the order of cancellation, which is clearly not permissible in terms of the law laid down by this Court in several of its decisions.

Learned Counsel for the appellant submitted that since all the pleadings, records, annexures filed before the High Court and also of this Court is available before this Court, this Court may dispose of the same on merits without remitting the matter to the High Court for fresh disposal as suggested by learned senior counsel for respondent No. 1. It is true that all the records, documents, annexures are available before us. At the same time, the High Court had no occasion to consider all these rival submissions and to render a categorical finding on all the issues. The High Court has disposed of the writ petition only on the ground of availability of alternative remedy. The High Court has not recorded its finding on the merits of the rival claim. Since elaborate arguments were advanced by learned senior counsel for the appellant and countered by learned senior counsel for the respondent, we extracted the entire argument in extenso in order to enable the High Court to consider all the above submissions made by both the parties on merits and dispose of the same within a period of 6 weeks from the date of receipt of this judgment. As already noticed the request for allotment of construction of multiplex was made on 18.05.2004 and the allotment was made by the Board's Resolution dated 03.06.2004. It is also a matter of record that both the appellants in the civil appeals have deposited several crores of rupees as and when directed by respondent No. 1. It is also pertinent to notice that commencement certificate to the appellants permitting them to start the construction was also made on 28.02.2005. However, the show cause notice was issued in July, 2005 and the allotment was cancelled subsequently which was challenged in the writ petition in the year 2006.

32. Since the matter is pending for a very long time before the High Court and also of this Court, we feel just and proper to request the High Court to restore both the writ petitions No. 9467/2005 and 9468/2005 to its original No. along with the pleadings which were already complete and request the High Court to decide the same in a time-bound manner preferably and on priority basis within 6 weeks from the date of receipt of this judgment. We make it clear that we have only extracted and reproduced the extensive arguments advanced by learned senior counsel appearing on either side which, in our opinion, would facilitate the High Court to decide the matter afresh on merits. While admitting the special leave petition, this Court on 24.7.2006 granted stay of dispossession pending further orders and also restrained the appellants from putting up any construction until further orders. The said order will be in force till the disposal of the writ petitions by the High Court. The Hon'ble Chief Justice of the High Court is requested to place the matter before a Division Bench for disposal of the same afresh on merits within 6 weeks from the date of the receipt of this judgment. This direction for early disposal is issued in the peculiar facts and circumstances of the case and in public interest.

Accordingly, the appeal is disposed of. No costs.

Alpesh Navinchandra Shah
v.
State of Maharashtra

AIR 2007 SC (Supp) 570: (2007) 3 SCALE 630
Writ Petition (Criminal) No. 114 of 2006
Decided on 26-02-2007

Coram: **Hon'ble Mr. Justice Altamas Kabir**
Hon'ble Dr. Justice AR. Lakshmanan

Judgment by: **Hon'ble Dr. Justice AR. Lakshmanan**

FACTS: The petitioner was detained under section 3(1) of the Conservation of Foreign Exchange and Prevention of Smuggling Activities Act, 1974 (COFEPOSA Act). The petitioner challenged the legality and validity of the detention order passed at pre-execution stage by a writ petition filed before the Supreme Court under Article 32 of the Constitution of India for issuance of a writ of *habeas corpus* or any other appropriate writ quashing and setting aside the order of detention under COFEPOSA Act, 1974 issued by respondent No. 2 - Principal Secretary (Appeals and Security), Government of Maharashtra, Mumbai.

ISSUE: Validity of the detention order under section 3(1) of the Conservation of Foreign Exchange and Prevention of Smuggling Activities Act, 1974.

HELD: It is true that normally before the execution of the detention order the same is not required to be quashed and set

aside. However, considering the peculiar facts and circumstances of the case no purpose will be served by continuing the detention order. It is pointed out that the appellant has ceased his activities in the field of import or export. He has already paid the tax with penalty as demanded by the authority. There is nothing on record that since the last five years the appellant has indulged in any such activity. The purpose of passing the detention order is to prevent the detenu from continuing his prejudicial activity but not to punish him. The writ petition is accordingly allowed and the impugned order is quashed and set aside.

JUDGMENT

Dr. AR. Lakshmanan, J.

1. The above writ petition was filed under Article 32 of the Constitution of India for issuance of a Writ of *Habeas Corpus* or any other appropriate writ quashing and setting aside the order of detention dated 12.01.2005 under COFEPOSA Act, 1974 issued against the petitioner by respondent No. 2 Principal Secretary (Appeals and Security), Government of Maharashtra, Mumbai.

2. The petitioner was detained under section 3(1) of the Conservation of Foreign Exchange and Prevention of Smuggling Activities Act, 1974 (hereinafter referred to as "COFEPOSA Act") in pursuance of the impugned order of detention. The petitioner by way of this writ petition is challenging the legality and validity of the impugned order of detention passed by respondent No. 2 at pre-execution stage in the peculiar facts and circumstances of this case. It is stated that two similar orders of detention dated 12.1.2005 and 31.1.2005 were issued under the COFEPOSA Act by respondent No. 2 against the petitioner Alpesh Navinchandra Shah and his brother Kamlesh Shah respectively. The detention order has already been served upon Kamlesh Shah. The grounds of detention order and the documents relied upon in the case of the petitioner are identical in content and material.

3. The brief facts of the case are mentioned in seriatim as under:

> In or about, August, 2004 M/s. Perfect Trading Co. (proprietorship firm of Shri Rajendra Mamgaim) imported Ball bearings in five containers. On 3.9.2004, consignments of miss-declared consignments were intercepted by the DRI officials. The petitioner and his brother were arrested on 4.9.2004 by the Intelligence Officers, DRI, Mumbai Zonal Unit primarily on the allegations that they have been indulging in import of high quality and high value Ball Bearing and were clearing the same by evading duty of custom.

4. The Addl. Chief Metropolitan Magistrate, 3rd Court, Esplanade, Mumbai *vide* Order dated 23.9.2004 directed to release the petitioner and his brother on bail imposing conditions including their regular attendance in the Department and the imposition of an embargo not to leave the country without the prior permission of the Court. Impugned Detention Order bearing No. PSA 1204/21 (2)/SLP-3(A) dated 12.1.2005 was issued by respondent No. 2 for detaining the petitioner ostensibly under the provisions of COFEPOSA Act, 1974. Similar Order No. PSA 1204/21 (1)/SLP-3 (A) dated 31.1.2005 was also issued to detain Shri Kamlesh Shah, the brother of the petitioner. Show Cause Notice dated 23.2.2005 was issued to the petitioner and his brother by the DRI, Mumbai Zonal Unit. Pursuant to the said show cause notice, the application for settlement under section 127B of the Customs Act, 1962, was filed on 19.4.2005 by M/s Perfect Trading Co. as Applicant and the petitioner, his brother and others as Co-Applicants before the settlement Commission, Mumbai. During the course of the admission hearing of the aforesaid settlement application, the petitioner came to know that the Order dated 27.12.2005 has been passed by respondent No. 2 for detaining him while invoking section 3(1) of the COFEPOSA Act, 1974. Accordingly, at the stage of the admission hearing, the Settlement Commission was urged to make recommendation to the Detaining Authority for the revocation of the Detention Order. The Settlement Commission, *vide* order dated 3.1.2006, rejected the prayer by adopting the reasoning narrated in the case of Vipul Gor, Proprietor of M/s Sonam Enterprises (Misc. Order No. 12/2005 - CUS dated 19.12.2005) wherein it was, *inter alia,* held that the Commission did not have any jurisdiction to make a recommendation to the Detaining Authority for revocation of a Detention order and further held that the petitioner and his brother would be at liberty to take recourse to any other legal remedy available to it for lifting of the detention order whether by the sponsoring authority, detaining authority or the courts. However, the Settlement Commission allowed the application for settlement to be proceeded with. The case was finally heard by the Settlement Commission on 1.3.2006.

5. *Vide* Final Order bearing No. 17/CUS/2006 dated 7.3.2006, the Settlement Commission allowed the Settlement Application and settled the case on payment of Customs Duty of Rs. 1,40,52,959. In terms of sub-section (1) of section 127H of the Customs Act, 1962, and in view of full and true disclosure, the Commission granted immunity to all the Applicants including the petitioner from any penalty that could be levied under the Customs Act and also from the prosecution under the Customs Act, 1962, as well as under IPC. It is evident from the Order that a copy of the said Final Order of complete settlement of the case, was also forwarded to the Detaining Authority by the Settlement Commission.

It is also pertinent to note that though the Settlement Commission *vide* section 127H of the Customs Act, 1962 is empowered to impose such conditions as it may deem fit for grant of immunities, deemed it fit not to impose any condition on the petitioner, in spite of the fact that detention Order having been issued against the petitioner, was before the Commission and granted full immunities and settled the case giving quietus to all issues. In spite of complete settlement of all disputes among the petitioner and the Revenue, after the case was fully settled by the said Final Order dated 7.3.2006 of 'compromise"/ "settlement" of the entire case, the officers of DRI apprehended the Petitioners brother and he was detained under the Detention Order dated 31.1.2005. The petitioner is also relying upon the copy of order dated 5th May, 2005 published in Gazette of Maharashtra Government at page 56, Page IV-A, *inter alia,* showing that the Order No. PSA 1204/21(2)/ SLP-3(A) was issued against the petitioner on 12th January, 2005 by the respondent. Being aggrieved by the said order of detention which is based upon the same grounds as reflected in the show cause notice and which were considered in the proceedings before the Settlement Commission, the petitioner preferred the above writ petition for quashing of the impugned detention order.

6. We heard Mr. Vikram Chaudhri, learned Counsel for the petitioner and Mr. Ravindra Keshavrao Adsure, learned Counsel for the contesting respondent. Learned Counsel for the petitioner, at the time of hearing, made the following submissions:

In the light of the fact that as per provisions of Customs Act, 1962, the case of the petitioner is 'settled' and he has been granted unconditional immunities by the Settlement Commission, chasing the petitioner for detaining him under the COFEPOSA Act would be contrary to the settled proposition of law that:

(i) the personal liberty is one of the most cherished freedoms more important than any other guaranteed under the constitution and in a democracy governed by rule of law the drastic power to detain a person, without trial, must be strictly construed.

(ii) Draconian power of detention must be exercised in rarest of rare cases and only as a preventive measure and not punitive.

(iii) The law pertaining to preventive detention must be meticulously followed with substantively and procedurally by the detaining authority.

(iv) Section 3(1) of the Act allows the detention of a person only if the appropriate detaining authority is satisfied that with a view to preventing such person from carrying on any of the offensive activities enumerated therein, it is necessary to detain such person.

(v) The satisfaction of the detaining authority is not a subjective one based on the detaining authority's emotions, beliefs or prejudices. There must be a real likelihood of the person being able to indulge in such activities, the inference of such likelihood being drawn form objective data based on surrounding circumstances.

(vi) The possibility of prosecution is having a direct bearing on the subjective satisfaction of the Detaining Authority.

(vii) Unsuccessful judicial trial may not operate as a bar to a detention order, but the discharge cannot be said to be entirely irrelevant and of no significance.

(viii) The detention power cannot be used to subvert, supplant or to substitute the punitive law of Penal Code.

7. At the time of hearing, the judgment rendered by this Court in *Hira Lal Hari Lal Bhagwati* v. *CBI, New Delhi* MANU/SC/0371/2003 (Brijesh Kumar and

Dr. AR. Lakshmanan, JJ) was also relied on and our attention was invited to paras 44 & 45 of the said judgment which read as under:

> 44... The declarant could not be dragged and chased in criminal proceedings after closing the other opening making it a dead end. It is highly unreasonable and arbitrary to do so and initiation and continuance of such proceedings lack *bona fides*.
>
> 45. In the background given above, there is every reason to legally infer that the position as it stood, in regard to the criminal prosecution and conviction on the date the declaration was filed, as conditions precedent to settlement under the Scheme, would also stand finalized on full and final settlement of the matter under the Scheme. That is to say the position that no criminal prosecution was pending against the declarant on the date of filing of the declaration nor he stood convicted for such an offence in relation to the matter covered under the declaration, it would stand finalized with acceptance of the declaration and settlement of the matter fully and finally. Later on, the declarant could not be or continued to be subjected to criminal prosecution to alter the position as it stood on the relevant date of the submission of declaration and get him convicted for such offences in respect of which, if he stood convicted earlier while filing statement he would not have been entitled to seek the benefit under the Scheme. The appellants virtually foreclosed their right to further pursue the proceedings before the authorities or courts of law challenging the legality, validity or the tax liability in terms of the Scheme. Undoubtedly, if the appellants' appeal which was pending in this Court against the order of CEGAT relating to the tax liability, had been allowed it might have affected the criminal proceeding too on merits. In certain circumstances, it could be put up as a defence by the declarant, in the criminal case but in terms of the scheme he was bound to withdraw his appeal. The criminal prosecution could not be allowed to proceed by putting an end to a possible defence, before hand. It certainly amounts to abuse of process of law. The appeals thus deserve to be allowed.

Placing reliance on the above judgment, learned Counsel for the petitioner urged that the detention order No. PSA 1204/21 (2)/SPL-3(A) issued against the petitioner be quashed and set aside without insisting the petitioner to undergo detention.

8. Learned Counsel for the petitioner further submitted that the impugned order of detention is contrary to the spirit of settlement and legislative intent behind the scheme of settlement enacted under the Customs Act, 1962.

i. The Settlement Commission came into being as a culmination of the report submitted by the Wanchoo Committee set up for toning up the administration of direct taxes.

Para 2.32 of the Wanchoo Committee's report reads as:

> This however, does not mean that the door for compromise with an errant tax-payer should forever remain closed. In the administration of fiscal laws, whose primary objective is to raise revenue, there has to be

> room for compromise and settlement. A rigid attitude would not only inhibit one-time tax-evader or an unintending defaulter from making a clean breast of his affairs, but would also unnecessarily strain the investigational resources of the Department in cases of doubtful benefit to revenue, while needlessly proliferating litigation and holding up collections. We would, therefore, suggest that there should be a provision in the law for a settlement with the tax-payer at any stage of the proceedings. In the United Kingdom, the 'confession' method has been in vogue since 1923. In the U.S law also there is a provision for compromise with the tax payer as to his tax liabilities. A provision of this type facilitating settlement in individual cases will give this advantage over general disclosure schemes that misuse thereof will be difficult and the disclosure will not normally breed further tax evasion. Each individual case can be considered on its merits and full disclosures not only of the income but of the modus operandi of its build up can be insisted on, thus sealing off chances of continued evasion through similar practices.

The recommendation of Wanchoo Committee has been quoted with approval by this Court in the case of *CIT (Central)* v. *B.N. Bhattacharjee,* MANU/SC/0301/1979.

9. On the above basis, in the course of the Budget Speech in 1992, Hon'ble the then Finance Minister announced as under:

A settlement Commission was established in 1976 under the Income Tax Act, 1961. I propose to set up a Settlement Commission, on similar lines, for dealing with Customs and Central Excise disputes between the Department and the assesses. I trust this will help in speedy settlement of tax disputes.

10. It is submitted that in spite of the above speech of the Finance Minister in 1992, it was only in the Finance Bill 1998 that provisions were made to insert Chapter XIVA in the Customs Act for creation of Settlement Commission and the provisions relating to the Settlement Commission came into effect *vide* Act 21 of 1998, section 102 w.e.f. 1.8.1998. In the Finance Bill of 1998, Clause 105 seeks to insert Chapter in the Customs Act, 1962 to provide for setting up of a Customs and Central Excise Settlement Commission on the lines of a similar commission already working under the Income Tax Act, 1961.

11. Learned Counsel for the petitioner further submitted that:

(i) Since the legislature itself has created Settlement Commission for generating Revenue and has also made provisions for release of the goods on payment of duty and has also made provisions for granting immunity from prosecution under the Customs Act, 1962 under the Indian Penal Code and also under the other Central Law, it is clear that the intention of the Legislature was more on Revenue aspect rather than prosecution and punishment aspect or in continuing with multiple litigations. He submits that it would be unjust unfair and unreasonable if a person is made to suffer preventive detention mainly after his application for settlement is allowed to be proceeded with, and after realisation of the Customs duties not only the goods are ordered to be released, but on considering the co-operation extended by him in the settlement proceedings, the Settlement Commission has also granted to him immunity from prosecution under the Customs Act, 1962 as well as under the IPC. He further submits that this Court in the case of *Sadhu Roy* has held that, if there is cast iron case against the person, then he should be prosecuted rather than detained under the preventive detention law, which is softer measure. He submits that when under the law the person is immuned from prosecution which is a stronger deterrent than detention, there is no reason as to why the same person should be detained preventively under a softer measure.

(ii) The act of detaining such person whose Settlement Application under the statutory provisions of Customs Act, 1962 has been allowed to be proceeded with and specifically whose case has been settled, would be discriminative and arbitrary as against the person who does not approach the Settlement Commission and does not settle their case and thus continue to damage the economy of the country. Learned Counsel submits that for the reason of discrimination and arbitrariness of the detention order against a person who is willing to or has settled the case against the petitioner, the detention Order is liable to be quashed and set aside because it would become punitive and how would the punitive Order would survive when the application for settlement of the case with prayers for immunity from prosecution has been allowed to be proceeded with and the case has been fully settled?

(iii) When the Settlement Commission grants immunity to a person under section 127H of the Customs Act, 1962, the Settlement Commission regularizes the act of the person which was supposed to be violative of the provisions of the Customs Act, 1962, meaning thereby that whatever was alleged to have been committed by the said person becomes *non-est,* as if he has not committed any breach of the Customs Act, 1962, the person becomes a person who has not at all committed any act or omission in respect of the goods under section 111 of the Customs Act, 1962 and therefore in such a situation where there is no act or omission on the part of the person who approaches the Settlement Commission and gets immunity from prosecution and penalty, a Detention Order under any clause of section 3(1)(i) to 3(1)(v) cannot sustain. Learned Counsel for the petitioner, therefore, submits since the petitioner's application for settlement of the case has been allowed to be proceeded with and his case has been finally settled, the impugned order of detention against the Petitioner has become an order which is not sustainable in law.

12. Our attention to the preamble of COFEPOSA Act, 1974 was invited which reads as under:

COFEPOSA Act, 1974, as per its Preamble is an Act to provide for preventive detention in certain cases for the purpose of conservation and augmentation of foreign exchange and prevention of smuggling activities and for matters connected therewith because the violations of foreign exchange regulations and smuggling activities are having an increasingly deleterious effect on the national economy and thereby a serious adverse effect on the security of the State.

13. Learned Counsel for the petitioner submits that it was clear from the Preamble of the COFEPOSA Act that only in certain cases the preventive detention is provided for conservation and augmentation of foreign exchange and preventing the smuggling activities which have deleterious effect on the national economy. He submits that the above objective of the COFEPOSA Act, 1974 is fulfilled by the Order of the Settlement Commission in as much as when a case is settled on payment of the Customs duty, there would be no deleterious effect on the national economy, on the contrary, even if after settlement of case the detention order is allowed to be continued, the legislative intent in introducing the settlement provision would be defeated which may have adverse and deleterious effect on the national economy.

14. It is further submitted that the Settlement Commission is a forum of legal criterion and the powers are drawn from the enacted statutes such as Customs Act, 1962 and Central Excise Act, 1944 in the case of eligible persons, who in addition to fulfilling the other criteria admit additional duty liability of a minimum of Rs. 2 lacs, the option of knocking the doors of Settlement Commission is available, *inter alia,* in the cases under the Customs Act. According to the learned Counsel, the functional mechanism of the Settlement Commission pertaining to the customs cases can be broadly described as follows:

15. On receiving an application, the statutory report is called for by the Settlement Commission from the jurisdictional Commissioner. The Commission considers the report and after hearing both the sides decides on the admissibility of the case. Again after hearing both the sides, the Settlement Commission, after being satisfied that a true and full disclosure has been made by the applicant, determines the duty liability, redemption fine in lieu of confiscation and the penalty on the persons. Further, the question of extending immunity from prosecution under the Customs Act, 1962, Indian Penal Code and any other Central Acts is also decided by the Commission. The Commission has got power to reject any application. Further the decisions of the Settlement are not appealable in the regular course. Above all, once the Commission admits a case, it is vested with the exclusive powers of all the Customs authorities till the finalization of the case.

16. In this regard it is apt to extract sections 127B to 127J of the Customs Act, 1962 which are as under:

> *127B. Application for settlement of cases.*—(1) Any importer, exporter or any other person (hereinafter in this Chapter referred to as the applicant) may, at any stage of a case relating to him make an application in such form and in such manner as may be specified by rules, and containing a full and true disclosure of his duty liability which has not been disclosed before the proper officer, the manner in which such liability has been incurred, the additional amount of customs duty accepted to be payable by him and such other particulars as may be specified by rules including the particulars of such dutiable goods in respect of which he admits short

levy on account of misclassification or otherwise of goods, to the Settlement Commission to have the case settled and such application shall be disposed of in the manner hereinafter provided:

Provided that no such application shall be made unless—

(a) the applicant has filed a bill of entry, or a shipping bill, in respect of import or export of goods, as the case may be, and in relation to such bill of entry or shipping bill or a show cause notice has been issued to him by the proper officer;

(b) the additional amount of duty accepted by the applicant in his application exceeds two lakh rupees:

Provided further that no application shall be entertained by the Settlement Commission under this sub-section in cases which are pending in the Appellate Tribunal or any Court:

Provided also that no application under this sub-section shall be made in relation to goods to which section 123 applies or to goods in relation to which any offence under the Narcotic Drugs and Psychotropic Substances Act, 1985 (61 of 1985) has been committed:

Provided also that no application under this sub-section shall be made for the interpretation of the classification of the goods under the Customs Tariff Act, 1975 (51 of 1975).

(2) Where any dutiable goods, books of account, other documents or any sale proceeds of the goods have been seized under section 110, the applicant shall not be entitled to make an application under Sub-section (1) before the expiry of one hundred and eighty days from the date of the seizure.

(3) Every application made under Sub-section (1) shall be accompanied by such fees as may be specified by rules.

(4) An application made under Sub-section (1) shall not be allowed to be withdrawn by the applicant.

127C. Procedure on receipt of application under section 127B.—(1) On receipt of an application under section 127B, the Settlement Commission shall call for a report from the Commissioner of Customs having jurisdiction and on the basis of the materials contained in such report and having regard to the nature and circumstances of the case or the complexity of the investigation involved therein, the Settlement Commission may, by order, allow the application to be proceeded with or reject the application:

Provided that an application shall not be rejected under this sub-section, unless an opportunity has been given to the applicant of being heard:

Provided further that the Commissioner of Customs shall furnish such report within a period of one month of the receipt of the communication from the Settlement Commission, failing which it shall be presumed that the Commissioner of Customs has no objection to such application; but he may raise objections at the time of hearing fixed by the Settlement

Commission for admission of the application and the date of such hearing shall be communicated by the Settlement Commission to the applicant and the Commissioner of Customs within a period not exceeding two months from the date of receipt of such application, unless the presiding officer of the Bench extends the said period of two months, after recording the reasons in writing.

(2) A copy of every order under sub-section (1) shall be sent to the applicant and to the Commissioner of Customs having jurisdiction.

(3) Subject to the provisions of sub-section (4), the applicant shall, within thirty days of the receipt of a copy of the order under sub-section (1) allowing the application to be proceeded with, pay the amount of additional duty admitted by him as payable and shall furnish proof of such payment to the Settlement Commission.

(4) If the Settlement Commission is satisfied, on an application made under sub-section (1) that the applicant is unable for good and sufficient reasons to pay the amount referred to in sub-section (3), within the time specified in that sub-section, it may extend the time for payment of the amount which remains unpaid or allow payment thereof by instalments, if the applicant furnishes adequate security for the payment thereof.

(5) Where the additional amount of customs duty referred to in sub-section (3) is not paid by the applicant within the time specified or extended period, as the case may be, the Settlement Commission may direct that the amount which remains unpaid, together with simple interest at the rate of eighteen per cent. per annum or at the rate notified by the Board from time-to-time on the amount remaining unpaid, be recovered as the sum due to the Central Government by the proper officer having jurisdiction over the applicant in accordance with the provisions of section 142.

(6) Where an application is allowed to be proceeded with under sub-section (1), the Settlement Commission may call for the relevant records from the Commissioner of Customs having jurisdiction and after examination of such records, if the Settlement Commission is of the opinion that any further enquiry or investigation in the matter is necessary, it may direct the Commissioner (Investigation) to make or cause to be made such further enquiry or investigation and furnish a report on the matters covered by the application and any other matter relating to the case.

(7) After examination of the records and the report of the Commissioner of Customs received under sub-section (1), and the report, if any, of the Commissioner (Investigation) of the Settlement Commissioner under sub-section (6), and after giving an opportunity to the applicant and to the Commissioner of Customs having jurisdiction to be heard, either in person or through a representative duly authorised in this behalf, and after examining such further evidence as may be placed before it or obtained by it, the Settlement Commission may, in accordance with the provisions

of this Act, pass such order as it thinks fit on the matters covered by the application and any other matter relating to the case not covered by the application, but referred to in the report of the Commissioner of Customs or the Commissioner (Investigation) under sub-section (1) or sub-section (6).

(8) Subject to the provisions of section 32A of the Central Excise Act, 1944 (1 of 1944), the materials brought on record before the Settlement Commission shall be considered by the Members of the concerned Bench before passing any order under sub-section (7) and, in relation to the passing of such order the provisions of section 32D of the Central Excise Act, 1944 shall apply.

(9) Every order passed under sub-section (7) shall provide for the terms of settlement including any demand by way of duty, penalty or interest, the manner in which any sum due under the settlement shall be paid and all other matters to make the settlement effective and shall also provide that the settlement shall be void if it is subsequently found by the Settlement Commission that it has been obtained by fraud, or misrepresentation of facts.

(10) Where any duty payable in pursuance of an order under sub-section (7) is not paid by the applicant within thirty days of the receipt of a copy of the order by him, then, whether or not the Settlement Commission has extended the time for payment of such duty or has allowed payment thereof by instalments, the applicant shall be liable to pay simple interest at the rate of eighteen per cent. per annum or at such other rate as notified by the Board on the amount remaining unpaid from the date of expiry of the period of thirty days aforesaid.

(11) Where a settlement becomes void as provided under Sub-section (9) the proceedings with respect to the matters covered by the settlement shall be deemed to have been revived from the stage at which the application was allowed to be proceeded with by the Settlement Commission and proper officer may, notwithstanding anything contained in any other provision of this Act, complete such proceedings at any time before the expiry of two years from the date of the receipt of communication that the settlement became void.

127D. Power of Settlement Commission to order provisional attachment to protect revenue.—(1) Where, during the pendency of any proceeding before it, the Settlement Commission is of the opinion that for the purpose of protecting the interests of the revenue it is necessary so to do, it may, by order, attach provisionally any property belonging to the applicant in such manner as may be specified by rules.

(2) Every provisional attachment made by the Settlement Commission under sub-section (1) shall cease to have effect from the date the sums due to the Central Government for which such attachment is made are discharged by the applicant and evidence to that effect is submitted to the Settlement Commission.

127E. Power of Settlement Commission to reopen completed proceedings.—If the Settlement Commission is of the opinion (the reasons for such opinion to be recorded by it in writing) that, for the proper disposal of the case pending before it, it is necessary or expedient to reopen any proceeding connected with the case but which has been completed under this Act before application for settlement under section 127B was made, it may, with the concurrence of the applicant, reopen such proceeding and pass such order thereon as it thinks fit, as if the case in relation to which the application for settlement had been made by the applicant under that section covered such proceeding also:

Provided that no proceeding shall be reopened by the Settlement Commission under this section after the expiry of five years from the date of application under sub-section (1) of section 127B.

127F. Power and procedure of Settlement Commission.—(1) In addition to the powers conferred on the Settlement Commission under Chapter V of the Central Excise Act, 1944 (1 of 1944), it shall have all the powers which are vested in an officer of the customs under this Act or the Rules made thereunder.

(2) Where an application made under section 127B has been allowed to be proceeded with under section 127C, the Settlement Commission shall, until an order is passed under sub-section (7) of section 127C, have, subject to the provisions of sub-section (6) of that section, exclusive jurisdiction to exercise the powers and perform the functions of any officer of customs or Central Excise Officer as the case may be, under this Act or in the Central Excise Act, 1944 (1 of 1944), as the case may be, in relation to the case.

(3) In the absence of any express direction by the Settlement Commission to the contrary, nothing in this Chapter shall affect the operation of the provisions of this Act in so far as they relate to any matter other than those before the Settlement Commission.

(4) The Settlement Commission shall, subject to the provisions of Chapter V of the Central Excise Act, 1944 (1 of 1944) and this Chapter, have power to regulate its own procedure and the procedure of Benches thereof in all matters arising out of the exercise of its powers, or of the discharge of its functions, including the places at which the Benches shall hold their sittings.

127G. Inspection, etc., of reports.—No person shall be entitled to inspect, or obtain copies of, any report made by any officer of the Customs to the Settlement Commission; but the Settlement Commission may, in its discretion, furnish copies thereof to any such person on an application made to it in this behalf and on payment of such fee as may be specified by rules:

Provided that, for the purpose of enabling any person whose case is under consideration to rebut any evidence brought on record against him in any such report, the Settlement Commission shall, on an application made in this behalf, and on payment by such person of such fee as may be specified by rules, furnish him with a certified copy of any such report or part thereof relevant for the purpose.

127H. Power of Settlement Commission to grant immunity from prosecution and penalty.—(1) The Settlement Commission may, if it is satisfied that any person who made the application for settlement under section 127B has co-operated with the Settlement Commission in the proceedings before it and has made a full and true disclosure of his duty liability, grant to such person, subject to such conditions as it may think fit to impose, immunity from prosecution for any offence under this Act or under the Indian Penal Code (45 of 1860) or under any other Central Act for the time being in force and also either wholly or in part from the imposition of any penalty, fine and interest under this Act, with respect to the case covered by the settlement:

Provided that no such immunity shall be granted by the Settlement Commission in cases where the proceedings for the prosecution for any such offence have been instituted before the date of receipt of the application under section 127B.

(2) An immunity granted to a person under sub-section (1) shall stand withdrawn if such person fails to pay any sum specified in the order of the settlement passed under sub-section (7) of section 127C within the time specified in such order or within such further time as may be allowed by the Settlement Commission, or fails to comply with any other condition subject to which the immunity was granted and thereupon the provisions of this Act shall apply as if such immunity had not been granted.

(3) An immunity granted to a person under sub-section (1) may, at any time, be withdrawn by the Settlement Commission, if it is satisfied that such person had, in the course of the settlement proceedings, concealed any particulars, material to the settlement or had given false evidence, and thereupon such person may be tried for the offence with respect to which the immunity was granted or for any other offence of which he appears to have been guilty in connection with the settlement and shall also become liable to the imposition of any penalty under this Act to which such person would have been liable, had no such immunity been granted.

127-I. Power of Settlement Commission to send a case back to the proper officer.—(1) The Settlement Commission may, if it is of opinion that any person who made an application for settlement under section 127B has not cooperated with the Settlement Commission in the proceedings before it, send the case back to the proper officer who shall thereupon dispose of the case in accordance with the provisions of this Act as if no application under section 127B had been made.

(2) For the purpose of sub-section (1), the proper officer shall be entitled to use all the materials and other information produced by the assessee before the Settlement Commission or the results of the inquiry held or

evidence recorded by the Settlement Commission in the course of the proceedings before it as if such materials, information, inquiry and evidence had been produced before such proper officer or held or recorded by him in the course of the proceedings before him.

(3) For the purposes of the time-limit under section 28 and for the purposes of interest under section 28AA, in a case referred to in sub-section (1), the period commencing on and from the date of the application to the Settlement Commission under section 127B and ending with the date of receipt by the officer of customs of the order of the Settlement Commission sending the case back to the officer of customs shall be excluded.

127J. Order of settlement to be conclusive.—Every order of settlement passed under sub-section (7) of section 127C shall be conclusive as to the matters stated therein and no matter covered by such order shall, save as otherwise provided in this Chapter, be reopened in any proceeding under this Act or under any other law for the time being in force.

17. Learned Counsel for the petitioner further submits that the Settlement Commission *vide* final order dated 7-3-2006 has allowed the settlement application and granted complete immunity to the petitioner as well as his brother from penalty and prosecution. In these circumstances, the detention of the petitioner in pursuance to the impugned order of detention would result in blatant infringement of Article 21 of the Constitution of India as the order has been rendered totally *non est* in the eyes of law. It is further submitted that in view of the acceptance of the settlement Application by the Settlement Commission, all matters stand concluded and settled. In these circumstances, the execution of the detention order is wholly uncalled for, unwarranted and absolutely illegal, being based on wrong reasons and the execution would be apparently *mala fide*. The very constitution of the Settlement Commission and insertion of the provisions relating to the settlement of the cases under the Act is to achieve the twin objective of collection of evaded revenue as well as the prevention of further evasion through similar practices. Necessarily implying thereby that by making true and full disclosure of his liabilities and settling them, the prejudicial activities of the evader are put to an end. Therefore, the detention order on the same accusations that have been considered by the Settlement Commission would be rendered otiose and not worthy of execution.

18. Learned Counsel would further submit that a perusal of section 127H would clearly reveal that the Settlement Commission has to arrive at a complete satisfaction that the Applicant before it has made a full and true disclosure of his duty liability and while granting the immunity from prosecution/penalty, the Commission is competent to impose "such conditions as it may think fit". It is therefore crystal clear that while allowing the settlement of the case, the Settlement Commission has comprehensively looked into the aspect of sealing the opportunity of any further indulgence of the Applicants in any such activity of evasion of duty.

19. Section 127J of the Customs Act, 1962, categorically stipulates that any matter that has been settled by the Commission would be conclusive and the same cannot be reopened in any proceeding under the Customs Act, 1962, or "under any other law for the time being in force". Viewed in this perspective, the detention of the petitioner on the same grounds that have been considered by the settlement Commission would tantamount to a gross abuse of the process of law.

20. Learned Counsel further submits that the deterrent effect inflicted by the settlement Commission is more effective and is foolproof than the method of preventive detention. Law has to select the method, which is objective, transparent and effective in preference over the method, which is subjective, unaccountable and ineffective.

21. Learned Counsel further invited our attention to the law that has been enunciated by this Court in *R.K. Garg* v. *Union of India* MANU/SC/0074/1981 which read as under:

> The Court must always remember that "legislation is directed to practical problems, that the economic mechanism is highly sensitive and complex, that many problems are singular and contingent, that laws are not abstract propositions and do not relate to abstract units and are not to be measured by abstract symmetry".... Every legislation particularly in economic matters is essentially empiric and it is based on experimentation or what one may call trial and error method and therefore it cannot provide for all possible situations or anticipate all possible abuses. There, may be crudities and inequities in complicated experimental economic legislation but on that account alone it cannot be struck down as invalid.... There may even be possibilities of abuse, but that too cannot of itself be a ground for invalidating the legislation, because it is not possible for any legislature to anticipate as if by some divine prescience, distortions and abuses of its legislation which may be made by those subject to its provisions and to provide against such distortions and abuses....

22. According to the petitioner's counsel, the case of the petitioner squarely falls with the said exceptions and thus the impugned detention order deserves to be set aside. He would also further submit that the case of the petitioner is squarely covered by the ratio laid down by this Court in *Additional Secretary to Government of India* v. *Smt. Alka Subhash Gadia,* 1992 SCC Supp (1) 496 wherein this Court, *inter alia,* has held as under:

> ...Thirdly, and this is more important, it is not correct to say that the courts have no power to entertain grievances against any detention order prior to its execution. The courts have the necessary power and they have used it in proper cases as has been pointed out above, although such cases have been few and the grounds on which the courts have interfered with them at the pre-execution stage are necessarily very limited in scope and number, *viz.,* where the courts are *prima facie* satisfied (i) that the impugned order is not passed under the Act under which it is purported

to have been passed, (ii) that it is sought to be executed against a wrong person, (iii) that it is passed for a wrong purpose, (iv) that it is passed on vague, extraneous and irrelevant grounds or (v) that the authority which passed it had no authority to do so....

This Court has further analysed and discussed the ratio laid down in *Alka Subhash Gadia* (*supra*) in the matter of *Subhash Muljimal Gandhi* v. *L. Himingliana* reported in MANU/SC/0835/1994 wherein this Court has held as under:

> 11. ...Bound as we are by the above judgments, we must hold that the other contingencies, if any, must be of the same species as of the five contingencies referred to therein....

23. Learned Counsel submitted that the law has to adopt a progressive approach and when an order of detention has been rendered infructuous by the supervening circumstances, as in the present case, permitting the execution of the same would be a draconian measure unacceptable to the settled tenets of justice, law and equity.

24. Learned Counsel cited the case of *Pawan Bhartiya* v. *Union of India* reported in MANU/SC/1512/2001 wherein this Court has held as under:

> 4... the custom duty which was required to be paid was paid by them before the execution of the detention orders. Despite this fact the detention order passed against the appellant was not revoked even though he has also paid the custom duty as demanded....
>
> 5...the fact of payment of duty in the cases detected against these persons may act as a deterrent against their chance of indulging in similar prejudicial activities in future since this may adversely affect their financial backbone....

25. Learned Counsel submitted that the ratio of the aforesaid case wherein the detention order was quashed at the pre-detention stage especially taking into account the need for execution of the order in view of payment of duties etc., is also applicable to the facts of the present case and in fact the petitioner is placed in a much better situation as his case has also been settled by the statutory process and has been granted complete immunities owing to true and full disclosure and full co-operation in the settlement proceedings. It is further submitted that the factum of settlement of the matter as well as the consequent grant of immunities had duly been conveyed to the detaining authority *i.e.,* respondent No. 2 by the Settlement Commission. The Detaining Authority was, therefore, bound to consider the desirability and need for execution of the impugned detention order in view of the dramatically changed scenario. According to the learned Counsel, after the settlement of the case, the entire controversy stands buried and settled warranting forthwith termination of the impugned detention order. Arguing further, he submitted that a citizen's right of personal liberty under Article 21 of the Constitution cannot be deprived of by the arbitrary decision of the statutory authority and, therefore, the order of detention so made is always subject to judicial scrutiny and review on the touchstone of relevance and reasonableness, fair play, natural justice, equality and non-discrimination. Considering the entire factual matrix in juxtaposition with the legal issues involved, the only inference according to the petitioner's counsel that can be legitimately drawn is that the execution of such null and void detention orders would only be punitive and not preventive in any manner whatsoever. Learned Counsel for the petitioner already invited our attention to the case of *Alka Gadia (supra)* to the effect that the writ petition at pre-execution stage is fully maintainable. The relevant observation of the extract of this Court is as under:

Thirdly, in the rare cases where the detenu, before being served with them, learns of the detention order and the grounds on which it is made, and satisfies the Court of their existence by proper affirmation, the Court does not decline to entertain the writ petition even at the pre-execution stage, of course, on the very limited grounds stated above.

It is, therefore, prayed that the detention order be quashed and set aside and directing the respondents to set the petitioner at liberty forthwith.

26. Mr. Ravindra Keshavrao Adsure, learned Counsel for the second respondent submitted that the Detaining Authority has exercised their powers conferred by section 3(1) of COFEPOSA Act and has issued detention order dated 12.01.2005. It is submitted that the detention order was passed after carefully considering the entire documents of the proposal sent by the sponsoring authority and after being subjectively satisfied that it is essential for preventing the detenu from indulging in prejudicial activities in future and accordingly the order of detention against the petitioner as well as his brother was passed. Learned Counsel also invited our attention to the judgment of this Court in *Naresh Kumar Goyal* v. *Union of India* reported in MANU/SC/2493/2005 wherein this Court has observed that Courts have power to entertain grievances against any detention order prior to its execution only in proper cases and the grounds on which the courts interfere the detention order at the pre-execution stage are necessarily very limited and in scope and number.

27. Therefore, when the courts are *prima facie* satisfied (i) that the impugned order is not passed under the Act under which it is purported to have been passed (ii) that it is sought to be executed against a wrong person, (iii) that it is passed for a wrong purpose, (iv) that it is passed on vague, extraneous and irrelevant grounds, or (v) that the authority which passed it had no authority to do so. Therefore, the impugned order does not suffer from any infirmity as stated above and accordingly, the present writ petition at pre-execution stage of detention order is not maintainable. Hence, the present writ petition is required to be dismissed.

28. Learned Counsel for the respondent further submitted that the admittance of the case and imposition/condonation of fine and/or penalty is the prerogative of the Settlement Commission and application praying immunity from fine, penalty and prosecution matters pertain to the jurisdiction of Settlement Commission. But, revocation of the detention order issued in respect of the detente is different issue and not governed by provisions of section 127F(2) of the Customs Act. It was submitted that in a representation made before Settlement Commission in *Shri Vipul Gor* v. *Sonam Enterprises,* the Settlement Commission in its order dated 15.12.2005 rejected the plea of the applicant therein, for making suitable recommendations to the Detaining Authority for revocation of his detention order. In the present case the petitioner relied upon the case of *Hiralal Harilal Bhagvati* v. *C.B.I* (*supra*). The said relied upon case was a case of duty evasion and the appellant therein was booked by Customs Department and thereafter, custom duty was paid under Kar Vivad Samadhan Scheme (K.V.S.S) and further in the criminal proceedings under section 120B and 420 of I.P.C initiated by C.B.I was quashed by this Court. The above cited case is different from the present case, as in the case in hand, the detention order was issued under COFEPOSA Act against the petitioner with objective to prevent the nefarious activities in future. Therefore the immunity is granted by Settlement Commission from fine, penalty and prosecution under the provisions of Customs Act, 1962 and I.P.C have no bearing on the order issued by the Detaining Authority which is very much legal and the same needs to be upheld.

29. We have carefully considered the rival submissions with reference to the entire pleadings and the provisions of section 127B-127J of the Customs Act and the provisions of the COFEPOSA Act. We have also perused the annexures and records filed along with the writ petition. In our opinion, the argument advanced by learned Counsel for the respondent merit acceptance. As rightly pointed out by learned Counsel for the respondent that the admittance of the case and imposition/condonation of fine or penalty is the prerogative of the Settlement Commission and application praying immunity from fine/penalty and prosecution are matters pertains to the jurisdiction of the Settlement Commission but the revocation of the detention order issued in respect of the detenu is different issue and not governed by the provisions of section 127F(2) of the Customs Act.

30. At the time of hearing, learned Counsel for the petitioner relied upon the case of *Hiralal Harilal Bhagwati* v. *C.B.I (supra).* According to learned Counsel for the respondent the said relied upon case was a case of duty evasion and appellant therein was booked by customs authority and therefore, customs duty was paid under KVSS and further in the criminal proceedings under section 120B and 420, IPC initiated by CBI was quashed by this Court. Therefore, it is admitted that the above cited case is different from the present case as in the case in hand the detention order was issued under the COFEPOSA Act against the petitioner with objective to prevent to the nefarious activities in future. Therefore, the immunity granted by the Settlement Commission from fine, penalty and prosecution under the provisions of the Customs Act and IPC have no bearing on the order of detention passed under the COFEPOSA Act. Therefore, it is contended that the detention order issued by the Detaining Authority is very much legal and the same needs to be upheld.

31. The Settlement Commission was constituted with the aim and objective of settling the tax evasion issues and by virtue of disclosure by tax offender; they gain immunity from fine/penalty which is otherwise mandatory under the provisions of tax laws. But, such opportunity is only extended to one tax offender but not available to habitual smugglers. For the persons involved in smuggling activities, other than the provisions made for the prosecution under the Customs Act, 1962, an equal deterrent is emphasized under the provisions of the COFEPOSA Act, 1974 *i.e.,* provisions for preventive detention. Such preventive detention prohibits smugglers from indulging in further smuggling activities. In the present case the investigation reveals the consistent involvement of the petitioner detente and his brother Kamlesh Navinchandra Shah in smuggling activities, therefore, the Detaining Authority on the basis of evidence placed before him felt it necessary to issue the detention orders in respect of both the detentes in order to prevent them from pre-judicial activities in future. Accordingly the impugned order is justifiable in the eyes of law and present Writ Petition deserves to be dismissed.

32. It is submitted that the orders of detention under COFEPOSA Act was issued in respect of the petitioner and his brother *vide* orders dated 12.1.2005 and 31.1.2005 respectively whereas they had made an application before the settlement Commission under section 127B of the Customs Act, 1962 on 19.4.2005. At the time of issue of the said Detention Orders, the Detaining Authority was not aware of the detentues' intention of approaching the Settlement Commission. The immunity from prosecution was granted to the petitioner and his brother by virtue of final order dated 8.3.2006 of Settlement Commission. Since the Settlement Commission is an authority to settle the duty liability with the discretion to grant immunity in respect of fine, penalty and prosecution, it cannot be construed that anybody approaching the Settlement Commission, ceases to take up Settlement Commission and the detention order under COFEPOSA Act both are distinctly different and objectives of both the orders are also different. Therefore, it is wrongly construed by the petitioner that once the Settlement Commission has granted unconditional immunities, the present detention order is contrary to the settled position of law.

33. Nowhere it is stated in. the provisions of section 127H of the Customs Act, 1962 and in the order of the Settlement Commission dated 08.03.2006 that the opportunity of further indulgence in smuggling activities is sealed or plugged. In our view, the Settlement Commissioner's order only dealt with true and full disclosure of the disputed duty and acceptance of the entire duty, liability by the petitioner and his brother. Nowhere it is mentioned in the Settlement Commission's order that the petitioner would not indulge in smuggling of goods in future. Therefore, in order to prevent the detenu from indulging in smuggling activities, the said detention order was passed and there is no illegality in the detention order. In the instant case, the customs duty of Rs. 1.4 crore was sought to be evaded by the petitioner and his brother was accepted in full by them. This acceptance of entire duty demanded in the impugned, show cause notice was interpreted as full and true disclosure by the Settlement Commission and as such the petitioner and the co applicants were directed to pay the said amount of duty during the Settlement Commission proceedings. The said customs duty of Rs. 1.4 crore was expected to be paid by the petitioner and others at the time of import of the impugned consignments during September, 2004. However, the said amount of evaded customs duty was ordered to be paid in the month of March, 2006 by the Settlement Commission. The Settlement Commission, while extending the benefits as envisaged in the true spirit of settlement, have granted immunity from fine, penalty and prosecution under the Customs Act, 1962 and IPC. The final order of the Settlement Commission has, by no means, undermined the surroundings of the offence committed by the petitioner and his brother. In the admission order No. 36/Customs/2005 of the Settlement Commission dated 3.1.2006, the Commission also distinctly demarcated the area of jurisdiction of the Settlement Commission and the matter of COFEPOSA. The Settlement Commission adhered strictly to the aspect of levy of customs duty and on the basis of the full and true disclosure by the petitioner and others, in that respect, settled the case by directing full payment of customs duty and having done so, extended the benefit of immunity from fine, penalty and prosecution.

34. Thus the matters of Settlement Commission and the COFEPOSA are altogether different issues, the orders of the respective authorities should not and cannot be binding or influencing each other. As such the outcome of the Settlement Commission order should not have any bearing on the detention order. Concluding his argument, learned Counsel for the respondent submitted that the preventive detention under COFEPOSA is distinctly different from the prosecution under the Customs Act, 1962 and IPC, the sanctity of the detention order issued by the second respondent as the Detaining Authority, should be upheld and the same should be ordered to be served upon the petitioner in the interest of justice.

35. Though the matter was argued by learned Counsel for the respondent on merits, learned Counsel for the respondent at the time of hearing in fairness placed before us the reported opinion dated 5.6.2006 of the Advisory Board constituted under the COFEPOSA Act, 1974 in respect of the detenu Kamlesh Navinchandra Shah, the brother of the petitioner.

36. Para 6 of the order dated 4.5.2006 of the Advisory Board constituted under section 8(a) of the Act 52 of 74 by the Government of Maharashtra was placed before us. We have perused the said order. In para 6, the Advisory Board has observed as under:

> ...After the final order passed by the Settlement Commission of Customs and Central Excise, the detention order has been executed. The detente and his brother had extended full co-operation and full customs duty as demanded by the Revenue has been paid and the case finally settled. The Commission had given unconditional immunity from prosecution as well as penalty. A copy of the order has been forwarded by the Commission to the Detaining Authority and yet the detention order was executed on his brother *i.e.,* detente Kamlesh Shah. He further stated that he challenged the order of his detention at pre-execution stage in the Supreme Court and Supreme Court has given Interim stay of the operation of impugned order.

It is thus seen that the Settlement Commission has, in its order, under the head 'penalty' and 'prosecution' granted immunity from penalty and prosecution to the co-applicant and in these circumstances the Advisory Board was of the opinion that there was no sufficient cause for the continued detention. Learned Counsel for the respondent has also placed before us the opinion of the Advisory Board which reads thus:

The Advisory Board is of the opinion that there is no sufficient cause for the detention of above named detente under section 3(1) of COFEPOSA Act, 1974.

37. The consequential communication dated 5-6-2006 and the order dated 5-6-2006 were also placed before us which read thus:

The Advisory Board has reported that there is no sufficient cause for the detention of Shri Kamlesh Navinchandra Shah. The government has accordingly revoked the detention order issued against him. The revocation order (in triplicate) is enclosed herewith. One copy of revocation order should be served on the detente concerned and the duplicate copy of the same alongwith signature of the detente with date should be returned immediately to the undersigned. Third copy should be retained for your record."

Order

Whereas, an order No. PSA-1204/21(1)/SPL-3(A), dated the 31st January, 2005, has been passed by the Principal Secretary (Appeals and Security) to the Government of Maharashtra, Home Department and Detaining Authority under section 3(1) of the Conservation of Foreign Exchange and Prevention of Smuggling Activities Act, 1974 (52 of 1974) for the detention of Shri Kamlesh Navinchandra Shah,

Whereas, the case of Shri Kamlesh Navinchandra Shah was placed before the Advisory Board, which is of the opinion that there is no sufficient cause for his detention; and

Whereas, the Government of Maharashtra has fully considered the report of the Advisory Board and material on record;

Now, therefore, in exercise of the powers conferred by section 8(f) of the aforesaid Act, the Government of Maharashtra hereby revokes the aforesaid Detention Order and further directs that said Shri Kamlesh Navinchandra Shah be released forthwith on receipt of this order.

38. Another decision cited by learned Counsel for the petitioner in *V.C. Mohan* v. *Union of India* reported in MANU/SC/0140/2002 and the observations made thereunder can also be usefully applied to the facts of this case.

In the case of *Pawan Bhartiya* v. *Union of India*, MANU/SC/1512/2001, the appellant challenged the detention order dated 30-7-1996 passed under section 3(1) of the COFEPOSA Act, 1974 before the High Court of Delhi. That petition was rejected by the High Court by holding that it is not a fit case where any interference is called for before the execution of the order of detention. At the time of hearing, learned Counsel for the appellant pointed out that similar detention orders were passed against 6 persons during the period from 07.12.1995 to 12.08.1996 and further pointed out that 5 out of 6 detention orders were revoked by the competent authority on the ground that the customs duty which was required to be paid was paid by them before the execution of the detention orders. Despite this fact the detention order passed against the appellant was not revoked even though he has also paid the customs duty as demanded. It has also been pointed out that the sponsoring authority submitted its report before the Detaining Authority to revoke the detention order which was passed against the appellant. The Joint Secretary to the Government of India, Ministry of Finance has filed an affidavit in this case wherein it is submitted that similar 5 detention orders were revoked. This Court (M.B. Shah and Brijesh Kumar, JJ) in para 6 & 7 observed as under:

> 6. In our view, there is no reason to discriminate the appellant and the reason given by the authority in not revoking the detention order could hardly be justified. It is true that normally before the execution of the detention order the same is not required to be quashed and set aside. However, considering the peculiar facts and circumstances of the case, in our view, no purpose will be served by continuing the detention order. It is pointed out that the appellant has ceased his activities in the field of import or export. He has already paid the tax with penalty as demanded by the authority. There is nothing on record that since the last five years the appellant has indulged in any such activity. It is to be noted that the purpose of passing the detention order is to prevent the detenu from continuing his prejudicial activity but not to punish him.
>
> 7. Hence, in view of the facts and circumstances of the present case, the impugned order dated 30-7-1996 passed by the Joint Secretary to the Government of India under section 3(1) of COFEPOSA is quashed and set aside. The appeal is allowed accordingly."

39. The above judgment, in our view, squarely applies to the facts and circumstances of the case on hand. In the instant case, the petitioner's brother has already been released on the ground there was no sufficient cause for the detention of the detenu under section 3(1) of the Act. The Government also accordingly revoked the detention order issued against him and the Government of Maharashtra, after considering the report of the Advisory Board and the material on record and in exercise of the powers conferred by section 8(f) of the COFEPOSA Act revoked the aforesaid detention order and further directed that Kamlesh Navinchandra Shah be released forthwith on receipt of the said order dated 5-6-2006. In our opinion, the petitioner before us who is also similarly placed and who has also paid the customs duty etc., pursuant to the order of the Settlement Commission and got the unconditional immunity by the Settlement Commission is entitled to the same treatment. At the time of hearing, it is pointed out that the petitioner has ceased his activities in the field of import or export and has already paid the tax with penalty as demanded by the authority and there is nothing on record that the appellant has indulged in any such activity in the recent past. It is settled by law that the purpose of passing the detention order is to prevent the detenu from continuing his prejudicial activity but not to punish him.

40. Considering the peculiar facts and circumstances of the case, no purpose will be served by continuing the detention order and we, therefore, allow the writ petition and quash and set aside the detention order bearing No. PSA 1204/21(2)/SPL-3(A) dated 12-1-2005. The writ petition is ordered accordingly.

Suraz India Trust
v.
Union of India

Writ petition (civil) no(s). 204 of 2010
Decided on 04-04-2011

Coram: **Hon'ble Mr. Justice Deepak Verma**
Hon'ble Dr. Justice B.S. Chauhan

Judgment by: **Hon'ble Dr. Justice AR. Lakshmanan**

ORDER

1. This writ petition has been filed under article 32 of the Constitution by the present petitioner claiming itself to be the registered Trust under the provisions of Rajasthan Public Trust Act, 1959. It has been established in the legal arena for the larger public interest. The Trust's motto is to challenge those provisions of law which are *ultra vires* and unconstitutional. Basically the petitioner has sought the review of the judgment by nine Judges' Bench of this Court in *Advocate on Record Association* v. *Union of India,* (1993) 4 SCC 441; so also in the case of Special Reference No. 1 of 1998 (reported in (1998) 7 SCC 739), whereby this Court declared the primacy of the collegium in the matter of appointment of the Judges of the Supreme Court and the High Courts.

2. As Mr. Rajiv Daiya, Chairman of the Trust appeared in person and was not able to render any assistance to the Court, thus, we requested Mr. A.K. Ganguli, learned Senior Counsel alongwith Mr. Bharat Sangal to assist the Court as *amicus curiae.* The petition raises large number of complicated issues. Meanwhile, we also sought assistance of the learned Attorney General for India.

3. Shri A.K. Ganguly, learned senior Advocate, has submitted:

That the method of appointment of a Supreme Court Judge is mentioned in Article 124(2) of the Constitution of India which states:

> "Every Judge of the Supreme Court shall be appointed by the President by warrant under his hand and seal after consultation with such of the Judges of the Supreme Court and of the High Courts in the States as the President may deem necessary for the purpose and shall hold office until he attains the age of sixty five years.
>
> Provided that in the case of appointment of a Judge other than the Chief Justice, the Chief Justice of India shall always be consulted."

It may be noted that there is no mention:

(i) for any Collegium in Article 124(2).

(ii) The word used in Article 124(2) is 'consultation', and not 'concurrence'.

(iii) The President of India while appointing a Supreme Court Judge can consult any Judge of the Supreme Court or even High Court as he deems necessary for the purpose, and is not bound to consult only the five seniormost Judges of the Supreme Court.

4. That by the judicial verdicts in the aforesaid two cases, article 124(2) has been practically amended, although amendment to the Constitution can only be done by Parliament in accordance with the procedure laid down in Article 368 of the Constitution of India.

5. That under Article 124(2) while appointing a Supreme Court Judge, the President of India has to consult the Chief Justice of India, but he may also consult any other Supreme Court Judge and not merely the four seniormost Judges. Also, the President of India can even consult a High Court Judge, whereas, according to the aforesaid two decisions the President of India cannot consult any Supreme Court Judge other than the four seniormost Judges of the Supreme Court, and he cannot consult any High Court Judge at all.

6. Shri Ganguli submits that the matter is required to be considered by a larger Bench as the petition raises the following issues of Constitutional importance:

(1) Whether the aforesaid two verdicts, *viz.* the 7-Judge Bench and 9-Judge Bench decisions of this Court referred to above really amount to amending Article 124(2) of the Constitution?

(2) Whether there is any 'Collegium' system for appointing Supreme Court or High Court Judges in the Constitution?

(3) Whether the Constitution can be amended by a judicial verdict or it can only be amended by Parliament in accordance with article 368?

(4) Whether the Constitutional scheme was that the Supreme Court and High Court Judges can be appointed by mutual discussions and mutual consensus between the judiciary and the executive; or whether the judiciary can alone appoint Judges of the Supreme Court and High Courts?

(5) Whether the word 'consultation' in Article 224 means 'concurrence'?

(6) Whether by judicial interpretation words in the Constitution can be made redundant, as appears to have been done in the aforesaid two decisions which have made consultation with High Court Judges redundant while appointing a Supreme Court Judge despite the fact that it is permissible on the clear language of Article 124(2)?

(7) Whether the clear language of Article 124(2) can be altered by judicial verdicts and instead of allowing the President of India to consult such Judges of the Supreme Court as he deems necessary (including even junior Judges) only the Chief Justice of India and four seniormost Judges of the

Supreme Court can alone be consulted while appointing a Supreme Court Judge?

(8) Whether there was any convention that the President is bound by the advice of the Chief Justice of India, and whether any such convention (assuming there was one) can prevail over the clear language of Article 124(2)?

(9) Whether the opinion of the Chief Justice of India has any primacy in thc aforesaid appointments?

(10) Whether the aforesaid two decisions should be overruled by a larger Bench?

7. Mr. G.E. Vahanvati, learned Attorney-General for India, supports the petitioner contending that the aforesaid judgments require reconsideration. However, he also submits:

(a) A writ petition under Article 32 is not maintainable at the behest of a Trust as the Trust cannot claim violation of any of its fundamental rights;

(b) Petitioner has no *locus standi* to seek review of the judgments of this Court. In fact, a petition under Article 32 of the Constitution does not lie to challenge the correctness of a judicial order; and

(c) A bench of two Judges cannot examine the correctness of the judgment of nine Judges Bench.

(d) A Bench of two Judges cannot refer the matter to the larger bench of nine Judges or more directly.

8. In *Coir Board Ernakulam* v. *Indira Devai P.S.*, (2000) 1 SCC 224, this Court while dealing with a similar reference by a Bench of two Judges doubting the correctness of seven Judges' Bench judgment in *Bangalore Water Supply & Sewerage Board* v. *A. Rajappa*, (1978) 2 SCC 213, held as under:—

> "The judgment delivered by the seven learned Judges of the Court in *Bangalore Water Supply* case, does not, in our opinion, require any reconsideration on a reference being made by a two Judge Bench of the Court, which is bound by the judgment of the larger Bench. The appeals shall, therefore, be listed before the appropriate Bench for further proceedings."

9. The Constitution Bench of this Court in *Pradip Chandra Parija* v. *Pramod Chandra Patnaik*, AIR 2002 SC 296, while dealing with a similar situation held that judgment of a co-ordinate Bench or larger Bench is binding. However, if a Bench of two Judges concludes that an earlier judgment of three Judges is so very incorrect that in no circumstances it can be followed, the proper course for it to adopt is to refer the matter to a Bench of three Judges setting out, the reasons why it could not agree with the earlier judgment. If, then, the Bench of three Judges also comes to the conclusion that the earlier judgment of a Bench of three Judges is incorrect, reference to a Bench of five Judges is justified.

10. In *Union of India* v. *Hansoli Devi*, (2002) 7 SCC 273, this Court reiterated the same view placing reliance upon its earlier judgment in *Pradip Chandra Parija* (supra).

11. However, Mr. Ganguli dealing with the issue of *locus standi* of the Trust has submitted that the petition may not be maintainable but it should be entertained because it raises a large number of substantial questions of law. In order to fortify his submission he places reliance upon a recent Constitution Bench judgment of this Court in *B.P. Singhal* v. *Union of India*, (2010) 6 SCC 331 wherein while dealing with the issue of removal of Governors, this Court held as under:

> "The petitioner has no locus to maintain the petition in regard to the prayers claiming relief for the benefit of the individual Governors. At all events, such prayers no longer survive on account of passage of time. However, with regard to the general question of public importance referred to the Constitution Bench, touching upon the scope of article 156(1) and the limitations upon the doctrine of pleasure, the petitioner has the necessary locus."

(Emphasis added)

Thus, Mr. Ganguli submits that considering the gravity of the issues involved herein, the matter should be entertained.

12. While dealing with the issue of reference to the larger Bench, Mr. Ganguli has placed a very heavy reliance of the recent order of this Court dated 30-3-2011 in Civil appeal Nos.4056-4064 of 1999 (*Mineral Area Development Authority* v. *M/s. Steel Authority of India*) wherein considering the issue of interpretation of the Constitutional provisions and validity of the Act involved therein, a three Judges Bench presided over by Hon'ble the Chief Justice has referred the matter to nine Judges' Bench.

13. At this juncture, Mr. Ganguli as well as Mr. Vahanvati have submitted that even at the stage of preliminary hearing for admission of the petition, the matter requires to be heard by a larger Bench as this matter has earlier been dealt with by a three Judges Bench and involves very complicated legal issues.

14. In view of the above, we place the matter before the Hon'ble Chief Justice for appropriate directions.

ARTICLES OF CONSTITUTION REFERRED

General

12. Definition.—In this part, unless the context otherwise requires, "the State" includes the Government and Parliament of India and the Government and the Legislature of each of the States and all local or other authorities within the territory of India or under the control of the Government of India.

Right to Equality

14. Equality before law.—The State shall not deny to any person equality before the law or the equal protection of the laws within the territory of India.

15. Prohibition of discrimination on grounds of religion, race, caste, sex or place of birth.—(1) The State shall not discriminate against any citizen on grounds only of religion, race, caste, sex, place of birth or any of them.

(2) No citizen shall, on grounds only of religion, race, caste, sex, place of birth or any of them, be subject to any disability, liability, restriction or condition with regard to—

(a) access to shops, public restaurants, hotels and places of public entertainment; or

(b) the use of wells, tanks, bathing ghats, roads and places of public resort maintained wholly or partly out of State funds or dedicated to the use of general public.

(3) Nothing in this article shall prevent the State from making any special provision for women and children.

(4) Nothing in this article or in clause (2) of article 29 shall prevent the State from making any special provision for the advancement of any socially and educationally backward classes of citizens or for the Scheduled Castes and the Scheduled Tribes.

(5) Nothing in this article or in sub-clause (g) of clause (1) of article 19 shall prevent the State from making any special provision, by law, for the advancement of any socially and educationally backward classes of citizens or for the Scheduled Castes or the Scheduled Tribes in so far as such special provisions relate to their admission to educational institutions including private educational institutions, whether aided or unaided by the State, other than the minority educational institutions referred to in clause (1) of article 30.

16. Equality of opportunity in matters of public employment.—(1) There shall be equality of opportunity for all citizens in matters relating to employment or appointment to any office under the State.

(2) No citizen shall, on grounds only of religion, race, caste, sex, descent, place of birth, residence or any of them, be ineligible for, or discriminated against in respect of, any employment or office under the State.

(3) Nothing in this article shall prevent Parliament from making any law prescribing, in regard to a class or classes of employment or appointment to an office under the Government of, or any local or other authority within, a State or

Union territory, any requirement as to residence within that State or Union territory prior to such employment or appointment.

(4) Nothing in this article shall prevent the State from making any provision for the reservation of appointments or posts in favour of any backward class of citizens which, in the opinion of the State, is not adequately represented in the services under the State.

(4A) Nothing in this article shall prevent the State from making any provision for reservation in matters of promotion, with consequential seniority, to any class or classes of posts in the services under the State in favour of the Scheduled Castes and the Scheduled Tribes which, in the opinion of the State, are not adequately represented in the services under the State.

(4B) Nothing in this article shall prevent the State from considering any unfilled vacancies of a year which are reserved for being filled up in that year in accordance with any provision for reservation made under clause (4) or clause (4A) as a separate class of vacancies to be filled up in any succeeding year or years and such class of vacancies shall not be considered together with the vacancies of the year in which they are being filled up for determining the ceiling of fifty per cent. reservation on total number of vacancies of that year.

(5) Nothing in this article shall affect the operation of any law which provides that the incumbent of an office in connection with the affairs of any religious or denominational institution or any member of the governing body thereof shall be a person professing a particular religion or belonging to a particular denomination.

Right to Freedom

19. Protection of certain rights regarding freedom of speech, etc.—(1) All citizens shall have the right—

(a) to freedom of speech and expression;

(b) to assemble peaceably and without arms;

(c) to form associations or unions;

(d) to move freely throughout the territory of India;

(e) to reside and settle in any part of the territory of India; and

(g) to practise any profession, or to carry on any occupation, trade or business.

(2) Nothing in sub-clause (a) of clause (1) shall affect the operation of any existing law, or prevent the State from making any law, in so far as such law imposes reasonable restrictions on the exercise of the right conferred by the said sub-clause in the interests of the sovereignty and integrity of India, the security of the State, friendly relations with Foreign States, public order, decency or morality or in relation to contempt of court, defamation or incitement to an offence.

(3) Nothing in sub-clause (b) of the said clause shall affect the operation of any existing law in so far as it imposes, or prevent the State from making any law imposing, in the interests of the sovereignty and integrity of India or public order, reasonable restrictions on the exercise of the right conferred by the said sub-clause.

(4) Nothing in sub-clause (c) of the said clause shall affect the operation of any existing law in so far as it imposes, or prevent the State from making any law imposing, in the interests of the sovereignty and integrity of India or public order or morality, reasonable restrictions on the exercise of the right conferred by the said sub-clause.

(5) Nothing in sub-clauses (d) and (e) of the said clause shall affect the operation of any existing law in so far as it imposes, or prevent the State from making any law imposing, reasonable restrictions on the exercise of any of the rights conferred by the said sub-clauses either in the interests of the general public or for the protection of the interests of any Scheduled Tribe.

(6) Nothing in sub-clause (g) of the said clause shall affect the operation of any existing law in so far as it imposes, or prevent the State from making any law imposing, in the interests of the general public, reasonable restrictions on the exercise of the right conferred by the said sub-clause, and, in particular, nothing in the said sub-clause shall affect the operation of any existing law in so far as it relates to, or prevent the State from making any law relating to,—

(i) the professional or technical qualifications necessary for practising any profession or carrying on any occupation, trade or business, or

(ii) the carrying on by the State, or by a corporation owned or controlled by the State, of any trade, business, industry or service, whether to the exclusion, complete or partial, of citizens or otherwise .

20. Protection in respect of conviction for offences.—(1) No person shall be convicted of any offence except for violation of a law in force at the time of the commission of the act charged as an offence, nor be subjected to a penalty greater than that which might have been inflicted under the law in force at the time of the commission of the offence.

(2) No person shall be prosecuted and punished for the same offence more than once.

(3) No person accused of any offence shall be compelled to be a witness against himself.

21. Protection of life and personal liberty.—No person shall be deprived of his life or personal liberty except according to procedure established by law.

24. Prohibition of employment of children in factories, etc.—No child below the age of fourteen years shall be employed to work in any factory or mine or engaged in any other hazardous employment.

Right to Freedom of Religion

25. Freedom of conscience and free profession, practice and propagation of religion.—(1) Subject to public order, morality and health and to the other provisions of this Part, all persons are equally entitled to freedom of conscience and the right freely to profess, practise and propagate religion.

(2) Nothing in this article shall affect the operation of any existing law or prevent the State from making any law—

(a) regulating or restricting any economic, financial, political or other secular activity which may be associated with religious practice;

(b) providing for social welfare and reform or the throwing open of Hindu religious institutions of a public character to all classes and sections of Hindus.

Explanation I.—The wearing and carrying of *kirpans* shall be deemed to be included in the profession of the Sikh religion.

Explanation II.—In sub-clause (b) of clause (2), the reference to Hindus shall be construed as including a reference to persons professing the Sikh, Jaina or Buddhist religion, and the reference to Hindu religious institutions shall be construed accordingly.

26. Freedom to manage religious affairs.—Subject to public order, morality and health, every religious denomination or any section thereof shall have the right—

(a) to establish and maintain institutions for religious and charitable purposes;

(b) to manage its own affairs in matters of religion;

(c) to own and acquire movable and immovable property; and

(d) to administer such property in accordance with law.

27. Freedom as to payment of taxes for promotion of any particular religion.—No person shall be compelled to pay any taxes, the proceeds of which are specifically appropriated in payment of expenses for the promotion or maintenance of any particular religion or religious denomination.

28. Freedom as to attendance at religious instruction or religious worship in certain educational institutions.—(1) No religious instruction shall be provided in any educational institution wholly maintained out of State funds.

(2) Nothing in clause (1) shall apply to an educational institution which is administered by the State but has been established under any endowment or trust which requires that religious instruction shall be imparted in such institution.

(3) No person attending any educational institution recognised by the State or receiving aid out of State funds shall be required to take part in any religious instruction that may be imparted in such institution or to attend any religious worship that may be conducted in such institution or in any premises attached thereto unless such person or, if such person is a minor, his guardian has given his consent thereto.

Cultural and Educational Rights

29. Protection of interests of minorities.—(1) Any section of the citizens residing in the territory of India or any part thereof having a distinct language, script or culture of its own shall have the right to conserve the same.

(2) No citizen shall be denied admission into any educational institution maintained by the State or receiving aid out of State funds on grounds only of religion, race, caste, language or any of them.

Right to Constitutional Remedies

32. Remedies for enforcement of rights conferred by this Part.—(1) The right to move the Supreme Court by appropriate proceedings for the enforcement of the rights conferred by this Part is guaranteed.

(2) The Supreme Court shall have power to issue directions or orders or writs, including writs in the nature of *habeas corpus, mandamus,* prohibition, *quo warranto* and *certiorari,* whichever may be appropriate, for the enforcement of any of the rights conferred by this Part.

(3) Without prejudice to the powers conferred on the Supreme Court by clauses (1) and (2), Parliament may by law empower any other court to exercise within the local limits of its jurisdiction all or any of the powers exercisable by the Supreme Court under clause (2).

(4) The right guaranteed by this article shall not be suspended except as otherwise provided for by this Constitution.

32A. Constitutional validity of State laws not to be considered in proceedings under article 32.— *Rep. by the Constitution (Forty-third Amendment) Act, 1977, sec. 3 (w.e.f. 13-4-1978).*

33. Power of Parliament to modify the rights conferred by this Part in their application to Forces, etc.—Parliament may, by law, determine to what extent any of the rights conferred by this Part shall, in their application to,—

(a) the members of the Armed Forces; or

(b) the members of the Forces charged with the maintenance of public order; or

(c) persons employed in any bureau or other organisation established by the State for purposes of intelligence or counter intelligence; or

(d) persons employed in, or in connection with, the telecommunication systems set up for the purposes of any Force, bureau or organisation referred to in clauses (a) to (c),

be restricted or abrogated so as to ensure the proper discharge of their duties and the maintenance of discipline among them.

34. Restriction on rights conferred by this Part while martial law is in force in any area.—Notwithstanding anything in the foregoing provisions of this Part, Parliament may by law indemnify any person in the service of the Union or of a State or any other person in respect of any act done by him in connection with the maintenance or restoration of order in any area within the territory of India where martial law was in force or validate any sentence passed, punishment inflicted, forfeiture ordered or other act done under martial law in such area.

35. Legislation to give effect to the provisions of this Part.—Notwithstanding anything in this Constitution,—

(a) Parliament shall have, and the Legislature of a State shall not have, power to make laws—

(i) with respect to any of the matters which under clause (3) of article 16, clause (3) of article 32, article 33 and article 34 may be provided for by law made by Parliament; and

(ii) for prescribing punishment for those acts which are declared to be offences under this Part,

and Parliament shall, as soon as may be after the commencement of this Constitution, make laws for prescribing punishment for the acts referred to in sub-clause (ii);

(b) any law in force immediately before the commencement of this Constitution in the territory of India with respect to any of the matters referred to in sub-clause (i) of clause (a) or providing for punishment for any act referred to in sub-clause (ii) of that clause shall, subject to the terms thereof and to any adaptations and modifications that may be made therein under article 372, continue in force until altered or repealed or amended by Parliament.

Explanation.—In this article, the expression "law in force" has the same meaning as in article 372.

PART IV

DIRECTIVE PRINCIPLES OF STATE POLICY

36. Definition.—In this Part, unless the context otherwise requires, "the State" has the same meaning as in Part III.

37. Application of the principles contained in this Part.—The provisions contained in this Part shall not be enforceable by any court, but the principles therein laid down are nevertheless fundamental in the governance of the country and it shall be the duty of the State to apply these principles in making laws.

38. State to secure a social order for the promotion of welfare of the people.—(1) The State shall strive to promote the welfare of the people by securing and protecting as effectively as it may a social order in which justice, social, economic and political, shall inform all the institutions of the national life.

(2) The State shall, in particular, strive to minimise the inequalities in income, and endeavour to eliminate inequalities in status, facilities and opportunities, not only amongst individuals but also amongst groups of people residing in different areas or engaged in different vocations.

39. Certain principles of policy to be followed by the State.—The State shall, in particular, direct its policy towards securing—

(a) that the citizens, men and women equally, have the right to an adequate means of livelihood;

(b) that the ownership and control of the material resources of the community are so distributed as best to subserve the common good;

(c) that the operation of the economic system does not result in the concentration of wealth and means of production to the common detriment;

(d) that there is equal pay for equal work for both men and women;

(e) that the health and strength of workers, men and women, and the tender age of children are not abused and that citizens are not forced by economic necessity to enter avocations unsuited to their age or strength;

(f) that children are given opportunities and facilities to develop in a healthy manner and in conditions of freedom and dignity and that childhood and youth are protected against exploitation and against moral and material abandonment.

41. Right to work, to education and to public assistance in certain cases.—The State shall, within the limits of its economic capacity and development, make effective provision for securing the right to work, to education and to public assistance in cases of unemployment, old age, sickness and disablement, and in other cases of undeserved want.

42. Provision for just and humane conditions of work and maternity relief.—The State shall make provision for securing just and humane conditions of work and for maternity relief.

43. Living wage, etc., for workers.—The State shall endeavour to secure, by suitable legislation or economic organisation or in any other way, to all workers, agricultural, industrial or otherwise, work, a living wage, conditions of work ensuring a decent standard of life and full enjoyment of leisure and social and cultural opportunities and, in particular, the State shall endeavour to promote cottage industries on an individual or co-operative basis in rural areas.

43A. Participation of workers in management of industries.—The State shall take steps, by suitable legislation or in any other way, to secure the participation of workers in the management of undertakings, establishments or other organisations engaged in any industry.

44. Uniform civil code for the citizens.—The State shall endeavour to secure for the citizens a uniform civil code throughout the territory of India.

45. Provision for early childhood care and education to children below the age of six years.—The State shall endeavour to provide early childhood care and education for all children until they complete the age of six years.

46. Promotion of educational and economic interests of Scheduled Castes, Scheduled Tribes and other weaker sections.—The State shall promote with special care the educational and economic interests of the weaker sections of the people, and, in particular, of the Scheduled Castes and the Scheduled Tribes, and shall protect them from social injustice and all forms of exploitation.

47. Duty of the State to raise the level of nutrition and the standard of living and to improve public health.—The State shall regard the raising of the level of nutrition and the standard of living of its people and the improvement of public health as among its primary duties and, in particular, the State shall endeavour to bring about prohibition of the consumption except for medicinal purposes of intoxicating drinks and of drugs which are injurious to health.

48A. Protection and improvement of environment and safeguarding of forests and wild life.—The State shall endeavour to protect and improve the environment and to safeguard the forests and wild life of the country.

PART IVA

FUNDAMENTAL DUTIES

51A. Fundamental duties.—It shall be the duty of every citizen of India—

(a) to abide by the Constitution and respect its ideals and institutions, the National Flag and the National Anthem;

(b) to cherish and follow the noble ideals which inspired our national struggle for freedom;

(c) to uphold and protect the sovereignty, unity and integrity of India;

(d) to defend the country and render national service when called upon to do so;

(e) to promote harmony and the spirit of common brotherhood amongst all the people of India transcending religious, linguistic and regional or sectional diversities; to renounce practices derogatory to the dignity of women;

(f) to value and preserve the rich heritage of our composite culture;

(g) to protect and improve the natural environment including forests, lakes, rivers and wild life, and to have compassion for living creatures;

(h) to develop the scientific temper, humanism and the spirit of inquiry and reform;

(i) to safeguard public property and to abjure violence;

(j) to strive towards excellence in all spheres of individual and collective activity so that the nation constantly rises to higher levels of endeavour and achievement.

(k) who is a parent or guardian to provide opportunities for education to his child or, as the case may be, ward between the age of six and fourteen years.

141. Law declared by Supreme Court to be binding on all courts.—The law declared by the Supreme Court shall be binding on all courts within the territory of India.

142. Enforcement of decrees and orders of Supreme Court and orders as to discovery, etc.—(1) The Supreme Court in the exercise of its jurisdiction may pass such decree or make such order as is necessary for doing complete justice in any cause or matter pending before it, and any decree so passed or order so made shall be enforceable throughout the territory of India in such manner as may be prescribed by or under any law made by Parliament and, until provision in that behalf is so made, in such manner as the President may by order prescribe.

(2) Subject to the provisions of any law made in this behalf by Parliament, the Supreme Court shall, as respects the whole of the territory of India, have all and every power to make any order for the purpose of securing the attendance of any person, the discovery or production of any documents, or the investigation or punishment of any contempt of itself.

143. Power of President to consult Supreme Court.—(1) If at any time it appears to the President that a question of law or fact has arisen, or is likely to arise, which is of such a nature and of such public importance that it is expedient to obtain the opinion of the Supreme Court upon it, he may refer the question to that Court for consideration and the Court may, after such hearing as it thinks fit, report to the President its opinion thereon.

(2) The President may, notwithstanding anything in the proviso to article 131, refer a dispute of the kind mentioned in the said proviso to the

Supreme Court for opinion and the Supreme Court shall, after such hearing as it thinks fit, report to the President its opinion thereon.

144. Civil and judicial authorities to act in aid of the Supreme Court.—All authorities, civil and judicial, in the territory of India shall act in aid of the Supreme Court.

226. Power of High Courts to issue certain writs.—(1) Notwithstanding anything in article 32, every High Court shall have power, throughout the territories in relation to which it exercises jurisdiction, to issue to any person or authority, including in appropriate cases, any Government, within those territories directions, orders or writs, including writs in the nature of *habeas corpus, mandamus,* prohibition, *quo warranto* and *certiorari,* or any of them, for the enforcement of any of the rights conferred by Part III and for any other purpose

(2) The power conferred by clause (1) to issue directions, orders or writs to any Government, authority or person may also be exercised by any High Court exercising jurisdiction in relation to the territories within which the cause of action, wholly or in part, arises for the exercise of such power, notwithstanding that the seat of such Government or authority or the residence of such person is not within those territories.

(3) Where any party against whom an interim order, whether by way of injunction or stay or in any other manner, is made on, or in any proceedings relating to, a petition under clause (1), without—

(a) furnishing to such party copies of such petition and all documents in support of the plea for such interim order; and

(b) giving such party an opportunity of being heard,

makes an application to the High Court for the vacation of such order and furnishes a copy of such application to the party in whose favour such order has been made or the counsel of such party, the High Court shall dispose of the application within a period of two weeks from the date on which it is received or from the date on which the copy of such application is so furnished, whichever is later, or where the High Court is closed on the last day of that period, before the expiry of the next day afterwards on which the High Court is open; and if the application is not so disposed of, the interim order shall, on the expiry of that period, or, as the case may be, the expiry of the said next day, stand vacated.

(4) The power conferred on a High Court by this article shall not be in derogation of the power conferred on the Supreme Court by clause (2) of article 32.

246. Subject-matter of laws made by Parliament and by the Legislatures of States.—(1) Notwithstanding anything in clauses (2) and (3), Parliament has exclusive power to make laws with respect to any of the matters enumerated in List I in the Seventh Schedule (in this Constitution referred to as the "Union List").

(2) Notwithstanding anything in clause (3), Parliament and, subject to clause (1), the Legislature of any State also, have power to make laws with respect to any of the matters enumerated in List III in the Seventh Schedule (in this Constitution referred to as the "Concurrent List").

(3) Subject to clauses (1) and (2), the Legislature of any State has exclusive power to make laws for such State or any part thereof with respect to any of the matters enumerated in List II in the Seventh Schedule (in this Constitution referred to as the 'State List').

(4) Parliament has power to make laws with respect to any matter for any part of the territory of India not included in a State notwithstanding that such matter is a matter enumerated in the State List.

340. Appointment of a Commission to investigate the conditions of backward classes.—(1) The President may by order appoint a Commission consisting of such persons as he thinks fit to investigate the conditions of socially and educationally backward classes within the territory of India and the difficulties under which they labour and to make recommendations as to the steps that should be taken by the Union or any State to remove such difficulties and to improve their condition and as to the grants that should be made for the purpose by the Union or any State and the conditions subject to which such grants should be made, and the order appointing such Commission shall define the procedure to be followed by the Commission.

(2) A Commission so appointed shall investigate the matters referred to them and present to the President a report setting out the facts as found by them and making such recommendations as they think proper.

(3) The President shall cause a copy of the report so presented together with a memorandum explaining the action taken thereon to be laid before each House of Parliament.

SEVENTH SCHEDULE

LIST II—STATE LIST

1. Public order (but not including the use of any naval, military or air force or any other armed force of the Union or of any other force subject to the control of the Union or of any contingent or unit thereof in aid of the civil power).

2. Police (including railway and village police) subject to the provisions of entry 2A of List I.

3. Officers and servants of the High Court; procedure in rent and revenue courts; fees taken in all courts except the Supreme Court.

4. Prisons, reformatories, Borstal institutions and other institutions of a like nature, and persons detained therein; arrangements with other States for the use of prisons and other institutions.

5. Local government, that is to say, the constitution and powers of municipal corporations, improvement trusts, district boards, mining settlement authorities and other local authorities for the purpose of local self-government or village administration.

6. Public health and sanitation; hospitals and dispensaries.

7. Pilgrimages, other than pilgrimages to places outside India.

8. Intoxicating liquors, that is to say, the production, manufacture, possession, transport, purchase and sale of intoxicating liquors.

9. Relief of the disabled and unemployable.

10. Burials and burial grounds; cremations and cremation grounds.

12. Libraries, museums and other similar institutions controlled or financed by the State; ancient and historical monuments and records other than those declared by or under law made by Parliament to be of national importance.

13. Communications, that is to say, roads, bridges, ferries, and other means of communication not specified in List I; municipal tramways; ropeways; inland waterways and traffic thereon subject to the provisions of List I and List III with regard to such waterways; vehicles other than mechanically propelled vehicles.

14. Agriculture, including agricultural education and research, protection against pests and prevention of plant diseases.

15. Preservation, protection and improvement of stock and prevention of animal diseases; veterinary training and practice.

16. Pounds and the prevention of cattle trespass.

17. Water, that is to say, water supplies, irrigation and canals, drainage and embankments, water storage and water power subject to the provisions of entry 56 of List I.

18. Land, that is to say, right in or over land, land tenures including the relation of landlord and tenant, and the collection of rents; transfer and alienation of agricultural land; land improvement and agricultural loans; colonization.

21. Fisheries.

22. Courts of wards subject to the provisions of entry 34 of List I; encumbered and attached estates.

23. Regulation of mines and mineral development subject to the provisions of List I with respect to regulation and development under the control of the Union.

24. Industries subject to the provisions of entries 7 and 52 of List I.

25. Gas and gas-works.

26. Trade and commerce within the State subject to the provisions of entry 33 of List III.

27. Production, supply and distribution of goods subject to the provisions of entry 33 of List III.

28. Markets and fairs.

30. Money-lending and money-lenders; relief of agricultural indebtedness.

31. Inns and inn-keepers.

32. Incorporation, regulation and winding up of corporation, other than those specified in List I, and universities; unincorporated trading, literary, scientific, religious and other societies and associations; co-operative societies.

33. Theaters and dramatic performances; cinemas subject to the provisions of entry 60 of List I; sports, entertainments and amusements.

34. Betting and gambling.

35. Works, lands and buildings vested in or in the possession of the State.

37. Elections to the Legislature of the State subject to the provisions of any law made by Parliament.

38. Salaries and allowances of members of the Legislature of the State, of the Speaker and Deputy Speaker of the Legislative Assembly and, if there is a Legislative Council, of the Chairman and Deputy Chairman thereof.

39. Powers, privileges and immunities of the Legislative Assembly and of the members and the committees thereof, and, if there is a Legislative Council, of that Council and of the members and the committees thereof; enforcement of attendance of persons for giving evidence or producing documents before committees of the Legislature of the State.

40. Salaries and allowances of Ministers for the State.

41. State public services; State Public Service Commission.

42. State pensions, that is to say, pensions payable by the State or out of the Consolidated Fund of the State.

43. Public debt of the State.

44. Treasure trove.

45. Land revenue, including the assessment and collection of revenue, the maintenance of land records, survey for revenue purposes and records of rights, and alienation of revenues.

46. Taxes on agricultural income.

47. Duties in respect of succession to agricultural land.

48. Estate duty in respect of agricultural land.

49. Taxes on lands and buildings.

50. Taxes on mineral rights subject to any limitations imposed by Parliament by law relating to mineral development.

51. Duties of excise on the following goods manufactured or produced in the State and countervailing duties at the same or lower rates on similar goods manufactured or produced elsewhere in India:—

(a) alcoholic liquors for human consumption;

(b) opium, Indian hemp and other narcotic drugs and narcotics,

but not including medicinal and toilet preparations containing alcohol or any substance included in sub-paragraph (b) of this entry.

52. Taxes on the entry of goods into a local area for consumption, use or sale therein.

53. Taxes on the consumption or sale of electricity.

54. Taxes on the sale or purchase of goods other than newspapers, subject to the provisions of entry 92A of List I.

55. Taxes on advertisements other than advertisements published in the newspapers and advertisements broadcast by radio or television .

56. Taxes on goods and passengers carried by road or on inland waterways.

57. Taxes on vehicles, whether mechanically propelled or not, suitable for use on roads, including tramcars subject to the provisions of entry 35 of List III.

58. Taxes on animals and boats.

59. Tolls.

60. Taxes on professions, trades, callings and employments.

61. Capitation taxes.

62. Taxes on luxuries, including taxes on entertainments, amusements, betting and gambling.

63. Rates of stamp duty in respect of documents other than those specified in the provisions of List I with regard to rates of stamp duty.

64. Offences against laws with respect to any of the matters in this List.

65. Jurisdiction and powers of all courts, except the Supreme Court, with respect to any of the matters in this List.

66. Fees in respect of any of the matters in this List, but not including fees taken in any court.

LIST III—CONCURRENT LIST

1. Criminal law, including all matters included in the Indian Penal Code at the commencement of this Constitution but excluding offences against laws with respect to any of the matters specified in List I or List II and excluding the use of naval, military or air forces or any other armed forces of the Union in aid of the civil power.

2. Criminal procedure, including all matters included in the Code of Criminal Procedure at the commencement of this Constitution.

3. Preventive detention for reasons connected with the security of a State, the maintenance of public order, or the maintenance of supplies and services essential to the community; persons subjected to such detention.

4. Removal from one State to another State of prisoners, accused persons and persons subjected to preventive detention for reasons specified in entry 3 of this List.

5. Marriage and divorce; infants and minors; adoption; wills, intestacy and succession; joint family and partition; all matters in respect of which parties in judicial proceedings were immediately before the commencement of this Constitution subject to their personal law.

6. Transfer of property other than agricultural land; registration of deeds and documents.

7. Contracts, including partnership, agency, contracts of carriage, and other special forms of contracts, but not including contracts relating to agricultural land.

8. Actionable wrongs.

9. Bankruptcy and insolvency.

10. Trust and Trustees.

11. Administrators-general and official trustees.

11A. Administration of justice; constitution and organisation of all courts, except the Supreme Court and the High Courts.

12. Evidence and oaths; recognition of laws, public acts and records, and judicial proceedings.

13. Civil procedure, including all matters included in the Code of Civil Procedure at the commencement of this Constitution, limitation and arbitration.

14. Contempt of court, but not including contempt of the Supreme Court.

15. Vagrancy; nomadic and migratory tribes.

16. Lunacy and mental deficiency, including places for the reception or treatment of lunatics and mental deficients.

17. Prevention of cruelty to animals.

17A. Forests.

17B. Protection of wild animals and birds.

18. Adulteration of foodstuffs and other goods.

19. Drugs and poisons, subject to the provisions of entry 59 of List I with respect to opium.

20. Economic and social planning.

20A. Population control and family planning.

21. Commercial and industrial monopolies, combines and trusts.

22. Trade unions; industrial and labour disputes.

23. Social security and social insurance; employment and unemployment.

24. Welfare of labour including conditions of work, provident funds, employers' liability, workmen's compensation, invalidity and old age pensions and maternity benefits.

25. Education, including technical education, medical education and universities, subject to the provisions of entries 63, 64, 65 and 66 of List I; vocational and technical training of labour.

26. Legal, medical and other professions.

27. Relief and rehabilitation of persons displaced from their original place of residence by reason of the setting up of the Dominions of India and Pakistan.

28. Charities and charitable institutions, charitable and religious endowments and religious institutions.

29. Prevention of the extension from one State to another of infectious or contagious diseases or pests affecting men, animals or plants.

30. Vital statistics including registration of births and deaths.

31. Ports other than those declared by or under law made by Parliament or existing law to be major ports.

32. Shipping and navigation on inland waterways as regards mechanically propelled vessels, and the rule of the road on such waterways, and the carriage of passengers and goods on inland waterways subject to the provisions of List I with respect to national waterways.

33. Trade and commerce in, and the production, supply and distribution of,—

(a) the products of any industry where the control of such industry by the Union is declared by Parliament by law to be expedient in the public interest, and imported goods of the same kind as such products;

(b) foodstuffs, including edible oilseeds and oils;

(c) cattle fodder, including oilcakes and other concentrates;

(d) raw cotton, whether ginned or unginned, and cotton seed; and

(e) raw jute.

33A. Weights and measures except establishment of standards.

34. Price control.

35. Mechanically propelled vehicles including the principles on which taxes on such vehicles are to be levied.

36. Factories.

37. Boilers.

38. Electricity.

39. Newspapers, books and printing presses.

40. Archaeological sites and remains other than those declared by or under law made by Parliament to be of national importance.

41. Custody, management and disposal of property (including agricultural land) declared by law to be evacuee property.

42. Acquisition and requisitioning of property.

43. Recovery in a State of claims in respect of taxes and other public demands, including arrears of land-revenue and sums recoverable as such arrears, arising outside that State.

44. Stamp duties other than duties or fees collected by means of judicial stamps, but not including rates of stamp duty.

45. Inquiries and statistics for the purposes of any of the matters specified in List II or List III.

46. Jurisdiction and powers of all courts, except the Supreme Court, with respect to any of the matters in this List.

47. Fees in respect of any of the matters in this List, but not including fees taken in any court.

TWO HUNDRED AND FOURTEENTH REPORT

LAW COMMISSION OF INDIA

PROPOSAL FOR RECONSIDERATION OF JUDGES CASES I, II & III – *S.P. GUPTA* v. *UNION OF INDIA* REPORTED IN AIR 1982 SC 149, *SUPREME COURT ADVOCATES-ON-RECORD ASSOCIATION* v. *UNION OF INDIA* REPORTED IN 1993 (4) SCC 441 AND SPECIAL REFERENCE 1 OF 1998 REPORTED IN 1998 (7) SCC 739

INTRODUCTION

In this Report the Law Commission of India opined that in the three Judges cases viz., *S.P. Gupta* v. *Union of India*, AIR 1982 SC 149; *Supreme Court Advocates-on-Record Association* v. *Union of India*, (1993) 4 SCC 441 and *Special Reference 1 of 1998* reported in (1998) 7 SCC 217, the Supreme Court has virtually re-written Articles 124(2) and 217 of the Constitution of India which pertain to appointment of Supreme Court and High Court Judges respectively.

In the second Judges case the Supreme Court evolved the concept of 'primacy' for the opinion of the Chief Justice of India, which itself was to be based on a consultative process amongst the senior colleagues of the Chief Justice of India. The Supreme Court's opinion in the *Special Reference* along with reinforcing the concept of 'primacy' of the Chief Justice of India's opinion also increases the number of Judges he must consult before providing his opinion. The Supreme Court also laid down a detailed set of guidance on the procedure to be followed in arriving at the opinion. The procedure in effect transferred the 'primacy' from the Chief Justice of India to the group of Judges to be consulted. The increased size of the group that has to be part of the consultation process has made the consultation process cumbersome and consequent delays in filling up of vacancies. Further the Chief Justice of every High Court is from outside the State as per the policy of the Government. The senior most Judges who form the collegium are also from outside the State and as such not conversant with the names and antecedents of the candidates. The appointments, thus, more often than not suffer from lack of adequate information.

The Law Commission of India in this Report recommended that no other alternatives are available to the Government than to seek a reconsideration of the aforesaid three judgments before the Hon'ble Supreme Court. Otherwise a law may be passed restoring the primacy of the Chief Justice of India and the power of the executive to make the appointments.

Dr. Justice AR. Lakshmanan
(Former Judge, Supreme Court of India)
Chairman, Law Commission of India

ILI Building (IInd Floor),
Bhagwandas Road,
New Delhi-110 001
Tel.: 91-11-23384475
Fax: 91-11-23383564

November 21, 2008

Respected Shri Bhardwaj Ji,

I am herewith enclosing our 214th Report on "Proposal for Reconsideration of Judges cases I, II and III – *S.P. Gupta* v. *Union of India* reported in AIR 1982 SC 149; *Supreme Court Advocates on Record Association* v. *Union of India* reported in 1993 (4) SCC 441 and Special Reference 1 of 1998 reported in 1998 (7) SC 739". The proposal was placed before the Members of the Commission at 3.30 p.m. today. The Members of the Commission after due discussion and deliberations have unanimously approved the report of the Commission. The Commission, as already stated, examined the law on the subject. Various recommendations of Parliamentary Standing Committees and law of foreign jurisdiction like America, Australia, Canada and Kenya, where the executive is the sole authority to appoint Judges or the executive appoints in consultation with the Chief Justice of the Country have also been considered.

I request you to consider this report and do the needful at the earliest.

Since the matter is of great importance, I am submitting this report today itself.

Yours sincerely,

(Dr. Justice AR. Lakshmanan)

Dr. H.R. Bhardwaj,
Union Minister for Law and Justice,

PROPOSAL FOR RECONSIDERATION OF JUDGES CASES I, II & III – *S.P. GUPTA* v. *UNION OF INDIA* REPORTED IN AIR 1982 SC 149, *SUPREME COURT ADVOCATES-ON-RECORD ASSOCIATION* v. *UNION OF INDIA* REPORTED IN 1993 (4) SCC 441 AND SPECIAL REFERENCE 1 OF 1998 REPORTED IN 1998 (7) SCC 739

Preface: Part 1

(1) Why reconsideration? The Supreme Court in *Subhash Sharma* v. *Union of India* [reported in 1991 (1) Supp SCC 594] presided over by Ranganath Misra CJ, M.N. Venkatachaliah and M.M. Punchi, JJ. had expressed, doubts about the correctness of the interpretation of the word "consultation" in regard to the appointment of judges in *S.P. Gupta* v. *Union of India* (reported in AIR 1982 SC 149) in the following words (in paras 43 & 45 of the said judgment):—

> "The word 'consultation' is used in a constitutional provision in recognition of the status of the High constitutional dignitary who formally expresses the result of the institutional process leading to the appointment of judges. To limit that expression to its literal limitation shorn of its constitutional background and purpose is to borrow Justice Frankfurter's phrase "to stick in the bark of words."

The judges in that case had opined that "Judicial Review is a part of the basic constitutional structure and one of the basic features of the essential Indian constitutional policy. The essential constitutional doctrine does not by itself justify or necessitate any primacy of the executive wing on the ground of its political accountability to the electorate. On the contrary what is necessary is an interpretation sustaining the strength and vitality of Judicial Review. It might under certain circumstances be said that government is not bound to appoint a Judge so recommended by the judicial wing. But to contemplate a power for the executive to appoint a person despite his being disapproved or not recommended by the Chief Justice of the State and the Chief Justice of India would be wholly inappropriate and would constitute an arbitrary exercise of power. Then again, whenever there might be difference of opinion between the Chief Justice of a state and the Chief Justice of India – Some of the weighty reasons in this behalf are set out by the other three Judges in their opinion – the opinion of the Chief Justice of India should have the preponderant role. We are of the view that the primacy of the Chief Justice of India in the process of selection would improve the quality of selection. The purpose of the 'consultation' is to safeguard the independence of the judiciary and to ensure selection of proper persons. The matter is not, therefore, to be considered that the final say is the exclusive prerogative of the executive government. The recommendations of the appropriate constitutional functionaries from the judicial organ of the State has an equally important role. "Consultation should have sinews to achieve the constitutional purpose and should not be rendered sterile by a literal interpretation. Who is able to decide the qualities of lawyers proposed to be elevated to the bench more than the judges of the Superior Courts before whom they practice? There are preponderant and compelling considerations why the views of the Chief Justices of the States and that of the Chief Justice of India should be afforded a decisive import unless the executive has some material in its possession which may indicate that the appointment is otherwise undesirable. (Para 44)

The View which the four learned judges shared in Gupta's case, in our opinion, does not recognize the special and pivotal position of the institution of the Chief Justice of India.(Para 45) The correctness of the opinion of the majority in S.P. Gupta case relating to the status and importance of consultation, the primacy of the position of the Chief Justice of India and the view that the fixation of Judge strength is not justiciable should be reconsidered by a larger bench. (Para 45)

Emphasis Supplied

The operative part of the order of reference is contained in para 49 "as in our opinion the correctness of the majority view in *S.P. Gupta* case should be considered by a larger bench we direct the papers of W.P. No. 1303 of 1987 to be placed before the learned Chief Justice for constituting a bench of nine Judges to examine the two questions we have referred to above, namely, the position of the Chief Justice of India with reference to primacy and, secondly, justiciability of fixation of judge strength". In para 51 the Hon'ble Bench has clarified:—

> *We clarify that apart from the two questions which we have indicated, all other aspects dealt with by us are intended to be final by our present order.* (Emphasis supplied)

Therefore, only two questions were referred to the bench of nine judges namely (1) The position of the Chief Justice of India with reference to primacy and (2) The justiciability of the fixation of the judge strength. It is important to note that no other question was referred to the larger bench.

2. The first judges case *S.P. Gupta* v. *Union of India*. At this point it may be relevant to know as to what was decided by the majority judgment in the bench presided over by P.N. Bhagwati, A.C. Gupta, S.M. Fazal Ali, V.D. Tulzapurkar, D.A. Desai, R.S. Pathak and E.S. Venkataramaiah, JJ., in *S.P. Gupta's* case the correctness of which was doubted in *Subhash Sharma's* case.

The relevant portion of the majority judgment delivered by Justice P.N. Bhagwati speaking for himself in regard to the expression "consultation" occurring in 217 of the constitution is extracted herebelow:

> "Each of the three constitutional functionaries occupies a high constitutional office and clause (1) of Article 217 provides that the appointment of a High Court Judge shall be made after consultation with the functionaries without assigning superiority to the opinion of one over that of another. It is true that the Chief Justice of India is the head of the Indian judiciary and may be figuratively described as paterfamilias of the

brotherhood of Judges but the Chief Justice of a High Court is also an equally important constitutional functionary and it is not possible to say that so far as the consultative process is concerned, he is in any way less important than the Chief Justice of India. In fact, under the constitutional scheme, the Chief Justice of a High Court is not subject to the administrative superintendence of the Chief Justice of India nor is under the control of supervision of the Chief Justice of India...........

If primacy were to be given to the opinion of the Chief Justice of India, it would, in effect and substance amount to concurrence, because giving primacy would mean that his opinion must prevail over that of the Chief Justice of the High Court and the Governor of the State, which means that the Central Government must accept his opinion. But it is only consultation and not concurrence of the Chief Justice of India that is provided in clause (1) of Article 217. (Para 29). (emphasis supplied) There must be a collegium to make recommendation to the President in regard to appointment of a Supreme Court or High Court Judge. The recommending authority should be in consultation with wider interests. If the collegium is composed of persons who are expected to have knowledge of the persons who may be fit for appointment on the Bench and of qualities required for appointment and this last requirement is absolutely essential – it would go a long way towards securing the right kind of Judges, who would be truly independent and who would invest the judicial process with significance and meaning for the deprived and exploited sections of humanity." (para 30)

Regarding fixation of judge strength the majority judgment was of the view that this was not justiciable and no Mandamus could issue. This aspect however has lost its significance because in the case of Subhash Gupta the Attorney General made a statement that the government had no objection to the Hon'ble Court going into the question.

3. The second Judges case *Supreme Court Advocates on Record Association* v. *Union of India* (reported in 1993 (4) SCC 441

It is in this backdrop that the nine judges bench was constituted and judgment was delivered on 06-10-1993. The judgment runs into 306 pages and travels far beyond the order of reference. Noted jurist Late H.M. Seervai in his Constitutional Law of India fourth edition Silver Jubilee Edition (Volume 1) has criticized this judgment and called it "*null* and *void*" for not following the mandatory provisions of Article 145(4) and (5) – (which is clear from the dissenting judgment of Justice M.M. Punchi, the relevant portion of which is reproduced in the succeeding para) – which are not a matter of form or technicality but a matter of substance as pointed out in *Mohammad Akill* v. *Azad-unnisaa Bibi's* case by Sir Barrnes Peacock C.J., speaking on this point for a bench of nine judges. "It is not a mere technical objection but is upon a fundamental principle essential to the due administration of justice that every judicial act which is done by the several judges ought to be completed in the presence of the whole of them... If after discussion, and after deliberately weighing the arguments of each other, the judges cannot agree, their several judgments ought to be delivered in open court in the presence of the others." (Wyman's Report Vol. 5, p.69 quoted in *Rohilkhand Kumaon Bank Ltd.* v. *Row,* (1884) 6 All 468 (474). (taken from Seervai's Constitutional Law of India, 4th Edn., Vol. 3).

The noted jurist calls the judgment "null and void" (please see page 2936 Constitutional Law of India by H.M. Seervai, Volume 3, 4th Edn.)

At this stage it is essential to note the lament contained in the opening paragraph of Justice M.M. Punchi's dissenting judgment at para 488 of 1993 (4) SCC 441 referred to in the preceding paras.

> "Para 488 – M.M. Punchi J. (dissenting) – This opinion is in the nature of epilogue, though not in stricto sensu. Much has already been written on the two topics under reference to this Bench, and on others as well without reference. I on my part would have liked to avoid making any addition thereto but it seems the turn of events leave me no choice. I feel it would be dereliction to withhold contributing and leave unsaid what needs to be said (emphasis supplied)
>
> Para 490 – "This nine judge bench sat from April 7, 1993, to hear this momentous matter concluding its hearing on May 11, 1993 close to the onset of the summer vacation. I entertained the belief that we all, after July 12, 1993, on the reopening of the Court, if not earlier, would sit together and hold some meaningful meetings, having a free and frank discussion on each and every topic which had engaged our attention, striving for a unanimous decision in this historic matter concerning mainly the institution of the Chief Justice of India, relatable to this Court. I was indeed overtaken when I received the draft opinion dated June 14, 1993 authored by my learned brother J.S. Verma, J. for himself and on behalf of my learned Brethren Yogeshwar Dayal, G.N. Ray, Dr. A.S. Anand and S.P. Bharucha, JJ. The fait accompli appeared a stark reality; the majority opinion an accomplishment. The hopes I entertained of a free and frank discussion vanished. But then came the opinion dated August 24, 1993 of my learned brother Ahmadi, J. like a pebble of hope hewn out of a mountain of despair, followed by the opinions of my learned Brethern Kuldip Singh and Pandian, JJ. dated September 7, 1993 and September 9, 1993 respectively. No meaningful meeting thereafter was possible as the views by that time seemed to have been polarized. So now the firm opinions of the eight Brethren, as communicated, are known to me. Loaded with these opinions, I set out to express my own, more as a duty to the venture embarked upon, for I owe it immeasurably, for being party to the referral."
>
> Para 491 – "At the outset, I must remove a misgiving pertaining to the contents and thrust of the order of referral re correctness of *S.P. Gupta* v. *Union of India*, the opinion of which was authored by the then Chief Justice of India, Shri Ranganath Misra, and concurred to by the present Chief Justice of India Shri M.N. Venkatachaliah (then as a puisne judge) and by me. We had referred only two questions to a Bench of nine Judges, namely, to test the correctness of the opinion of the majority in *S.P. Gupta* case relating to the status and importance of consultation and the primacy of the position of the

Chief Justice of India, and whether fixation of Judge strength was not justiciable, clarifying in the ultimate paragraph that apart from the two questions aforeindicated all other aspects dealt with were intended to be final by the said order. As I view it, due to the rigidity of its terms, except for the two questions specifically referred, no other matter was open to canvass as has seemingly been done. (full text is not extracted for the sake of brevity." Please see page 712 of the judgment).

In the penultimate para of his concurring judgment Kuldip Singh, J. whose judgment came as late as September 7, 1993 (when the original majority judgment was signed on 14th June, 1995) makes the following observations "Before parting with the judgment it would be appropriate to say that the opinion circulated by Verma J. was based on elaborate discussion amongst the Brother Judges who were available and participated in the discussion. Although Verma, J. incorporated various suggestions in his original draft but a feeling left lurking in my mind that I have something more to say in support of the conclusions reached by Verma, J. and that is how I ventured to embark upon writing a separate opinion".

It is therefore clear that there was no discussion, no meeting of minds and no consensus among the 9 judges on 14 of June 1993 when the final draft judgment was signed by Justice Verma who spoke for himself and on behalf of Yogeshwar Dayal, G.N. Ray, Dr. A.S. Anand and S.P. Bharucha, JJ. The judgment therefore plainly is Per Incuriam.

4. What was decided by the majority judgment headed by Justice Verma?

Following the suggestion made by Justice Bhagwati in the *S.P. Gupta* case that there should be a 'collegium' which should be consulted by the Chief Justice of India in every appointment the nine judge bench, speaking through Justice Verma laid down fourteen conclusions which are as follows:—

1. The process of appointment of Judges to the Supreme Court and the High Courts is an integrated 'participatory consultative process' for selecting the best and most suitable persons available for appointment; and all the constitutional functionaries must perform this duty collectively with a view primarily to reach an agreed decision, sub serving the constitutional purpose, so that the occasion of primacy does not arise.
2. Initiation of the proposal for appointment in the case of the Supreme Court must be by the Chief Justice of India, and in the case of a High Court by the Chief Justice of that High Court; and for transfer of a Judge/Chief Justice of a High Court, the proposal has to be initiated by the Chief Justice of India. This is the manner in which proposals for appointments to the Supreme Court and the High Courts as well as for the transfers of Judges/ Chief Justices of the High Courts must invariably be made.
3. In the event of conflicting opinions by the constitutional functionaries, the opinion of the judiciary symbolised by the view of the Chief Justice of India, and formed in the manner indicated, has primacy.

4. No appointment of any Judge to the Supreme Court or any High Court can be made, unless it is in conformity with the opinion of the Chief Justice of India.
5. In exceptional cases alone for stated strong cogent reasons, disclosed to the Chief Justice of India, indicating that the recommendee is not suitable for appointment, the appointment recommended by the Chief Justice of India may not be made. However, if the stated reasons are not accepted by the Chief Justice of India and the other Judges of the Supreme Court who have been consulted in the matter, on reiteration of the recommendation by the Chief Justice of India, the appointment should be made as a healthy convention. (Emphases Supplied).
6. Appointment to the office of the Chief Justice of India should be of the seniormost Judge of the Supreme Court considered fit to hold the office.
7. The opinion of the Chief Justice of India has not mere primacy, but is determinative in the matter of transfers of High Court Judges/Chief Justices.
8. Consent of the transferred Judge/Chief Justice is not required for either the first or any subsequent transfer from one High Court to another.
9. Any transfer made on the recommendation of the Chief Justice of India is not to be deemed to be punitive, and such transfer is not justiciable on any ground.
10. In making all appointments and transfers, the norms indicated must be followed. However, the same do not confer any justiciable right in anyone.
11. Only limited judicial review on the grounds specified earlier is available in matters of appointments and transfers.
12. The initial appointment of a Judge can be made to a High Court other than that for which the proposal was initiated.
13. Fixation of Judge strength in the High Court is justiciable, but only to the extent and in the manner indicated.
14. The majority opinion in *S.P. Gupta* v. *Union of India* in so far as it takes the contrary view relating to primacy of the role of the Chief Justice of India in matters of appointments and transfers, and the justiciability of these matters as well as in relation of Judge strength, does not commend itself to us as being the correct view. The relevant provisions of the Constitution, including the constitutional scheme must now be construed, understood and implemented in the manner indicated herein by us. (para 486).

Para 487 states that this summary has to be read alongwith the earlier part, where in the conclusions are elaborately stated with the reasons which in effect means that para 487 has to be read and incorporated in to the conclusions enumerated above. The said para provides as follows:—

> "What is the meaning of the opinion of the judiciary 'symbolised by the view of the Chief Justice of India?"

"This opinion has to be formed in a pragmatic manner and past practice based on convention is a safe guide. In matters relating to appointments in the Supreme Court, *the opinion given by the Chief Justice of India in the consultative process has to be formed taking into account the views of the two seniormost Judges of the Supreme Court. The Chief Justice of India is also expected to ascertain the views of the senior-most judge of the Supreme Court whose opinion it likely to be significant in adjudging the suitability of the candidate, by reason of the fact that he has come from the same High Court, or otherwise. Article 124(2) is an indication that ascertainment of the views of some other Judges of the Supreme Court is requisite. The object underlying Article 124(2) is achieved in this manner as the Chief Justice of India consults them for the formation of his opinion.* This provision in Article 124(2) is the basis for the existing convention which required the Chief Justice of India to consult some Judges of the Supreme Court before making his recommendation. This ensures that the opinion of the Chief Justice of India is not merely his individual opinion, but an opinion formed collectively by a body of men at the apex level in the judiciary.

In matters relating to appointments in the High Courts, the Chief Justice of India is expected to take into account the views of his colleagues in the Supreme Court who are likely to be conversant with the affairs of the concerned High Court. The Chief Justice of India may also ascertain the views of one or more senior Judges of that High Court whose opinion, according to the Chief Justice of India, is likely to be significant in the formation of his opinion. The opinion of the Chief Justice of High Court would be entitled to the greatest weight, and the opinion of the other functionaries involved must be given due weight, in the formation of the opinion of the Chief Justice of India. The opinion of the Chief Justice of High court must be formed after ascertaining the views of at least the two seniormost Judges of the High Court.

The Chief Justice of India, for the formation of his opinion, has to adopt a course which would enable him to discharge his duty objectively to select the best available persons as judges of the Supreme Court and the High Courts. The ascertainment of the opinion of the other Judges by the Chief Justices of India and the Chief Justice of High Court, and the expression of their opinion, must be in writing to avoid any ambiguity.

For a full coverage of all details and reasons which are summarized in the conclusions aforementioned which are not being repeated for the sake of brevity, Please see page 702 to 706 of the judgment (*Supreme Court Advocates on Record Assn.* v. *Union of India* reported in 1993 (4) SCC 441).

Clearly the court has transgressed far beyond the order of reference and covered many aspects which were not in the contemplation of the referring order. Instead of clarifying matters the judgment of nine judges has created more ambiguity than before.

5. The third judges case: (special reference No.1 of 1998) reported in (1998) (7) SCC 739.

The President of India who required clarification and light on the second judges case made a reference to the Supreme Court under Article 143 of the Constitution which is as follows:—

"Whereas the Supreme Court of India has laid down principles and prescribed procedural norms in regard to the appointment of Judges of the Supreme Court [Article 124(2) of the Constitution of India], Chief Justices and Judges of the High Court [Article 217(1)], and transfer of Judges from one High Court to another [Article 222(1)], in the case of *Supreme Court Advocates-on-Record Assn.* v. *Union of India;*

And whereas doubts have arisen about the interpretation of the law laid down by the Supreme Court and it is in public interest that the said doubts relating the appointment and transfer of Judges be resolved.

And whereas, in view of what is hereinbefore stated, it appears to me that the following questions of law have arisen and are of such a nature and of such public importance that it is expedient to obtain the opinion of the Supreme Court of India thereon;

Now, therefore, in exercise of the powers conferred upon me by clause (1) of Article 143 of the Constitution of India, I, K.R. Narayanan, President of India, hereby refer the following questions to the Supreme Court of India for consideration and to report its opinion thereon, namely:—

1. Whether the expression 'consultation with the Chief Justice of India in Articles 217(1) and 222(1) requires consultation with a plurality of Judges in the formation of the opinion of the Chief Justice of India constitute consultation within the meaning of the said articles;
2. Whether the transfer of Judges in judicially reviewable in the light of the observation of the Supreme Court in the aforesaid judgment that 'such transfer is not justiciable on any ground' and its further observation that limited judicial review is available in matters of transfer, and the extent and scope of judicial review;
3. Whether Article 124(2) as interpreted in the said judgment required the Chief Justice of India to consult only the two seniormost Judges or whether there should be wider consultation according to past practice;
4. Whether the Chief Justice of India is entitled to act solely in his individual capacity, without consultation with other Judges of the Supreme Court in respect of all materials and information conveyed by the Government of India for non-appointment of a Judge recommended for appointment;
5. Whether the requirement of consultation by the Chief Justice of India with his colleagues, who are likely to be conversant with the affairs of the High Court concerned refers to only those Judges who have that High Court as a parent High Court and excludes Judges who had occupied the office of a Judge or Chief Justice of that Court on transfer from their parent or any other court;
6. Whether in the light of the legitimate expectations of senior Judges of the High Court in regard to their appointment to the Supreme Curt referred to in the said judgment, the 'strong cogent reason'

required to justify the departure from the order of the seniority has to be recorded in respect of each such senior Judge, who is overlooked, while making recommendation of a Judge junior to him or her;

7. Whether the Government is not entitled to require that the opinions of the other consulted Judges be in writing in accordance with the aforesaid Supreme Court judgment and that the same be transmitted to the Government of India by the Chief Justice of India along with his views;
8. Whether the Chief Justice of India is not obliged to comply with the norms and the requirement of the consultation process in making his recommendation to the Government of India;
9. Whether any recommendations made by the Chief Justice of India without complying with the norms and consultation process are binding upon the Government of India?

New Delhi — Narayanan, K.R.

Dated: 23-7-1998 — President of India

A bench of nine Judges was constituted comprising of S.P. Barucha, M.K. Mukherjee, S.B. Majumdar, Sujata V. Manohar, G.T. Nanavati, S. Saghir Ahmad, K. Venkataswami, B.N. Kirpal and G.B. Pattanaik, JJ and the court answered the said reference unanimously in the following manner in para 44 of the reference:

"The questions posed by the reference are now answered but we should emphasize that the answers should be read in conjunction with the body of this references

1. *The expression "consultation with the Chief Justice of India" in Articles 217(1) and 222(1) of the Constitution of India required consultation with a plurality of judges in the formation of the opinion of the Chief Justice of India. The sole individual opinion of the Chief Justice of India does not constitute "consultation" within the meaning of the said articles.*
2. *The transfer of puisne Judges is judicially reviewable only to this extent that the recommendation that has been made by the Chief Justice of India in this behalf has not been made in consultation with the four seniormost Judges of the Supreme Court and/or that the views of the Chief Justice of High Court from which the transfer is to be effected and of the Chief Justice of High Court to which the transfer is to be effected have not been obtained.*
3. *The Chief Justice of India must make a recommendation to appoint a Judge of the Supreme Court and to transfer a Chief Justice or puisne Judge of a High Court in consultation with the four seniormost puisne Judges of the Supreme Court. Insofar as an appointment to the High Court is concerned, the recommendation must be made in consultation with the two seniormost puisne Judges of the Supreme Court.*
4. *The Chief Justice of India is not entitled to act solely in his individual capacity, without consultation with other Judges of the Supreme Court, in respect of materials and information conveyed by the Government of India for non-appointment of a Judge recommended for appointment.*

5. *The requirement of consultation by the Chief Justice of India with his colleagues who are likely to be conversant with the affairs of the High Court concerned does not refer only to those Judges who have that High Court as a parent High Court. It does not exclude Judges who have occupied the office of a Judge or Chief Justice of that High Court on transfer.*
6. "Strong cogent reasons" do not have to be recorded as justification for a departure from the order of seniority in respect of each senior Judge who has been passed over. What has to be recorded is the positive reason for the recommendation.
7. *The views of the other Judges consulted should be in writing and should be conveyed to the Government of India by the Chief Justice of India along with his views to the extent set out in the body of his opinion.*
8. The Chief Justice of India is obliged to comply with the norms and the requirement of the consultation process, as aforestated, in making his recommendations to the Government of India.
9. Recommendations made by the Chief Justice of India without complying with the norms and requirements of the consultation process, as aforestated, are not binding upon the Government of India (emphasis supplied)

PART II

ANALYSIS OF THE JUDGES CASES I, II & III – *S.P. GUPTA* Vs. *UNION OF INDIA* REPORTED IN AIR 1982 SC 149; *SUPREME COURT ADVOCATES-ON-RECORD ASSOCIATION* Vs. *UNION OF INDIA* REPORTED IN 1993 (4) SCC 441 AND SPECIAL REFERENCE 1 OF 1998 REPORTED IN 1998 (7) SCC

1. In the three judges cases, I, II & III – *S.P. Gupta* v. *Union of India* reported in AIR 1982 SC 149; *Supreme Court Advocates on Record Association* v. *Union of India* reported in 1993 (4) SCC 441 and Special Reference 1 of 1998 reported in 1998 (7) SCC 739, the Supreme Court has virtually re-written Articles 124(2) and Articles 217 which pertain to appointment of Supreme Court Judges respectively. The text of Article 124(2) is as follows:—

> 124(2) Every judge of the Supreme Court shall be appointed by the President by warrant under his hand and seal after consultation with such of the Judges of the Supreme Court and of the High Courts in the States as the President may deem necessary for the purpose and shall hold office until he attains the age of sixty-five years:
>
> Provided that in the case of appointment of a Judge other than the Chief Justice, the Chief Justice of India shall always be consulted:
>
> 217(1) Every Judge of a High Court shall be appointed by the President by warrant under his hand and seal after consultation with the Chief Justice of India, the Governor of the State, and, in the case of appointment of a Judge other than the Chief Justice, the Chief Justice of the High Court, and shall hold office, in the case of an additional or acting judge, as provided in Article 224,

and in any other case, until he attains the age of sixty-two years. The word "collegium" is no where present in the constitution. It was first used by Bhagwati J in the majority judgement of *S.P. Gutpa* v. *Union of India* (4:3) In Para 29 "There must be a collegium to make recommendations etc." ...... (already extracted in Para 2 of Part 1) Again in the Presidential reference the expression "collegium" and "collegium of judges" has been freely used (Paras 15 and 22 to cite a few instances)

It is submitted that any addition of words in the constitution would not be permissible under the interpretive jurisdiction of the Supreme Court. The Supreme Court has to interpret the constitution as it is.

2. The advisory opinion in the guise of clarifying doubts raised regarding the norms laid down in the Judges II case has virtually reviewed its earlier decision.

It is respectfully submitted that the opinion expressed in an advisory opinion is contrary to the plain language of Article 124(2). What the article says is that the President shall consult the Chief Justice of India and such of the judges of the Supreme Court or the high court as he deems necessary. The article does not place any ceiling or limitation on the number of judges other than the Chief Justice of India to be consulted. The President should always act on the aid and advice of the Council of Ministers (Article 74). However, contrary to what was said in the Constitution, both the Judges II and Judges III cases have laid down that consultation with the Chief Justice of India means a collegium consisting of the Chief Justice of India and two or four judges as the case may be. Further, in both the cases it was stated that it is the Chief Justice of India who should consult with collegium of judges, whereas Constitution says that the President should consult the Chief Justice of India and such judges as he deems necessary.

3. The three judges cases, *i.e.* the two judgements of the Supreme Court and one opinion on a Special Reference have all dealt with the scope of "consultation" and it was in the Second Judges Case that the Supreme Court evolved the concept of 'primacy' for the opinion of the Chief Justice of India, which itself was to be based on a consultative process amongst the senior colleagues of the Chief Justice of India. At the hearing of the Special Reference for the opinion of the Court about the extent of the 'consultative' process, it was conceded on behalf of the Executive (and recorded in the Court's opinion) that the Government was not seeking a review or reconsideration of the judgement in the Second Judges case and that it would accept as binding (although an opinion and not a decision) the answers of the Court to the questions incorporated in the Special Reference.

4. The Supreme Court's opinion in the Special Reference not only strongly reinforced the concept of "primacy" of the Chief Justice of India's opinion but also increased the number of judges the Chief Justice of India must consult before providing his opinion and laid down a detailed set of guidelines on the procedure to be followed in arriving at the Chief Justice of India's opinion to which "primacy" was attached. The procedure in effect transferred the "primacy" from the Chief Justice of India to the group of Judges to be consulted.

5. The collegium is now to consist of the Chief Justice of India and four (instead of two) senior-most judges of the court in the appointment of a High Court judge,

the Supreme Court judge acquainted with that particular High Court should also be consulted raising the number to six. The increased size of the group that has to be a part of the consultation process with several interests being involved has made the consultation process cumbersome and delays in filling up of vacancies is bound to arise. The Presidential Reference also provides that every communication with the consultee has to be in writing and the views should be communicated to the Government. There is no indication as to what happens if there is no consensus among the consultees or if the majority dis-agrees with the Chief Justice of India. S.P. Gupta has laid down that the entire correspondence and communication between various authorities are open to public scrutiny (since the entire record was summoned, perused and made public in that case).

PART III

RECOMMENDATIONS

1. From what has been stated above it is clear that an entire reconsideration I, II & III judges cases – *S.P. Gupta* v. *Union of India* reported in AIR 1982 SC 149; *Supreme Court Advocates-on-Record Association* v. *Union of India* reported in 1993(4) SCC 441 and Special Reference 1 of 1998 reported in 1998(7) SCC 739, is urgently and immediately called for in order to bring about clarity and consistency in the process of Appointment of Supreme Court and High Court Judges.

2. The Eighty-Fifth Report on Law's Delays: Arrears in Courts has expressed the same view.

The same is extracted here below:

> "The Committee is aware that for this state of affairs the Union Law Ministry is not blameworthy, as the entire process of initiation of proposal for appointment of new judges is no longer the responsibility of the Executive as a result of a decision of the Supreme Court. Though it was not contemplated in the Constitution, responsibility for judicial appointments now rests in the domain of the judiciary. The Union Law Minister is accountable to Parliament for the delay in filling up of the vacancies of judges but he has functionally no contribution to make. The Supreme Court read into the Constitution a power to appoint judges that was not conferred upon it by the text or the context. The underlying purpose of securing judicial independence was salutary but the method of acquiring for the Court the exclusive power to appoint judges by the process of judicial interpretation is open to question. Against this backdrop the Committee recalls a recent discussion in the Rajya Sabha in which the Government was asked regarding alternate arrangements to fill up the vacancies and whether there was any scope for having a fresh review of the Supreme Court's judgment.
>
> The position as it exists in different countries may be noticed at this stage. On a scrutiny of several constitutions of other countries it may be seen that in all other Constitutions either the executive is the sole authority to appoint judges or the executive appoints in consultation with the Chief Justice of the country. The Indian Constitution has followed the latter method. However, the 2nd judges case *Advocates-on-Record Association* v. *Union of India*, 1993 (4) SCC 441, as we have seen in the discussion above, has completely eliminated and

excluded the executive and the opinion of the Hon'ble Supreme Court in the Presidential reference (Special Reference 1 of 1998) has reaffirmed this view with slight modifications.

In America the State judges are elected. When they are not elected their appointment is subject to legislative concurrence. In the Supreme Court it is the President who nominates the Judges but the nomination has to be confirmed by the Senate. In Australia it is the executive that appoints judges. In Canada the Governor General makes the appointment of judges.

In New Zealand the Chief Justice is appointed on the recommendations of the Prime Minister by the President. The Prime Minister in turn consults the Attorney General; the A.G. informally consults the President of Court of Appeal and other judges.

As for High Court Judges, Chief Justice recommends after consulting other Judges and gives the list to the AG for scrutiny. AG scrutinizes the list, consults New Zealand Law Society and then candidate's consent is sought. Thereafter the Cabinet finally recommends the names to the Governor General who issues the appointment letter.

Recently, the judges from the Apex Court and the High Court of Kenya came to the Supreme Court and they addressed the Supreme Court Bar. They confirmed that they have a National Judicial Commission which undertakes the selection process. In this National Judicial Commission there is the Attorney General and the Chief Justice, two senior most judges of the Apex Court and an expert.

Thus it may be seen that in all the Constitutions, the executive has a role to play and in some countries a major and exclusive role. The Indian Constitution provides a beautiful system of checks and balances under Articles 124(2) and 217(1) for the appointment of Judges of the Supreme Court and High Courts where both the executive and judiciary have been given a balanced role. As already stated this delicate balance has been upset by the 2nd Judges case (*Advocate-on-Record Association* v. *Union of India* 1993 (4) SCC 4412 and the opinion of the Supreme Court in the Presidential Reference (Special Reference No.1 of 1998). It is time the original balance of power is restored.

The above recommendation for the need for an urgent and immediate review of the present procedure for appointment of judges is further fortified by the views expressed by Justice J.S. Verma, who wrote the lead judgment in *Advocates-on-Record* v. *Union of India,* 1993 (4) SCC 441, by his fortright views expressed in an interview in the Front Line Magazine dated 10.10.1998. The relevant portion is reproduced below:

When asked "you said in one of your speeches that judicial appointments have become judicial disappointments. Do you now regret your 1993 judgement? Justice Verma stated "My 1993 judgement, which holds the field, was very much misunderstood and misused. It was in that context I said the working of the judgment now for some time is raising serious questions, which cannot be called unreasonable. Therefore, some kind of rethink is required. My judgement says the appointment process of High Court and Supreme Court Judges is basically a joint or participatory exercise between the executive and the judiciary, both taking part in it. Broadly, there are two distinct areas. One is the area of legal acumen of the candidates to adjudge their suitability and the other is their antecedents. It is the judiciary, that is, the Chief Justice of India and his colleagues or, in the case of the High Courts, the Chief Justice of the High Court and his colleagues (who) are the best persons to adjudge the legal acumen. Their voice should be predominant. So far as the antecedents are concerned, the executive is better placed than the judiciary to know the antecedents of candidates. Therefore, my judgement said that in the area of legal acumen the judiciary's opinion should be dominant, and in the area of antecedents the executive's opinion should be dominant. Together, the two should function to find out the most suitable (candidates) available for appointment."

The views of the Parliamentary Standing Committee on Law & Justice recommended the scrapping of the present procedure for appointments and transfers by Supreme Court and High Court Judges are of great relevance in this context. As reported in the Hindustan Times of 20-10-2008 "the Law Ministry has agreed to review the 15-year-old system after the Parliamentary Standing Committee on Law & Justice recommended doing away with the committee of judges (collegium). Presently, the collegium decides the appointments and transfer of judges. Interestingly, the recommendations come close on the heels of recent cases of corruption against judges of the top courts in the country. Law Minister H.R. Bhardwaj told Hindustan Times that the House Committee's recommendation had been accepted, and an action-taken report prepared by the Ministry would now be placed before Parliament. "Collegium system has failed. Its decisions on appointments and transfers lack transparency and we feel courts are not getting judges on merit.(......) The government cannot be a silent spectator on such a serious issue", Bhardwaj said. The House Committee had said:

"Through a Supreme Court judgment in 1993, the judiciary wrested the control of judges appointments and transfers. The collegium system has been a disaster and needs to be done away with". H.R. Bhardwaj, Minister for Law & Justice, said "It is the right time to review this important matter".

"There was no problem till 1993 when the judiciary tried to re-write the Article of the Constitution dealing with appointments. They created a new law of collegium which was wrong. In a democracy, the primacy of Parliament cannot be challenged", he said.

The Chairman of the Departmental Related Parliament Standing Committee of Personnel, Public Grievances Law and Justice in its 28th Report presented to the Hon'ble Chairman of Rajya Sabha on August 2008 has stated thus:—

"I would like to conclude by saying that the Government should expeditiously see to it that appointment of Judges in High Courts and Supreme Court are done in a transparent way. We have recommended in two ways: One is, we have to see to it that the collegium system has to be done away with, since appointments will be delayed, we have said that from the very beginning of identifying the eligible persons, the various places of recommendations, be it at the level of the High Courts, or, at the Governor's level or at the level of the Departments, and finally be the Supreme Court, should be transparent, and this should be put up in the web site then and there so that the person, who is going to occupy the Constitutional place, is known to the public, and their background should be allowed to be discussed by the public and, finally, it has to go through the process of issuing warrant by the President of India. But, what is happening presently is that from the day one of identifying the person till the issuance of the warrant, nothing is known to anybody except to the persons who are involved in it. Even the persons, who are identified and who are going to be made as judges of the High Court or of the Supreme Court, may not know about it. This type of secrecy is not good for democracy".

It may be noted in this context that in every High Court the Chief Justice is from outside the State as per the policy of the Government. The senior most Judges who form the collegium are also from outside the State. The resultant position is that the judges constituting the collegium are not conversant with the names and antecedents of the candidates and more often than not, appointments suffer from lack of adequate information.

Two alternatives are available to the Government of the day. One is to seek a reconsideration of the three judgments aforesaid before the Hon'ble Supreme Court. Otherwise a law may be passed restoring the primacy of the Chief Justice of India and the power of the executive to make the appointments.

•••